ENGLISH
AND
AMERICAN
TEXTILES
1790 to the present

ENGLISH
AND
AMERICAN
TEXTILES

from 1790 to the present

Mary Schoeser
Celia Rufey

Thames and Hudson

For my colleagues at Warners,
and for Anna and Ellen Rufey

Frontispiece: Simple damask used to
stunning effect in the home of Peter
Leonard, founder of the influential
London firm, Soho Design

Copyright © 1989 by Mary Schoeser and Celia Rufey

First published in the United States in 1989 by Thames and Hudson Inc,
500 Fifth Avenue, New York, New York 10110

Library of Congress Catalog Card Number: 89-50543

This book was designed and produced by John Calmann and King Ltd, London

Designed by Harold Bartram
Picture research by Susan Bolsom-Morris
Typeset by Rowland Phototypesetting Ltd, Bury St Edmunds, Suffolk, England
Printed and bound in Singapore by Toppan Ltd

Contents

Acknowledgments

Every book is a team effort, and we have been fortunate in having the excellent combination of Susan Bolsom-Morris, who never flagged in the face of the complexities involved in the picture research, Sophie Collins at Calmann and King, who resourcefully drew together the elements of this book and guided it through production, and Eleanor Van Zandt, whose intelligent and informed editing was of enormous benefit to the finished text. We are also grateful to Harold Bartram for his excellent design, and to Tim Imrie and Graydon Wood for their photographic work.

For assistance, encouragement and accommodation during the research stage we would like to thank Rita Adrosco, Diane Affleck, Mary Ashton, Joanna Banham, Linda Baumgarten, Vivienne Bennett, David Black, Dennis Boyce, Chris Boydell, Syd Chase, Mike Cutliffe, Frank Davies, Phyllis Dillon, Murray Douglas, Audrey Duck, John Faulder, Lynn Felcher, Merri Ferrell, Dale Gluckman, Alan James, Clare Jameson, Julie Harrison, Mary Ellen Hern, John Hunter, Keith Lambourn, Betty Leviner Hyman, Santina Levy, Pamela Lewis, Edward Maeder, Joanna Marschner, Melissa Marsh, Jessica Nicoll, Richard Nylander, Lorna Poole, Deborah Price, Shaun Roberts, Rodris Roth, Barbara Schellenberger, Margaret Schoeser, Richard Slavin, Judy Straeten, Jolyon Tibbitts, Edward Turnbull, Nancy Waters, Mary Whiteley, Ron Wilkey, Alice Zrebiac and, especially, Dilys Blum. So many other people assisted by answering enquiries, allowing access to their collections and facilitating photography that we could not name them all; we nevertheless hope that they will also accept our thanks.

Introduction

Beginning with the 1790s, this book examines furnishing fabrics and their use in Britain and the United States up to the present day. At every level of society the use of fabrics in interiors provides a commentary on the interplay of fashion, technology and social change. The force of these changes on interior styles was felt equally in manor house and cottage, for a significant feature of the last two hundred years has been the increased expectation that all should desire the 'home beautiful' – to such an extent that an unwillingness or inability to decorate was, by the mid-nineteenth century if not earlier, interpreted as a symbolic withdrawal from society. From the 1790s onwards, textiles provided the means by which ever-larger sections of the community could participate in this 'ritual' of decorating; when furniture itself was expected to last a generation or more, renewed textiles kept abreast of fashion.

While the impact of fashion can be observed on textile usage at any period, irrespective of wealth and class, different sections of society responded each in their own way. When we look at interiors of the past, we therefore have to try to see them through the eyes of their contemporaries as well as our own. What fabrics looked like in a particular period and the way they were used depended on many factors: the available raw materials, the state of technology, whether a given fabric was profitable to manufacture, how much it cost, whether it was perceived as attractive and, if so, *why* it was perceived as attractive (which had as much to do with fashion as with how appropriately it portrayed the occupants' social position or aspirations). The modern student of furnishing textiles approaches the subject with all these aspects in mind. However, it is not only the restorer or the social historian for whom these issues are significant. The current retrospective furnishing style (a corollary of Post-Modern architecture) has made them relevant to the work of interior designers as well, and of interest to anyone furnishing a home in a traditional manner. In the following pages we have set out to answer the questions that, as historian and journalist, we most commonly confront with regard to furnishing fabrics – that is, the relationship between 'what', 'how' and 'why'. The subject is so enormous that we have chosen to focus on the dominant influences of each period and to suggest various lines of enquiry.

The starting-point for our study, the 1790s, has been selected for several reasons. One reason is that this is the point at which one begins to find parallels in the design and manufacture of English-made and American-made furnishing textiles. Of course there were some resemblances between the appearance and use of some English and American furnishing fabrics before this time – even as early as the mid-seventeenth century; but for another century or so, substantial differences remained. For example,

1 Langley Walter's evocative oil 'Day Dreams' was painted in 1914, and has the hallmarks of an artist's romantic view of the past. Nevertheless it contains factual information on the use of fabrics in interiors – and even humble ones such as this. The child's coverlet shows the practical, functional role of textiles, whereas most of the other fabrics indicate the desire to participate in the social ritual of decorating one's environment. The simple muslin curtain, hung by a rod at the window, and (even more so) the mantle's lambrequin serve as indications of the household's propriety. This is further emphasized by the child's pillow, which has been carefully laundered and ironed.

2 Two printed cottons depicting horseracing at the Turf Inn, the red one hand-printed by flat copperplate in England between 1780 and 1790 and the brown version designed from it by G. P. & J. Baker of London in 1973 and produced, until 1988, by rotary (machine) screens, the dominant method of printing textiles today. In 1937 the historian Ada Longfield established that the first known use of engraved plates for printing fast-dyed cotton or linen and cotton cloth was by Robert Nixon, in Ireland, in 1752. The process spread rapidly, and between 1760 and about 1800 it was used to produce very fashionable furnishing fabrics, characterized by their fine line details and, with a few exceptions, single colours (red, blue, black-brown or purple) on an undyed ground. Although many designs were used – including exotic flowering S-shaped stems, scrollwork, floral bowers and birds – it was the scenic designs which in later years came to be associated with copperplate prints. These were (and are) often called 'toiles', since the printing process was for so long thought to have been perfected in France. Scenic toile patterns have been imitated by every other printing process and have returned to fashion periodically over the last 200 years.

the fine French and English hand-woven silks that adorned great European houses throughout the eighteenth century were rarely found in Colonial homes before 1760. Instead, inventories reveal that wool was the principal fibre in elegant American bed hangings, upholstery and curtains. The majority of these were imported from England, where they were also used in the homes of prosperous landowners and merchants, but where their status was not of the first rank. Common to both countries were homespun, home-woven cloths, which varied according to local materials and skills. Rural production methods also formed the basis of Britain's silk, calico, worsted and woollen industries. Highly organized though some British cottage industries were, they nevertheless bore little resemblance to the factory system which was emerging at the end of the eighteenth century.

The industrialization of textile manufacture about this time precipitated a substantial change in the furnishing of interiors. This is not to suggest that pre-1790 decorating styles disappeared entirely, for both survivals and revivals assured the continued importance of eighteenth-century patterns and furniture forms. Nevertheless, the relative importance of mass-produced printed and woven cloths increased. Accompanying this trend was the substitution of informality and comfort for grandeur and formality. The result was that the late eighteenth century witnessed the final disappearance of the great differences in the use of furnishing fabrics by comparable classes in England and America; in particular, wealthy Americans now more often used silks.

In 1790 we also find in existence for the first time all the basic principles that govern today's industry. Among the most significant of these is the acceptance of changing fashions in interior decoration, the pace of which accelerated from about a thirty-year lifespan in the late seventeenth century to about seven years two centuries later. The ease with which information was disseminated played an important role in establishing this quickened pace. From the beginning of the eighteenth century an increasing number of engraved plates were issued, singly or in sets, showing fashionable interiors and draperies – inspired mainly by French decorating styles, if not actually produced by French engravers. These were used by English and, later, American upholsterers (both of whom produced – in addition to upholstery – curtains, bed hangings and loose covers or 'cases'). After the middle of the eighteenth century, these sources were supplemented by entire books on the subject, including those by the English furniture designers Thomas Chippendale, George Hepplewhite and Thomas Sheraton. Such publications, however, still served mainly those in the trade; the general public's knowledge of fashionable furnishing styles more often came indirectly, from other engravings, such as English satirical and political prints. In the United States, a surge of journal publishing followed the establishment of a national postal service in 1794, and promoted the circulation of an estimated 500–600 new magazines between 1800 and 1825. Although most were short-lived and few dealt specifically with decorating, many contained topical engravings which illustrated fashionable interiors. Published in London, Rudolph Ackermann's magazine, *The Repository of Arts*, was the first English-language journal to achieve both a relatively long life – from 1809 to 1828 – and considerable influence on interior decor on both sides of the Atlantic. But it was only with the subsequent widespread introduction of books and magazines on decorating that a greater public was able to gain an immediate familiarity with – and therefore a taste for – the newest fashions in textiles and their use in the home.

Although some late eighteenth- and early nineteenth-century American furniture and drapery styles were of French origin, most followed the English taste. Of the fashionably patterned furnishing textiles, a few were made in America (most based on English designs) and the remainder were predominantly English imports. In fact, in the 1790s – and at several other points in the century – English fabrics were more readily available in the United States than the products of American manufacturers. Various factors contributed to this state of affairs, including the minute size of America's industry in relation to that of England. Furthermore, technology that was entirely new to America in 1790 was already fairly well established in Britain. After 1800 the difference grew less apparent; and although for several more decades the British and American industries differed significantly in size, their respective contributions to the economy of their countries was comparable.

In tracing the development, design, manufacture and distribution of furnishing fabrics, we have tried, so far as possible, to indicate the longevity of certain styles and their use over the past 200 years by different classes. These matters become important when studying the economic or social significance of textiles and are equally useful for those who restore or re-create historical interiors. With this in mind, the main text, although organized chronologically, discusses fabrics in the context of their use in the home, and therefore includes revivals as well as new styles. Some groups of textiles have had such lasting importance in interiors that these have been termed 'basic cloths' and are given a separate chapter.

Any authors who collaborate on a book owe their readers some explanation of their respective contributions to it. Besides writing the last chapter, Celia Rufey has, for the remainder of the text, played the role of both reader and critic – prompting discussion of points I might otherwise have overlooked and contributing information along the way. In the same manner, we have together written many of the captions. These, supplemented by the appendix, provide much of the information on changing techniques, dyestuffs and design styles. In preparing this book we have been assisted by scholars, both past and present, who have dealt in depth with various influences on furnishing textiles and their use, and also by the many journalists whose trenchant observations on decorating fashions over the past 200 years have so often illuminated the subject. The important contributions of all these professionals must be acknowledged at the outset.

Mary Schoeser

Chapter One

Basic Cloths

'In what beauty consists the philosopher and the artist are alike
unable to determine, for it is impossible to find a judge.'
(H. W. Arrowsmith, in *The House Decorator and Painter's Guide*[1])

It is tempting to discuss furnishing fabrics of the past only in the context of
the most fashionable interiors and the most novel textiles prevailing at any
time, and to give scant acknowledgement to the large body of textiles that
change little or evolve slowly. These basic cloths, however, form a
consistent strand running through a great diversity of interiors from the
eighteenth into the twentieth century. They are the mainstay of fabric use
and the points of departure for novelty and invention. Long outliving the
normal cycle of fashion, their use has extended across a wide range of
tastes and social classes. The basic cloths include classic patterns which
transcend changing fashions, unpatterned woven fabrics (including plain
– or tabby – weaves, velvets, satins and taffetas) as well as fabrics with
small-scale woven or printed designs. It would be an unusual house in any
period from 1790 to 1990 that did not include in its furnishings one or more
of these basic fabrics or patterns.

Many of the classic patterns were designed well before our starting date of
1790. Dominant among them are those originating from late seventeenth-
and eighteenth-century silk damasks, which have survived in forms both
very close to the originals and freely adapted from them. Such silk damask
patterns were quickly copied by makers of other types of fabrics and by
wallpaper printers. Subsequently the popularity of these designs must
have been due partly to their initial use on silks in palatial surroundings,
which made them emblematic of a gracious, assured lifestyle.

The perpetuation of such patterns and the establishment of silk damask
itself as a classic textile was aided by the long period these fabrics often
remained *in situ*. Some, having been applied to walls, remained unchanged for over two centuries. For example, an Italian crimson damask
wall covering, ordered by William III in about 1689 for one of the presence
chambers in Hampton Court Palace, was not replaced until 1923. The new
silk was a duplicate of the old. Prolonged use of silk damask was undoubtedly due not only to its relative scarcity but also to its high cost – a fact to
which even the wealthiest could be sensitive. When Grosvenor House, the
London home of the Dukes of Westminster, was altered and redecorated
by William Porden in 1807–8, 'with an eye to economies, crimson damask
from Eaton Hall, the Grosvenor country house in Cheshire, was rehung
on some of the walls.'[2]

1 Shown within an 1818 room from
Duncan House, Haverhill, Massachusetts
(now installed in the Metropolitan
Museum of Art, New York), this carved
bed of c.1795, probably by John Seymour,
was refurnished in the 1940s in a manner
faithful to Hepplewhite's 1787 *Upholsterer's
Guide*. The room was reinterpreted and
redecorated in 1980, but the 1940s
interpretation of a late-eighteenth-century
bed is not without interest. It serves as a
reminder that every era interprets the past
in the light of contemporary taste
(compare this to the 1933 interior, Chapter
6, Fig. 43), while the basic cloths provide
compelling evidence that plain-coloured
fabrics are equal to the most elaborate of
settings.

First woven in Europe, luxurious yet hard-wearing damasks were also fashionable in America, where they were imported and, later, manufactured. Two damask patterns, still available in England and North America, typify the history of classic damasks. The first of these, a boldly delineated Palladian design, originated in about 1730, and the same pattern was also used on a flocked wallpaper in the Queen's Drawing Room at Hampton Court Palace and in the Offices of H.M. Privy Council in about 1735. An original piece of the silk survives on a bed originally from Belhus, Essex, which is now in Christchurch Mansion, Ipswich. During the eighteenth century the damask was also used at Hopetoun House, near Edinburgh; in Corsham Court, Chippenham; and elsewhere. Early in the nineteenth century a variation of it was being blockprinted on cotton, and throughout the century this pattern was still being produced, in slightly altered form, as both fabric and wallpaper.

The other pattern, featuring a be-ribboned basket of flowers, dates from 1775–85. It was still fashionable in 1810 and was again being woven in the

2 Furnished in the early 1980s by a New York interior designer, this living room has walls and one chair clad with an eighteenth-century style damask, similar to Figs. 9 and 11. Used without restrictive reference to the original period, as it has been for over 200 years, the damask is perfectly at home with the mid-nineteenth-century-style chairs, one upholstered in an appropriately 'muscular' chintz. Note also the curtains with stripes, another basic pattern which has no limiting historical niche.

3 Plain linen has been used in various weights for bedding, bed hangings and bedroom curtains over the past two centuries. This valance was accompanied by three 34-inch-wide bed curtains, and its netted cotton fringe was very typical of 1790–1825. This particular linen piece is judged to be very late eighteenth century and may have been spun and woven by the Copp family in America. Linen is still highly regarded (for its coolness of touch and dispersal of moisture) by those who have slept between pure linen sheets.

1840s, in Spitalfields, reflecting the then-current fashion for rococo revival. Like the first design, it was very slightly altered, in this case having now a broader, more horizontal arrangement (see p. 21).[3]

In this century both designs have been continuously available as silk damasks, and although recently their production has been supported by restoration projects, they nevertheless remain important elements of the exclusive decorator's vocabulary. Both have also been printed, and woven in other fibres.

Damask can be made from any fibre, alone or in combination with another; in late-eighteenth-century America these patterns appeared far more often in woollens and worsted damasks, primary furnishing fabrics imported into the country in quantity from English manufacturers. Damask patterns were also stamped or embossed on worsteds by hot molds or metal rollers, producing cloths then known as harateens, camlets, moreens or cheneys. The same methods were used to stamp linen with damask patterns but it is the woven linen damasks which are perhaps the most universally known and continuously popular versions of late seventeenth- and eighteenth-century patterns. Variations on these classic linen damasks have continued to appear alongside fashionable contemporary linen designs in every period. In *The Art of the House*, 1897, Rosamond Mariott Watson noted that 'the feminine love of linen – a taste strangely pure and civilized – survives, in some degree, with almost all women, straying, like the lady in Comus, unmoved amid all manner of ugly and foolish fads and fancies.'[4] In fact, the association between a 'civilized' household and good table linen held true until after World War II.

Linen, alone or in combination with other fibres, was also used for another basic pattern, the check. Checked furnishing fabrics had already enjoyed 100 years of popularity by the late eighteenth century, when they were still in widespread use as cases (loose covers) and bed hangings. At this date checks made entirely of cotton were normally distinguished as such in inventories, since they were relatively uncommon. By the mid-nineteenth century the situation had reversed, and the most important was the cotton check, a well established member of the gingham family. Although nineteenth-century gingham – always all cotton – included stripes, plaids and checks, it was the balanced check (with equal-width stripes in both warp and weft) that eventually became a standard furnishing cloth. Unlike damask patterns, the use of which implied a degree of social eminence or, at the very least, social aspirations, checks have always been practical, informal fabrics. Today they are commonly seen at kitchen windows and on oilcloths, tablecloths and kitchen towels. Blue, red or brown, combined with natural or white, have remained the most widely produced colour combinations reinforcing associations with similarly coloured home-produced linen checks.

The long pre-eminence of linen fabrics for tablecloths, napkins and towels can be attributed to its strength, particularly during washing. It remained the standard fabric for sheets and pillowcases until well into the nineteenth century, when cotton of acceptable strength, and in adequate widths, began to be manufactured.

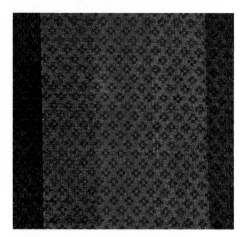

4 The bands of colour seen in this modern haircloth – produced by John Boyd, England's last remaining haircloth manufacturer (the United States has none) – are colour options and not part of the pattern. As the English upholsterer J. S. Croften revealed in *The Upholsterer's Companion*, haircloth, normally plain or with small non-directional patterns such as this one, was also liked because it could be cut economically, 'which will effect a saving of one third of a yard in a set of [eight] chairs. But this cannot be done when chintz or damask is used, because the pattern will run one way; unless, indeed, it be running patterns, stripes, etc., which may be cut in the same manner, and to the same advantage.' The number of horses declined in the years around 1930 due to the increased use of automobiles and this, together with the loss of Russian horsehair supplies (an important export until the Revolution in 1917), dramatically curtailed haircloth production.

Strength is also one of the characteristics that made horsehair an important upholstery fibre well into the second half of the nineteenth century. By about 1900 horsehair fabrics or haircloths (with warps of cotton, linen or wool) were regarded as suitable only for the homes of artisans and labourers; but for the previous century and more this moderately priced, sturdy, yet richly coloured fabric had appealed to the growing middle class. It was often used for upholstering dining room chairs – indeed, almost to the exclusion of other uses in the second half of the nineteenth century – because it was easy to keep clean. For some people its additional advantages – resistance to the effects of heat, humidity and sunlight and immunity to insect attack – outweighed all other considerations. Haircloth was not, however, valued solely for its serviceability; its sheen made it especially fashionable between about 1765 and 1825, when other glossy fabrics, including plain silks, such as taffeta and satin, and damasks with large unbroken areas of satin ground, were also in vogue.[5] It was thought particularly suitable for mahogany furniture.[6]

As in the case of haircloth, a fabric's colour and surface (reflective or matt, smooth or textured) plays a significant part in determining its popularity at a given time. We can see this in our own century's reproductions of the nineteenth-century floral designs that had become classic patterns. At times – notably during the 1980s – these benefitted from the general fashion for revivals and have been reproduced more or less intact, and in great numbers; but when modern design was in the ascendant, nineteenth-century floral patterns were adapted by being applied to contemporary textures (as in the 1920s and '30s) or interpreted in new colours (as in the 1950s and '60s). Many traditional damask patterns also underwent the same treatment.

The cloths that have adapted to changing fashions most readily are cut-pile fabrics, which are unique in their chameleon-like surface qualities – smooth in appearance yet textured to the touch; glowing with saturated colour which darkens when viewed in the direction of the slant of the pile – qualities that may account for their unbroken popularity since the late sixteenth century. Among the plain velvets, those made of silk have always been the most expensive (and approximately twice the cost of a silk damask at any period), but their price was justified by their beauty. In the highly cost-conscious period of the mid-nineteenth century, the Philadelphia decorator J. Arrowsmith recommended 'rich and ample' purple or claret-coloured library curtains of silk velvet, 'splendid beyond any other material; their lustre by candlelight has a magnificent effect. . . .'[7]

More expensive still were the velvets patterned in the loom (rather than embossed, printed or painted afterwards). Often called Genoa velvets, after their seventeenth-century Italian antecedents, these cost between 10/6 and 50/0 a yard in April 1891, when James Shoolbred & Company of Tottenham Court Road, London, advertised them 'in various beautiful designs and colourings, 21 inches wide'. The same catalogue listed 27-inch-wide corduroy for curtains at 2/6 a yard, or 2/9 if embossed. Also available either plain or embossed were Utrecht velvets and silk plushes, the latter at 22/9 plain. One might feel safe in assuming that, at this date,

5 Damask and brocade patterns have often been adapted to twentieth-century tastes by being produced in modern colours or a different texture. These two examples represent a further adaptation, in that both are printed. The larger sample is a version of 'Hampton Court Palace' (see Fig. 8), screen-printed in 1962, when matt, bright colours were fashionable. Overlying it is a swatch with brocade pattern, block-printed in the 1930s, when textured, indistinct effects were desired. (The base cloth is a dobby-woven cotton, then called dimity, due to its 'bird's eye' design, offset to form a narrow stripe.)

the Utrecht velvet was a wool or mohair pile, but the terminology relating to different fibre contents and pile lengths is still a contentious issue. One can only assume from their price that Shoolbred's 'Mecca Furniture Velvets, 24 inches wide, 5/9 per yard', their 'Bokhara plush, a perfect draping material, 50 inches wide, 5/6 a yard' and 'The New Deep Pile Velvets from 8/9 a yard, 24 inches wide', were of cotton, as would also have been the inexpensive corduroy already mentioned. The great variety of slightly differing plain or embossed cut-pile fabrics – Shoolbreds' mention thirteen – is typical of the entire period under review, and gives some indication of their importance as furnishing fabrics.[8] Suggesting both luxury and sobriety, pile fabrics even entered speech in the early nineteenth-century American phrase 'neat as plush'.[9]

At the opposite end of the spectrum from cut piles in terms of their draping qualities, weight and use, are muslins, cloths woven of very finely spun cotton yarns. Originally made only in India, muslins were subsequently woven in England after the production of these fine yarns was made possible by the invention of the spinning mule (patented in 1779). Originally the name 'muslin' referred to the yarn itself, as well as to the variety of fabrics made from it. In 1827 John Bradshaw, a muslin manufacturer in Bolton, listed eleven categories of muslin cloth, including cambric, dimity and gingham, descending in price from 39 to 7 shillings a yard for 45-inch-wide cloth. Among the cambrics were 'dart', 'spot' and 'flock' (small patterns powdered across a semi-transparent ground), which were more expensive than muslinett, dimity, cotton broad, tape cambric and gingham (available in white, full-colour and 'plad'). Twenty-two jaconets (firm cloths, varying in width and density, with small all-over patterns) cost between 6 and 39 shillings, while fourteen similarly varied plain cambrics ranged from 7 shillings to 21/9.[10]

6 Within John Bradshaw's 1827 sample book of muslins – fabrics woven from finely spun cotton yarns – were these two cloths, probably the 'gingham plad' (*sic*) that he sold for 12s 6d. Bradshaw was the warehouseman for Brown & Villing, in Bolton, near Manchester. For just under £1 a week he managed the warpers, weighed yarn for the winders and took work to out-weavers, as well as keeping the books for the firm's three spinning mills. He wrote to his father in July, 1827, that his 'prospects were not very flattering', and considered emigrating to the United States, where 'many keep going and many more would go if possible, weavers [there] get $1 a day'. His notes also suggest that the Bolton 'yard' measurement was, in fact, 30 inches, making the 6/4 yard-wide cloth common to that area 45 inches wide.

Today the word 'muslin' is applied only to plain cambric. This firm, gauze-like fabric, in white or off-white, became a standard cloth, particularly for sheer curtains. Their appeal was summed up in 1944 by the American decorator Dorothy Draper: 'Your undercurtains, or glass curtains, should be of some thin crisp material . . . Fresh book muslin is practically a classic here. Just as the well-tailored Scotch tweed suit is in style for years, so white muslin glass curtains are always fashionable. You may have to let the hem of your suit up or down, but you won't have to worry about your muslin curtains at all.'[11]

Muslin sub-curtains formed an important part of decorative window schemes in the first third of the nineteenth century, and again later in the century, when continued drapery (including several windows in one treatment) was revived; but even when less than fashionable, these useful and inexpensive curtains never quite disappeared. According to J. C. Loudon, writing in 1839, the purpose of muslin sub-curtains was to exclude insects and in some degree to soften the light of the sun.[12] Over 100 years later H. G. Hayes Marshall, the influential head of Fortnum & Mason's interior decoration department, was more concerned with the visual advantages of such curtains: 'Most people use them to prevent people peering into their parlours, but their greatest attraction is to prevent people seeing out, most of our outlooks are so ugly.'[13] Even during the height of fashion for machine-made lace curtains (c.1850–1915), writers such as Arrowsmith (1852) recommended muslin curtains alone (or, alternatively, pearl white damask trimmed with white silk) as 'handsome and suitable' for a lady's boudoir.[14] F. A. Moreland suggested in 1889 that in addition to full lace curtains, short lace or glass (i.e. muslin) curtains should be hung next to the window,[15] a fashion still prevalent in 1902, when it was decried by Edith Wharton in *The Decoration of Houses*.

Wharton's dislike of curtains of all types stemmed mainly from their masking of the details of internal architecture; her belief was that the better the house, the less need there was for curtains.[16] In fact, it was perhaps not in fine houses but in simple country dwellings that muslins and other plain lightweight cotton curtains had their greatest sustained use. In plentiful supply and washable, muslins also quickly became one of the least expensive curtain fabrics available; in Shoolbreds' 1891 catalogue they were about one-quarter the price of corduroy if printed and less if plain. Muslin curtains were often used with blinds or, alternatively, as the only covering to windows, particularly in homes where the occupants generally rose at sunrise and retired at sunset.

Cotton dimity shared the practical aspects of cambric muslin, being washable and relatively inexpensive (in the 1850s about half the price of a woollen damask). By about 1800 most dimities were corded, with woven vertical ribs or alternating plain and ribbed stripes, but they could also be patterned with small woven motifs dotted over the surface. It was probably an imitation dimity being referred to when, in 1797, the Peels of Church & Bury printed 'pin striped chintz, the pin to represent muslin'.[17] *Cassell's Household Guide* of the early 1870s recommended dimity in each of its four volumes and it was approved by virtually all the writers so far

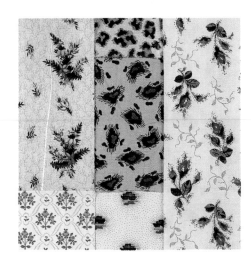

7 This group of printed cotton furnishing fabrics typify the small floral, stylized and abstract patterns which have been produced over the last two centuries. All have been block-printed, with the exception of the sample at lower left, which was roller-printed in about 1912. The leopard-spot patterns were printed in about 1800 (top) and 1820, and were revived again in the inter-war years and, as a screen print, in the late 1980s. The small 'shawl' pattern with a pinned, or dotted, ground was also fashionable early in the nineteenth century; this sample was printed in the 1920s from blocks first used in about 1840. The floral patterns (upper left and far right) were fashionable in the second and third quarters of the nineteenth century, respectively, and represent the type of pattern most often revived since. The rosebud chintz was used in 1863 as a wall covering in one of the English royal palaces.

mentioned. Wharton went so far as to say that it was easy to make 'tinted walls, deal furniture and dimity curtains more beautiful, because more logical and more harmonious, than a ball-room lined with gold and marbles'.[18] Her comment implicitly underlines the 'ordinary' status of dimities by the beginning of the twentieth century, but earlier, at the beginning of the ninteenth century, this was one of the fashionable cloths made from fine 'muslin' yarns. Like muslins, dimities were often printed.

Small 'all-over' patterned weaves and prints can also be considered basic cloths. Typically including no more than three colours, their simple striped, floral, geometric or irregular forms are far more resistant to changing fashions than large-scale designs, possibly because the differences between them are scarcely distinguishable. Small prints were naturally used for linings. In 1839, for example, Loudon noted that chintz was preferred for bed curtains, and that such curtains were 'generally lined with cotton of a different colour, sometimes plain, and sometimes spotted'.[19] For elegant drawing rooms in 1808, George Smith allowed small chintz patterns as a choice for curtain material (after damasks and plain satins and lustrings), and in 1852 J. Arrowsmith thought them particularly suitable for drawing rooms 'which are confined or low'.[20] A glance at surviving records of high-quality furnishing fabric printers working at Bannister Hall, near Preston between 1799 and 1893 and of Stead McAlpin & Co. (at Cummersdale near Carlisle from 1835 to today) indicate that block printers consistently received orders for small-scale floral prints. These could actually be more expensive to produce than larger patterns, because the blocks had to be 'laid' many more times to complete a length of cloth. The most inexpensive method of producing small prints was by wooden 'surface' or engraved metal rollers, used by furnishing fabric manufacturers from the beginning of the nineteenth century. Since the same types of machine were used to print fabrics for clothing, all inexpensive 'calico' dress prints were potentially furnishing fabrics, particularly in households where availability and price were of paramount importance.

In fact, all of the other fabrics mentioned so far were also originally used for clothing. Even denim (since the late eighteenth century firmly associated with rugged clothing) was used in interiors. In 1904, for example, an American writer suggested a blue denim bedspread to replace a white one in a boy's bedroom that had no couch. This knowledge should make us wary of classifying textiles rigidly as 'dress' or 'furnishing' fabrics. In the past, as today, people have shown great ingenuity in using dress fabrics for furnishing, and vice versa – a fact frustrating to the historian and the restorer.

Despite such ambiguities, we do have some fairly reliable guides to the appearance and use of fabrics in furnishing over the past two centuries – in the form of contemporary publications, manufacturers' records, inventories and decorators' accounts (generally available only for upper- and upper-middle-class homes). These document what fabrics were available and how they were used in specific settings, while pictorial sources show us the final result. From these it is possible to build up a picture of the

8 Silk designs of c.1680–1800 are the source of many subsequent patterns, whether direct copies or simplified adaptations. These three twentieth-century silks, hand-loom Jacquard-woven by Warners, typify the main pattern types. 'Hampton Court Palace' (left) copies a Genoese crimson damask ordered in 1689 by William III for the walls of one of the Presence Chambers in the palace. This pattern represents the last stage of Near Eastern influence, with its highly organized, formal foliate designs. By 1775–85 ('Farleigh', centre) all that remained similar was the repeat height; the several-centuries-old ogee structure also appears, but interpreted as graceful curving garlands in characteristic Rococo style. Typical of many designs up to the mid-nineteenth century are the two main motifs within similar 'frames', one above the other. Intended for use in long drops, such patterns were necessarily halved as ceilings became lower in the second half of the nineteenth century. Richly brocaded with additional colours by the use of small hand-held bobbins, 'Farleigh' is in the style of Philippe de Lasalle, a Lyons silk designer (1723–1805). Patterns with similar structures were also manufactured as damasks. At the end of the eighteenth century, fashion demanded light, lustrous fabrics. Few brocades were being made, and the damasks of this period, such as 'Mentmore' (right) tended to have well-spaced design elements to show off large areas of satin ground.

typical interiors of each period; and this, together with the developments in textile design, manufacture and distribution, forms the basis of the following chapters. The 'basic' fabrics will be mentioned again but, for obvious reasons, not in proportion to their use. Changing their colours in response to changing fashions, these fabrics have acted as a foil for more boldly patterned textiles or wallpapers, as complements to polished woods, understated modern interiors or cottage furniture, and as linings or for other practical purposes. They therefore form a continuing thread that runs through interiors over the past 200 years.

9 The curtains on this bed of c.1775 have a damask design in the Palladian style, fragmented by the introduction of finely etched areas of infill patterns inspired by details from 1720s and '30s plasterwork cornices, picture frames and other architectural embellishments. Its first known use in Britain was in the 1730s, and immediately after its appearance variations became available. This pattern has since enjoyed widespread and constant use, especially in British houses, appearing – as did many other damasks – in widths of both 21 and 25 inches by the early years of the nineteenth century. The bed itself, at Blickling Hall, Norwich, has been restored several times; note that several damask patterns have been used.

10 This damask design developed from the 'Farleigh' type of rococo-influenced brocade, but its leopard-spotted ribbon framework repeats itself exactly, making it half the vertical height. It was probably first produced in the last quarter of the eighteenth century, and has been in production ever since. In 1810, a blue damask in this pattern was used for chair coverings and window hangings in a New York house, and it was being woven in the years around 1840 by the Spitalfields silk weavers Bailey & Jackson. In the

9

10

11

second half of the nineteenth century, the English silk-weaving firm Daniel Walters & Sons also produced an almost identical damask. The sample shown here, probably woven in France, was in the range of H. Scott Richmond, an English

firm active from about 1840 to 1930. In East London, in 1871, Warners began producing a design only marginally different, and it is still in their hand-wovens range. Scalamandre have produced it in America.

11 These block-printed impressions on paper, from a volume that probably records the cotton furnishing textiles of the block printer E. B. Dudding, 1811–16, show a portion of a damask pattern similar to that seen in Figs. 2 and 9.

12 An American lambrequin of about 1860–80, made of English moreen, a worsted stamped or embossed in imitation of a damask. Damasks derive their effect from the contrast between matt and glossy, or light and shaded areas, and over the last 200 years their patterns have often been simulated on cloths (by printing or embossing) and on wallpapers (by flocking or printing).

13 Mary Ellen Best produced this watercolour of her dining room in York in 1838, shortly after it was redecorated. This middle-class interior shows the persistence of a number of nineteenth-century themes: the red curtains – probably (since Yorkshire was the major centre for their production) a woollen or worsted cloth; the haircloth-covered dining chairs, identified by their sheen; and the linen tablecloth (note also the napkins used as side plates). The somewhat haphazard arrangement of the pleats in the curtain valance was typical of homemade or a provincial upholsterer's work. The dominant pattern – on the walls – could be either wallpaper or fabric. If the latter, it would also certainly have been a printed cotton (used as late as the 1860s for covering walls), for a weave would have been too elaborate for this room.

14 Velvet was chosen for an important Gothic-style oriel window, illustrated in Ackermann's *Repository of Arts* in 1826. A stamped or cut-pile silk or 'Manchester' cotton velvet, it was recommended for its jewel-like colours (see Fig. 15 for surviving stamped velvets). The pattern is appropriately Gothic, being a fifteenth-century quatrefoil design. The textured richness of the fabric is matched by the trimmings.

15

15 Now under the care of the British National Trust, Penrhyn Castle, in North Wales, has an important collection of stamped velvets. In the drawing room (restored in 1985–6) the 1830s chairs retain their original stamped velvet upholstery. Stamped and printed velvets duplicated the richness of effect obtained in the more costly voided velvets. Leather and leather-cloth was also stamped with similar patterns. The curtains and wallcovering have been made in a three-colour silk lampas, re-woven in France from a fabric found on a sofa in the same room.

16

16 A collection of Pennsylvanian artifacts are accompanied by curtains and a tent bed canopy newly made from mid-nineteenth-century indigo and white ginghams and fringe; the 1840s quilt also includes basic stripes and small prints.

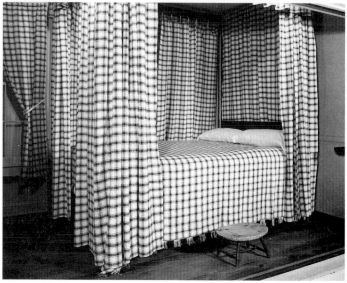

17

17 A collection of household textiles used by the Copp family in late eighteenth-century America includes these bed hangings, coverlet and pair of curtains, all hand-woven in single-ply linen, possibly by the Copps themselves. Approximately 50 yards of 34-inch-wide fabric were used in the complete set, which was woven with blue and undyed yarns. Such large, boldly shaded checks (this one is 2½ by 2¾ inches) remained popular well into the 1840s, by which time they were being power-woven. Plaid-like checks in richer colours were popular again in the second half of the nineteenth century (when they were associated with Queen Victoria's Scottish residence, Balmoral). Between about 1930 and 1960, homespun-looking checks and plaids were also favoured.

18

19

20

18 Unlike checked ginghams, stripes – another basic pattern – have never been relegated to 'country' or informal settings. This 'in-town' living room, from *Modern Homes Illustrated* (London, 1947) makes clever use of painted red lines, red and blue piping, and striped furnishings. The linen curtains were hand-screen-printed with blue stripes (the same screen used horizontally created the plaid) and red dots. Used separately the same two stripe and dot screens have created the fabrics for the loose-covered furniture.

19 Plain-weave cotton cloths, patterned in various ways by dyeing some of the yarns, were called 'ginghams' for much of the nineteenth century. Six such cottons are shown on a page from the Lancaster Mills' 1848 sample book. Numbers 2, 5 and 6 would today be called ticking, whereas the remainder have retained the name gingham. When America's textile factory system developed in the 1790s, fabrics such as these were among the first to be produced.

20 A certain indication of the popularity of a woven pattern is its imitation by printing. In this 1885 American example, checks have been machine-printed on cotton by the Cocheco Manufacturing Company of Dover, New Hampshire.

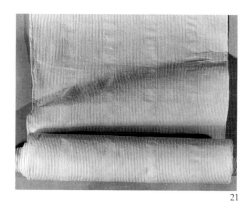

21 The Copp family history records that this cotton dimity was bought in New York in 1800. It would have been intended for window curtains, bed hangings or clothing. Part of the roll still exists; the cloth is 25 inches wide, woven with intermediate narrow and wide stripes. Other patterns (such as 'bird's eyes') were in some cases called dimity, but the taste of the times for striped fabrics no doubt made this type of dimity the most fashionable.

23 From the introduction of muslins into interiors at the beginning of the nineteenth century to the re-appearance of watercolour-like furnishing prints in contemporary interiors, the influence of fashionable dress has been a perennial factor in furnishings over the past two centuries. Often the same fabrics or designs have served both purposes. Here an elaborate tented bed has been created by Zandra Rhodes, using 'Star Wars', a screen-printed pleated net of her own design and manufacture which was part of her fashion collection of 1977.

22 Promoting style without money, this 1938 interior was illustrated in *Decorating is Fun!*, written in 1944 by the influential American decorator Dorothy Draper. The table setting is 'from the Five-and-Ten-Cent Store', and includes lettuce-green china, red-handled cutlery and a tablecloth and napkins of green-dotted white organdie (stiffened muslin) bought by the yard (probably from among the dress fabrics) and hemmed at home. These and the green taffeta homemade dress curtains, magenta satin upholstery and muslin glass curtains all have a shiny or crisp handle, which has always imparted an aura of expense (which has probably also contributed to the continued popularity of glazed cottons).

24 The decoration of this unmistakably modern Paris flat belonging to the British architect Richard Rogers – with leather for upholstery and firmly woven cotton for blinds – relies entirely on two basic cloths which have been used in interiors over the past two centuries in the same way, although seldom with such a stark effect.

26 This Manhattan apartment, designed in 1986 by the architect Stephen Forman, demonstrates the versatility of pile fabrics, which, despite their luxurious surface and historical associations, have never been entirely eliminated from modern interiors. Here the owner's involvement in the film business has been evoked by selecting 1930s-style setting, upholstered in cinema fashion with commercial-weight mohair velvet produced by Boris Kroll, a leading American wovens manufacturer founded in 1938.

24

25

26

25 The muslin of these 1839 curtains (illustrated in J. C. Loudon's *Encyclopedia of Farm, Villa and Cottage Architecture*) was more similar to cambric lawn in its fineness – it is said that forty layers were required to make it opaque. Here, a sheer fabric was required so as not to detract from the architectural detail. This means of draping them – together at the top, pulled to one side and held by cords or around metal curtain pins – was a practice already established in the eighteenth century, and it has remained one of the accepted ways of deploying muslin and lace curtains ever since.

Chapter Two

Revolution

1790–1825

'Change in fashion becomes a source of wealth and commerce.'
(George Smith, in *A Collection of Designs for Household
Furniture*[1])

In the textile industry, as in political life, the years around 1790 were a watershed. On the 4th of July, 1788, the newly independent United States celebrated the recent ratification of their Constitution, and in the following month 'privilege' was condemned by a French nobleman, Mirabeau, as 'the mortal enemy of the "nation"', giving notice to the shrewd observer of the impending French Revolution.[2] Meanwhile Britain had developed a thriving cotton industry, which derived its strength from its lead in yarn-spinning technology. John Kay's flying shuttle – invented in 1733 but not widely applied until after the middle of the century – had simplified the hand-weaving of wider cloths but also increased from three to twelve the number of hand spinners needed to supply one weaver. This demand was effectively met first by James Hargreaves' jenny, a hand-operated multiple-spindle machine patented in 1770. In the following year Richard Arkwright established the first water-powered spinning mill, employing the water frame, which he had patented in 1769.

Unlike the jenny, the water frame was capable of producing coarse cotton yarns, which for the first time were strong enough to act as a warp. The natural consequence of this development was to jeopardize the manufacture of fustian, a cloth (made with a linen warp and cotton weft), which since 1736 had enjoyed a monopoly as the only legally sanctioned 'cotton' fabric that could be woven and printed in Britain for home consumption. The so-called 'Manchester Act' of 1736, which had provided this protection, indicated the growing force of the cotton industry, for it was a reversal of part of a 1721 act (sponsored by weavers of medium-priced silks, half-silks, worsted and woollens) which had prohibited the sale, use and wear of *all* British printed calicoes. By securing the rights to print on fustian in 1736 (and on cotton if exported), the calico printers regained the use of the best base-cloth produced in Britain at the time.

By the 1770s the cotton industry had such power that in 1774, only three years after Arkwright began spinning cotton suitable for warps, the remaining prohibition on the home consumption of all-cotton cloths was also removed. Accompanying this repeal was the institution of heavy excise duties placed on printed goods and intended to continue a degree of protection for the woollen and silk industries. Despite this, the British

1 A copperplate print depicting George Washington in a chariot of state, Benjamin Franklin and Liberty led by Minerva towards the Temple of Fame and, on Minerva's shield, thirteen stars representing the thirteen states of the newly formed American republic. Although produced specifically for the American market (in Britain in about 1785), this print appealed to the popular interest in democracy and was sold in other countries as well. Many Europeans, particularly the French, looked to America for a republican model. At least three versions are known – in blue, red and purple, with minor changes in details, on cloths of varying widths, on all-cotton and fustian (linen and cotton), and with and without blue threads in the selvage (the latter indicating manufacture for export from Britain between 1774 and 1811).

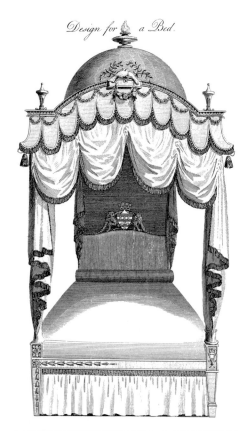

Design for a Bed.

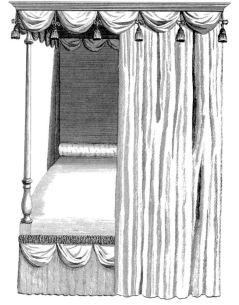

2

cotton industry grew rapidly, adding to its technical prowess Samuel Crompton's spinning mule (patented in 1779 and developed in the 1780s) and Thomas Bell's engraved roller printing machine (patented in 1783–4 but in limited use until the 1810s). James Watts's steam engines (patented in 1769) were applied to mule and jenny spinning from 1781. With the patenting of power looms by Edmund Cartwright in 1787 and of the cotton gin by the American Eli Whitney in 1793–4, the last technical bottlenecks were cleared. Although the wool and silk industries applied some of the new technologies, such as mule spinning and steam power, it was the cotton spinners, weavers and printers who used it most effectively and with the greatest impact in the years around 1790. Cottons became more widely available, cheaper and, not surprisingly, even more fashionable.

The coincidence of these three revolutions – two political and the other industrial – affected the commercial alliance which one would have expected to find between America and her ally, France. The French textile industry dominated the intangible force of fashion, and French weavers in Lyon and printers in Jouy, Rouen, Nantes and elsewhere were renowned for their leadership in design. Ironically, the depression which had followed France's entry into the American war in 1778 had already precipitated a crisis in the French textile industry. The annexation of the Mulhouse area to France's eastern border in 1789 added an important textile-printing centre to French domains; but being preoccupied with its internal struggles, France in the 1790s could do little either to promote the industrialization of its industry or to prevent Britain from establishing itself as the principal supplier of textiles for America. By 1795 North America (including Canada) accounted for over half of Britain's cotton exports, and these were equalled – if not slightly exceeded – by the number of British woollens sold to America. Thus furnishing fabrics were similar in these English-speaking countries.

The growing importance of cotton fabrics from the fourth decade of the eighteenth century onwards can be seen especially in the furnishings for beds, which throughout this period were the principal vehicle for displaying the art of upholstery. In *The Cabinet-Maker and Upholsterer's Guide* (published in 1788, 1789 and 1794) George Hepplewhite described bed furnishings as predominantly of cotton: white dimity, 'plain or corded, [was] peculiarly applicable', Manchester (cotton) velvets could be used 'with good success' and printed cottons and linens were 'very suitable'. Only in state rooms, 'where a high degree of elegance and grandeur are wanted' could Hepplewhite envisage figured or plain silk or satin, or gold velvet with gold fringes.[3]

A corresponding shift towards cotton furnishing fabrics was also occurring in America, according to Abbott Lowell Cummings' survey of inventories and accounts in Suffolk County, Massachusetts. Although about 90 per cent of the beds listed had unspecified fabrics, the remaining noted between 1760 and 1770 were predominantly worsteds, such as harrateen and cheney; between 1800 and 1810 no cheneys and only five harrateens appear (three of the latter described as 'old'), and in their place were copperplate prints and other cottons and linens – accounting for about 65 per cent of the fabrics named. One entry for silk occurs in each period.[4]

Fabrics for window draperies and furniture show a similar, although less emphatic, trend towards cotton. Silks and velvets continued to be recommended in influential publications such as George Smith's *Collection of Designs for Household Furniture*, 1808, and Rudolph Ackermann's journal, *The Repository of Arts*, 1809–1828, but it was generally understood that these were appropriate 'where grandeur and show are necessary' and chintz or calico could be substituted 'according to choice'.[5]

Well into the 1820s, cottons seemed less acceptable only in libraries and dining rooms; for these the preferred fabrics were 'cloth', 'stuff' and moreen – all worsteds, the last-named having a horizontal rib and, usually, a stamped or watered pattern. The inclination towards such fabrics may have arisen out of the belief that, as Hepplewhite asserted, dining rooms should be 'plain and neat'[6], or out of the growing tendency to regard both libraries and dining rooms as masculine domains. Further, woollen or worsted fabrics were complementary to haircloth or Moroccan leather, both of which were often recommended for upholstering furniture intended for these rooms. Woollens and worsteds were not, of course, excluded entirely from drawing rooms; George Smith, for example, proposed curtains 'of silk, to have a rich effect, or else of fine

2 Two beds from Hepplewhite's 1787 *Cabinet Maker and Upholsterer's Guide* showing the popular late-eighteenth-century use of swags. The first illustrates working festoons, drawn up by means of cords. Below it is a bed of simpler construction with decorative swags which maintain the fashionable theme and serve to cover the pole on which the straight-hanging curtains are suspended. Dimity, cotton velvets, printed cottons or linens were usual on such beds, and only the more elaborate and costly beds (such as plate 100) were described as 'proper for satin or velvet furniture' (meaning the textile elements). Bed draperies could require up to 50 yards of cloth, and window draperies were expected to match them.

3 A counterpane hand-block printed by John Hewson of Philadelphia, 1790–1800, demonstrating that American block printing could be of high quality. The design shows awareness of developments in the European decorative arts, with the slightly scalloped edging with tassels printed in imitation of a swagged bed or curtain drapery. Its *Indienne* motifs would also have been equally appreciated by British tastes. The fabric is printed in black, brown and two shades of red, with blue and yellow drawn on by hand, a process known as 'pencilling'. The golden brown or butternut colour is particularly interesting because it may have been produced from the American oak – a dye not widely used in Britain until the early 1800s.

3

cassimere' (a soft, twilled woollen of medium weight).[7] Nor was haircloth confined to 'masculine' rooms, as we can infer from Hepplewhite's general recommendation that 'mahogany chairs should have seats of horsehair, plain, striped, chequered, etc. at pleasure, or cane bottoms with cushions, the cases of which should be covered the same as the curtains.'[8]

The concept of integrated schemes of furniture and internal decoration, alluded to by Hepplewhite, had previously been introduced in the houses designed by British architects such as Robert Adam. It generally meant matching window and upholstery fabrics or, if different (as was necessary when upholstery was of leather or haircloth), the use of similar hues. Fabrics on walls were also included in this 'en suite' fashion, which persisted into the middle of the nineteenth century. The wide circulation of publications such as Hepplewhite's *Guide* no doubt contributed to the longevity of this eighteenth-century fashion, acting as a link between what could have been seen in many grand English houses prior to 1790 and what became standard practice in fashionable interiors in Britain, the United States and elsewhere for several decades thereafter.

English writers recommended silks for these ensembles, and this advice was followed by the most fashionable American and British upholsterers. Never created in vast numbers of houses during this period, silk-laden interiors remained costly and therefore socially desirable. One needs little imagination to suppose the impact of an American house in which the 'First Drawing Room' described in an early nineteenth-century inventory contained a sofa, ten chairs and two armchairs, all covered 'en suite' in blue silk and each with a linen loose cover. In addition there was a set of blue silk curtains and cornices (which may suggest the style of drawn-up festoons with an 'upholstered' cornice) and another set of muslin and

4 This Buckinghamshire interior was recorded in watercolours by one of the Drummond children, whose schoolroom it was. Although painted in 1828, it shows muslin-curtained windows embellished with festoons – probably fixed in position – which differ little from draperies found in a variety of French engraved sources, including copperplate-printed toiles of c.1790. Similarly, striped cotton or linen loose covers had been fashionable over the same period. One can only guess what type of fabric was used to upholster the furniture, but haircloth cannot be ruled out: across the Atlantic the young American Sophie du Pont recorded in her letters and diaries of 1823–33 that their horsehair sofa had been 'robed in full attire of white dimity' because the upholstery had lost its sheen.

5 A group of designs produced at Bannister Hall in 1800 or 1806, comprising a 'pillar' print, a chair seat and a border (for the sides of a chair cushion or for edging curtains). These sets were very popular; for each border shown there was a coordinating seat and pillar print. The 'pillars' were printed as stripes or, as instructed on another, placed up the middle of the cloth with a filling pattern on either side. The small designs proposed as fillings appear with the lower pillar.

linen curtains and blinds (possibly for the summer).[9] The muslin curtain set was not valued, but the remainder totalled £289 (American), a considerable sum in a period when few estates were worth more than £2,000.

Ackermann's *Repository* was probably – according to a recent study – 'the first publication to promote the [*en suite*] idea forcefully for middling houses'.[10] By 1825, however, Ackermann had observed signs that 'the fashion of making the coverings of furniture similar in point of colour to the walls of the room has at length subsided, and the colour now chosen for them is such as will form harmonious combinations. . . .'[11]

Loose covers (or cases) provided one of the easiest ways to unify furniture, particularly if the pieces were of varying ages. The fabrics used for cases were linens and cottons (which were, of course, washable) with woven or printed patterns. Cases might also serve to protect a fine upholstery fabric or conceal an inferior one. The use of cases to protect upholstery is well documented in both Britain and the United States. There is evidence that – in Britain at least – cases were still made, as they had been in the seventeenth century, to cover chairs which had no 'final' upholstery, but only the canvas normally used as a foundation under a finer cloth. Conventional upholstery had two fabric surfaces, as described in the records of the London furniture makers Gillow, when, in 1817, they made two 'chairs in thin . . . canvas with fast [fixed] covers in Print' for a Colonel Wilkes.[12] Hepplewhite's description of a 'Saddle Check, or easy chair [which] may be covered with leather, horse-hair; or have a linen case to fit over the canvas stuffing as is most usual and convenient' may, however, suggest a loose cover over canvas.[13] Upholsterers may have provided canvas-covered chairs for the owner to cover later, perhaps with her own petit point or embroidery, but this custom also served as a means of economizing. It therefore appears equally likely that cases were put on for special occasions if the covering beneath was merely canvas, and taken off for special occasions if the cloth below was of finer quality. The first of these situations evidently obtained in Edinburgh's Assembly Rooms in about 1800, when 'a Lady Helen Hall was demanding that the Directors of the Assembly Rooms "permit the covers of the sofas & benches . . . to be given out on the nights of the Dancing school balls . . . for nobody likes to sit upon dirty canvas with nails standing out, to tear their cloaths every time they move".'[14]

The fashion for *en suite* fabric was also reflected in the sets of matching curtains, chair seats and borders which could be hand woven to order and to shape. In 1790 a Spitalfields weaver produced 'tailor-made' chair seats for the Prince of Wales's Chinese Drawing Room at Carlton House; the room was subsequently illustrated in Sheraton's *Drawing Book*. Specialized work of this kind had always been the province of hand-weavers, and the practice continues, although on a very limited scale since about 1930. Block printers quickly demonstrated that their work was equally flexible, as can be seen among the records of high-quality block printers operating at Bannister Hall, near Preston, Lancashire, throughout most of the nine-teenth century. Between about 1800 and 1825, numerous sets of chair seats, borders, 'furnitures' and 'fillings' were produced there – many at the instigation of Richard Ovey, a London merchant-warehouseman. Ovey often sent designs to the printers, annotated with relevant com-ments; one of 3 March 1806 reads: 'This chair seat is designed to match the . . . Pillar [a "furniture" print depicting a plain marble pillar swatched in a spiralling garland of lilacs, roses, convolvulus, wheat-ears etc.] and hope [you'll] get on with it as [soon as] possible – as [I] can't sell the Pillar without it. . . .' The practice of printing sets was also mentioned in 1793 by Sheraton, with regard to a chair that 'may be finished in japan painting . . . The covering of the seat is of printed chintz, which may now be had of various patterns on purpose for chair-seats, together with borders to suit them.' Sets of English printed fabrics such as borders and fillings were also known to have been used in the United States.[15]

Although *en suite* curtains and upholstery were the ideal, many homes on both sides of the Atlantic had no curtains to match their furniture. During the first decades of the nineteenth century this seems to have been by choice as often as by necessity. In the inventories of three members of Samuel Crompton's family (for whom fabric could not have been scarce), bedsteads and hangings are mentioned in 1799, 1802 and 1805, but only in the 1805 account does one window curtain also appear. Inventories, descriptive accounts and pictorial sources demonstrate the gradually increasing use of curtains in this period, but even as late as 1824, when the wealthy Pennsylvanian Isaac Pennock died, only one of his six bedrooms had curtains, and his otherwise expensively furnished parlour and dining room had none.[16]

However, many otherwise undressed windows had blinds (as did

6 John Harden, a gentleman and amateur watercolourist, painted this informal family scene at his home in the Lake District in 1827. The house, Brathay Hall, had been rented by Harden in 1804, and the room shown here was probably furnished soon afterwards (the Hardens purchased items new, from a house sale at Rydal and possibly from their landlord, who in 1805 sold the furniture originally in the house). The same velvet, or, more likely, woollen stuff, appears as curtains and on the furniture, as was fashionable at the beginning of the nineteenth century. Of particular interest is the sun blind composed of two frames containing pleated silk and hinged inside the recessed shutters. When closed they filtered the light coming through the window, as had their precursors, sash curtains (for which both plain and copperplate-printed silks had been used).

curtained windows). These took several forms. The simplest had been known in the late seventeenth century, and in crude form was described by Thomas Martin in 1813 as 'the cheapest kind of blind . . . formed of green canvas fixed to two sticks either of mahogany or walnut and hung by a couple of rings and hooks screwed to the lowermost sash frames'.[17] Both paper and flat or pleated silk sun screens were similar, occupying the lower portion of the window, but these were more costly; painted or varnished, they were usually framed, and hinged from the side of the window. It is thought that the 'paper curtains' in General Salem Towne's kitchen in his Charlton, Massachusetts, house in 1799 were probably of this construction, but they may equally have been paper roller blinds.[18]

Direct sunlight was considered too harsh, and its effects on furnishings – specifically fading and rotting – were already well known. In the last quarter of the eighteenth century, Susanna Whatman, wife of James Whatman, a prosperous paper-maker in Kent, created her own precise written instructions on housekeeping. They included cautions against knocking painted chairs together or breaking the plaster between the dado and skirting board. The arrival of the sun was noted for each room: 'The sun comes into the Library very early. The window on that side of the bow must have the blind let down. . . . Drawing room. The blinds always closed in the morning and window up. Kept dusted . . . and the mahogany rubbed. The covers shook.'

The Whatmans had wooden Venetian blinds, probably very similar in construction to blinds known by that name today: 'When let down . . . pull the longest string to turn or close them quite.'[19] The Venetian blinds advertised by James Barron in *Modern and Elegant Design of Cabinets and Upholstery Furniture*, London, 1814, differed, and were 'made in pairs if not ordered otherwise: if in 3 parts . . . please give the exact distance of the Bars of the Sash, that the Frame of the Blinds may come opposite them.' The wooden-slat blinds described as most fashionable by Sheraton in his

Dictionary of 1803 correspond to Barron's Venetian blinds: 'the frame . . . is of mahogany. The blind part is either composed of upright or horizontal narrow laths which are an eighth part of an inch thick, painted bright green, and move by means of a lever, to any position for admitting more or less light.'[20] Although Venetian blinds were most fashionable, they were far too costly for widespread use (which may explain why some among the wealthy chose them over curtains). Barron's Venetian blinds were 49/9 for 5 by 2½ feet; much more economical were his cloth patent roller blinds, which, at the same size, cost 21/6. These blinds could be fixed to the top of the window with sliding brackets – to allow for the removal of the blind – or with spring brackets. In 1808 George Smith recommended these newly invented spring blinds 'of the same colour as the principal draperies'.[21] Blinds were also made of printed or painted fabrics. However, both Sheraton and Martin (who copied much of his information on blinds from the formers' *Dictionary*) agreed that the most commonly used blinds were plain rolling blinds without springs, normally made of white silesia, woven to the standard widths of windows (2¼–4½ feet). Silesia was initially a stout linen, but at about this time the name began to be applied to a coarse cotton cloth of similar appearance. The replacement of linen yarn by cotton typified many cloths of the early nineteenth century. The name 'fustian', for example, was now adopted by cotton weavers of the period for an all-cotton fabric which imitated the linen-warp and cotton-weft fustian of the eighteenth century. Such inexpensive cotton fabrics were the main factor behind the increased use of curtains and blinds in the early nineteenth century by people of modest means.

The increased use of curtains during this period was paralleled by an increase in the amount of fabric recommended for individual window schemes. Because the tax on British printed cottons, established in 1774, was applied equally, irrespective of cloth quality or the number of colours, the cost of low-priced prints increased by 70–80 per cent, while those of higher quality, with more elaborate patterns, had only 10–15 per cent added. This evened out the prices in Britain, and possibly contributed to

7 Window curtains for a boudoir, designed by Mr. Allen of Pall Mall, a London decorator and draper who was congratulated by Ackermann for his stock of 'most chaste and elegant patterns of calicoes'. Illustrated in the *Repository of Arts* of April 1809, the curtains were of ruby-coloured calico printed in various black hues and were lined with 'a newly invented [cotton] print of an azure colour, strictly resembling a figured silk'. The mantle or central valance of blue silk was a variation of continued draperies, which linked together two or more windows. The pole – described as suspended by silken cords attached to metal pins – is surmounted by implements of war, alluding to a military tent. War in Europe was almost continuous from the late 1790s until about 1815, ensuring the popularity of designs and interior schemes based on allegories of both peace and war.

8 French influence dominates the boudoir at The Deepdene, the Surrey house owned by Thomas Hope, author of *Household Furniture and Interior Decoration* (1807). The room was furnished between 1806 and 1818 (when W. H. Bartlett painted this watercolour). The work may have been carried out by George Bullock, an influential furniture designer and decorator who popularized Mona marble fireplaces such as the one shown, and whose work was often illustrated in Ackermann's *Repository of Arts*. Ackermann's May 1816 (p.307) description of Bullock as a man of 'genius and science' in an age when the fashion made rooms 'dependent on a display of elegant furniture and draperies, rather than on those features which are peculiarly and legitimately architectural' also marries well with Hope's boudoir decoration. The loose-covered sofa, its baldequin with gathered fabric interior and Roman drapery, the walls and two small movable items of furniture are all covered in the same pattern, which may be a chintz with a leopard-spot design. French influence is most noticeable in the enclosed sofa, reminiscent of a fashionable French treatment for beds, and in the Roman draperies, with their conical pleats and embroidered or appliquéd neo-classical wreaths.

the sluggish introduction of machine printing (which produced prints more cheaply, but lost part of this advantage due to taxation). A 'drawback' or refund was obtained on exports, but shipping costs had a similar effect on the purchase price of imported printed cottons in the United States. Nevertheless, from about 1805 the relatively low cost and practicality of cottons contributed substantially to the large amounts of yardage in more elegant British and American interiors. Some idea of the amounts required for a fashionable 'suit of curtains' in 1810 can be obtained from a Boston advertisement offering 168 yards of cambric chintz and the same amount of light blue cambric for lining.[22]

One fashionably lavish use of material was in additional draperies fixed at the top of the windows over newly fashionable floor-length divided curtains. This style incorporated – visually though not functionally – features of two earlier styles: the elegant single festoon curtains, which were drawn up into swags by means of cords and pulleys; and the equally fashionable divided swag-type curtains, which consisted of two pieces of fabric drawn diagonally upwards to create swags with 'tails' at either side.

Swagged effects were not confined to windows: they were also added between chair and sofa legs, behind bookcase doors, to bed cornices and around the edges of small tables – manifesting in fabric an already existing decorative motif employed in plasterwork, marquetry, wall painting and relief carving. So similar were the effects created that engravings for decorators could be misleading. In 1793 Sheraton added to his notes concerning two sets of cornices, curtains and draperies for drawing room windows a caution that 'the French strapping and tassels in the right-hand design is no part of the cornice, as some cabinet-makers have already mistaken it to be. It is the upholsterer's work, and is sewed on within the valance or ground of the drapery.'[23]

In time, a more reserved form of upper drapery began to appear. This consisted of widely spaced conical pleats, which were drawn marginally upwards to create shallow curves in between – a style fashionable in France at the turn of the century (most notably in Madame Récamier's bedroom, 1802, where the same drapery technique was also used to cover the walls). George Smith's 1808 *Collection of Designs for Household Furniture* showed several examples, 'commonly called Roman drapery . . . in fact taken from the Roman Standards'. One of these consisted of an under curtain of muslin worked with an ornamental border and bound with silk (drawn to the left) and a curtain (drawn to the right) and upper Roman drapery of satin or damask 'to be bordered with velvet, cut out and neatly sewn on.' The cornice, finished in bronze or gold, took the form of a large carved rod with three leopard-heads, two as finials and one above the elevated centre pleat. In 1810 Ackermann illustrated a less ostentatious version of lemon-coloured silk, hanging from large rosette pins and, five years later, the same construction hanging from rings on an exposed pole. The latter was also of silk, in this case 'interwoven in gradations of tints . . . termed "shot"'.[24] Since this style often left the top of the fabric exposed, necessitating skilful cutting, and since the recommended materials were usually the most expensive, suggestions such as Ackermann's and Smith's were not intended for any but the most experienced upholsterers and their wealthy clients. However, James Arrowsmith's *Analysis of Drapery* of 1819 included patterns for Roman drapery, and by the 1820s the means of achieving such effects were more widely understood.

The emphasis throughout this period remained at the top of the window, where carved gilt or japanned cornices were often combined with fixed upper draperies. The curtains beneath could either be fixed (closed)

9 Belton, Lincolnshire, as decorated by Gillow's in 1810–11, demonstrates the early-nineteenth-century fashion for red interiors, which persisted, though with diminishing incidence, for another eighty or ninety years. Here both the walls and the furniture are covered in a silk damask, which showed little signs of wear by the 1840s when this watercolour was painted. The portière and tablecloth were relatively new additions to the interior, and indicate a popular way in which interiors were updated without substantial alteration to the original decoration.

at the top and draped open or, more fashionably, hung from a 'French rod'. Introduced in about 1790, the French rod operated in a manner similar to the traverse rod or cording set of today, pulling open by means of cords. The French rod was the first device that allowed curtains to open without lifting from the floor, but like spring blinds, these did not become common until the second half of the nineteenth century, partly due to the fashion – noticeable by about 1810–15 for large elaborately decorated exposed rods with rings.

By about 1810 the fashion for both plain and embroidered muslin sub-curtains also became established as an integral part of fashionable, fully dressed window treatments, which now included what George Smith and others called continued draperies (with upper draperies and rod or cornice extended across two or more windows on the same wall). In this way cottons came to be used with silks, when they did not replace them entirely. In their continued campaign to increase the appeal of cottons, calico printers, not content with imitating woven upholstery 'sets', began to produce 'moiré' and 'damask' prints, the latter acknowledged by Ackermann in 1809 as 'equal to silk, particularly in the richer and more brilliant colours. . . . Should silk become objectionable from its expense, we strongly recommend the use of these new patterns. They need only be seen to become approved, and are particularly calculated for candle-light effect.'[25]

Against the competition of cottons, the silk weavers fared badly (particularly with respect to fabrics for clothing). French silks had been banned from sale in Britain since 1766 in order to protect the British weavers, but from about 1790 to 1815 the plight of London's Spitalfields weavers was particularly severe: competition of cheaper labour in the provinces and the use of steam power in the lower branches of silk weaving (i.e. plain, lightweight and mixed cloths) combined with existing difficulties which had already driven down wages, especially for hand weavers of simpler fabrics. Concern was such that in 1816, for example, the *Repository of Arts* illustrated a bed with hangings of light blue silk, lined and ornamented in 'a tender shade of brown'; and while noting that 'it would, however, be suitable to draperies of the usual [cotton] material', Ackermann urged the use of silks, which 'in the present state of our silk-manufactories . . . would prove a national advantage.'[26]

Throughout this difficult period the silks most consistently recommended for window and bed draperies were predominantly plain (and therefore less expensive). Satin-striped silk tabarets (with ribbed or watered alternate stripes) were often used for upholstery, but were said to make 'indifferent draperies'.[27] Plain silks were both recommended and used as linings for silk satin or damask curtains, but they also were inexpensive enough to be proposed as linings for cottons; Hepplewhite, for example, suggested green silk for lining a dark-patterned cotton print; white cotton he found appropriate for lining only light patterns. Much of the effect of draperies relied on a similar use of contrasting linings, fringes and borders, with dark edgings and/or linings often used on a light-coloured curtain.[28]

Many of the suggested colour schemes of the time reflect the growing interest in colour theory, which had been stimulated partly by the recent discovery that classical architecture had been coloured. Colour schemes thought to have been favoured in ancient and medieval periods were adopted, at first along with their corresponding decorative styles, then later without them. Combinations of the primaries in full or muted shades, of tertiaries, such as lilac with bright green and fawn, and of complementary colours, such as lavender with amber or light green with pink, were recommended by Ackermann between 1809 and about 1825, irrespective of the Grecian, Roman, Egyptian or Gothic allusions intended. For bedrooms, however, he favoured blues for bed hangings, often recommended with white and buff, fawn or gold.

It is difficult to know how carefully upholsterers followed the advice offered by the various 'directories' – not least because clients could supply their own fabrics, as did Lord Brownlow when Gillow's redecorated the Red Drawing Room at Belton in 1810–11, covering the walls and furniture with a red silk damask obtained by the client. Many wealthy Americans obtained fabrics directly from Europe and often gave very specific directions to their upholsterer. The majority of published engravings show unpatterned fabrics, or at most a generalized indication of surface design. Possibly this was to allow for individual taste. It may also have been intended to prevent plates from dating too quickly, for by 1800 fashions in printed furnishing patterns were changing routinely – a tradition established early in the eighteenth century by fine dress-silk weavers. Nevertheless, furnishing fabrics – particularly silks – were never subjected to the extreme pressure of fashion which led one silk merchant in 1769 to advertise 'a quantity of flowered and striped [dress] silk of last year's pattern [which] will be sold extremely low'.[29]

The fashionable patterns of the eighteenth, nineteenth and twentieth centuries are well charted with respect to their date of introduction, although many would have continued to be made for some time afterwards. In this period the source of some design types is fairly easy to trace, since they drew their inspiration from the prevailing interest in ancient and exotic cultures. The use of Indian styles was maintained through the importation of Indian shawls and already familiar Indian chintzes and the continuing influence of infill patterns with stylized and abstracted flowers.

Although many different designs appeared on textiles of the period, the dominant influence in interiors throughout was classicism. This trend took three related forms: the French Empire style (alive both before and after Napoleon's Imperial court of 1804–1815), the equally influential and related English Regency style and the American Federal style. The emergence of textiles based fairly accurately on classical motifs, around 1800, lagged several decades behind the developing interest in Egyptian, Etruscan, Greek and Roman archaeology, which had begun in the mid-eighteenth century with the discoveries at Pompeii and Herculaneum. One of the reasons for this delay may have been the initially high cost of the erudite publications in which these discoveries were presented. Several of them were re-issued in cheaper form in the first years of the nineteenth century.[30] In 1812 the upholsterer and decorator George Smith prefaced his *Collection of Ornamental Designs after the Manner of the Antique* with the observation that 'Many works have been published exhibiting faithful copies of the remains of the grandeur of ancient Architecture, as well as Ornament, yet . . . most of such publications are of great cost, and consequently not within the reach of general inspection'.[31] Surviving textile designs of the 1800s indicate that Smith's remarks were slightly out-dated, but they nevertheless explained the rather haphazard 'classical' styles (including European, Indian or Chinese motifs) which preceded and co-existed with more accurate archaeological interpretations that began to appear in about 1804.

The use of published sources for designs was not, of course, new; for many engraved roller-printed textiles continued the practice of copper plate printers, who often used images closely related to engravings.[32] Also of lasting importance to textile designers were the publications illuminating patterns for marquetry and carving. Although Robert Adam's two-volume *Works in Architecture* (1773–79) was not the first of these, it proved one of the most influential, establishing 'grotesque' scrollwork and classical motifs (and their Etruscan variants), arranged around a vertical axis, as perennial design types. The popularization of embroidered, appliquéd, painted and printed curtain and drapery borders in the 1780s and '90s owed a great deal to the 'grotesque' style, because it was widely used for long narrow sections of painted wall decorations, plasterwork mouldings and woodcarvings.

A more philosophical, less literal style in textiles followed the promotion of Grecian interiors by Thomas Hope in 1807[33] and Ackermann, who themselves were indebted respectively to the French publications of Charles Percier and Pierre-François-Léonard Fontaine[34] 1801–1812 and the journal *Meubles et Objets de Goût*.[35] At first glance the many floral textiles of the period may seem to spring from an entirely separate impulse, yet many fit well within this neo-classical idiom when viewed as emblematic designs. The longest entry in Sheraton's *Drawing Book* concerned the 'iconology' of a state bed, and includes references to motifs found on furniture and textiles of the period, together with a discussion of their symbolism. As well as pomegranates, grain, laurel wreaths, oak leaves and acorns, baskets of fruit and rose garlands, Sheraton mentioned cinnamon garlands, images of which were to 'signify that Chastity is a virtue both pleasant and valuable.'[36] 'Delicate conceits and comprehensive allusions' were approved by Ackermann, and were extended to colours. In 1814 he noted that 'azure and white . . . are the colours of the legitimate dynasty of France'[37] – a comment that may explain his preference for these colours in French-style bed hangings (used to frame both freestanding and sofa-like beds with conical or rounded domes).

Distinctive colour combinations were one of the most notable features of cotton furnishing prints of this period. Although not immediately apparent in full-colour chintzes of the 1790s, late eighteenth-century prints were primarily based on madder red. Printing was only one step in the elaborate process involved in producing a fast colour on fabric. Prepared cloth was

10 An increased understanding of the chemical properties of chlorine led, in the early nineteenth century, to the finely controlled creation of white dots by printing a bleaching agent either before or after dyeing the cotton with its background colour. In this example, block-printed in Britain in about 1805, the black background is probably a combination of an iron mordant and madder. Producing stripes and all-over background patterns was a great challenge because it required exact placement of blocks (here the slight mis-registration of the block can be seen in the centre area). One can conjecture that the anticipation of competition from cylinder printing (perfected in 1783 and capable of producing exact outlines, stripes and graded tones through varied spacing of dots) encouraged block-printers to pursue this more difficult style.

printed, not with a coloured substance but with a mordant (carried in a thickening agent), which attracted dye to the fibres. Madder red was the dye most commonly used in this way, and so this type of mordant-dyeing process was often called 'madder-style'. Several different mordants (such as alum and iron), or the same mordant in solutions of varying strengths, could be applied prior to immersing the piece in dye. Where they had been printed, the mordants reacted with the dyestuff to create different colours. Pinks, reds, purples, browns and black could therefore be obtained in a single madder dye bath, and these colours remained the basic underlying colours in many prints up to the middle of the nineteenth century. After dyeing, the cloth went through several further stages, including 'clearing', or removing the traces of colour from unmordanted areas.

If other colours were called for, weld (yellow) and indigo (blue) were the dyes generally used by eighteenth- and early nineteenth-century printers. In order to avoid dyeing the fabric a second time to create yellow areas (or oranges where placed over reds), weld could be applied to a madder-dyed cloth directly, by means of an artist's paint brush (traditionally called a 'pencil' and thus the technique's name, 'pencilling'). The drawback was that pencilled yellow was not fast. True greens could be created only by overlapping yellow and blue, although olive could be obtained by printing an iron mordant and dyeing in weld or another yellow dye. All natural dyes could be used in the madder-style, except indigo, which needed no mordant, but instead developed its colour on contact with oxygen. It therefore had to be treated in a completely different and often complex way if large areas of blue were required, and in madder-based prints it was usually pencilled on to avoid complications and reduce costs. By skilful use of mordants, using only red, yellow, and blue dyes, and by applying one colour over another, the block printer could produce deep lakes of colour with a wide range of subtle blends of shades and tones.

The appearance in 1799 of a predominantly green/brown/yellow-gold (or 'drab') palette is linked to the expiration of Dr. Edward Bancroft's 15-year patent on the manufacture of quercitron yellow (from the bark of the North American oak, *Quercus tinctoria*). 'Drabs' were highly fashionable until about 1806 and remained in use until the 1820s. Late eighteenth-century improvements in bleaching led to greater use, in about 1800, of backgrounds dyed indigo-blue and, after 1813, of backgrounds dyed Turkey-red (a very bright red derived from madder). Both of these colours were extremely fast and therefore required a strong bleach to re-create areas of pure white which were then re-printed. Improved bleaching methods also made possible elaborate variations of discharge printing, involving application of a bleaching agent combined with a mordant to create, for example, a red pattern on a blue ground. During the 1810s other complex dye styles evolved, many based on mineral dyes (first introduced in the 1790s for wools) and producing shades of buff, orange-red, brown and blue.

Each extra colour – if separately dyed – added considerable cost; and therefore many colour combinations arose out of attempts to provide a range of colours in one dye bath. Printing prices quoted by Peels in 1806

11 This English block-printed glazed cotton typifies both the 'pillar prints' and 'Gothic' trelliswork grounds which were the height of fashion in the years around 1805. Like many other designs of the period, it is printed in 'drab style' ('style' was the contemporary term for colour, rather than pattern). The various shades of brown and golden yellow were produced in the same quercitron (oak) dye bath after the cloth was printed with different mordants for each colour (probably iron for brown and alum for yellow). The blue was added afterwards by hand. Such single dye-bath styles were often referred to as 'demi-chintzes'.

included 141 (pence?) for purple, 310 for light pink with fawn (both possible from madder) and 1,710 for Saxon green (a fairly fast green obtained by pre-mixing indigo with a new yellow 'drug').[38] By 1817 his price list was still predominantly for two-colour/one dye-bath combinations – all in the 1806 price range except 'Chintz furniture', which at 3,010 must have involved an elaborate three-stage printing and dyeing process (for red, yellow and blue), or alternatively, have employed the new 'single' green (the first green obtained without overprinting indigo and yellow, developed in 1809). Few could have afforded such expensively-coloured chintzes. Printing/dyeing was still an inexact science, and results varied according to ingredients, skills and knowledge. In the opinion of Elijah Bemis, writing in the United States in 1815, 'Many dyers can work with success in a number of colours only which depend on each other, and are entirely ignorant of the rest, or have but a very imperfect idea of them.'[39] He himself was unaware of the 'single' green – as probably were many British dyers at this date. Colour-matching was also very difficult. Pieces from the same printer or dyer varied with changes in temperature and imprecise measurements of dyestuffs, and regional discrepancies occurred due to un-standardized working practices, different water and the use of local dyestuffs. For example, the American colour palette consistently used the 'butternut' colour, from the American oak, much earlier than did the British.

Little is known about the British designers of this period, apart from evidence in government enquiries and surviving patterns signed by such designers as William Kilburn, J. Pearman, Daniel Goddard, John Polley and H. Mills. It does seem clear, however, that designs were acquired in two different ways. The most fashionable patterns were probably purchased from freelance designers by linen-drapers such as Richard Ovey, Atkinson and Clarance, and George Anstey (all in London), or Bateman & Todd in Manchester – all of whom may also have employed in-house designers. Although these firms often described themselves as 'furniture printers' ('furniture' meaning furnishing fabrics), the printing was actually done elsewhere – as is known from surviving designs associated with the printers Vint & Gilling in Crayford and Clarksons at Bannister Hall. Less expensive prints, produced by the majority of printers, followed the formula of the Burys of Pendle Hill, calico printers who sold finished cloth to drapers (often by auction) through their London agent, Lloyd, or through other warehousemen. These uncommissioned prints may have been created by skilled designers, but more often they were the work of copyists. In 1807, for example, Joseph Peel sent a sample from a nearby printer to his firm, instructing them: 'This plate is new today. Draw some similar.' Regarding another, his request was to 'Copy it as near as you dare.'[40]

By 1805–10 many more prints were being produced by wooden surface or engraved metal cylinders. A machine on which the two were combined was known as a 'mule' or 'union' machine. In 1813 John Bury wrote to his father from London that 'good block work is usually so much in demand and so scarce, that a print house who has the means of doing it in quantity

12 This page is contained in a book of 1806–1817 that belonged to Jonathan Peel's print works at Church Bank, near Accrington, Lancashire, and contains prices, orders and notes, many from his brother Joseph Peel at the family's Bury printworks. These unfaded samples indicate the colour palette which could be obtained by skilful use of different mordants, overprinting and discharge (bleaching). Among them is also an imitation moiré (number 113). The Peels dominated the Lancashire cotton-printing industry in the early nineteenth century and were the first to bring pauper children from London to tend the machines. The Church Bank works are also thought to have first combined copper and surface rollers, the latter perfected in about 1805 by a Peel employee called Burch.

and the reputation of doing it well, may almost engage with what commission houses [linen-drapers] he pleases. . .' .[41] By this time a further hindrance to the supply of fashionable furniture prints in London was the growing importance of Manchester as a centre for trade. As early as 1808 there is evidence that this was causing a decline of the London linen-drapers' practice of commissioning designs, except for the most fashionable furniture prints.[42] London merchants complained that only unpopular or expensive prints were sent to London, and since a greater proportion of the Lancashire cottons after 1800 were cheaper varieties of cloth, advice from London agents and linen-drapers became less valued. The proximity of Manchester to the Liverpool docks also decreased the importance of London-based agents as exporters to America, for all types of cloth. An increasing number of northern English firms also dealt directly with the United States. By 1800 a dozen or more manufacturers had partners, agents or members of the family established in North America, taking orders and sending advice.

The transfer of technology from Britain to the United States initially relied on emigrants. In *Transatlantic Industrial Revolution*, David Jeremy charts America's acquisition of newly developed machines and manufacturing techniques, commenting that 'patriotic merchants and tradesmen also promoted textiles mills based on English models. By 1790, however, these efforts had advanced little further than the advertisements of aspirations in local newspapers.'[43] The United States was, of course, trying to develop its own industry, although it was not until after the War of 1812 that American political leaders were convinced of the necessity to develop self-sufficiency in manufacturing. The efforts to establish a textile industry in the United States centred – as in Britain – on spinning, and the first 'revolutionary' machine-made cloths, such as those produced by Samuel Slater, were actually composed of machine-spun yarns, hand-woven, typically, in checks, plaids and stripes.[44]

Spinning aside, in weaving and printing (except bleaching), the two countries were capable of producing similar goods. Until about 1805–10 all weaving – whether British or American – was done primarily by hand, and hand printing by wood blocks or, less commonly, copper plates, was the norm. Between 1774 and 1800 in the Philadelphia area (for many years the centre of the American textile industry), there had been numerous individual fringe and cloth weavers and dyers, two calico- and linen-glazers, seventeen calico printers and eleven copperplate printers, few of whom are known to have survived in business for more than four or five years. The copperplate presses may have been occupied in printing on paper, but even if they did not supply printed linens and cottons, those working at the turn of the century would no doubt have produced ink-printed silk chair backs of the type mentioned by both Sheraton and Hepplewhite.

Documented examples from two pre-1800 Philadelphia calico-printing establishments – Walters & Bedwell and John Hewson – indicate that fine workmanship and up-to-date fashions could be provided by American textile printers. A pattern book from Archibald Hamilton Rowen's print works, operating from 1797 to 1799 in nearby Wilmington, Delaware, shows an equally high standard. Whether or not these examples are typical is impossible to establish, for there are no other documented surviving pre-1800 American printed textiles or designs. Of the three firms, John Hewson is exceptional, for his business continued from c.1773 (when he emigrated from England) through his retirement in 1810 and for a further fifteen years under the direction of his son, also named John. Hewson was alone in surviving three particularly difficult periods for the American textile industry: the Revolution, the period between 1793 and 1796, and the years immediately after the War of 1812.

During these periods, some American textile ventures closed due to lack of capital, inexperienced management or possibly even poor workmanship. Further, some printers left their trade as soon as they had enough capital to buy a farm. However, it was the glut of imported British fabrics that contributed most to the high failure rate during the 1790s and again in the 1810s. This glut was caused by both defensive and offensive tactics on the part of British merchants and politicians. In the 1790s, a need to develop the American market was generated by Britain's increased difficulty in exporting to the Continent – particularly after 1793, when war broke out with France. However, the British had already recognized that the importing of their fabrics by Americans could help to stifle the growth of a competing textile industry in the United States. After the 1812 War, some Members of Parliament even advocated a certain amount of loss on textile exports in an attempt to cripple the young American industry. This pattern was maintained into the middle of the nineteenth century (although with decreasing effects), and virtually every time a sharp slump occurred in the British home trade, or selling to other export markets became difficult, America was encouraged to absorb Britain's surplus fabrics. (This may account for the greater number of surviving British chintzes in America. These fall into several main groups: dark-ground florals, patterned stripes and pillar prints from the late 1790s; game-bird patterns from the mid-1810s and elaborately engraved two-colour prints with net and lace-like grounds in the years just after 1820.)

As a further obstacle, British textile agents instructed American merchants that their credit would be withdrawn if they also stocked locally-made textiles. Many American manufacturers were thus left with only peddlers and local fairs as outlets – a method of selling that was already dying out in urban Britain. American traders with the East Indies also imported textiles to compete with those made domestically (although fine Indian cloths, such as muslins, had been ousted by British-made versions by about 1820). Finally, American printers had to contend with discounting practices, including sales such as one organized by the New York merchant Robert Robertson in 1791, when 'a large assortment of those damaged calicoes and chintzes, of the cargo of the brig Betsy [were] to be sold very reasonable.' By such means importers frequently had better sales outlets than American printers, who often had to rely for orders on 'pattern books lodged in different places for the convenience of the public.'[45]

Although Britain led in the manufacture of the high-quality worsted and silk furnishing fabrics used in America during this period, it was her control of the cotton industry which had most influence. In particular, the combination of widespread mechanized cotton spinning with power weaving (there were 14,000 power looms in England in 1820) significantly reduced linen as a yarn used in first British and then American furnishing fabrics, except for specialized products. Writing of Maine agriculture, Clarance Day observed that 'Flax was the first crop to be abandoned:

13 Three from a set of five hand-painted silk valances, probably for a bed and made in England or on the Continent between about 1790 and 1810. Although the mass production of printed textiles was accelerating throughout the first quarter of the nineteenth century, an enormous number of hand-decorated textiles were still used in interiors. They could be as simple as stencilling or as elaborate as these examples, with roundels containing scenes including one, upper right, showing a fashionable festooned bed. Every roundel is different, as is each intermediate motif. With mass production, patterns lost the visual interest provided by such varying elements.

Farmers and their wives gladly gave up the drudgery of preparing flax and weaving linen as soon as factory-woven cloth made from cotton was priced within their reach.'[46] Since British intervention had delayed full mechanization in America until the 1830s, it inadvertently gave all American home-spun and home-woven cloths an extended period of production.

Although by 1825 the industrialization of the textile industry was well on its way, standardization as yet found no place in either British or American homes. Interiors in both countries, whether employing fabrics produced by traditional or new methods, still depended otherwise on hand labour. In the pages of the guides and directories of the period one can find ample reminders of the variety of hand finishings expected: embroidery, fringing, appliqué (either sewn or glued) and patterns hand-drawn in ink or watercolour.[47] Hand painting was done on velvet, worsted and woollens, and occasionally on silk satin and taffeta. In America the use of stencils and oil colours for pictorial purpose, known as 'theorem painting', was popular well into the mid-century.

The textile revolution that took place between 1790 and 1825 was as much social as technical. Regional differences and class distinctions – although still apparent – were no longer manifested so obviously in furnishings as they had once been. Even quite modest houses now contained decorative fabrics, either commercially-made or home-made from machine-spun yarns. These differences continued to break down in the years between 1825 and 1860, during which time the 'classical' fashions launched early in the century continued to filter down to successively less affluent households.

14 Three carved pilasters illustrated in Thomas Sheraton's *Drawing Book* in 1793 show the 'grotesque' style, with circular coiling stems, lozenges and ogee shapes arranged on a vertical axis. Throughout the 1790–1825 period such patterns were often transferred to textiles, as shown on the drawing-room window curtains illustrated by Ackermann in *The Repository of Arts*, December 1818. These were described as 'arranged and decorated in the style of Vatican embellishments, and are suspended from a cornice by silk cords and tassels; the curtains are . . . exquisitely fine woollen cloth, on which the border is painted by hand, as is frequently done on velvet; and the cornice is decorated in a similar way . . .' Both the curtains and muslin sub-curtains appear to be fixed at the top. The overcurtains just touched the floor when closed.

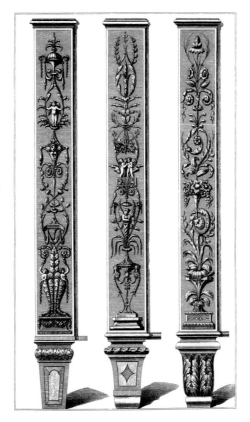

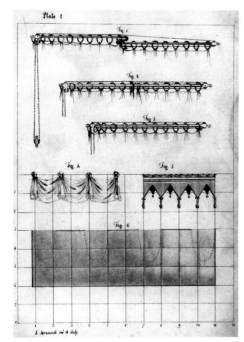

15 In 1819 James Arrowsmith published *An Analysis of Drapery*, in London, not 'to attempt at competition with the superb Designs which constantly appear in periodical and other publications, but to render assistance where it is required [so that] such Designs should be brought into effect . . .' Among his diagrams and instructions for cutting and draping were these drawings of French rods, which were still an uncommon method of opening curtains. He also included Roman draperies in plan (with dots indicating gathers) and in finished form (figures 6 and 4). These, he noted, were frequently used for the inside of a bed or for bedroom curtain drapery, adding that they were 'useful for temporary purposes, as the material will be little injured by the operation'. Figure 5 shows a double 'Vandyke' valance, suggested as suitable for a low window, since it barely obstructed the light. Both Roman draperies and Vandyke valances were to become more widely used in the 1820s and '30s.

17

17 This plate, depicting two alternative curtain treatments, was published by Thomas Sheraton in June 1792 and appeared in his influential work, *The Cabinet-Maker and Upholsterer's Drawing-Book*. The curtains were described as drawn on French rods, which allowed them to be opened and closed by means of cords at the side, and without lifting from the floor, as was more common (see p. 48 for a diagram). The valance served to replace the fabric element below the cornice which had previously been provided by curtains which drew upwards into swags. The 'French strapping' and tassels on the right-hand valance, Sheraton noted, had been mistaken by cabinet makers as carved elements.

18 With a deep yellow ground and red and brown pattern, this block-printed cotton was probably made in England, but is known to have been used as bed or window curtains in the United States in the early nineteenth century. The cloth is 26 inches wide and the border just over 9 inches wide. Its circular format and oak and acanthus leaves are similar to borders in George Smith's 1812 *Collection of Ornamental Designs*, which were described (plate 4) as 'capable of being worked in carpet, wood, metal, paper, or silk: and equally serviceable to the Ornamental Painter & Japanner'.

16 An English chintz, block-printed in 1792 for Francis & Crook, linen drapers in Covent Garden, London, then the centre of the fashionable furnishing fabric trade. The elaborate pattern employs 'grotesque' plasterwork-like motifs combined with a large roundel derived from marquetry. The pattern has been carefully designed so that when the fabric is seamed in lengths, the small medallion aligns with the large one. This arrangement, known as a half drop, had also been used by copperplate printers, although in making-up, many upholsterers did not bother to match the sideways repeat. (This remained true throughout most of the nineteenth century.) The deterioration in those areas coloured light brown has been caused by the use of an iron mordant. Other examples of this design, in different colours, are in the Victoria & Albert Museum, London, and at Winterthur, in Delaware.

18

19 More than 100 chintz designs by William Kilburn (1745–1818) survive. This example, of about 1792, is similar to another produced for the London linen-drapers Brown, Rogers & Co. With a printworks at Wallingford, Surrey, Kilburn was one of five or six designers at that time who were also master printers. He also sold drawings and engravings to print shops and produced some of the plates for William Curtis's *Flora Londinensis* (1777). This was not an unusual practice; John Edwards, for example, was a flower painter who in 1770 published *The British Herbal* and who also designed for block-printers. This design has been skilfully arranged so that the outer stripe or border reads both horizontally and vertically. In 1787 Kilburn explained to a Parliamentary committee (investigating the need for copyright of designs) that cutting such patterns cost between £10 and £20. Kilburn's designs were quickly copied by Northern printers, among them Peel & Co.

20 This hand-woven linen curtain, measuring 30 inches selvage-to-selvage, by 53½ inches, was made in the last quarter of the eighteenth century for a window in the Stephens Robbins House, a saltbox built in East Lexington, Massachusetts, in about 1750. The stencilled pattern (in red, indigo and green) was applied after the curtain was hemmed and fitted with tape loops, from which it would hang. When in place it would have been drawn to one side.

19

20

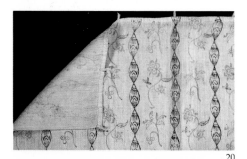

21

21 Striped patterns were fashionable for both prints and weaves throughout the 1790–1825 period. Like this English block-printed glazed cotton of about 1805, most were 'double stripes', with two alternating patterned bands separated by decorative edgings.

23 An American hand-woven linen curtain, measuring 30¾ inches selvage-to-selvage, by 53½ inches, of about 1800, patterned with red, gold and indigo-dyed warp stripes, the latter colour only partially covering some threads to give a shaded or chiné effect. Vertical stripes are one of the simplest means of patterning a woven textile, since once the warp is placed in the loom, the weaving process is the same as for an unpatterned cloth, requiring only the passage of the weft from left to right, without any change of colour.

22 An English furnishing chintz block-printed at Fordingbridge, Hampshire, in about 1790. The combination of a variety of flowers and leaves on one meandering stem was commonly found in Indian printed and painted textiles, an association further emphasized in this chintz by the inclusion of a pineapple. The use of a dark ground, as seen in the narrower stripe, was popular into the first years of the nineteenth century.

24 With the exception of the late-eighteenth-century English worsted (second from top, right), these striped and checked fabrics are silk bourettes (employing a coarse, slubbed silk made from silk waste). Cloths such as these, typically between 19 and 21 inches wide, enjoyed long popularity; included here are examples from the second half of the eighteenth century (third and fourth down, right) and the mid-nineteenth century (top right and left). The checked bourette dates from the late eighteenth century.

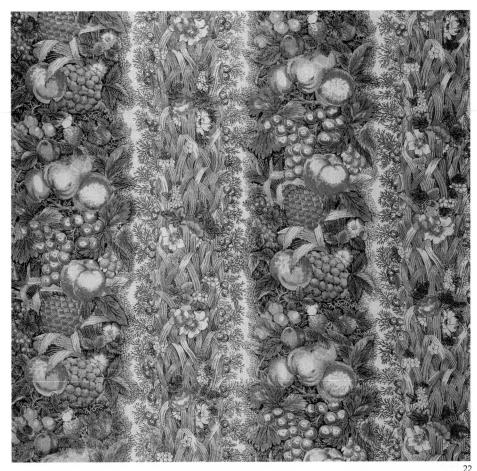

22

23

24

25

26

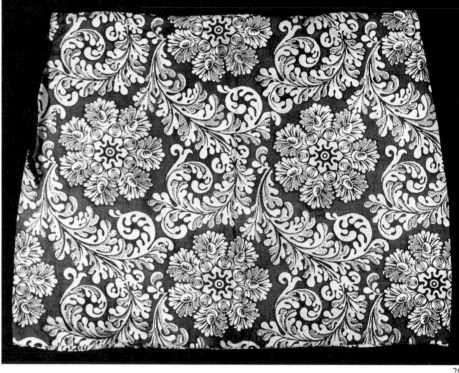

28

27

27 Two drawing-room chairs included in Thomas Sheraton's *Drawing Book* of 1793. The right-hand chair 'is intended to be finished in burnished gold and the seat and back covered with printed silk'. Such silks were probably printed by flat copperplate, with the design engraved to match the shape of the seat. They were typically produced by printers who normally printed on paper, and could therefore have also been made in the United States, where plate presses were established and where publications such as Sheraton's were influential. The chair on the left is covered with a chintz, also block-printed to shape and with 'borders to suit'. Chintzes were often thought appropriate for painted wood furniture such as this japanned chair – the chintz was chosen first (in theory) and determined the colour of the painting.

25 This copperplate-printed silk satin chair seat and border employ a 'single' green (not dependent on overprinting blue on yellow), identical in colour to that perfected in 1809. Since copperplate printing on silk generally used inks instead of dyes, and since stylistically these pieces could be from the 1790s, they could therefore be contemporary with Sheraton's reference to such chair coverings (see Fig. 27). Equally, they could have been printed at any point up to about 1825.

26 This late-eighteenth- or early-nineteenth-century copperplate-printed silk is thought to have been produced in India and would have been suitable for a chair or cushion cover, or the centre of a patchwork quilt. Indian fabrics were imported into both Britain and America throughout this period.

28 This small chair pad is made from a cotton chintz, dyed indigo and printed with a bleaching agent to create the pattern, into which yellow was added. It is probably English and made in about 1820, when small, densely placed designs were also used by weavers (this print has a vertical repeat of 9½ inches). The acorn medallions and oak-leaf scrolls are a reminder of the popularity of these motifs as symbols of the mighty oak, an image which appealed equally to the French, British and Americans.

29 One of a set of twelve mahogany side chairs made for George Washington by John Aitken of Philadelphia in about 1800. The covering is an example of very high quality French or English haircloth, with white horsehair wefts (always substantially more expensive than grey or black) and a gold silk warp with an extra pattern warp of blue-green silk, the fineness of which assisted in the production of such a detailed pattern. Because the maximum length of horsehair is about 27 inches, it was used only as a weft, and combined with a warp of cotton, linen, wool or silk. Most haircloth weaves were much simpler, or plain, but being a particularly fashionable cloth at the beginning of the nineteenth century, it merited the more elaborate patterning shown here.

29

30

30 A group of designs commission-printed at Bannister Hall, Lancashire, between September 1803 and May 1804, for the London merchant-draper Richard Ovey. The chair seats are labelled 'The Egypt Mummy chair seat' and 'Black and Orange Egyptian chair' and are 11 and 9 inches in diameter, respectively; the colours illustrate what is now called the Pompeian style. Ovey instructed that these should be placed so that as many as possible could be printed. The trompe l'oeil design reflects both the interest in swagged draperies and the eclectic tastes of the period, which supported the production of patterns as diverse as these.

31 This late eighteenth-century fragment
of a linen valance illustrates the simplest
form of hand-block printing. A mordant
applied by wooden block makes the fabric
receptive to a dye, in this case madder.
The outline of the 9 by 11-inch block can
be seen on the left-hand edge. Small dots
just above the two identical outcrops are
pin marks, indicating the position of the
metal prong attached to the block as a
guide to placement. Note that the
'grotesque' pattern (similar in design to
fabrics produced in the Alsace area of
eastern France) has been used on its side.

32 A design for a Bannister Hall block
print of 1806, showing two different
colour schemes, of which the yellow and
green was cheaper, since it did not require
the addition of red. The leopard-spot
pattern was popular throughout the
period between 1790 and 1825, while the
'fat' trelliswork was characteristic of the
first ten or fifteen years of the nineteenth
century.

31

32

33

34

33 Meandering vines with elaborately patterned flower-heads had been a popular type of textile design since the 1770s, but the dramatic combination of sallow green (pencilled blue over yellow) and black dates this block-printed cotton to about 1800.

34 Two prints from a group of drab style designs in a pattern book of 1803–4, attributed to Vint & Gilling (or Vint & Dixon, as this Crayford block printing firm became in 1804). Both were 'engaged', or produced exclusively, for Richard Ovey, a leading London furnishing fabric merchant from 1790 to 1831. The all-over floral pattern was designed by Daniel Goddard, as probably was the pillar print, since it also employs Goddard's characteristic thick black line which shades one side of the patterns.

35 There are forty-one pieces in this bed hanging set, and it is one of the most elaborate to remain intact. Nevertheless, the construction is relatively simple, with the draperies suspended from poles through open-ended upper hems, and the fabric has been economically used (the most dominant element in the pattern repeat does not match across all widths). Originally from the George R. Curwen family house in Salem, Massachusetts, these hangings were made in about 1818, when pillar prints were still popular, and when beds were still often the most expensively furnished objects in a house. Although the very wealthy would have had beds with silk hangings, most beds at this date were dressed with cotton fabrics such as these, which were both washable and fashionable.

35

36

37

38

36 This discharge print of about 1810 began as a dyed blue cotton cloth, from which white areas were bleached out. Then dyed yellow, to create green over blue or yellow over white, the cloth was finally printed with a mordant and dyed in red (madder), creating the dark trellis as well as the bright red. The American textile historian Florence Montgomery has recorded that this pattern and a similar one in the Smithsonian Institution were owned by the Malcolm Westcott Hill family of Alexandria, Virginia.

37 Two block-printed impressions on paper from a pattern book labelled 'Duddings' Furnitures at Reduced Prices . . . being designed by Artists of celebrity, and peculiarly adapted to Rooms of every Class, with appropriate Taste . . . Any Quantity may be printed to order.' The volume itself was purchased no earlier than 1811 and probably contains impressions of the block-printed cotton furnishing fabrics made by E. B. Dudding, who was in business in London from 1811 to 1816. Both designs rely on two dyes, madder for the reds and (in D37 only) black, and weld or quercitron for the yellow and olive. Olive was a commonly used alternative to the richer green created by blue and yellow.

38 Three designs for block printing, ordered by Richard Ovey from Bannister Hall printworks near Preston, Lancashire, between June 1804 and February 1805. These Indian-style designs, with characteristic detailed infills within each pattern, were probably all by 'Pearman', the first of several designers of that name, who appear frequently in the Bannister

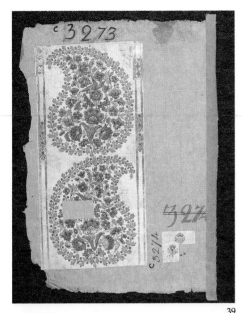

Hall books, and who may have been employed there. (His signature appears on one of the two colourways on the right.) Ovey noted on the reverse of one design, 'Don't let your yellow ground be too deep – but as pale as you can without hurting the greens', a reference to the fact that pure green relied on the overlaying of blue and yellow.

39 A design for a block print from the Bannister Hall records (now held in the Stead McAlpin private archive, in Carlisle), dated 18 January 1806. This so-called 'Paisley' or *boteh* pattern is a very close approximation of the Indian shawls fashionable in the early 1800s, finely woven with plain grounds and elaborate borders, and therefore an ideal choice for a border print. Note the alternative edgings in the upper left and right stripes.

The flexibility of block printing also allowed the border patterns to be printed several times across the fabric, as a stripe.

40 Isolated 'islands' were a distinctive feature of block-printed cottons in the years around 1815, having previously been characteristic of copperplate-printed fabrics. This type of design must have been extremely popular, since many examples survive, particularly in the United States (suggesting that such designs were among those 'dumped' on the American market in the attempt to stifle the development of their textile industry after the War of 1812 ended, in December 1814). The background is the so-called tea ground prevalent at this time, as was the practice of separating the ground from the design by a narrow uncoloured band.

39

40

41–3 The production of the same pattern in different colours is not a new invention, as demonstrated by these three examples of the same design. Single-colour roller-printed versions are known in red, green and blue (which can be seen lining the chest). Additional colourways were created by adding colours to these by block or surface roller printing, as was the case with the length of cotton, which has yellow and buff surface printing added to the basic pattern, roller-printed in red. Produced in the second decade of the nineteenth century, the design employs fashionably draped windows to form a central column, which from a distance reads as a pillar print.

44 This yellow and pink French silk and its matching tassels were originally part of drawing room curtains in Charles Russell Codman's house in Boston. Ordered in 1824 from Samuel Welles, a Boston merchant living in Paris, these were made up as continued draperies (with an inner curtain of white silk) before being shipped to America. The small pattern is typical of many silks of the period, which often also employed widely spaced motifs to emphasize the gleaming satin ground. These furnishings were designed to impress Boston society; and correspondence held at the Society for the Preservation of New England Antiquities indicates that Codman expected to pay close to £200 sterling for the curtains, two

sofas and six chairs. All were to be in 'the best style – rich but not gaudy'.

45

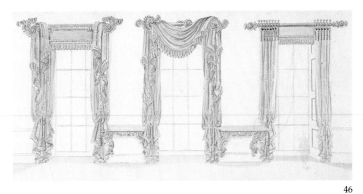

46

47

45 Three chairs illustrated in the *Repository of Arts* in July 1823, of which the red morocco (goat skin)-covered chair on the right was the most utilitarian, although none would have been inexpensive. The left-hand chair was to have green velvet upholstery with blue or black applied bands, or 'rich silk' coloured to suit (*not* to match) the drapery. The central chair was the most costly – the frame burnished gold; the upholstery light blue figured silk with broad gold lace at the lower back and Persian fringe. The silk may have been English, for only 20 months later Ackermann illustrated an elaborate armchair with similar upholstery, described as British-made blue ground satin with a gold-coloured pattern.

46 These three upper window treatments sketched by Gillow's in about 1820, as part of a scheme for Mr. West's third drawing room, include, on the right, the 'modern' Grecian exposed rod which became an alternative to elaborate Regency festoons at about this time. Since the beginning of the nineteenth century the lack of elaborate upper draperies has invariably denoted modernity.

47 A border and filling design for a block-printed cotton, produced in two versions, one with the royal garter motif (shown) and one without. First made in 1820 for T. Smith & Co., it proved a very popular pattern and was ordered until 1835. It was printed on buff and tea grounds in monochrome schemes (blue, red or green), in red and black, or in full colour, described in the records as chintz colouring. The small filling was sometimes replaced with a stripe.

48

48 A chair-cushion case, or loose cover, decorated with needlework and applied block-printed chintzes of the first decade of the nineteenth century. Oriental motifs such as temples, towers and rock-scapes had been popular since the 1760s, when they appeared on copperplate-printed textiles and other decorative ware, such as ceramics.

49 Cotton roller-printed fabrics such as this example of about 1820, probably produced by John Marshall & Sons of Manchester, had begun to replace flat plate-printed 'toiles' in the previous decade. The squashed scenes are characteristic of roller prints, which had a maximum vertical repeat of about 22 inches, the circumference of a roller. Printed in red, the design is thought to represent England, Ireland, Scotland and Wales, although individual scenes from it are found on other examples produced in France.

50 The daybook of Joseph Lockett, an engraver and cylinder-maker in Salford and Manchester, contains a pattern similar to this, executed for George Palfreyman, Manchester, in 1816. This pattern, just over 21¾ inches high (the full width is not known), has been lengthened by the addition of the two polar bears; other motifs have been rearranged. Active in the first four decades of the nineteenth century, Lockett was said to be the best engraver of his day.

51 This handkerchief was made from a printed cotton furnishing fabric designed from aquatints published by Rudolph Ackermann, produced to commemorate the death of Lord Nelson, whose funeral procession took place on 9 January 1806. Note the fashionable festoons and swags on the funeral carriage. The brown appears to be from an engraved roller, whereas the red was probably added by flat copper plates.

52 Six block-printed impressions on paper from a volume that probably records the cottons printed by E. B. Dudding, 1811–16. The large border and its smaller variant owe much to French design, particularly that of Napoleon's principal architects, Charles Percier and Pierre François Léonard Fontaine, whose complete *Recueil de Décorations Intérieurs, comprenant tout ce qui a rapport à l'ameublement* appeared in 1812. The small patterns may have been intended as fillings for the borders, and were probably derived from woven fabrics.

49

50

53 The Green Pavilion at Frogmore, shown in a 1819 watercolour by Charles Wild, has curtains that may well have been retained by Queen Charlotte's daughter, Princess Augusta, who used the pavilion as a dining room. In the 1841 inventory, taken on Princess Augusta's death, they were described as 'printed merino curtains and drapery to the Venetian windows, lined [in] green tammy and fringed, [with] loops, hooks and fixings'. Queen Charlotte's exceptionally early use of merino would not be surprising, since it was her husband, King George III, who introduced the merino sheep into England in 1786 and was praised in Ackermann's *Repository of Arts* (March 1809, p.189) for his 'unwearied and patriotic effort for their increase and diffusion.' Loose covers appear to have been made from the same material. Interiors such as this had great influence on contemporary fashions, for, like many other houses, it was open to viewing by 'respectable parties'. Now under the care of English Heritage, Frogmore is being restored.

51

52

53

54 Included among James Barron's *Modern and Elegant Designs of Cabinet and Upholstery Furniture* (London 1814) were several designs for continued drapery, one of which is shown here. Exceptionally for a pattern book, it includes patterned fabrics. The muslin sub-curtains, which had recently become fashionable, are depicted with a small pattern 'powdered' over the cloth, probably during weaving (although often decorative edgings were run in by hand).

54

55

56

57

58

55 A border and filling, produced at Bannister Hall for T. Smith & Co. and signed H. Mills (probably the designer), 15 May 1817. This colour scheme – produced from mineral dyes – was not unusual. It appears that such border prints were designed with loose covers in mind, so that the pattern on the finished cases appeared upright just above the floor. A Grecian couch loose cover (now owned by the Society for the Preservation of New England Antiquities) in the same colours and another similar Bannister Hall pattern was made up in Boston between 1815 and 1825.

56 The lack of distinction between furnishing and dress fabrics is especially noticeable in patchwork coverlets. This example (detail), worked by Mrs. George Austen (mother of Jane Austen), is composed of block- and roller-printed cottons produced in the first quarter of the nineteenth century.

58 A ruled paper or 'point paper' such as this was used to translate a design for figured draw-loom or Jacquard weaving. This pattern of about 1824 belonged to Stephen Wilson, who had introduced the Jacquard harness into South London in 1820. Since the terminology used for draw looms and Jacquards was often the same, it is impossible to determine for which technique this point paper was intended. Nevertheless it may well represent one of the earliest English Jacquard weaving designs.

57 One of the easiest ways for printers to create colourways in a multi-coloured design has always been to change the background colour. The pattern on this block-printed English chintz of about 1825, with a repeat of 12¼ by 13 inches, derives much of its impact from its clear blue ground; its effect is very different on a sample at Winterthur which has a brown ground.

59 This asymmetrical Etruscan curtain echoes the draping of a Grecian peplos and the painted or appliquéd kneeling figure and flowers are taken from fifth-century BC Grecian painted 'red ware' pottery. Made of lightweight fabric edged with a delicate fringe, the casually draped, unstructured style belies the skill of the cutter. The figurative pins at the top clasp the fabric and hold the pleating in place. The curtains were made so that when open they swept the floor. Looping the curtain back over a curtain pin was a common method which survived in use beyond the middle of the nineteenth century.

60

59

61 A design for a painted velvet ottoman cover, reproduced in *The Repository of Arts* in January 1821. As James Roberts, portrait painter to the Duke of Clarence commented in 1809, 'Painting has long been considered as a graceful accomplishment for the dignified and opulent, and also an useful acquirement for those who compose the middle ranks of society. Most, if not all the elegancies of polished life, have the art of Design for their basis.' This attitude encouraged many middle-class women to paint or produce needlework, which was often used to embellish furnishings.

61

60 Although small printed velvet samples can be found in some British manufacturers' pattern books of the period, few complete examples survive. This block-printed cotton velvet seat cover of about 1825 retains its original printed cotton velvet border, used to disguise the tacks which held the seat cover in place. The light areas have been created by printing a bleaching agent.

Chapter Three

Exuberance

1825–1860

'Not everything in the Early Victorian period was equally bad. Among the textile patterns of the time, especially the printed materials, there were some very attractive, unaffected, cheerful and pleasing designs.' (Hermann Muthesius, in *The English House*[1])

The English Regency period ended, strictly speaking, in 1820, when the Prince Regent became King George IV. However, the Regency style (and many of the textiles associated with it) continued beyond this date, as did the related American neo-classical or Federal style, which also lost its namesake with the demise of the Federal party during the 1824–28 administration of President John Quincy Adams. No convenient label exists for the years between the end of the Regency and Federal periods and the emergence, around 1860, of movements aimed at reforming design. This is partly because the lingering neo-classical styles were freely intermingled with several other revival styles, gothic and rococo most prominent among them. Perhaps the most apt summary of the years between 1825 and 1860 was provided by H. W. and A. Arrowsmith in 1840, when they commented that 'the present age is distinguished from all others in having no style which can properly be called its own.'[2] Yet the various textile designs of this period do share certain characteristics: bold juxtapositions of colour, vigorous outlines, overlapping motifs or trompe l'oeil effects. The resulting exuberant eclecticism suited the new architecture of the period, which exhibited, as the historian Mark Girouard has noted, a 'growing taste for the primitive and the powerful, in line with a general . . . taste for toughness. At the time, the nickname for it among architects was "muscular".'[3]

The heterogeneous character of 'muscular' textile designs attracted a good deal of disapproval from both contemporary and later critics. Later writers, on both sides of the Atlantic, tended to condemn these fabrics on aesthetic grounds, attributing the perceived decline in standards to increased mechanization or the new harsh dyestuffs. However, this approach overlooks the emergence of the middle class and skilled working class as significant purchasers of fabrics, which both supported and influenced the wide variety of designs made available. Up to the beginning of the American Civil War in 1861 and the Cobden Treaty, enacted in England in 1860 (which removed high tariffs on French textiles imported into the United Kingdom), both the British and the American textile industries expanded considerably, introducing new technologies or re-

1 The brilliant green ground on this English printed and glazed cotton has been 'padded', a term used to indicate that the entire ground has been mordanted or dyed prior to the application of additional colours. Here the ground has been dyed twice, first in indigo and then in yellow. The areas not requiring blue were probably bleached out, and the non-yellow areas most probably were protected from the dye by first printing a resist. The cloth has then been roller-printed with various mordants which, when dyed madder, give a range of reds and purple-browns. Produced in about 1830, this elaborate combination of techniques and rich colour scheme resulted in the most expensive type of chintz available at the time, one that epitomized the 'muscular' style.

2 A point paper for a hand-woven silk of about 1825, probably produced by Stephen Wilson. On the reverse it is described as a '3 comber', indicating that the pattern repeated three times (side by side) across the width of the fabric, which was probably 21 inches wide. It is also labelled 'The Chintz', identifying the source of design as a printed cotton. Narrow meandering thorny stems with small flower-heads were popular chintz patterns during the mid-1820s, having been revived from the last quarter of the eighteenth century.

fining existing ones. The standard of spinning, weaving and printing was not necessarily lowered, but broadened to serve the more specific markets which were developing. 'The trade may therefore be said to have changed from an artistic employment to a staple manufacture, using taste as one of its elements.'[4]

New technology did, of course, promote changes in the appearance and use of cloths, and this was nowhere more apparent than with the introduction of new weaving technology. The Jacquard system, perfected by the Frenchman Joseph-Marie Jacquard in 1801, had effectively replaced the draw-boy (who had previously manipulated the patterning mechanism from the side of the loom) with a connected series of punched cards, from which every warp thread could be controlled. Although the initial investment was high and many months might be required to prepare a design for weaving, once the cards were in place the weaving required only one man. Fancy patterns therefore eventually became more economical. Exchanging existing sets of cards could be done relatively quickly – another advantage unknown to draw-loom weavers. This system revolutionized the stock of patterns offered by the figured furnishing fabric weaver, who could now combine the production of 'staple' designs (which could be repeatedly woven over a lifetime) with a series of more short-lived, fashionable designs.

Knowledge of the Jacquard's working mechanisms eluded the British until 1820, when Stephen Wilson obtained the necessary information through an industrial spy. Wilson's patent of 1821 was followed two years later by a patent of an improved version. Both of these versions were first applied to hand silk-weaving looms. Similarly, the first recorded Jacquard looms in the United States were employed by hand silk weavers in Philadelphia in 1824, although the Americans did not use them in any numbers for furnishing-silk weaving until the 1860s.

Jacquard weaving required fine warp threads and was thus ideally suited to silk and finely spun worsted and cotton yarns, and to patterns featuring thin lines, shading, or realism – in other words, to 'muscular' designs. Warps of coarser spins (which excluded silk) were better suited to the dobby loom, patented for hand weaving in 1818 and for power looms in 1824 by Taylor and Potter respectively. The dobby, worked from a cylinder or barrel of pegs, produced small patterns, and was suited to the manufacture of all-over designs such as trellis-based patterns, single motifs 'powdered' or dotted over the surface, figured warp-striped fabrics and textural weaves. After mid-century, dimities were produced on dobby looms, which accounted for the slightly coarser yarns found in many of them.

Fashion operates within the realm of possibilities; the new technologies introduced or refined during this period extended the variety of wovens – that is, non-printed fabrics – available in the middle price range and also attracted attention to existing types of weaves. Writers increasingly recommended wovens in the years surrounding the British patenting of the dobby and Jacquard looms. Early in 1821 Rudolph Ackermann reported that 'the loom of our country is now in that state of advanced perfection,

3 *An Encyclopaedia of Domestic Economy* by Thomas Webster (London 1844 and New York 1845), shows the 'modern' preference for perpendicular folds or piped detail, here also employed with 'massive brass rods and large rings [that] have been much in fashion' and a 'cornice and valance in the style called Louis XVI, now much in fashion.' For drawing rooms Webster recommended silk satin, figured damask, lutestring (*sic*, a silk taffeta with a glossy dressing), Salisbury flannel, fine cloth or cassimere; moreen was suitable in dining rooms and libraries. Stiffened materials, such as chintzes, were unsuitable. Such advice differed little from that of George Smith in 1808, save Webster's emphasis on perpendicular folds, which harboured less dust.

that damasks of the most magnificent kind, in point of intensity of colour and richness of patterns, are manufactured at prices that permit their free use in well-furnished apartments. . . .'[5] In the following year he recommended 'the richest style of decoration by silk or velvet draperies [referring to a sofa] . . . now so admirably produced by the British loom. . . .'[6] By September 1824, when he illustrated a Grecian-style sofa designed by John Taylor (an upholsterer working in Covent Garden, London), the sofa and its pillows were to be covered 'in the prevailing taste' with silk or merino damask and trimmed with silk cords and tassels.[7] Irrespective of whether Ackermann was referring to Jacquard or dobby-woven fabrics or, rather, defending the existing draw-loom trade, his remarks reflect the renewed interest in patterned weaves of all types which accompanied the introduction of new loom-patterning devices.

Hand in hand with the appreciation of weaves came a more full-bodied, straighter, style of window and bed draperies, also called Grecian or 'modern'. These featured tubular, vertical pleats, and were a simplified variant of the widely spaced conical pleats in Roman drapery. The 'modern' variety had the advantage of being simple enough for an amateur to construct; valance or curtain fabric could be nailed directly to the supporting bed or window frame and the nail-heads covered by a cornice. An even simpler variant dispensed with upper draperies, completely exposing the curtains, which hung in unstructured pleats from large rings on massive exposed rods. Gothic, rococo and neo-classical overtones could be suggested by the choice of cornice or rod finials.[8] Vertical pleats were recommended for curtains and bed hangings in both Britain and the United States up to the early 1850s; aside from being adaptable to any style, they were thought to harbour less dust than swags and to be better suited to moreen[9] and, by inference, to any of the firmer, weightier fabrics such as cotton or woollen piles and dobby weaves.

As in previous decades, many of the guides of the 1820s and '30s continued to illustrate furnishing ideas with unpatterned cloths, so it is difficult to know whether they intended Jacquard and dobby-woven patterns for particular schemes. The Jacquard was, in any case, only moderately successful in Britain for the first ten years or so after its introduction, and draw-loom weavers continued to produce damasks in tried and tested designs. In fact, Wilson had installed his Jacquard machines in Streatham High Road, several miles away and across the River Thames from Spitalfields, perhaps in anticipation of resistance from draw-loom weavers established there.[10]

The patterns first produced by Jacquards were small, since the design width was limited by the relatively small number of controlling hooks. A larger motif size was necessary to compete with the draw-loom, and the Jacquard was gradually modified and improved to make this possible. By the late 1830s medium-sized, elaborately figured designs could be Jacquard-woven by hand, and the Jacquard began to be integrated with draw-looms in Spitalfields.[11] Jacquard hand-weaving had already been introduced into the quality British worsted trade, which was increasingly dominated by Yorkshire weavers.[12]

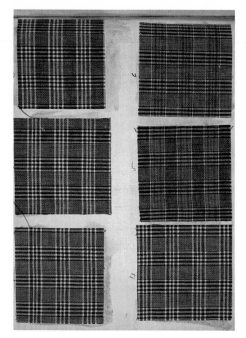

4 Checked worsteds, produced in the American Lancaster Mills at Clinton, Massachusetts, in 1848. These were principally for men's suiting, but certainly were substantial enough to have been used for upholstery. In the 1840s, supply routes over many areas were so poor that any available fabrics were used in interiors. These checked cloths, apart from being sturdy, came in shades also fashionable in interiors of the day.

'Muscular' aptly describes the bold floral bunches, heavily shaded scrollwork and densely detailed patterns produced by early Victorian Jacquard weavers. Such patterns were often more effectively displayed when flat, and it seems no coincidence that stiffened pelmets – sometimes offered as alternatives to valances from about 1825 – grew into large, arching lambrequins in the late 1830s. One of the earliest representations of this window treatment – in *The Workwoman's Guide*, 1838 – is described as suitable for Gothic windows in a study or library. Lambrequins were to remain a popular device into the 1880s, for – even more so than the 'modern' pleated valances – they were 'very simple, and may be formed to any shape, according to the style of the room'.[13] 'Gothic' could be suggested by a pointed arch and 'rococo' by S- or C-shaped curves.

Since the American textile manufacturers in the 1820s and 1830s were concentrating on building an industry that would produce low-cost dress and furnishing fabrics for a population that was still largely rural and living just above subsistence level, their main interest was in fairly simple power-woven cloths. (The Jacquard was not taken up by American worsted weavers, for example, until about 1850.[14]) William Morris, a British weaver who emigrated to America in the 1820s, wrote from Rockdale, Pennsylvania, on 8 March 1834, that 'handloom weaving being irregular on account of the wonderfull [sic] increase of powerlooms, we concluded to try the power looms. . . .' A friend of Morris's in Philadelphia got work on the first day of looking, 'at $1 per day and the priviledge [sic] of working piece work at nights' and was earning $7–9 per week.[15] The type of cloth being woven had been described five years earlier by another member of the emigrant Morris family: 'There is not any fine work wove in this country yet there is various kinds of coarse such as check gingam, wooling, cloak flannell [sic] and many other kinds but it is all very good to learn.'[16] He also noted that beef, veal and mutton cost five cents a pound, and whiskey thirty-six cents a gallon.

The concentration in America on the production of commodity cloths meant that Americans with more expensive tastes still sought out the more elaborate imported prints and weaves. This helped to support British Jacquard weaving, in particular, but even as the technology was being introduced, competition for customers – both in Britain and in the United States – was increasing from the French. In 1826 new British legislation was passed, allowing the importation of French fabrics into Britain. With this and the 1824 repeal of the Spitalfields Act (which had protected journeyman silk-weavers' wages) London's fine silk-weaving trade temporarily floundered. The tariff levied on imported French silks did, however, protect the remaining weavers to some extent; and they also survived the 1837 panic in the American and English financial markets, which caused 'great stagnation in the manufacturing business' and was (according to William Morris, now writing from Ohio on 30 December 1838) 'no great loss [in America] because few depend on it, unlike England.'[17]

The ups and downs in trade did nothing to replenish the numbers of British silk designers, greatly depleted since about 1800 (and traditionally

5 A silk damask of the same design was used for the hangings in Westminster Abbey at Queen Victoria's Coronation in 1838 and varies only very slightly from a French silk of about 1806. The sample shown here was woven by Daniel Walters & Sons, who moved from London to Braintree, Essex, in 1820, gradually establishing a large hand silk-weaving factory which was taken over by Warners in 1895. It is not known whether Walters wove the silk for Westminster Abbey or acquired the design at a later date, for patterns such as these remained fashionable into the 1860s (being compatible with neo-Gothic furnishings) and in less dramatic colourings persisted to the end of the century.

the source of the most fashionable patterns). Many weaves from c.1820 to the 1840s therefore employed restrained, rather compacted foliate wreaths, 'bosses' and trellises, based to a large extent on French designs of 1805–12. Since the latter had limited circulation when originally produced, their subsequent use in England and America was less a revival than a case of exceptionally slow dispersal of a fashion. Like many floral 'muscular' designs, these patterns were often vigorously shaped or broken by strong outlines, suiting both the prevailing taste and the continued production of Empire-style furniture. There was also often very little difference between the English 'Gothic' and the French 'Empire' patterns.

The use of old French Jacquard designs by British and American manufacturers new to the machine must also have been common. Having introduced Jacquard weaving to his Halifax worsted mill in 1834 for example, James Ackroyd proudly described the cloths as 'most beautiful and exact . . . French figures'.[18] Even on the most British of occasions an appreciation of French patterns was evident; for Queen Victoria's coronation in 1838, an unidentified firm supplied Westminster Abbey with silk drapery fabric only marginally different from a surviving French silk of about 1806. Another early nineteenth-century French-style design was used on the walls of the State Rooms at Woburn Abbey in about 1841.

The Empire pattern types appeared on British prints of the 1820s and '30s, as did more recent French designs. From the testimony given to a Parliamentary select committee set up in 1840 to investigate reforming the British copyright laws, one can easily detect a general belief that French designs were superior to English ones – a belief difficult to dispel with so many French-inspired designs in production. However, at issue was not the British vanity, but the concern that export business might be lost to the French. The vexed question of the need to improve British design arose both with regard to the extension of copyright (made law in 1842) and as part of the moves to establish appropriate industrial design schools, but little is known of individual designers of the period, perhaps because many more were now employed by manufacturers and therefore worked anonymously. Certainly in Manchester, where there were an estimated 500 designers in 1841, the number of those working freelance was declining.[19] It must have been galling to the remaining British freelance designers that during the late 1830s and '40s British firms were willing to pay twice the price for a design from a Parisian studio. (James Thompson of Clitheroe even retained a designer in Paris for four or five years during this period.) The Americans, with no large export markets and a continued reliance on European patterns, had no commercial incentive to promote indigenous designers.

The textiles exported by the French to Britain and North America throughout this period were costly. When the Englishwoman Isabella I. Bishop toured America in 1854,[20] she visited drapers' and mercers' shops, 'which go by the name of "dry goods" stores [and] are filled with the costliest production of the world. The silks from the looms of France are to be seen side by side with the products of Persia and India, and all at an advance of fully two-thirds on English prices.' Possibly because few

6 One of the reasons why registration of British printed furnishing fabric designs was extended in 1842 to three years was that copying was rife. Although British firms tended to deny being guilty of this practice, they openly acknowledged their use of foreign or old patterns as a source of design. Competition between French and English block printers was particularly fierce in the mid-nineteenth century, resulting in rapid copying of each others' designs. The design of the block-printed cotton shown here was printed by the French Alsatian firm Schwartz Huguenin in 1856 and by the northern English printers Stead McAlpin a few years later. (This piece was printed from the original blocks c.1896.) A similar example is Fig. 41, designed by J. U. Tournier for Schwartz Huguenin in the first half of the 1840s and appearing at virtually the same time in England.

people could afford such luxuries, French textiles and French drapery and furnishing styles in general had an added cachet. French prints, also, were more expensive. When, in 1841, the Hartford, Connecticut, dry goods dealer N. Ritter & Co. advertised American, English and French calicoes at 6¼ to 37½ cents a yard, the latter price was almost certainly for French cloths.[21] However, French patterns were also available on fabrics from England, whether copied or purchased.

Style aside, it was the English worsted – cheaper in general than either French or English silks – that benefitted most from the return to favour which weaves and heavier draperies were experiencing during these years. Improved breeds of sheep also stimulated interest in wool-based cloths. The finest-quality European wool came from the merino, a Spanish sheep which had been introduced into Britain in 1786 and into America in 1802, and again between 1809 and 1811, in larger numbers. In 1809 Ackermann described 'new and curious . . . Anglo-Merino cloth' as 'the closest imitation of the real India shawl fabric . . . nearly as fine as muslin in its texture . . .'.[22] Merino cloth tended to be used as a dress fabric until the 1820s. In that decade George Smith's *Cabinet-Maker and Upholsterer's Guide* (published in London in 1828 but largely prepared in 1826) noted the use of merino damask for upholstery and curtains, the latter now recommended for use in the drawing room as well as the dining room, long a favoured position for worsteds. In the opinion of the writer Miss Eliza Leslie, handsomely furnished houses in Philadelphia in 1841 had curtains of silk and worsted damask, figured satin and merino cloth.[23] Of these, the wool-based cloths were most commonly used, for, as another American commented in 1834, a house 'well furnished [with] silk damask window curtains and other furniture to correspond . . . is quite unusual in this country'. He could equally have been speaking of the 1840s and '50s, and of Britain for that matter.[24]

Woollen velvets and plushes, both plain and figured, were upholstery fabrics which gained in popularity as middle-class householders increasingly valued durability. Although damasks, dobby-weaves and velvets made of cotton had the advantage of being washable, wools took dyes more readily. As curtains, worsted fabrics had additional advantages: merino damask, for example, was recommended by George Smith (whose 1828 publication was well used by American upholsterers) because it made up 'beautifully, not requiring a lining'.[25] In 1829 a similar point was made to Americans by Mrs. William Parkes in *Domestic Duties: or Instructions to Young Married Ladies*,[26] with reference to the stamped or watered worsted cloth, moreen. Discussing bed hangings, she noted that it was 'very serviceable' because it was well-suited to the cold climate and required no lining, making it less expensive than chintz, 'though not so pretty'.

Wovens were now so popular that Miss Leslie confidently recorded in 1841 that 'chintz curtains are now seldom seen in America, except for bedrooms', where rich silk, broad-striped dimity or damask were also allowed. The bed curtains 'would of course be of the same material, and corresponding in form'. 'Damask' could well have included worsteds or

7   Although recorded in watercolours by Edmond Darch Lewis in 1857, this parlour in the John Bohlen House, in Philadelphia, has two features that were typical of many middle-class interiors of the previous thirty years. The first is that most of the furnishing fabrics appear to be of wool. The blue cloth at the window may well be merino, since this fabric was thought suitable for unlined curtains; the armchair on the right is probably covered with red woollen velvet or plush; the neo-rococo side chair appears to be upholstered in French tapestry; and the table may be covered with one of the many printed felted-wool tablecloths produced during this period. The other feature is the great variety of furniture, scattered around the room and yet contained by the plain walls and curtains (compare this to a completely different impression given by the patterned curtains and wallpaper in the Farnsworth parlour, shown in Fig. 54). Among all the features in the room it is the presence of three lace antimacassars which identify it as an 1850s interior.

mixtures, such as silk and wool; it certainly embraced 'figured or damasked brown linen', which as bed hangings Miss Leslie thought not handsome but very lasting and economical, and which could be 'set off with a bright coloured fringe or binding'.[27]

The debate regarding cloths suitable for bed hangings, which was well under way by the late 1820s, reveals much about attitudes of the period. John Claudius Loudon summarized the advanced view in London in his influential 1833 publication, *An Encyclopedia of Cottage, Farm & Villa Architecture:* 'Moreen used to be employed for the hangings of best beds and bedrooms; but it is now considered as apt to harbour moths and other vermin; and therefore, in these economical times, it is much less used than formerly.' Also on the grounds of health, many people now used low post bedsteads, dispensing with curtains altogether, although Miss Leslie felt that 'the winter climate of most parts of America is such as to render curtains highly desirable at that season, to all who can conveniently procure them. It is not necessary to draw them closely all round; but if the heads of the sleepers were always screened from the cold air of a cold room, there would, perhaps, be fewer tooth-aches, rheumatic pains, coughs and sore throats.'[29]

The half-tester bed provided a reasonable compromise between freely circulating air and stuffy curtains around the sleeper's head; in addition, its cantilevered canopy helped perpetuate the tradition of decorating beds to match window treatments. Its upper embellishments might be festoons, pleated valances or flat edgings, cut out in piped V-shaped 'Vandykes' or scallops. The flat edgings were preferred by the author of *The Workwoman's Guide* of 1838, being 'pretty and simple' and light in appearance.[30] Half-testers were used in rooms both great and small throughout this period. Made with an iron frame, they were cheaper than iron-framed tent beds (which Loudon described as still in universal use in the 1830s) and also required less fabric. For small cottage rooms half-

8 The beds illustrated in *The Workwoman's Guide* (London, 1838) were described by the anonymous author as typical of the period and therefore included folding and inexpensive beds such as the trestle (27) and stump (31) beds, which had no hangings. Numbers 21–25 are French-style beds; a Vandyked flat valance can be seen on the half-tester (20). Bed hangings, she noted, were thick stuff, moreen, damask or linen, unlined chintzes and, less often, dimities lined with glazed calico, the colour harmonizing with the bed furnishings and the wallpaper (fringe and other decorations matched the lining). Stripes and small patterns were for small rooms, large flowers or patterns for large rooms and, she continued, best beds and draperies for sitting rooms (although, in fact, the practice of placing beds in sitting rooms was no longer fashionable).

testers could, Loudon advised, be folded up 'with little trouble . . . and the curtains drawn round them'. Thus concealed, said Loudon, 'they are by no means unsightly . . . but they are quite inadmissible in a kitchen or a parlor' (a reference to the custom, common in the eighteenth century, of putting beds in these relatively warm rooms). Many half-testers, certainly, were hung with chintzes, muslin and dimity, but it seems unlikely that wool-based fabrics disappeared from use – wool being cheaper, if unlined, and warmer. Woollen fabrics also retained the advantage, acknowledged by Loudon, 'of not taking fire so readily as chintz or dimity', although cottons could be made somewhat fire resistant by being dipped, after washing, in a solution of alum in water. The danger of candlelit bedrooms was regarded by Miss Leslie as the 'one serious objection to bed curtains, in the rooms of children, or of any persons that are not habitually careful'.[32] Gaslight, although widely used by 1860, seems not to have been used in many bedrooms, which may account for the persistance of light-

9 An American coverlet, designed and woven in New York by Harry Tyler and now in the American Museum, Bath. Dated 1836 and produced for L. A. Wright, whose name was woven into the corner, this coverlet of indigo and bleached white machine-spun wool was produced by hand on a Jacquard loom. (Tyler did his own dyeing and is also known to have used cochineal for red, which, at over 31 cents per ounce, more than twice the cost of indigo, was used less often.) The pattern is a 'point' repeat, folding outwards from the centre and causing the inscription to be reversed on the left. Here, the often-seen close relationship between coverlet and flat-woven or ingrain, carpet designs is not surprising, since Tyler also wove the latter.

coloured bedhangings and curtains which otherwise would have shown the effect of the fumes.

Even the folding half-tester was a bed of reasonable luxury; in 1838 *The Workwoman's Guide* described two beds which were for 'cottagers and men-servants, and require no drapery'. One of these, the trestle bed, was the 'most simple and most common kind of bedstead made'. A concentration of expenditure on beds and bedding, previously noticeable in the most fashionable houses, became by the 1830s and '40s a feature of urban lower-middle-class and rural homes. In otherwise unheated rooms bed curtains were a sensible expedient, but the very possession of a furnished bed distinguished the poor from the impoverished. In acknowledgement of this, writers often provided tips for 'cheap and very good-looking' bed curtains. Miss Leslie recommended thick domestic shirting muslin, dyed a fine buff and trimmed with worsted fringe or a binding of purple, dark brown, green or crimson.[33]

A manifestation of the continued symbolic importance of bedding was the Americans' application of the Jacquard, which was almost exclusively used prior to 1860 for the manufacture of coverlets with complex patterns (the other main use was in coach trimmings). Typically woven with cotton warps and woollen wefts, these were manufactured from about 1830 by professional hand-weavers, many of whom gradually moved westward – staying just behind the frontier and just ahead of the good supply routes from Eastern and European mills. Nevertheless, some eastern areas, such as Pennsylvania, continued to have some Jacquard coverlet weavers up to about 1870.

Reversible Jacquard woven coverlets were expensive – about $10–12 each in the 1840s – especially compared to 'over-shot' coverlets with floating-weft patterns (woven in America since the late eighteenth century on four-shaft looms) which cost about $2–3 in the same period.[34] These prices can be compared to a Pennsylvania inventory of 1841, which valued quilts and woollen blankets at $1 each, twenty linen sheets at $5, a set of diaper-patterned bed curtains (probably consisting of 25 to 35 yards) at $3, a professional weaver's loom, complete with diaper 'rigging', at $10, a desk at $12 and a featherbed and under (or trundle) bed at $16. No window curtains were listed.[35]

On the surface the interest in weaves was not auspicious for printed cottons, which since 1800 had been declining in price with each successive improvement in manufacturing processes and the supply of cotton, which now came increasingly from the American South. In Britain, with the removal in 1831 of the iniquitous taxation on prints, the one- and two-colour unglazed designs became very inexpensive – as low as fourpence a yard. Plain calico was about 2½ pence a yard. In his chronicle of British cotton manufacturing, published in 1835, Edward Baines (who, since 1818, had also been editor of the *Leeds Mercury*) reported with satisfaction that the typical English peasant's cottage was as handsomely furnished with cotton fabrics for beds, windows and tables as the house of a substantial tradesman had been in 1775.[36] Linen, although less used than previously, also fell in price.

In the United States, in areas near ports, manufacturing centres or trading centres, the cost of mass-produced cottons and linens was also dropping. An American inventory of 1849 exemplifies the continued reliance on unglazed cottons and linens in middle-class homes in both Britain and the United States. Polly and Nathan Bennett, both from families of prominence but not great wealth, were married in 1840 and lived in Bridport, Vermont. Their late Empire, or 'Victorian classical', furniture was purchased in New York City, Boston and Troy, New York. All of their identifiable curtains and upholstery fabrics were cotton or linen, with the exception of the horsehair-covered sofa and mahogany chairs bought in New York in 1846. The kitchen and sitting room had white curtains, the latter possibly of dimity – as probably were the single set of bed hangings (five beds were listed). The single curtain to the door window was dotted muslin, the hall window curtain was muslin with a ruffled edge and one bedroom had three plain muslin curtains. Three other bedrooms had more decorative curtains: a painted curtain (possibly a blind) was combined with a calico curtain in the first, four painted curtains were used in the second; the third had one copperplate-printed curtain, which presumably matched the dressing table and stool, both also with copperplate covers.[37] The latter (of linen or cotton) may have been cut down from an older set of bed hangings or curtains, although flat plate prints were still available in the 1840s. Alternatively, the term 'copperplate' could have referred to a one- or two-coloured roller-printed cotton with a scenic design, a style produced by many manufacturers in both Britain and America by this date. By becoming lower in price such fabrics ceased to be the most fashionable, but their use decreased only in terms of status, not in volume.

10 A roller-printed cotton, 1848–50, depicting scenes from the battle of Resaca de la Palma during the Mexican–American War. The coarsely spun and woven cloth and the limited colour palette suggest that it was made in the United States, since the similarly 'scenic' designs produced by British printers generally used finer cloths and more colours. Images for such patterns were readily available in the popular engraved prints, which depicted current events and reproduced paintings.

11 The Clinton Manufacturing Company manufactured this 'pantaloon cloth' in 1846 or '47. It was intended for trousers, as its name implies, but is not dissimilar from the striped upholstery worsteds being produced at the same time in Yorkshire, where they were known as calimancoes.

Home-woven cloths were also declining in status, perhaps partly because many were difficult to distinguish from the inexpensive stripes and checks now being factory made.[38] However cheap the latter were, added transportation costs made even the simplest store-bought fabrics something many could not easily afford. For example, in Jefferson County, Iowa, in 1846, a yard of plain calico cost 25 cents (or, in barter, five pounds of butter, an amount not easily obtained in surplus on a small farm). Muslin, with its more finely spun yarns, was 60 cents a yard, or the price of twenty eggs. This was about three times the price of muslin nearly twenty years earlier in Montgomery County, Pennsylvania.[39] So the occupants of the more isolated areas of Britain and the United States continued to weave significant amounts of checked, striped and plain furnishing cloths. They also continued to use the more economical styles of curtain, such as drawn-up eighteenth-century-style festoons, curtains barely gathered on rods or wires or tacked to the window frame, or simple blinds, rolled up by means of a piece of string.

The status of fabrics of this period was summarized by an English writer in *The Workwoman's Guide* (1838). Discussing bed hangings, the writer stipulated that linen or cotton checks and stripes, prints or stuff (all inexpensive, and most also capable of being home-woven) were 'for common use'. Dimities, full-colour glazed chintzes, fine stuff, moreen and damask (probably not including those of silk) were for hangings on beds 'for better purposes' and were to be lined with glazed calico or muslin of a suitable colour. These cloths were obtainable only from mercers or dry goods stores. Further, although dimities and chintzes were washable, they required special treatment: dimity was not meant to be ironed, but stretched in the direction of the warp until flat, and chintz had to be re-glazed and re-lined, which would cost as much as the fabric itself. Only state rooms warranted fine silk, satin or velvet.[40] Essentially the same divisions applied to fabrics in rooms other than the bedroom. In 1852, for example, J. Arrowsmith's Philadelphia publication, *The Paper-Hanger's Companion*, recommended striped silk tabaret or silk damask for spacious and lofty rooms, but chintz for drawing rooms that were small or low.[41] (He made no suggestions for rooms in very modest houses.)

For both prints and patterned weaves, elaboration was the factor distinguishing 'common' from 'better' fabrics. In North America production of the more complex fabrics was promoted partly by changes in British laws. In 1824 skilled British artisans, including textile workers, were no longer forbidden to emigrate; and the bans on exportation of British copper cylinders and calico-printing machinery were lifted in 1825 and 1830 respectively (although an export licence was required for these items until 1842.) Thenceforward British-engraved rollers were exported to America in large numbers; Joseph Lockett, an English engraver and cylinder-maker based in Salford and Manchester, exported from a stock of 20,000 designs (few of which had originated in England).[42] Prior to 1842 some machines, for all aspects of textile manufacture, were also smuggled into America in pieces or were built there from drawings made illicitly in England.[43]

12 Vivid colours characterized many British calicoes produced specifically for export between about 1835 and 1855. Mineral colours – which allowed mordant mixed with dye to be printed directly and then 'aged' (fixed) by steaming – were crucial to the export trade, since they greatly increased the speed of production and reduced the cost of the finished fabric. First used in the 1790s on wool, they were introduced to cotton printing between 1820 and 1830. By 1844, according to E. A. Parnell, author of *Applied Chemistry in Manufactures* (London), they were still generally added to cloths already partly printed in the madder style. This cotton typifies the madder-mineral palette, with mordants for red and purple applied by roller before immersion in madder, followed by block printing of mineral dyes (probably Prussian blue, Persian berries for yellow and a direct green based on quercitron liquor mixed with Prussian blue and often called 'spirit green'). Here the design appears to be too wide for the cloth, suggesting second-hand production.

The influx of British labour, combined with the greater availability of textile machinery, soon produced noticeable results. The acquisition of the Jacquard loom in 1824, within months of the British relaxation on emigration, was paralleled by a surge in fabric-printing. By the mid-1830s American printers provided about 120 million yards of finished cloth (just over one-third the amount printed in Britain). Although many were producing small-patterned two- or three-colour machine-printed dress fabrics, there were a number of American firms producing more ambitious 'muscular' patterns. Among these was the Hudson Calico Print Works (founded in 1826 by Joseph and Benjamin Marshall at Stockport, New York) which in 1836 had forty-two hand-block printers, two four-colour printing machines and three that printed in three colours. Each machine (imported from England) could produce the same amount of printed cloth in a day as could the forty-two hand-block printers, who probably equalled in number the total that could have been found in the United States at any one time in the early 1800s. The total production of the works in 1836 was 5.4 million yards, a vast increase on the 100,000 yards roller-printed by the Taunton Manufacturing Company of Massachusetts only ten years earlier. Very few American printed textiles of this period can be firmly documented, but the close relationship between the British and American industries must have led to many similarities in pattern in the two countries.

Machine-printing technology had first been developed in the late eighteenth century, but it was only after about 1825 that it began to be applied in earnest. The combined wooden and copper roller machines, known as 'mule' or 'union' machines, inspired many remarkable textiles, with fine-line engraving or etching contrasted with intense areas of overlapping colours provided by the wooden rollers. Hand-block printers were also employed to finish colouring roller-printed cloths (the Hudson Calico Print Works probably used their block printers in this way) and it is often difficult to distinguish between wooden surface rollers or hand blocks when used in conjunction with engraved rollers. Also utilized was a method (introduced in Manchester in 1808) of repeatedly engraving the entire cylinder from one very small 'mill' or steel cylinder. This system, which did not become common until the 1820s, used a small hand-engraved cylinder (or die) to mould the steel 'mill' cylinder with the pattern in relief, thus making possible detailed 'fancy ground' patterns. Die-and-mill grounds were often added to block-printed cloths, the completed block work being over-printed with a protective paste before passage through the machine. They were also used with roller- and union-printed designs. Although David Smith commented, in *The Practical Dyer's Guide* (1850), that dyers did not base their practices on scientific principles,[44] control of dyestuffs was then being improved, allowing a greater range of mineral-based colours (fixed by steaming) and multicolour printing in a single application, including 'rainbow' stripes. A mechanized form of warp printing (putting the pattern on the warp prior to weaving, producing designs with shaded or fuzzy outlines) was perfected in 1837. Rather in the same way that the invention of the sewing machine induced the proliferation of ruffles, the improved printing techniques brought out the 'look what I can do' spirit. In keeping with the youth of the textile-printing industry, a bold, uninhibited approach was characteristic. Low-priced labour and raw materials further encouraged an extravagant approach to design.

The increased volume of production demanded more patterns. In his study of *The Textile Manufacturers of Great Britain* (1844), George Dodd observed that 'the drawing of . . . designs is an extensive branch of employment at Manchester', also noting the 'rapid succession of novelties . . . on which the calico printer relies for success'.[45] The need for a constant supply of new designs was more pressing in the dress fabric trade, but it was also felt among furnishing fabric printers, particularly since they were now competing with the newly fashionable patterned weaves. One solution was to resuscitate and revamp old patterns, a practice encouraged by the prevailing taste for furniture in revival styles. During the late 1820s and '30s, many prints, as well as weaves, were based on designs of the years around 1800. Both pillar prints and patterns based on Berlin woolwork (a florid style of canvas embroidery) were popular revivals, the former surviving in fair quantities as bed hangings.[46] Designs such as these may never actually have gone out of production, due to the continuing demand created by compatible Gothic-style furniture. By the 1840s the taste for revivals was looking farther back, to patterns popular in the mid- to late eighteenth century.

Cheaper paper and printing methods encouraged copying by printers and weavers. For example, *Knight's Unique Fancy Ornaments*, published in London in 1834, advertised itself as a 'Compilation of splendid Ornamental Designs, from Foreign Works of recent Production'. It was intended to be 'equally useful to the architect, the upholsterer, the decorative painter, even the manufacturer of cloths and papers', and its publication was hailed as 'the commencement of an era of good and cheap architectural publication, which workmen may afford to purchase, as well as architects'. Others were not so optimistic. In the same year *Locke, Johnson, and Copland's Ornamental Designs* – 'intended for the ornamental painter, carver and gilder, and printed paper and printed cotton manufacturer' – was reprinted. Originally issued in the 1770s, the plates were intended 'to supply the present demand for the grotesque fanciful ornaments commonly said to be in the style of Louis XIV'. The London *Architectural Magazine*'s reviewer of this volume found 'a good deal of fancy [but] of the most inferior kind', concluding that 'this book is abundantly cheap, which is the best thing we can say of it.'[47]

Engravings of scenes were also a natural source of patterns for roller printing – and a style which weavers could not successfully imitate. The cloth printers' interpretations of Landseer and Delacroix paintings, hunting and war scenes, railway stations and Gothic ruins continued a tradition established by flat copperplate printers. The products of fine presses also influenced textile designers. For example, Audubon's *Birds of America*, published in London between 1827 and 1838, was the source of a group of roller-printed textiles engraved between 1830 and 1834.[48] The fashion for

13 In an era when the natural sciences were of great interest to amateurs as well as scholars, it was not surprising that textile designers used images obtainable from the many botanical and ornithological publications of the day. This roller-printed cotton, probably engraved by John Potts of New Mills, Derbyshire, includes birds taken from Audubon's *Birds of America*, published in London between 1827 and 1838. The combination of realism and unnatural colouring (created here by the use of a discharged manganese ground and the inclusion of bright mineral dyes) is typical of the 1820s and '30s.

14 This small sample (4¾ by 3½ inches) is one of a number that were inserted into the *Journal of Design*, a mid-nineteenth-century English periodical which was an important forum for discussion, advice and criticism on the decorative arts. Included in the May 1850 *Journal* and described as 'one of the most lively and tasteful chintzes issued this season', this glazed cotton was printed by Hargreaves for Liddiards, an English wholesale firm. The conventionalized flowers line up on a complex grid of vertical and diagonal lines; such patterns were therefore praised as 'geometric'.

bird prints continued into the early 1840s, supplemented by revived patterns with game birds, first produced just after 1810.

Owen Jones's *Plans, Elevations, Sections and Details of the Alhambra* (published in London in two volumes, 1836–45) and his *Grammar of Ornament*, 1856, influenced designers of weaves and prints alike. Some patterns, especially those in the chromolithographed *Grammar*, were copied directly (contrary to Jones's intentions), but many realistic florals, block-printed, for example, by Clarksons' and Stead McAlpin, simply adapted the trellis and ogival arrangements found in Jones's highly stylized Moresque, or Moorish-style, patterns. Under this influence floral bunches seldom remained isolated, but were joined by vines or flowering sprigs. This fashion soon spread to roller-printed fabrics, and remained an important method of arranging printed patterns into the 1880s.

Flowers remained the most common source of designs, and water-coloured stipple engraving such as Pierre-Joseph Redouté's widely admired 'Les Roses' (published in Paris in thirty parts between 1817 and 1824) probably contributed to the use of dotted shading as well as to the highly naturalistic woven and printed florals of the period. Real flowers also came indoors; conservatories attached to the drawing room were no longer unusual (particularly after 1845, when the tax on glass was removed); knowledge of flowering plants and gardening skills became socially desirable. In a less scientific spirit, the 'language' of flowers was carefully documented.[49] Many chintzes were publicly criticized for being too close to nature, but they nevertheless formed the core of printed textile design, and some have continued in and out of production ever since.

The mid-century British *Journal of Design* discussed the finer points of 'correct' floral patterns in virtually every issue, promoting 'merely likeness of form without absolute identity'.[50] The *Journal of Design* was one of many

15 This hand-woven silk brocatelle, employing two warps to create slightly raised surface areas, was designed by A. W. N. Pugin in the mid-1840s. Woven by Daniel Keith & Co., successors in the early 1840s to Stephen Wilson, this silk was probably produced for the influential London decorator J. G. Crace, who collaborated with Pugin during this period. The formal, stylized pattern is characteristic of 'pure' neo-Gothic designs.

books and magazines dealing with the newly recognized need for aesthetic criteria appropriate to machine-made goods. In keeping with the tough, 'muscular' tastes of the time, critics were thoroughly uncompromising, and none more so than John Ruskin, author of *The Stones of Venice* (1853), and A. W. N. Pugin, the architect, designer and writer, both of whom rejected all other styles in favour of the Gothic. Jones's *Grammar of Ornament* set down principles for good design, the majority relating to the proper use of colour. No one treated this issue lightly. According to the *Journal of Design*, the appropriate decoration and furnishing of dwellings was a 'momentous question'.[51] J. G. Crace, of the influential London decorating firm, also entered the fray; the *Journal of Design* quoted his comment that 'in silk manufactures . . . it is distressing to see so valuable a material too often woven in tasteless and unsuitable patterns.'[52] Nevertheless the same journal noted that many people thought textile design had improved after the British copyright act of 1842 had extended protection from one to three years. With much wider circulations than earlier in the century, such books and journals became the vehicle for a dialogue among designers, manufacturers and educators.

Lower publishing costs also made possible a proliferation of 'etiquette' books relating to interiors, aimed increasingly at the legions of housewives, who – away from cities or unable to afford the services of an architect or high-class decorator – selected and made up their own soft furnishings. The issue of appropriate pattern was not generally discussed in depth in these publications. Webster and Parke's *Encyclopedia of Domestic Economy*, for example, concentrated on guiding the reader through the maze of revival styles, taking 'modern' Grecian as the norm. Published in London in 1844, it was reprinted in New York soon afterwards and again in 1849 by Henry Bill of Norwich, Connecticut, selling in large numbers in the Midwest. Loudon's *Encyclopedia* of 1833 was never published in the United States, but it was widely circulated and influenced the American A. J. Downing, author of *The Architecture of Country Houses* (1850). Louis Antoine Godey's journal, *Godey's Lady's Book*, also drew on Loudon's work, and had, in 1850, a circulation of 62,500. Publications such as these both disseminated and perpetuated what was essentially an 1830s style, ensuring its use in middle-class homes in Britain and the United States up to about 1860. Nevertheless, as canal, road, rail and sea links improved in the 1840s and '50s, new ideas spread more rapidly both within and between the two countries. By 1850 even the well-to-do in the recently annexed states of Texas and California were following Eastern styles, which themselves were European and, increasingly, rococo in derivation.[53]

The application of such terms as 'Gothic', 'rococo' and 'Empire' to textiles of this period should be interpreted loosely. For example, the rococo style – generally regarded as French – included accurate (and inaccurate) copies of English patterns of the last quarter of the eighteenth century, when rococo had given way to neo-classicism. Many floral designs were made 'rococo' by the addition of elaborate lace or lace-like bands of leaves, inspired by early eighteenth-century textiles. A similarly

16 When the sixth Duke of Devonshire redecorated this bedroom at Hardwick Hall in the 1840s, he was part of a force that created a new fashion, being among the first to use tapestry almost like wallpaper and to re-use Elizabethan embroidery, as shown here. The application of original embroideries (quite possibly from one of the Duke's other properties, such as Chatsworth) to new velvet was probably undertaken by Crace, the influential London decorator who carried out much of the redecoration at Hardwick in the 1840s. The long decorative bands of gold lace (closer to what today would be called braid) were precursors of 'paning', or the application of patterned bands, which was widely practised (or simulated) within a decade on upholstered furniture and tablecovers with 'Gothic' or 'medieval' pretensions.

broad interpretation of 'Gothic' prevailed, except in designs by purists such as A. W. N. Pugin (who designed Gothic furnishings for the Houses of Parliament in 1836–7) and Owen Jones. The term 'Gothic' often referred to any pattern inspired by pre-eighteenth-century textiles or architectural ornament, freely adapted or combined with other more recent historical styles as well as with the ubiquitous florals. The designs of this period are easier to characterize by their 'sharp focus', crisp lines or realistic shading – the forte of both roller printing and Jacquard weaving. Incongruous combinations and an apparent horror of unpatterned areas typify most of the less expensive patterned textiles. Colours are bold and clear, with vivid blues, greens and yellows often used as backgrounds.

The complexity of many designs was compounded by the upholstery and curtaining treatments for which they were used. The application of springed seating and deep-buttoning in the 1830s changed the shape of upholstered furniture. Closely associated with rococo-revival chairs and sofas (although not confined to them), deep-buttoning distorted patterns, especially stripes. 'Paning' (the practice of applying vertical bands of decoration to another textile surface) was perceived as a medieval or Renaissance practice. Bands of embroidery were stitched to plain velvet, an effect simulated by printed pile fabrics; weavers produced mock paning by juxtaposing patterned and plain bands in the same cloth (often using rococo-style motifs). Printers revived the boldly patterned double stripes of the 1790s; and taste arbiters of the period also recommended turning the lining over the front of curtains, to provide a banded edge.[54] Piping, fringes and tassels added further detail to upholstery and curtains.

Despite the lack of restraint in many fabric patterns, the overall appearance of many British and American homes well into the 1850s was often much simpler than one would imagine. Although in practice, the use of loose covers, blinds and muslin or lace curtains (whether year round or only in the summer) might add extra colours, the principal fabrics in any one room were still supposed to be the same colour, if not the same material, and in harmony with the colours of the walls and carpets. Red continued to be a favourite colour for furnishing fabrics. It was virtually the only colour approved by Mrs. Parkes, whose influential book *Domestic Duties* was in its tenth edition by 1846. Once gathered, curtains read as a mass of colour, and the contrast between bright or deep-toned fabrics and adjacent walls was minimized by 'dusky' wallpaper or paint in shades of drab, grey, greyish pink or pale olive, pea or sea green.

In the late 1840s a new fashion for un-matched, though still harmonizing, fabrics began to appear – except in bedrooms. Fabrics here were generally lighter in colour than in other rooms, and throughout the mid-1800s they were expected to match exactly – so much so that patchwork, according to Miss Leslie, was no longer fashionable, having been replaced by coverlets made from seamed lengths of the material used in the bed hangings and/or curtains.[55]

A measure of harmony was also achieved by not combining the various revival styles in the same room. In 1840 H. W. and A. Arrowsmith, decorators to Queen Victoria, suggested that the 'Tudor style is well suited for a dining-room, the arabesque [Empire or Grecian "modern"] for sitting rooms, and the gorgeous French [neo-rococo] styles for drawing-rooms, and although some of these may be employed for other purposes than those we have mentioned, it is for these that they seem most appropriate.'[56] Loudon, in 1833, felt that rococo-revival styles were essentially for the fairly wealthy,[57] and this remained true until about 1860, when neo-rococo furniture began to be mass-produced in great quantities (particularly by the American manufacturers based in Grand Rapids,

17 When Samuel Rayner depicted this British townhouse bedroom in a watercolour of about 1855, he provided an excellent example of the way in which a colour scheme could moderate a multi-patterned interior. Although the bed and chairs are covered in the same chintz, the wallpaper, carpet, rugs, curtains and lace-topped dressing table add eight additional patterns to the room. Nevertheless, all are held together by the harmonious colour scheme, based on a soft golden brown, blue and white. These light colours emphasize the rococo theme of the room and override the presence of furniture made in other styles. The use of 'modern' or Grecian straight-hanging curtains in a neo-rococo interior was not uncommon. If the artist is to be believed, these curtains hang from behind a purely decorative rod. The blue gathered fabric inside the curtains is an inner valance; a plain blind can be seen in the far window.

Michigan). The Arrowsmiths qualified their own advice (which was probably aimed at their wealthiest clients), by acknowledging that the Grecian 'modern' style was most suited to 'the social habits and intercourse of the great mass of the British public who require a cheerful and pleasing but not a gorgeous style of decoration.' It also suited the majority of Americans. As a result, irrespective of the pattern, fabrics were most often treated in the rather austere Grecian style, imparting a solidity which averted much potential visual confusion.

Although complex patterns were made more economical by improvements in yarn preparation and cloth finishing, there were still many fabrics made in single colours or with restrained patterns. Writers of the period consistently included these in their recommendations – regardless of the cost of the proposed interior. Loudon suggested glazed self-coloured calico as 'a very cheap yet tasteful' loose sofa cover, Mrs. Parkes maintained the superiority of moreen and crimson or scarlet cloth for the dining room, and Downing, the American author of *The Architecture of Country Houses* (1850), suggested satin and velvet – as well as brocades – for villa or townhouse curtains.[58] Dimity and cambric muslin in bedrooms and horsehair or leather upholstery remained popular throughout the period.

An almost austere effect resulted, in many cases, from leaving windows uncurtained. In 1826, Ackerman still found it necessary to point out that curtains were 'a very essential part of interior decoration'.[59] *Godey's Lady's Book*, published in Philadelphia from 1830 to the end of the century, admonished his American readers in 1851 to use curtains, complaining that Philadelphia gave a cold, 'unwinking, unwelcome stare to the passer-by', as a result of 'the prevalence of a uniform style of stone-coloured or green window shades'.[60]

Venetian blinds, louvred interior shutters and roller blinds continued to predominate in homes in both Britain and the United States, although by mid-century Venetian blinds were no longer fashionable. Plain roller blinds were the cheapest and easiest to maintain, and therefore the most common. Typically made of linen, they were also made of canvas, gauze and calico, or fine so-called 'Scotch' or cambric lawn.[61] Painted 'transparent' cloth blinds were also popular, initially with all-over landscapes or architectural details, such as representations of stained glass. After a vogue for plain blinds between about 1840 and 1850, they were generally painted with borders and a wide choice of central designs. The trade was substantial enough in London in the 1830s to support at least four specialist blind-painting firms (Joseph Stubbs, Jones & Sons, John Fawley and William Bacon, all recommended in J. S. Croften's *The London Upholsterer's Companion*, 1834) and furnishing fabric shops also stocked block- and roller-printed fabrics with designs suitable for blinds. Every taste was catered for; in 1854 Carryl's, the Philadelphia shop so often cited in *Godey's Lady's Book*, could offer painted cloth blinds from $2 to $20.

The desire to provide for all tastes and income levels can be seen in much that was manufactured during this period. At the 1853 Industrial Exhibition in New York, for example, fancy printed cassimeres (medium-weight twilled woollens) were described as suiting 'a large class of buyers,

18 This oil-painted cloth 'Tontine Shade Roller' or 'transparent blind' was produced in the United States between 1830 and 1840. An example of the period's liking for trompe l'oeil decoration, blinds with landscapes or all-over architectural details were also popular and were sometimes hung with the painted side facing outwards. Thomas Webster's *Encyclopaedia of Domestic Economy* (1844 and 1845) described these as sun blinds, which were 'particularly convenient when it is desirable to exclude the view of disagreeable objects'. A homemade substitute was wallpaper pasted onto linen or paper, but these were more opaque and could not, therefore, give the desired stained glass-like effect. The blind measures 42 by 26⅜ inches.

particularly . . . the western markets, as being at once low in price and showy in character'.[62] The New York exhibition was a response to the Great Exhibition, held in London in 1851. Both exhibitions set out to demonstrate new, more useful and cheaper machine-made goods, as well as superior skills in established crafts, such as block printing.[63] Celebrating the new use of known methods or materials, as well as new methods and materials themselves, the 1850s also witnessed the application of power to Jacquard weaving and the development of the first synthetic dye – but these occurred too late for either exhibition. Events such as these generated a greater taste for 'showy' ornament, and at the same time galvanized those already concerned about standards of design. Two distinct groups began to take shape: those who valued comfort, complexity and richness of effect, and those committed ideologically to honest use of materials and appropriate ornament. By 1860 these two views had become polarized, setting the stage for developments over the next forty years. At the same time the furnishing textile industry was passing out of its exuberant adolescence and into maturity.

19 With their delicate stems and finely drawn mixture of flowers, both of these patterns are reminiscent of designs of the last quarter of the eighteenth century – so much so that the block-printed chintz on the left could date either from about 1790 or from 1825–30. The chintz on the right is certainly of the later period, since the reds and purples have been roller-printed, with the remaining colours supplied by blocks. It is not clear how the background stripe has been applied.

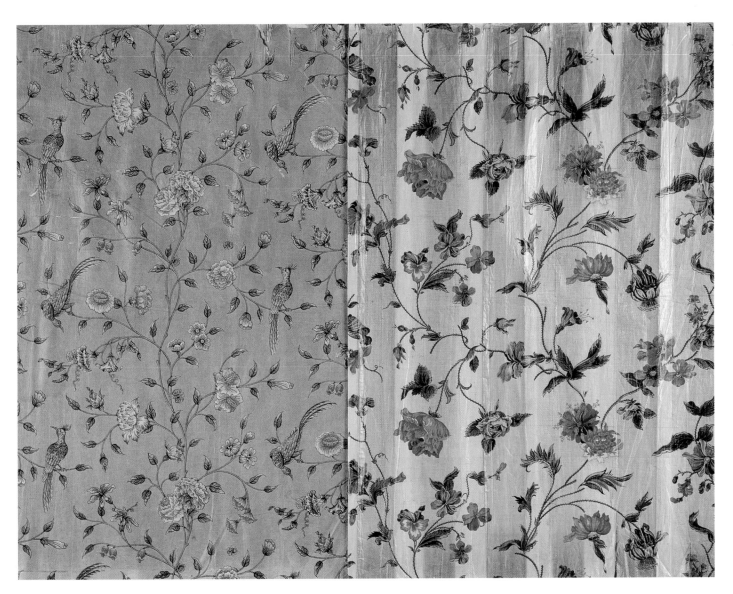

20 and 21 Two *en suite* bedrooms, on the right a scheme drawn in about 1825 by Gillow & Co., Oxford Street, London. The seemingly casually placed draperies of the bed and windows are a last reminder of asymmetrical treatments of the previous two decades. The floral-printed cotton was similar in colouring to the filling in the chintz seen in the room on the left, the 'Queen of Scots' bedroom at Chatsworth. The bed in the latter room shows the shallow, more controlled draperies fashionable in the late 1820s, whereas the window had a double set of fossilized 'drawn up' festoon curtains. The chintz on the Chatsworth bed was printed at Bannister Hall in 1830, at the time the bed was made. Note that here the border has been placed at the top of the upholstered headboard, footboard and sofa. Permanent upholstery in chintz became more common in this period (particularly in bedrooms and informal day rooms); by contrast, the Gillow interior appears to compromise, with what is probably a fixed cover on the chair and a loose cover on the chaise longue.

20

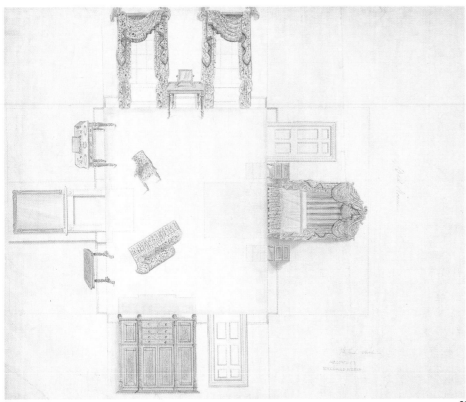

21

22 An 1829 design by the architect J. B. Papworth for the dining room at Little Grove, East Barnet (now Barnet, London), which contained Grecian 'modern' furniture, also designed by Papworth. With 20 and 21, it illustrates the transition from the late Regency to the 'muscular' style, with cylinder-shaped folds in the continued drapery. The straight cornice and measured use of tassels emphasize the symmetrical arrangement of the window treatment and the furniture, which is shown arranged (possibly for the convenience of the drawing) against the walls in eighteenth-century fashion. It is not known whether this interior was ever installed, but the drawing suggests muslin curtains and red stuff or velvet draperies, the latter still often recommended for dining rooms.

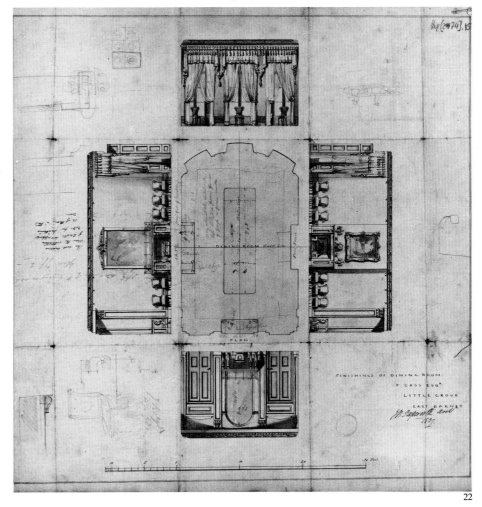

22

23

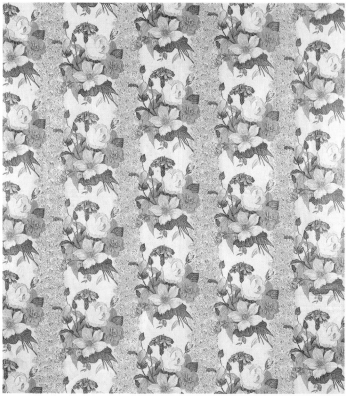

24

23 and 24 Employing only four colours, these English printed cottons were produced in the first half of the 1830s on a union machine, which combined engraved copper and wooden 'surface' rollers. Here brown and red were supplied by the engraved rollers, with yellow and blue added by surface rollers. (The consistent misalignment of the yellow over the red flower indicates mechanized printing.) A meander, stripe or all-over 'fancy' ground pattern was often added to floral prints of 1825–60. The mixture of perennials and annuals suggests that the designer was familiar with John Claudius Loudon's *Gardener's Magazine* or one of his many other publications which together promoted such flowers as fashionable for middle-class gardens (labourers' cottage gardens were expected to contain mainly fruit and vegetables). The similarity of drawing and colouring suggests that the same designer or firm created both fabrics.

25 This madder-style union-printed cotton was produced in Britain in about 1835. The background imitates a woven fabric with its 'moiré' or watered pattern. Note the sideways repeat, which offsets the dominant motif so that it does not form a diagonal line. One of a pair of curtains, the piece retains several simple tape loops from which it was hung. It was not lined.

25

26 and 27 These two designs are so
similar that one must have been copied
from another, or both from a common
source. Pillar prints such as these were
extremely popular patterns in the years
around 1830, and the numerous surviving
examples of both of these designs indicate
the way in which roller printers continued
to produce varied cloths by altering the
number of colours or the background.
Other pieces of the pattern seen in 27
include three at the Winterthur Museum
(printed in red only, on a tan ground and
with a brown and yellow vertical stripe
over the entire design) and another at the
Metropolitan Museum, with a trelliswork
ground. At the Musée de l'Impression sur
Étoffes, in Mulhouse, are two examples:
one, like 26, with discharged lace, cords
and tassels in the background and the
other without, but covered completely
with a block printed textured ground.
Both of the examples shown here were
produced in Britain on union machines.

28 A comparison between this design for a block-printed furnishing chintz of about 1792 by William Kilburn and Fig. 29 shows the typical similarities and differences between the original designs and their revivals.

29 Registered by William Benecke & Co., in April 1848 (design number 51491), this roller-printed cotton displays passion flowers and blossoms of the type found in late eighteenth- and early nineteenth-century designs. The desire for authenticity extends even to the old technique of using an outline to disguise misregistration of blocks and bleeding, although neither was technically necessary in the 1840s. Benecke's offices were in Manchester, where during the 1840s some ninety other cotton-printing firms were also based.

28

29

30 When compared to the delicately drawn flowering vines of the mid-1820s, the large, robust flowers on this hand-block-printed cotton (first produced at Bannister Hall in 1845) indicate the change in taste which had accompanied the development of 'muscularity' in architecture and the decorative arts.

30

31 This machine-printed cotton was registered in Britain by Kershaw, Leese & Sidebottom in August 1848 (design no. 53809) and is typical of the last phase of what could be called 'toile' designs. The scene has here been reduced to a vignette within a floral roundel, which retains the squashed proportions more typical of earlier roller-printed scenic designs. Vivid (and non-fast) steam colours have been used, and the pattern is arranged to repeat sideways in a half-drop.

32 The watercolourist Mary Ellen Best made this record of her newly decorated late Empire-style drawing room at No. 1 Clifton, York, which she occupied between November 1837 and March 1840. The fully gathered lambrequin (a form illustrated by Loudon in 1833 and popular before superseded by flat lambrequins) is made from a printed cotton which matches the curtains, loose sofa-cover, and chair and stool upholstery. Also fashionable is the use of the lining, folded forwards to edge the drapery and loose cover, as well as the only partial use of *en suite* furnishings. The armchair upholstery and tablecloth which introduce different fabrics may well be of stamped woollen velvet. Both the design of the wallpaper and the printed cotton are revivals from some forty years earlier.

31

32

33

34

33 Sketched in watercolours by Suzanne Roy, c.1936, this chintz was part of a set of four-poster bed curtains and window curtains bought for an 1834 wedding in Bergen, New York. Of unknown origin, it is nevertheless similar to the first prints produced by the Cranston Mills, in Rhode Island, where more than fifty textile mills existed in the mid-nineteenth century. The design's interpretation of embroidery – in this case, crewelwork – is typical of many 1830s prints.

34 Gothic designs, particularly those employing images of stained glass windows, were popular throughout the 1830s and '40s. This glazed cotton example, roller-printed in madder red and purplish-brown, is similar to chintz designs known to have been used as window blinds.

35 A design for an eight-colour hand-block-printed cotton produced in February 1857 for the Oxford Street, London, retailers Messrs. Hindley & Co., by Stead McAlpin (known as J. H. McAlpin, Stead & Co. from 1848–60). Naturalistically drawn floral bunches have been 'Gothicized' by the addition of a 'carved' ogival framework.

36 Conservatories were not uncommon additions to Victorian houses, and often, as depicted here in 1852 at Blithfield Hall, Staffordshire, led from the morning room or boudoir. The plain velvet (or, less

35

36

probably, stuff) curtains hanging from a large wooden pole with exposed rings were in keeping with the Gothic style of the conservatory. The banquettes are covered with a floral chintz, with naturalistically drawn flowers. Note the two different table covers, the right one almost certainly of velvet with applied 'panes' or bands in medieval style, the left of velvet or baize with a similarly 'antiquated' deep embroidered or woven

border and fringe. By 14 March 1856, George Wallis could report in *The Journal of the Society of Arts* that cloths such as seen here – plain surfaces, with borders 'of an elegant character' or small patterns dotted or 'powdered' over the surface – were, 'as compared with those in vogue eight to ten years ago . . . preferred to the "all-over" patterns, which were pronounced as the only things which would ever sell in the English market'.

37 'The Yankee Pedlar', by an unknown artist, illustrates the interior of a fairly prosperous rural American kitchen in the early 1840s. The plain sheer muslin half, or sash, curtain is the only curtain seen and probably hangs on a wire fixed to the window frame. It may be embellished with a hand run-in lower border. The cloth being offered is a check almost certainly of American manufacture. Pedlars of diverse stocks, such as depicted here, were often agents, many operating as did the W. A. Currier agents who went to houses within a 12-mile radius of Haverhill, Massachusetts, accepting payment in articles such as shoes, apples, feathers, old newspapers, rags, metals and ox horns, as well as in cash. However, there were other types of pedlars during this period. Correspondence from the United States in April 1846 indicates that William Morris, a wool-jean weaver, hired a peddling wagon to sell his own wares.

37

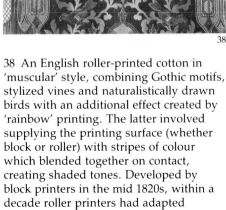

38

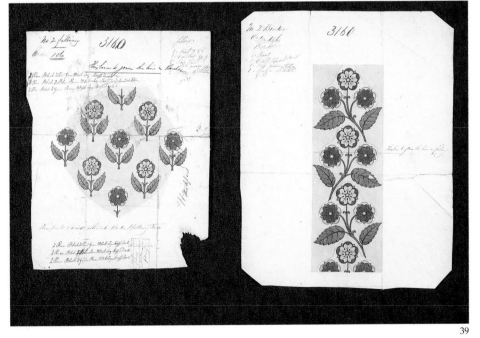

39

38 An English roller-printed cotton in 'muscular' style, combining Gothic motifs, stylized vines and naturalistically drawn birds with an additional effect created by 'rainbow' printing. The latter involved supplying the printing surface (whether block or roller) with stripes of colour which blended together on contact, creating shaded tones. Developed by block printers in the mid 1820s, within a decade roller printers had adapted 'rainbow' stripes to their own process, which could produce only stripes running up the cloth, as in this example of about 1840–45.

39 This 1854 design for a block-printed cotton is typical of the simpler patterns favoured by design reformers. The flower shape itself would have been regarded as Gothic. Employing only three colours in addition to the ground, the single conventionalized flower in the filling is arranged in a manner referred to as a 'half drop'. Note the line marked in both border and filling to indicate where they were to align. The notes on the filling suggest that the two patterns alternated in vertical stripes.

40

41

40 This arrangement of floral patterns –
with a 6- to 8-inch border and a trelliswork
filling – was particularly popular in the
late 1850s and early 1860s. The example
shown here was hand block-printed by
Steads in about 1859. Note that the
trelliswork running from upper left to
lower right has been altered. Originally
both strands in the trellis were the same.
Combined with a different border, this
design was produced in several shades of
green only in the same year (both designs
are recorded as engaged to Soper).

41 In 1852 an exhibition intended to
demonstrate 'False Principles of Design'
was organized by Henry Cole at the
Museum of Ornamental Art, Marlborough
House, London. This design of 1840–45
was included as an example of direct
imitation of nature (False Principle No. 11)
and represented the growing consensus in
avant-garde circles that life-size, three-
dimensional, realistically drawn motifs
were unsuitable for carpets, wallpapers
and textiles. Despite such criticism, block-
printed textiles continued to employ
naturalistic designs, and this and other
Victorian floral chintzes have continued in
production ever since (latterly more often
as screenprinted adaptations). The pattern
and dark ground colouring is similar to
designs of about 1800, and the blue-green
leaves even imitate the appearance of an
early 'double' green from which the
yellow has faded.

42 These two late-Empire window
treatments were drawn in 1826 and
included in George Smith's 1828
publication, *The Cabinet Maker and
Upholsterer's Guide*. Both were intended for
use in a drawing room, and show two of
the several ways Smith incorporated
drapery with large rods without rings.
Other plates show similarly raised (left) or
toga-like (right) draperies elongated to
encompass two or more windows. Raised
draperies were still thought 'handsome' in
1838, when *The Workwoman's Guide* was
published, but A. W. N. Pugin illustrated
similar draperies in *The True Principles of
Pointed or Christian Architecture* (London,
1841) as examples of decoration as 'a
surprising vehicle for bad and paltry
taste.'

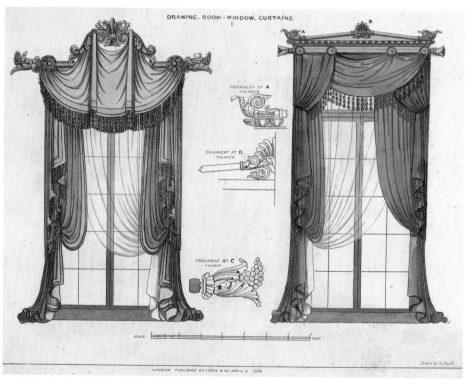

DRAWING · ROOM · WINDOW · CURTAINS.

ORNAMENT AT A ENLARG'D

ORNAMENT AT B ENLARG'D

ORNAMENT AT C ENLARG'D

SCALE   FEET

LONDON PUBLISHED BY JONES & CO APRIL 8 1826

42

43

44

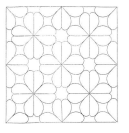

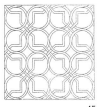

45

43 This all-over design of roses and leaves was roller-printed in the United States by Maquestion & Co., who received an award for their 'premium' damask and furniture chintz prints from the American Institute, New York, in 1850. With bright colours and a padded, discharged ground, this chintz demonstrates the improved understanding of dyeing and printing techniques that manufacturers in the United States had gained during the 1830s and '40s. This piece was probably produced soon after 1850, when such well-ordered floral designs became popular.

44 The effects of rainbow printing were often very subtle, as in this elaborate block-printed cotton of about 1855. Careful study of the block-printed leaves shows that the colour changes from green to blue-green (from left to right). Just visible is the faint vertical band of silhouetted budding vines set into a 'pinned' ground. Designs such as this were produced in both France and Britain.

45 These four geometric design exercises were included in the *Drawing Book of the Government School of Design*, written in 1842–3 by William Dyce, who in 1838 had been appointed Director of the Government School (the first official institution in Britain for teaching design). Grids such as these were used alone as textile designs but also acted as guides for placement of motifs.

46 In the early 1840s Charlotte Bosanquet made watercolour sketches of the interiors of her own and her relations' houses, including this drawing room at Meesdenbury, Hertfordshire (1843). Of interest in this interior is the abundance of needlework, the majority used as upholstery for 'Tudor' furniture (with spiral-turned legs more accurately described as late-seventeenth-century in origin) which, together with the Empire-style pieces, probably date from the 1830s. The curtains hang from exposed rods set, as was fashionable in the 1840s, in front of a flat valance embellished with a deep fringe.

46

47

47 Queen Victoria's bedroom and dressing room at Osborne was decorated in a combination of rose-pink and apple green which had been approved by John Claudius Loudon in 1833 and remained popular into the 1850s. The same chintz has been used on the half-tester and bed curtains, for loose covers and at the window, where the lambrequin is gathered rather than flat. The 'paned' dressing-room portière is related to the bedroom by its fringe, and also presents a vivid contrast to the rest of the furnishings, illustrating a fashion still very new when J. Roberts painted this watercolour in 1854. Note the embroidered details on the stool (the bands on the portière may also be embroidered, but their 'shawl' patterns could equally be woven or printed).

48 Similar to the fabric depicted in Fig. 17, this English chintz employs a limited colour range often found on block prints of the 1850s. Although the pattern is related to those produced in France at mid-century, *The Art Journal Illustrated Catalogue* of the Great Exhibition, 1851, (p. XVIII) noted that the predominance of browns or greys was a feature of many prints produced by firms based in and around Manchester.

48

49 The continued practice of hand-weaving silks for a specific use is exemplified by this silk damask, in which the hand-brocaded floral motifs were worked in sideways on the loom, so that the finished piece could be used horizontally. This mid-nineteenth-century silk, thought to have been woven by Charles Norris & Co. of London, was probably intended as a flat valance or lambrequin. Earlier in the century, patterns woven sideways were generally for sofa backs, which could thus be constructed without seams.

49

50

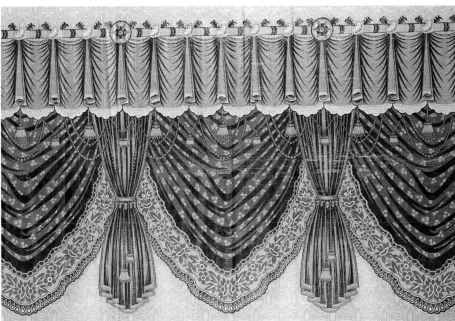

51

52

50 This silk brocatelle, woven by Keith & Co. in about 1855, has a double-striped pattern which echoes the contemporary fashion for 'panes' (applied or inset vertical bands). Although paning seems initially to have been associated with neo-Gothic schemes, it was also interpreted, as here, in neo-rococo motifs and naturalistically drawn flowers (see Fig. 6).

51 Like Fig. 49, the design on this roller-printed cotton has been placed sideways. Here, the trompe l'oeil valance makes the intended use clear, and the imitation moiré ground was probably produced alone as separate lengths so that matching bed or window curtains could complete the effect. Possibly by James Burd of Mount Zion Works, Radcliffe, near Manchester, the arrangement of the Roman draperies with swags beneath suggests that this was produced between 1825 and 1840.

52 The designs employed on this chair seat and border are typical of French patterns of the early nineteenth century, but these English-woven pieces were probably not produced until about 1825–35. Both were hand-woven for furniture in Windsor Castle and have linen warps and worsted wefts, with the two-colour pattern hand-brocaded in cream worsted and gold (border) or white (seat) silk. The use of worsted illustrates the renewed popularity of this fibre during the second quarter of the nineteenth century (these fabrics were later replaced with similar patterns woven in silk).

53 This English townhouse drawing room, depicted in watercolours by Samuel Rayner in the mid 1850s, illustrates the type of Louis XV-inspired furniture that was probably the decade's most popular historical style. It was promoted by many mid-nineteenth-century furniture designers and manufacturers in both Britain and the United States and was possibly the first middle class *en suite* furniture. Soon mass-produced, especially in the United States, this style remained popular until the late 1880s, although it was seldom used with the gold-and-white rococo setting seen here. Note the modest lambrequins, with banding vaguely echoing the arabesques decorating the walls and ceiling.

53

54

54 This parlour in the Farnsworth Homestead, Rockland, Maine, exemplifies the surfeit of boldly coloured patterns which began to be apparent in some interiors after about 1850. The suite of neo-rococo furniture (which includes a sofa not seen) was upholstered in three different silks; a peach brocatelle was used on the pair of armchairs, a red, green and white tissue on the side chairs and a blue and gold damask on the sofa. Also typical of the mid-nineteenth century is the eclectic combination of the fashionable suite with bobbin-turned 'Tudor' furniture, popular since the 1830s, and the 'modern' simply hung curtains. The latter are of red, black and white silk and wool in a 'paned' design of roses and pseudo-Gothic ornament.

55 Aniline dyes, first manufactured in 1856, were quickly taken up by block printers of wool, many of whom were

55

56

56 This two-colour printed cotton of about 1840–45 was roller-printed, the design having been stippled (hammered with a blunt point) rather than engraved with a sharp tool. This technique, which was particularly popular from about 1825 to 1845, required a high degree of skill, and was often done by specialists such as Joseph Lockett of Manchester. Completed rollers were then sold to printers – in Lockett's case many went to the United States.

57

based in or near Mulhouse, in eastern France. Already prized for the depth of colour that it radiated, wool, when printed with an aniline colour, was a glowing cloth that enjoyed widespread use in upholstery and curtains. The design, with its lattice-work of rococo scrolls, is typical of the compartmentalization found in many 1850s patterns.

57 The Public Records Office in Kew, near London, holds sample books of registered designs for furnishing fabrics which begin in 1842. This damasquette (with two colours in the warp, one of which matches the weft in order to create solid-coloured areas where they cross) was registered by Daniel Keith & Co. on 23 October 1859. Four years earlier Keith's (a hand silk-weaving firm based in London) had advertised their range as including plain satins and plain striped and figured tabarets at 2–4 shillings a yard, carriage linings, carriage blinds, velvets and (at 5–30 shillings a yard) damasks, brocatelles, tissues and brocades. This example, close to a damask in construction, probably cost about 8–10 shillings.

58 This small boudoir is furnished with lambrequins and curtains which appear to be made from a brocatelle. When Carl Haag painted this watercolour in 1847, *en suite* furnishings were no longer fashionable, so although the same curtains are used in the adjacent room and the portière has been made double to match both aspects, the sofa and chair are upholstered in different fabrics in related shades of blue. Note that the lambrequin has been cut to echo the shape of the neo-rococo sofa-back.

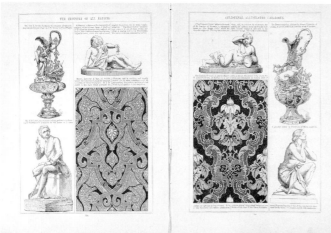

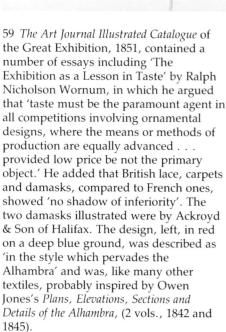

59 *The Art Journal Illustrated Catalogue* of the Great Exhibition, 1851, contained a number of essays including 'The Exhibition as a Lesson in Taste' by Ralph Nicholson Wornum, in which he argued that 'taste must be the paramount agent in all competitions involving ornamental designs, where the means or methods of production are equally advanced . . . provided low price be not the primary object.' He added that British lace, carpets and damasks, compared to French ones, showed 'no shadow of inferiority'. The two damasks illustrated were by Ackroyd & Son of Halifax. The design, left, in red on a deep blue ground, was described as 'in the style which pervades the Alhambra' and was, like many other textiles, probably inspired by Owen Jones's *Plans, Elevations, Sections and Details of the Alhambra*, (2 vols., 1842 and 1845).

60 A cotton and worsted power-driven Jacquard-loom cloth, possibly made by H. C. McCrea & Co. of Halifax, Yorkshire, employs rococo-revival scrollwork and filigree details, but with a bolder effect, heightened by the choice of black and cream yarns. The repeat is also more ordered or mechanical than original rococo patterns.

61 From the Morse-Libby House in Portland, Maine, these silk-over-wire flowers (probably of French manufacture) on curtain tie-backs were part of an elaborate neo-rococo interior of about 1860. They illustrate the love of overlaid detail which was an essential part of mid-century taste.

62 This design for a drawing-room curtain comes from George Smith's 1828 London publication, *The Cabinet Maker and Upholsterer's Guide*. A rococo style is suggested by the cornice, but the same valance could as easily have been finished with a cornice carved with Gothic ornament.

63 P. and M. A. Nicholson's *Practical Cabinet Maker, Upholsterer and Complete Decorator* (London, 1826) begins with an introduction to perspective drawing and geometry, the latter related by Nicholson to Greece, the 'source of unrivalled excellence and universal admiration'. The authors nevertheless included neo-Gothic designs, including the lower two footstools. The five stools demonstrate how, to suggest different historical styles, cabinet-makers often depended on variations in carved detail and the choice of upholstery and trimmings. Their introduction makes clear that their work was for professionals and not the public.

61

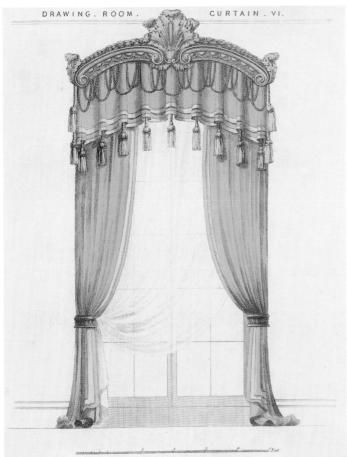

62

63

Chapter Four

Renaissance

1860–1890

'We next approach the important subject of beauty in reference to the decoration of houses. For while the aesthetic element must be subordinate to the requirement of physical existence . . . it yet holds a place of great significance among the influences which make home happy and attractive, which give it a constant and wholesome power over the young, and contributes much to the education of the entire household in refinement, intellectual development, and moral sensibility.'
(Harriet Beecher Stowe and Catharine E. Beecher, in *The American Woman's Home*[1])

Many individual elements found in interiors of the 1840s and 1850s were still in evidence in the 1880s: designs based on fifteenth- and sixteenth-century fabrics or exotic hothouse flowers, deep-buttoned parlour suites and lambrequins, machine-made lace curtains, needlework, tassels and fringe – all continued to play a prominent role.

Yet the 1860s witnessed a number of events which, taken together, marked the beginning of a new era and a new ethos. The enactment of the Cobden Treaty in Britain, in 1860, removed the protective tariff on French silks and so signified a more liberal trading spirit. The opening of the Suez Canal, nine years later, not only facilitated travel and trade between Europe and Asia but symbolized the whole idea of freedom of movement. Even the great tragic upheaval of the 1860s, the American Civil War, achieved, ultimately, freedom for an enslaved people – and, in the process, a new maturity for the nation that had oppressed them.

The spirit of optimism and self-determination engendered by these events inevitably manifested itself in the decorative arts. New criteria were tempering and supplanting the preoccupation with technology which had characterized the Industrial Revolution. The establishment, in 1861, of the firm of Morris, Marshall, Faulkner & Co., which produced a variety of high-quality furnishings, and behind which William Morris was the prime force, marked the coming of age of a movement for artistic reform, in which respect for craftsmanship was to be a central theme. Loosely related to this 'Arts and Crafts' movement (as it was later called), but guided primarily by a belief in 'art for art's sake', irrespective of function, was the 'Aesthetic' movement, which emerged a few years later. The decorative arts thus became the subject of lively debate, with such words as 'beauty', 'usefulness', 'honesty' and 'appropriateness' brandished like so many banners. A renaissance in design was clearly under way.

It was, however, a renaissance inspired by many sources – some ancient

1 William Morris's first emboidery was worked in 1857, and his bed at Kelmscott Manor, Gloucestershire, has hangings and a cover designed before 1890 by his daughter May. The cover was embroidered by Morris's wife Jane and the hangings by May and others. The natural dye-based colour palette seen here was to be as influential as the patterns and techniques Morris promoted. Equally influential was the emphasis on stems and attenuated lines, seen here and on many other contemporary embroideries and soon to be adopted by avant-garde designers for repeating textile patterns.

2 Increased urbanization put greater emphasis on both privacy and exterior appearances from the mid-nineteenth century onwards, resulting in lace and net-laden windows such as this, illustrated in *Beautiful Homes* (1878, New York), a book by William Jones. This layered effect was to be achieved by drapers using expensive tasselled, fringed, bordered and embroidered silks, lace curtains and finely embroidered muslin blinds (which appear to pull up like Austrian blinds). Alternatively, the style could be made at home with lightweight wool (lined with coloured cambric), Nottingham lace curtains and coarse muslin blinds. Cigar colour was recommended for the lambrequin and curtains, in keeping with the Renaissance-revival embroidery and strapwork on the lambrequin and border and the motifs on the curtain.

and exotic, others drawn from the recent past. The Gothic revival and the appetite for pattern matured into a taste far more akin to that of the Renaissance in its cosmopolitan roots. Like the dress of a sixteenth-century courtier, the interiors of 1860–90 were richly encrusted with textures, colours and patterns which openly acknowledged their indebtedness to several cultures, combining the classicism of Greece, the dark splendour of the Levant and the silken surfaces of the Far East. The High Renaissance and the mid-Victorian period were also similarly materialistic eras, when power, privilege and patronage were strongly evident. The prevailing materialism was manifest in mid-Victorian interiors, even the most modest, as the rising lower and middle classes took greater pride in the embellishment of their homes.

The picturesque arrangement of a multitude of objects, which characterizes this period, was beneficial to all those involved in the supply of fabrics or yarns, for the fashionable interior demanded more textiles, whether hand-made, antique or mass-produced. The principal instrument of this increase was mass production – against which the use of hand-made or antique fabrics was largely a reaction. Not until the 1860s, however, did the requisite mass market exist in both Britain and the United States. Most of Britain's market lay beyond its shores, but a more substantial domestic market had come into being as a result of the urbanization associated with the Industrial Revolution, so that by 1851 an estimated two-thirds of the country's population of two-and-a-half million lived in towns of more than 2,000 inhabitants. Thus, machine-made goods were within the geographical, if not always financial, reach of the majority.

In the United States the situation was reversed: its market for manufactured goods was largely domestic and rural. In 1850 there were twenty-three million Americans; by 1890 the population had increased to sixty-three million, but only one-third of them lived in towns. The isolation of these rural Americans, however, was increasingly alleviated by the rapid extension of the railways, which, even more than in Britain, played an important role in linking consumers and suppliers. A crucial event for the United States was the joining of the East and West coasts by rail in 1869. Fashionable décor therefore became more feasible, as furnishings became both cheaper and more accessible.

The mass-production of printed fabrics led to their standardization, and to a significant decrease in the number of techniques that had previously been applied to the same cloth. By 1889 English block printing had decreased in quantity to 8.5 per cent of its 1840 level, eliminating with it many of the more elaborate hand-controlled techniques, such as the shaded colours of rainbow printing. Block prints remained dependent on naturalistic floral motifs, many following the fashions in gardening, with rhododendrons, lilies, large roses and poppies, chrysanthemums and azaleas, often connected by trailing vines or ribbons. Grounds were often plain white, or a striking colour such as plum or Prussian blue. Because so few were produced, block prints were desired for their rarity and gradually became less influenced by fashion, becoming classic designs which have since remained in use.

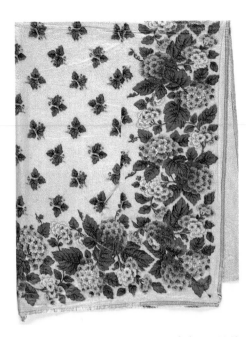

3 This English glazed cotton of about 1860 has been roller-printed in dark purple, providing the outlines, shading and 'pinning', and subsequently block-printed in two shades of red and a dark blue-green. With the pattern completely protected by a block-printed paste, the cloth was returned to a machine and roller-printed with a vermicelli-patterned fancy ground. The lining of this curtain or bedcover was printed in blue from the same roller. The lower, applied border has been cut from a separate length of cloth.

Because so few were made, block prints now became much more expensive than roller prints. In 1862 when the silk weaving and wholesale firm, Daniel Walters & Sons of Braintree and London, ordered a block print from Stead McAlpin ('the Poppy', shown at the 1862 London International Exhibition) they were charged 17 pence a yard for a white-ground cloth and an additional penny for a coloured or 'fancy' ground. (Where block printing survived it was still often put onto machines for the addition of small background patterns.) One-colour machine prints from the same manufacturers were about one-sixth this cost, and an elaborate nine-colour mule machine print was about eightpence.[2] The use of block-printed fabrics therefore became less common. When Catharine and Harriet Beecher proposed a green glazed English furniture print for lambrequins and upholstery in a room to be furnished for $80, they were referring to a machine print, which could be purchased in the United States in 1869 for 25 cents a yard.[3]

Between mid-century and 1890, the annual volume of roller printing trebled, and its quality improved. A greater understanding of 'the nicety of adjustment to bring all the cylinders to print at the proper places'[4] had made it possible to increase the number of colours printed at any one time – formerly only two or three – to as many as fourteen, though the usual number was five or six. Since large areas of roller-printed colour could not be overlapped easily, the majority of prints produced after about 1860 relied for effect on clear, contrasting adjacent colours or, alternatively, muted closely-related shades which gave a damask-like effect. Other unprinted fabrics, or 'weaves' – still the most fashionable cloths – were also mimicked by the use of paisley patterns, broad ribbon-like stripes or entire backgrounds which appeared ribbed, watered or dobby-woven.

The appearance of many cloths was also affected by the scientifically-based dyestuffs industry, which had developed rapidly after 1856, when the Englishman William Perkins isolated from coal tar the first widely used dye with an organic structure unknown in nature. Contrary to later popular belief, this new red-violet aniline dye (named from a substance used in its synthesis but popularly known as Tyrian purple or mauvine) was an improvement on the old dye of the same colour, and faded less rapidly. It was in use by London silk-dyers by 1857, and subsequently by cotton-dyers and then calico-printers. Mauvine was replaced by aniline magenta in 1866, when a patent battle was resolved and the price fell to one-tenth that of 1860. Other chemically related dyes quickly followed: bright aniline blue for wool, orange azo dye (for wool) and, by 1877, red azo, the first real challenge to cochineal. Lightweight wools printed in these new bright colours (including many exported from Mulhouse, France), were widely used for furnishings in middle-class homes, since they were less expensive than silk but equally brilliant. Several shades of violet, green, black and yellow were also introduced for silks and wools, and in the 1880s several new blues were added, together with a direct red dye for cotton.

The various tertiary shades popular in this period – magenta, blue-

4 This union machine-printed glazed cotton may well have been dyed with cutch, which was capable of producing the three reddish-brown shades seen (black has been added separately). Although the pattern is typical of neo-rococo textile designs, the combination of red, black and tan was associated with neo-Renaissance interiors. Cottons printed with designs such as this were produced in both the United States and Britain throughout this period.

violet, aqua, bronze or olive, copper, and sienna – were made much easier to obtain by the new synthetic dyes.[5] Home dyeing was also revolutionized: in 1875, for example, Judson's Simple Dyes for the People sold in London for sixpence a bottle – enough to dye feathers, ribbons, fringes, and clothing.[6] Larger items had to be professionally dyed. One of the advantages of wool damask curtains, according to *Cassell's Household Guide*, was that they could be re-dyed and calendered (machine pressed) after four years and would 'look like new'.[7]

New colour schemes reflected these developments. The so-called 'Manchester brown', a tannish-brown azo dye introduced to silk dyeing in 1865, inspired a fashion for a red-and-tan colour scheme, which (often with the addition of black) was closely associated with neo-Renaissance interiors. Such rooms, fashionable up to the mid-1880s, were characterized by squared-off architectural details, massive dark furniture and Renaissance motifs, such as strapwork, interpreted as broad bands appliquéd a few inches from the outer edge of curtains. Strapwork also appeared on printed and woven textiles, either alone or in combination with other motifs. The interest in the Renaissance owed a great deal to London's South Kensington Museum which had been founded as the Museum of Manufactures at Marlborough House in 1852 and later became the Victoria and Albert Museum. Its collections in 1860 were drawn predominantly from the Renaissance. The London International Exhibition of 1862 reflected this taste in the many textiles that emulated sixteenth-century embroideries, tapestries, silks and decorative motifs found in the museum's objects.

Another development observable at the Exhibition was the accelerating mechanization of the weaving industry, which was bringing down the price of previously very expensive goods. For example, James Houldsworth & Co. exhibited embroideries, silk damasks, brocatelles and other furnishing fabrics which had all been produced on power-driven machines. These were described as sufficiently wide for curtains without seaming (probably 63 inches wide, allowing the old 21-inch-wide designs to be used 'three over'; or 50 inches wide, allowing 25-inch designs to be used side-by-side). A contemporary observed that 'the recent application of power to their manufacture places them within the reach of large classes hitherto unable to obtain such goods'. Cloth for an entire window curtain in one of the exhibited brocatelles (a fabric employing two sets of warps to create raised, repoussé-like areas) could be purchased for £8 8s to £10 10s, exclusive of making up and lining. The same report noted with some satisfaction that 'the French have not yet succeeded in applying steam power to . . . such goods'.[8] The application of power to Jacquard weaving was elsewhere fairly universal by the 1870s. Hand weaving as a commercial enterprise virtually disappeared, taking with it the hand-woven Jacquard coverlet in America and all but the most successful English hand-weaving firms. (Of the latter, those that survived the Cobden Treaty's provision for duty-free French silks experienced something of a renaissance themselves – aided in 1870 by the disruption caused by France's defeat in the Franco–Prussian War.)

5 This 21-inch-wide handwoven silk is one of several neo-Renaissance textiles exhibited by Walters at the 1862 London International Exhibition (see also Fig. 38). Its design was derived from the Vatican loggia by Raphael, perhaps the best-known Renaissance artist in the mid nineteenth century. The extremely long repeat (84 inches) is unusual for the period.

Associated with mechanization was specialization, or what is today known as horizontal structuring of the industry. Whereas textile mills previously often wove, printed and dyed cloth, they increasingly performed only one of these processes. The American Civil War did much to hasten this process in the cotton industry, since it cut off the major supply of raw cotton from 1862 until 1866, the year after the war ended. The cotton shortage brought grief to the calico-weaving, -dyeing and -printing firms in New England and in Philadelphia. Those that survived reduced their functions to dyeing and printing other's fabrics, appearing in the 1870 census as smaller firms.[9] For some Lancashire firms the War was the last in a series of events leading to the same result. (The Civil War also contributed to the demise of Jacquard coverlet weaving, since the casualties included many experienced weavers, as well as young men who might otherwise have taken up the craft.)

The 'cotton famine' affected that industry's weaving and spinning most seriously, and encouraged the combination of linen, hemp or jute with cotton. Cretonne reappeared in a modified version, differing from its eighteenth-century predecessor (which had a warp of hemp and a weft of linen) in combining hemp, jute or linen with cotton and invariably being printed. In 1868 an English writer described 'the new cretonne' as 'now used for bed furniture, etc, [and] a good substitute for chintz, in so far as it will wash, and does not depend for effect on a high glaze'.[10] A relatively loosely woven, textured cloth, cretonne subdued the effect of any dyestuff, however bright. According to Mrs. H. W. Beecher, writing in 1879, the 'softness of the cloth, the delicacy of colour . . . make it one of the most desirable and attractive materials for furnishing a country, or summer, home'.[11]

Crash, a firmer linen-based fabric, was now also printed, and large amounts of plain hand-woven Russian crash were imported into the

6 Warners, like some other English silk-weaving firms, also supplied printed fabrics to their customers. The nine samples shown here, which date from about 1890, show a variety of base-cloths (including a cotton dobby weave, bottom centre) and a representative selection of the patterns and colours available at that time. Typically, all the greens have a strong yellow cast. Note the absence of any chintzes, which had become less fashionable under the influence of the reform movement.

United States in the 1870s and '80s, to be used 'as is' or as a base for embroidery or appliqué. The increased demand for printed wool, wool–cotton blends and silks was another result of the cotton shortage. In 1878 one writer commented that there were 'no end of cretonnes, crashes and other fabrics to choose from when the time comes'. The same author was still recommending home-made blinds, but now included 'cheap and coarse' materials, which 'may be left quite unadorned, or decorated with simple horizontal bands of various widths. . . . jute-cloth, costing thirty or forty cents per square yard, answers very readily. . . . Even common burlaps, with a small outlay of money and a large outlay of ingenuity, may be made very charming in effect.'[12] During the 1860s jute and hemp replaced cotton as the fibres for the most humble interiors, and by printing on these as well as on cretonnes, printers added a measure of textural variety to offset the reduction in techniques.

A separate but related form of specialization was the division between production and selling. Commissioned production became much more common after about 1860; many manufacturing firms originated far fewer speculative designs than in previous years, waiting for the retailer or wholesaler to order them. Some designs were still commissioned by private individuals. Design choices were therefore more often made outside the mill or print works, a situation that helped to counteract the standardization within the industry itself.

Retailers became more powerful, not only in terms of design choice, but also with regard to influencing customers' choices. When Owen Jones complained in 1863 that 'the furnishing of our houses has been handed

7 One piece of a moderately priced American parlour suite, 1885–90. Essentially in rectilinear Renaissance-revival style, the crest rail is embellished with imitation bamboo and a semi-circular half-daisy – allusions to Japan and the 'aesthetic' style. The use of two different colours of upholstery cloth – in this case crushed mohair plush – was often found on 'aesthetic' and 'Eastlake' furniture.

over to [the upholsterers]' by architects, 'whose duty it is to make this question their own',[13] he was referring to the more expensive interiors. The majority were now falling under the influence, not of upholsterers, but of the large furniture shops and department stores, which took advantage of improved postal services to circulate catalogues to their customers. America's first department store was A. T. Stewart's (now defunct) in New York; soon there were Wanamaker's in Philadelphia, Marshall Field's in Chicago and many others. In London's Tottenham Court Road alone there were half-a-dozen influential department or furniture stores, including Shoolbreds, Heals and Maples. All offered delivery of goods to customers in the country, and some London firms also shipped overseas. However, it was an American, Aaron Montgomery Ward, who, in 1872, founded the first entirely mail-order-based firm.

Although many American country stores continued to accept payment in feathers, metals, fruit, old newspapers or rags (accounting for the limited survival of textiles), they now increasingly faced competition from urban stores which offered credit terms. Advertising also increased, as did 'high-pressure' selling. Mrs. Beecher found it necessary to caution her readers that they should buy 'to suit individual taste, comfort, and circumstances, and must not permit a salesman to solicit or urge any purchase'.[14]

The styles promoted to the middle classes by many catalogues, advertisements and shop windows were the curvilinear neo-rococo and the more robust neo-Renaissance. These styles actually differed only in their superficial details; otherwise both consisted of suites of furniture, lambrequins, opaque fabric and lace curtains, often combined with glass curtains or blinds. With the further development of mass-produced furniture, roller-printed textiles and stiff, carpet-like, pile upholstery cloths, plus the introduction of power-woven Jacquard fabrics in these styles, they ceased to be an exclusive fashion in the 1860s and remained popular into the 1880s.

Mass-production, standardization and specialization generated great wealth, and the increasing prosperity of many people in both Britain and America generated, in turn, a noticeable increase in conspicuous consumption. Despite Mrs. H. W. Beecher's caution in 1879 that no room must be crowded,[15] the over-dressed room became the norm. Scarves, shawls, and embroidered or lace antimacassars ensured that almost no surface remained un-draped; fringe was added to all types of furniture; tables were covered with carpet-like cloths, both printed and woven; and valances or lambrequins were added to shelves, brackets and mantles. Many fireplaces were covered with curtains, instead of fire-boards, when not in use.[16]

Whether indulged in by the vastly rich, whose rooms continued to rely on commissioned hand-made silks and hand-block printed chintzes, or by the modestly well-off, who bought from an upholsterer's or retailer's stock, elaborate decoration was more than merely a show of wealth. It was also – even more than in most periods – an expression of individuality. Because, according to the Victorian view, interior decoration contributed

8 Dressing or toilet tables remained a focus of elaborate decoration, as this make-it-yourself version from William Jones's *Beautiful Homes* of 1878 indicates. The top is an old blanket, table cover or other heavy cloth, covered with stretched dimity and edged with lace hangings interlined in rose. The rest of the skirt could be in any material (cretonne was suggested) with a 'Swiss ruffle' to cover the seam of the flounce. The chair and curtains complete the neo-rococo setting. These curtains, to the horror of reformers wishing to reduce dust, would puddle on the floor when opened. The chair is probably covered with machine-simulated 'Beauvais' tapestry, complete with scrolls and naturalistic flowers.

to the occupants' refinement, intellectual development and moral sensibility, it seemed to follow naturally that the more the room contained, the more refined it was. Thus even the homes of the less well-off became crowded with furnishings, albeit crudely home-made. In an age that was experiencing profound social, political and economic changes, the home became a sanctuary, or castle, within which quantity suggested both social and financial security. Quantity also more readily expressed the occupants' identity; the sheer multiplication of objects within a room helped to distinguish it from others whose basic furnishings would have been similar, due to the uniformity imposed by mass production.

Women were expected to maintain or organize the household; whereas in the home – according to *The Young Ladies' Treasure Book* – the business of men 'is to make work for others, not to do it themselves'.[17] Against such placid acceptance of the *status quo*, enjoined upon young women in the early 1880s, there were stirrings of a counter-movement, encouraging originality in women, and exemplified by Henry James's heroine in *The Portrait of a Lady* (1881), who expressed her individuality by giving 'an impression of having intentions'.[18] For many neo-Renaissance women, however, embroidery, beadwork, lace-making or knitting were the only means of self-expression. This was encouraged by writers, especially (but not exclusively) when addressing the middle and lower classes. Silk or wool embroidered onto velvet for a wall panel was described by Mrs. Haweis in 1889 as 'a really beautiful ornament and occupation'; other writers' suggestions ranged from knitted curtain tie-backs to lambrequins made from cardboard and covered with pine cones, open beech-nut hulls and acorns.[19] The result of such efforts was to ensure that even if two houses had been furnished mainly with identical store-bought items, the finished rooms would have varied considerably.

The interiors of 1860–90 therefore both embraced and rejected standardization and mass-production, and it was within this context that the ideas of the earlier design reformers were re-interpreted. During the 1840s and '50s Pugin, Ruskin and Owen Jones were among the most articulate of many writers who had searched for principles of design. In 1840, for example, H. W. Arrowsmith had proposed that certain decorating styles were suitable for specific rooms.[20] The related idea – that all ornament must be appropriate to the purpose for which it was to be employed – was advanced by the reform movement as it consolidated in the 1860s and '70s. To begin with, the voices raised on this issue were almost entirely within the professions of architecture, design and education.

The publication that did most to stimulate the popular debate on design issues was Charles L. Eastlake's *Hints on Household Taste*. Originally drawn from articles that first appeared in the London journal *The Queen* in 1865, Eastlake's book was published four times in London between 1868 and 1878 and six times in the United States between 1872 and 1881. Eastlake was a trained architect – as was the Bostonian Charles W. Elliott, whose *Book of American Interiors* (1876) publicized a similar style; but the principles proposed by Eastlake were rapidly adopted by many writers on decoration who were from other disciplines.[21]

The Eastlake style was called 'modern Gothic' by some American writers; he himself called it 'austerely picturesque'. In some respects 'modern Gothic' resembled the 'modern' Grecian, for Eastlake also preferred weighty curtains hanging straight from rings on poles (and the curtains were not to sweep the floor). Valances were allowed if used to exclude draughts, but decorative cornices and over-large poles and finials were in 'execrable taste'.[22]

Among the major decorative styles popularized by Eastlake and his followers were the use of horizontally striped curtain fabrics and the elimination of fringe, except when it could be produced by fraying one end of a fabric. (A similar and more widely used effect was achieved by adding fringe that matched the upholstery in colour, something made easier by the new synthetic dyes.) Among the most favoured striped fabrics was Algerian or Algerine. Originally a woollen fabric made in Algiers, but made by the French during this period, it was described in 1882 as having

9 When Charles Eastlake included this sketch in *Hints on Household Taste* (London, 1868) as an example of 'furniture designed upon thoroughly artistic principles', he could hardly have imagined that it would result in numerous versions which continued to be popular until the Second World War and were always known as 'Knole' sofas, after the house near Sevenoaks, Kent, in which he sketched them. Eastlake particularly liked the lack of curves, the extra fixed cushions and the faded velvet upholstery. He illustrated his own furniture designs, and these were also widely copied, often upholstered, unlike his original pieces, in 'Knole' style, with divided or banded areas.

10 Made from four spiralling threads with horizontal tufts caught between the twists, chenille yarns could be constructed so that when the yarn was used as a weft, the different-coloured tufts created a pattern. Being double-sided, chenille cloths were particularly suitable for portières and became especially popular in the United States in the late 1880s, when Philadelphia weavers introduced power-woven cotton chenilles. These were normally woven to a standard length of three yards and turned forward at the top, as has been done in this unidentified interior, photographed in the 1890s by H. F. Preston of Athol Center, Massachusetts. Portières were a long-lived aspect of the 'Eastlake' style; the pair in the photograph are similar to Sears, Roebuck & Co.'s 'very heavy' chenille curtains (second best, illustrated over a doorway) which in 1897 sold for $4.69, a price that remained virtually unchanged until just before the First World War.

alternating stripes of undyed rough 'knotted' cotton and undyed or scarlet gauze-like silk. Yet Eastlake referred to Algerine as made chiefly of cotton and therefore washable, and there certainly must have been a variant firmer than the silk gauze, since a cloth of the same name was recorded, in 1887, as being used for upholstery as well.[23] The latter may perhaps have been what *Cassell's Household Guide* referred to as 'Timbuctoo', which was 'a stout kind of curtain', also made in France and 'striped horizontally in white, scarlet, black, and yellow, on a green, red or blue ground.'[24] Horizontal stripes were thought more agreeable because they were not lost in the folds of a curtain, but they did make a low room look lower, and Eastlake therefore also recommended a red or green damask with vertical figured stripes woven with gold-coloured silk.

Eastlake preferred furniture of simple construction, with tight-fitting upholstery. Although he was a proponent of the Gothic style, his favourite forms of seating were the Renaissance pieces at Knole, in Kent, covered in rose-coloured velvet (faded to silver-grey), with the backs and seats subdivided vertically into panels by a firm silk and gold lace (similar to braid); the backs, arms and seat edges had extra bands of horizontal fringe (of which, in this context, he evidently approved).

Portières, already in limited use in Britain by 1850, were also popularized by Eastlake. These door curtains were the focus of even greater invention than window curtains, and were often made double-sided to suit adjoining rooms of different colours. Many types of portière were recommended by writers on both sides of the Atlantic; some incorporating the device of 'paning', but with horizontal rather than the vertical bands intoduced earlier in the century. Typically of a soft 'full' cloth such as velvet or chenille, portières were thought particularly appropriate for appliqué and embroidery, generally applied in horizontal bands which echoed the tripartite division of walls into a dado at the bottom, a filling and a frieze at the top. One, described by an American writer in 1882, was of dove-coloured all-wool 'diagonal cloth' (presumably with a diagonal stripe), lined with pale pink silesia (a lightweight cotton twill) and bordered at the top and bottom with crazy quilting in blue, green, dove and rose.[25] (Cassell's had noted the revival of patchwork in the 1870s, and suggested that patchwork made from silk and satin pieces was 'handsome, especially if arranged with taste; and may be used for quilts, sofa and chair covers, cushions and ottomans. . . . The pieces can generally be begged, but all good upholsterers' shops will sell, and even give, cuttings to good customers.'[26] Patchwork was also simulated in roller prints.)

Eastlake's stance on honesty of construction and appropriate pattern owed a good deal to the English Arts and Crafts movement, for which the key figure was William Morris. Morris also trained as an architect, but, like Eastlake, never practised, turning instead to poetry, the decorative arts and the dissemination of his socialist views through lectures, publications and his own working practices. The first textiles he produced, in the late 1850s, were embroideries. It was not until the late 1860s that printed fabrics began to be sold by his firm, Morris, Marshall, Faulkner & Co. (founded in 1861 and re-organized as Morris & Co. in 1875), and the first

11 'Honeysuckle', designed by William Morris in 1876, was block-printed onto a wide variety of fabrics, including linen, silk, challis and velveteen. It typifies Morris's use of a small subsidiary pattern over which conventionalized flowers seem to grow naturally from meandering stems. The size of the repeat is 30 by 36 inches.

weave was sold by the firm in 1871. These were mainly patterns selected rather than created by Morris, but from 1873 until his death in 1896 he designed many fabrics, all based on principles developed from his study of fifteenth- and sixteenth-century textiles.

If the age needed a 'Renaissance man' they found it in Morris, who was undoubtedly the most influential designer of the century. Together with Thomas Wardle, he re-established interest in natural dyes, particularly indigo and madder. (Wardle himself travelled to India to study unadulterated dyeing methods and imported Indian silks on which to print.) Morris also taught himself to weave and embroider and became an authority on Persian and Turkish carpets. His understanding of the techniques and styles of the sixteenth and earlier centuries was gained partly through the collections at the South Kensington Museum, where he was a member of the acquisitions committee. Like Owen Jones, he used the principles of the patterns he admired, rather than copying them directly. Flowers and stems, he believed, should be seen to be growing naturally. Patterns were definite and evenly distributed across the surface, and motifs were firmly outlined, simplified, but recognizable flowers and animals from the English countryside, scrolling acanthus leaves or figured strapwork arranged in ogees or meandering lines.

Morris's interest in the patterns and working methods of the pre-industrial period was in part the result of John Ruskin's influence. Set out in greatest detail in *The Stones of Venice* (1853), Ruskin's arguments – both moral and emotional – focused on the evils of division of labour, unnecessary production of goods, superfluous ornament and copying. Others were reaching similar conclusions. In 1849 William H. Kanlet, an American architect and author, based his comment that 'cheerfulness and amiability could hardly be compatible with a dark blue ceiling and dingy brown walls'[27] on the assumption that behaviour was influenced by environment. The correlation between state of mind and surroundings was central to both Ruskin's and Morris's condemnation of mid-Victorian working conditions and standards of workmanship.

The notion that good design was a force for society's benefit was not far removed from the belief that an interest in good design was beneficial to one's social standing. This rather free interpretation of the high moral and political tone adopted by design reformers created an acceptable rationale for interior design as a vocation, whether practised by passionate amateurs or by respected professionals. In a similar way, the acknowledgement of rooms as 'environments' led to the creation of 'stage set' interiors – rooms within a single house that differed according to the desired atmosphere. Although the use of different styles in different rooms had been proposed earlier, by the 1860s it was a well-established practice, and one which accommodated the continued use of neo-rococo, neo-Gothic and 'modern' Grecian styles, as well as the new interest in Renaissance, 'Aesthetic' and Arts and Crafts furnishings.

Even within the same room, however, styles were now often mixed; it was thought that portières, for example, 'should not repeat the curtains of the room, but represent a separate idea . . .'[28] and that the 'practice of modelling rooms too severely upon a single period is open to grave objections'.[29] Although the principles of the reform movement were in opposition to the neo-rococo and neo-Renaissance interiors, the *styles* created by the reformers were often adapted by manufacturers or added by householders to existing furnishings – 'medieval' portières, for example, appearing in rooms with 'rococo' lambrequins. The result was that for some thirty years, between 1860 and 1890, most rooms were at best a *mélange* and at worst a chaotic hodgepodge of different styles.

Despite this eclecticism, the overall effect did have its own distinctive character. The dominant note was late medieval/Renaissance, with the jewel-box quality of juxtaposed patterns, colours and textures. In those interiors designed with artistic principles in mind, this was a carefully judged style, but it easily became hackneyed when mass-produced. The reformed 'Eastlake style' (as it was called by American manufacturers who capitalized on the popularity of his book) included furniture that inevitably mixed two cloths – for example, a plush on the sides of a square, unbuttoned seat, a patterned fabric on the top and piping or braid in between. In Britain the reform style came to be associated with 'Queen Anne' architecture, in which so many devotees of the aesthetic movement lived.

Mrs. H. R. Haweis declared 'the keynote of all these "Queen Anne" rooms is quiet and morally severe. The chairs are few, hard, square and heavy, and covered with dingy velvets laboriously made to look poor and imperfect in web and recalling in colour mud-mildew-ironwood. . . .'[30] Certainly the reformers cared little for comfort. Angela Thirkell (novelist and granddaughter of the artist Edward Burne-Jones) recalled the Burne-Jones homes, decorated in the mid- to late-1860s with goods from Morris & Co. (to which Burne-Jones contributed designs). These had 'sofas' which were 'long low "tables" with a little balustrade round two, sometimes three sides' onto which were placed 'rigidly hard squabs covered with chintz of blue linen . . . a small bolster apparently made of concrete and two or three unyielding cushions'.[31] Nevertheless, in reality, 'Queen Anne' came to represent the well-furnished interiors of the period, which for comfort retained the low, often armless and completely upholstered 'Turkish' chair – usually deep-buttoned and always finished to the floor with a deep fringe or fabric valance. The term 'Queen Anne' with reference to interiors is thus an imprecise but useful one, embracing not only English furnishing styles of the reign of Queen Anne (1702–14) and the previous century's Stuart kings, but also various nineteenth-century styles inspired by it, as well as Morris's work, and the rustic, 'Eastlake' and 'Aesthetic' fashions.

With so much to choose from, it became easier for the amateur decorator to go wrong. However, there was no shortage of advice. To help prospective purchasers, stores began to use room sets (which also promoted the mass-produced suites of furniture characteristic of the period and often consisting of six to nine pieces). Since the total effect was crucial, magazine articles and books on decorating now rarely illustrated isolated objects. Photography gave precise details of real houses, and photographic anthologies, such as the American publication *Artistic Houses* (1883), provided glimpses into the homes of the wealthy.

The common concern for appropriateness in furnishings apparent in many writings of the time was not matched by a consensus as to what 'appropriate' meant. For example, Mrs. Beecher declared in 1879 that 'Eastlake patterns, for the most part, look faded and old . . . and the designs are as ungraceful and untrue to nature, and disagreeable to the eye, as can well be imagined.' Despite Beecher's dislike of 'reformed' patterns (she generally preferred chintzes), she found a use for the Burne-Jones type of sofa, described above, recommending a similarly constructed cosy corner as a form of home-made furniture, appropriate to the 'hard times' many Americans were experiencing in the late 1870s.[32]

Portières also came in for some criticism. Robert Edis found, in 1881, that 'in London halls [they] are generally objectionable as traps for dirt and dust' – although he had no similar qualms about a length of coloured stuff or silk thrown over a divan or seat on the landing.[33]

Similarly, lambrequins received mixed reviews; the Beechers were 'for' and Eastlake 'against'. In 1882 Almon C. Varney reported that they had been 'superseded by a valance which will shove aside with the curtains.' (Curtains and portières began to be made in standard lengths of about 9 feet, with fringes at both ends. The upper end was folded forward to create the 'valance' and obtain the correct length.) The stationary character of lambrequins, Varney continued, 'and the fact that they exclude the light from the top, whence it is so desirable, has served to make them unpopular'. He nevertheless added that 'they are still made in rich material, cut in

12 Designed by Louis C. Tiffany, this morning room or lady's parlour was illustrated in Constance Cary Harrison's *Woman's Handiwork in Modern Homes* (New York, 1881). The two chairs are plainly upholstered – perhaps to provide a resting place for the eye as well as for the room's occupants. The velvet curtains appear to be embroidered and appliquéd or stencilled, since the pattern differs on each. Although this interior was never actually realized, the combination of stained-glass panels at the top of the window, muslin curtains and simply hung over-curtains was also used in a dining room that he decorated for Dr. William T. Lusk in about 1880; it, like other records of Tiffany's influential 'aesthetic' interiors, survives only in black-and-white photographs – in this case in *Artistic Houses*, published in New York in 1883.

all manner of forms, and trimmed with fringe and heavy gimp'.[34] Even a simple lambrequin, however, could give some distinction to a plain room. A twentieth-century American writer described how her mother – originally from an elegant middle-class Iowan home – attempted, as a young bride in the Dakota territory, to give her house a little charm; how she 'decorated the sad little room with dried grasses, wild rose haws and golden rod from the prairie . . . and made the low windows look higher and more elegant with red flannel lambrequins'.[35] Lambrequins also provided a cheap but acceptable form of window dressing when used without heavy curtains above the ubiquitous lace or muslin curtains.[36]

Sheer glass curtains were one of the few subjects on which most writers agreed. Cassell's referred to the muslin and lace varieties as 'one of the ornaments and glory of summer'.[37] Although expensive lace curtains sweeping above inexpensive ingrain carpets were thought in 1878 to lack 'harmony', machine-made Nottingham laces were actually relatively cheap at 3–6 per cent the cost of Brussels lace. Curtains made of the latter cost between $35 and $100 a pair, depending on the pattern, in 1883.[38] Eastlake preferred '"Swiss lace" . . . made of stout thread-cotton, and worked in two or three small but well-defined patterns' to muslin, 'on what semi-naturalistic foliage and nondescript ornament is allowed to meander after an extravagant and meaningless fashion.' (Swiss lace, or net, was a Nottingham machine-made coarse cotton lace, with patterns based on sixteenth-century lace.) Robert Edis admired 'Crete muslin, printed in light shades of yellow pink'; the Beechers, muslin, no matter how coarse, so long as it was white and hung in graceful folds. They further suggested the addition of a strip of gingham or chambray to the hem.[39]

Together with dimity and printed cottons, muslins, bobbinet (machine-made hexagonal mesh net) and other laces were also popular bedroom fabrics, especially for dressing or 'toilet' tables. These were often confections of a sheer fabric or lace over a solid-coloured cambric, lawn or chintz, with bows or ribbons added for good measure.[40]

Although upholsterers continued to illustrate four-poster beds in their catalogues, these were undoubtedly intended as showpieces, and beds on the whole ceased to be a subject of much debate. Cassell's dismissed the subject with the comment that 'bed curtains are necessary or not according as a sleeping-room is draughty or otherwise . . . Very often it is sufficient to drape the window [to cut out light and cold air] and unless unmistakeably needful, the bed is better without.'[41]

Most writers agreed on colour – not necessarily on specific schemes but on its importance in creating a 'harmony of general effect'. Owen Jones advised against matching upholstery 'when the amount of colour produced . . . would give too much of a particular colour. As a general rule, the covering of the furniture should be of a darker tone than the curtains, this because the curtains are seen against the light.' Patterned curtains, he felt, should have small borders, and 'on plain colours a small inner border is a still further improvement, as it prevents the eye from running out at the sides'.[42]

A scheme typical of those based on related shades suggested either red

13 In this hand-woven silk tissue, designed by H. Scott Morton and woven by Warners in 1883, Italian Renaissance-style strapwork has been combined with highly stylized 'pomegranate' forms and conventionalized flowers. The colours illustrate the complex schemes which arose during this period from the application of colour theory. With the 'enbrowned' red ground balanced by tertiaries ranging from turquoise through olive-gold to apricot, this is a complementary-tertiary scheme employing aniline dyes.

plush curtains lined with a lighter tone, sateen curtains embroidered in many shades of red (the sateen to be darker than the walls of pale terra cotta), or curtains made of horizontal bands, with the lightest of three shades of red at the top. The sofa's upholstery was to be in many shades of red, some 'inclined to embrowned-purple', and the cushions also in several reds, including light terra cotta. The tablecloth was to be red velvet embroidered with lighter tones and the furniture made of rosewood.[43] This was a harmonious tertiary scheme, embracing all shades from terra cotta to plum (i.e. orange-red to red-purple; it could equally have been gold to terra cotta, olive to turquoise or turquoise to blue-violet). Decorators also devised more complex schemes, always using at least one of the tertiary colours. Darker schemes were thought best for a modest parlour, whereas a magnificent reception room required similarly related colours but based around lighter shades – cream, yellow, blue, pink or rose. Such schemes were popular regardless of the style of decoration.

Disagreement arose, however, on the starting point for colour schemes. Varney, in 1882, thought the curtains and wallpaper should be bought first, 'and the carpet selected as a quiet accessory', whereas *The Decorator and Furnisher* (published in New York but often expressing British views) based schemes on carpets throughout the late 1880s and into the 1890s.[44] The latter view probably reflected the growing appreciation of Persian and Turkish carpets and the production of similarly patterned new carpets by Morris & Co. By about 1890 some people, such as the fashion-conscious Mrs. Haweis, were tiring of the intense subtleties of 'harmonious' colour combinations and issuing a 'sigh for something neither blue-green or green-blue' but less offensive than 'the old red and gold business'. Despite such differing views, however, colour – in particular solid or inconspicuously patterned areas of colour – remained an important decorative element throughout this period, drawing together the multitude of objects in a room.

The social importance of successful room schemes is underlined by the shift in terminology during the 1870s from 'upholsterer' to 'interior decorator'. For some upholsterers it was simply a change in name, and interior-decorating services continued to be provided by cabinet-makers. However, independent decorators also appeared; and besides advising on room treatments, they collected antiques or designed reproductions. The complexity of interiors no doubt encouraged many middle-class people to rely on decorators, whether personally or through their magazine articles and books.

Antique textiles were also prominent in many interiors of this period. This trend, however, was not approved of by Mrs. Haweis, who thought that 'the recent fashion of covering chair-seats with exquisite antique silks, old brocades and delicate featherwork, is a waste of good things which were better applied elsewhere'. She nevertheless believed that, as a background, old tapestry could not be bettered (except in Empire-style rooms, where it was inappropriate).[46] Antique lace, embroideries and shawls were also pressed into service, whether to drape mantels, pianos or easels, on which framed paintings were displayed.

Naturally, many 'antique' textiles were newly made. The term 'tapestry' was broadened in this period to apply to a heavy, mainly woollen cloth (machine-made in Britain from the late 1850s) with a warp-faced pattern and also to machine-made pictorial hangings. Embroideries were also made in historical styles although imitations of eighteenth-century *gros point* (the ubiquitous Berlin work) ceased to be fashionable in the late 1860s. Instead, seventeenth-century-style crewelwork was preferred – a boon to manufacturers of the unbleached linen and crash used as a base. New styles of embroidery evolved, which were also indebted to pre-eighteenth-century styles; fine examples were produced by members and followers of the Arts and Crafts movement, including Morris & Company in England and Associated Artists in the United States (founded by Louis Comfort Tiffany as a decorating firm in 1879 and from 1883 principally supplying textile and wallpaper designs and embroideries under the direction of Candice Wheeler).

The interest in embroidery, lacemaking, knitting and tapestry was partly due to the reformers' support of hand craftsmanship, but it also reflected the general interest in surface texture associated with hand-made goods and therefore imitated by machine processes. This interest was apparent in the rougher surface qualities of hemp-cloth, burlap, linen, wool, crash and cretonne and the prevalence of unglazed printed cottons (although the exclusive block prints were still glazed, since in this period they seem to have been most often used in wealthy homes as loose covers, for which this finish was appropriate).

The same interest was expressed in the extensive use of pile fabrics – plain, embossed or figure-woven velvets, brightly coloured inexpensive 'carpet' upholstery, chenilles and plushes (including the newly machine-made mohair plush) – and textured weaves such as the horizontally ribbed wool or silk fabric, rep. 'The best material to cover chairs is Utrecht plush', was Cassell's verdict. However, perhaps because it would 'last excessive wear for twenty years' Cassell's added that 'it has never been made popular in England by furniture makers'. (With more rapidly changing fashions in mind, some writers joined upholsterers in encouraging the use of cheaper fabrics in order to change them more often.) Plush of all kinds nevertheless became a widely used fabric, since it was 'the most economical, even if the expense be greater in the first instance than woollen rep, which is the next best thing to it'. The latter, continued Cassell's, 'must be all wool, otherwise there is no wear in it; very good can be had for 6 shillings a yard, double width'.[47]

Embossed piles such as 'Utrecht plush' had an impeccable pedigree. A mohair plush embossed with a seventeenth-century 'Utrecht' pattern was 'discovered and revived' by William Morris in about 1871; ten years later Gillow's received praise from Robert Edis for their use of furniture covers and hangings of tapestry and sage-green embossed velvet.[48] By the early 1880s plain and stamped furniture plushes were also being made in the United States, greatly reducing their price and increasing their availability. These were solid-coloured fabrics, now available in a wide range of synthetic colours, as were velours (a term that included a variety of pile

14 This embossed mohair plush or 'Utrecht velvet' was sold by Morris & Co. in at least fourteen colours. In her book, *William Morris Textiles*, Linda Perry notes that it was 'discovered and revived' by Morris in about 1871, probably adopted from the range of J. Aldam Heaton, Manchester. The size of the repeat is 26 by 24 inches and the cloth is 24 inches wide, selvage to selvage.

fabrics, but at this date typically a cotton with a stiff, coarse looped pile) and velveteens, a weft-pile form of cotton velvet (which has a pile made from the warp). Brushed cottons, flannels (sometimes called 'art draperies') and wool (as opposed to worsted) damask had the requisite blurred surface, while the more elaborate weaves, such as brocatelles and tissues (which simulated hand-brocading), often incorporated areas of 'textured' pattern, as did prints. In 1888, the Southport, Connecticut, department store D. M. Read Co. announced that 'popular fabrics for portières and window curtains at present are plush, brocatelle and velours'. These were equally popular in Britain, no doubt because, 'These all make suitable hangings, as they give a rich and luxurious appearance.'[49]

The quality appreciated in many old, or seemingly old, fabrics extended to traditional non-European textiles. Varney described 'very odd portières . . . brought home by travellers from the East, including Smyrna, and imported in great quantities' into the United States. 'Stripes of old woolen [*sic*] stuff, loosely caught together by coarse woolen cord, and embroidered evidently by hand [in] odd combinations of red, black and white,

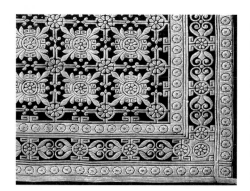

15 A fine cotton machine-woven coverlet designed in 1878 by Christopher Dresser for Messrs. Barlow & Jones, manufacturers of woven cottons based in Bolton, Lancashire, and known for their fine quilt-like marcella coverlets. The Japanese 'bosses' which make up the main elements of this pattern bear a close relationship to the flattened sunflower and daisy motifs found in many 'aesthetic' textiles of the period. Dresser, a botanist who collaborated with Owen Jones on the production of *Grammar of Ornament* in 1854, made a first-hand study of Japanese textiles in 1876. Author of *The Art of Decorative Design*, 1862, Dresser also sold textile designs to F. Steiner & Co., Turnbull & Stockdale, Wardles, Warners, J. W. & C. Ward and several other firms, but few of his textiles survive.

can be seen in fashionable houses.'[50] The British could obtain similarly exotic fabrics from sources such as Arthur Lasenby Liberty, an importer of Near- and Far-Eastern goods who opened his London shop in 1875, or from G. P. & J. Baker, a London firm which later designed and manufactured furnishing fabrics, but which imported carpets and other goods from Istanbul in the 1880s and '90s. Many ingrain carpets, prayer rugs, saddle bags and Turkish rugs (all but the first made in the Near East, often to European specifications) were also used as upholstery and portières in rooms with a Near-Eastern or Moorish aspect. The colours of many of these also contributed to the fashion for 'Nile green', 'old red' and 'Gobelin blue' and to the appreciation of shades that 'faded handsomely'.[51] (Fading was still a recognized problem, and already-subdued shades were easier to integrate with an existing and inevitably faded interior.)

Travel affected interiors in other ways. Ships, trains and American hotels and steamboats were themselves lavishly decorated. In 1854, Isabella Bishop, an Englishwoman travelling in the United States, reported that in Stewarts' Broadway department store 'the damasks and brocatelles for curtains and chairs were at almost fabulous prices. Few gentlemen, the clerk observed, give less than £3 per yard. . . . The most costly are purchased by the hotels . . .'[52] Such establishments therefore provided models as persuasive as any shop display or publication.

Travel also influenced the design of textiles. Owen Jones had already displayed the fruits of his grand tour in the patterns contained in *The Grammar of Ornament*. Jones was one of the first architects to become actively involved in mass production – designing stamps, foreign banknotes and wrappers for biscuit tins, as well as carpets, wallpapers and furnishing textiles. His earliest known textiles date from the 1850s and his last from c.1872, two years before his death. Jones drew his principles of pattern-making from so many cultures of the past that his designs are difficult to describe, save their highly organized repeats and sophisticated colour relationships, based on mathematical proportions. However, near the end of his life his interests turned towards Indian and Chinese patterns, the latter as a result of his study of Alfred Morrison's collection of porcelain (which culminated in Jones's *Examples of Chinese Ornament* in 1865). His publications influenced textile design in his day, and his example encouraged the involvement of architects in industrial design.[53]

Apart from the Chinese, Indian and Turkish textiles so influential in this period, there was a flood of objects from the newly opened ports of Japan, which made their way into (and virtually defined) aesthetic Queen Anne-style rooms: blue and white china, embroideries, lacquer, bamboo and woodwork (often inset with patterns in straw). Japanese objects were displayed in exhibitions in both England and the United States, and their patterns were admired by several English textile designers, including Jones, Bruce Talbert, E. W. Godwin, Walter Crane, G. C. Haite and Christopher Dresser (who, in 1876 and 1877, was the first of his generation of English designers to travel to Japan).[54] Birds, insects, blossoms and patterned discs or other shapes characterized these textiles, which often had very small repeats consisting of overlapping or adjacent areas of

16 Japanese motifs were ideal for small-scale prints and from about 1875–1890 were often incorporated into roller prints (themselves suited to small designs). This example, produced by the Hamilton Manufacturing Company of Lowell, Massachusetts, in 1881, includes conventionalized blossoms overlaid with patterned circles which freely interpret Japanese 'badges'.

different patterns, rather like a patchwork. Such textiles were often used with black wood furniture, including those with lacquer and/or bamboo-like details. They were an important aspect of British and American silk manufacturers' business, since the essence of the Japanese style was a rich, restrained lustre, so appropriate to silk. Manufacturers of other fabrics also made good use of Anglo–Japanese patterns, employing brilliant colours, exotic birds and flowers, and Oriental emblems.

The quality of British design temporarily ceased to be an issue; in Eastlake's fourth English edition of *Hints* (1878), he announced 'happily', that 'a great improvement has taken place within the last few years in the character of almost every kind of textile fabric used for curtains and upholstery. Patterns, often of great artistic excellence and based upon a legitimate adaptation of form in vegetable life, are to be seen in the shop windows; and skilful combinations of colour in secondary and tertiary tints, which it would have been impossible to procure a few years ago, may be found in portières and window-hangings in many varieties of material, and produced at a price which is quite within reach of ordinary means.'[55] He included his own designs for Cowlishaw, Nicol & Co. of Manchester and Jackson & Graham of London as of 'moderate cost', while Edis recommended Morris fabrics as inexpensive, the 'tapestry' (woven fabrics) and cretonnes selling, in 1881, at 3 to 12 shillings a yard.[56]

The relationship between price and design became important during this period. Thus the expensive French fabrics displayed in the influential Centennial Exhibition held in Philadelphia in 1876 were praised for their 'brilliant contrasts of colour, the harmonious blending of tints and shades, and the grace and elegance of the patterns [because] elaborate decoration is appropriate . . .' to their costliness.[57] Location also became important. Mrs. Beecher proposed in 1879 that 'heavy damask curtains with rich white lace over-curtains sweeping the floor may be endured in the city, and by some eyes will be regarded as the crowning glory of the room. They are doubtless a great protection from bold-eyed gazers passing by, but in the country they are surely a great mistake. Aside from being very expensive, we cannot think them half so elegant and tasteful as more simple curtains'.[58]

Throughout the late 1870s and '80s there was a growing sense that cheap versions of expensive, elaborate furnishings were inappropriate. In addition, resistance to the production of well-designed mass-produced textiles decreased as the markets for these fabrics grew; any stigma attached to designing specifically for low- and middle-priced cloths had, by 1890, virtually disappeared. The reform movement had by then reached many manufacturers, and it was their desire to make fabrics appropriate to the means and habits of their customers which made the years around 1890 a turning-point. The newly enlightened middle classes and manufacturers emerged from the design renaissance of the 1860s to '90s prepared to take a more active role in the creation of tastes and fashions in interiors.

17

17 In 1853 work began on the rebuilding of Balmoral Castle, the Aberdeenshire royal residence, and was completed in 1855, the interiors having been decorated by Thomas Grieve, a set designer who had recently completed designs for Charles Kean's *Macbeth*. Queen Victoria found the house charming, although one of her courtiers observed that, although appropriate, the décor was not pleasing to the eye. Shown here is the drawing room (depicted in watercolours by James Roberts in 1857), which has Royal Stewart carpeting and Dress Stewart curtains and upholstery. Despite Prince Albert's death in 1861 and Queen Victoria's retirement into mourning, fashions set by British royalty continued to influence interiors on both sides of the Atlantic. A drawing of the same room at Balmoral was illustrated in the American magazine *The Graphic* in 1882, although by this time the vogue for tartans as furnishing fabrics or elements in printed designs was passing.

18 This block-printed wool of the early 1860s employs aniline purple, one of the new synthetic dyes first developed from coal tar extracts in the second half of the 1850s. Wool receives dyes readily, and, like silk, it did not require a mordant when printed with aniline colours. Ribbons had been incorporated into many printed designs since the 1830s and remained a popular device for the next half-century, although the depiction of plaid-patterned ribbons was – as a result of changing fashions in contemporary dress – seldom seen after about 1875.

18

19 'Sultan', a silk tissue designed by
Owen Jones in 1870, illustrates
Proposition 18 of his *Grammar of Ornament*,
which stipulated that the harmonious
balance of colours was three parts yellow,
five red and eight blue. Secondary and
tertiary colours were harmonious in the
same proportions – five parts red, for
example, being balanced by eleven parts
green (the sum of yellow and blue), as
seen here. 'Sultan' was first woven in
September 1870 by Warners (in another
colourway) for use on the walls in James
Gurney's billiard room in his Regent's
Park, London, home.

20 One of the most enduring patterns for
printed textiles in the nineteenth century
was the 'paisley' pattern derived from
Indian shawls and their European
imitations. Produced in Dover, New
Hampshire, by the Cocheco
Manufacturing Company, this example is
dated 28 February, 1883, by which time
the company (which began mass-
producing prints in the 1820s) was
producing over twenty-five million yards
of printed textiles each year.

21 A machine-printed furnishing cotton
produced by Cocheco in about 1882.
Cassell's Household Guide had noted in the
previous decade that patchwork was
being revived, and fabrics such as this
were produced for most of the last quarter
of the nineteenth century, providing a less
laborious substitute. This particular
example is a very good rendition of early
nineteenth-century patterns.

19

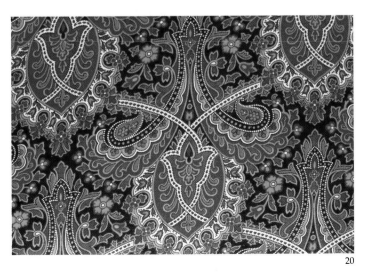

20

21

22 After the middle of the nineteenth century, many more American roller-printed cottons can be positively identified. This example, printed in five colours by Maquestion & Co., dates from about 1855–65, when 'busy' floral sprays were often surrounded or connected by swagged bowers in neo-rococo style.

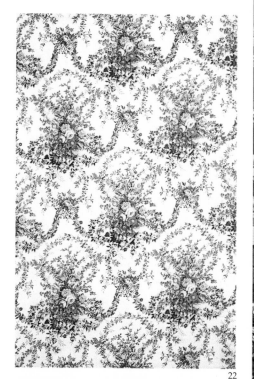

24 In the second half of the nineteenth century, silk weavers maintained their practice of eliminating one part of a long narrow design. 'Poppy', shown here, employs a large floral bunch taken from a silk that had two different floral sprays, each set within an oval framework which – in slightly altered form – also appears on 'Poppy'. The earlier silk (with yellow-gold in place of the purple) was used for upholstery and curtains at Calke Abbey, Derbyshire, in 1857 and was probably woven by Charles Norris & Co., whose business and designs were acquired by Warners in 1885. Within months, Warners were producing 'Poppy'. The two shades of purple are an illusion created by the different reflective qualities of satin and twill weaves.

23 Retaining its original silk cords and tassels, this drapery panel – used in Boston in the mid-1860s – is a French silk lampas or tissue (green warp and cream and olive weft) with naturalistic floral bunches highlighted by the addition of shades of pink, white and olive, alternating in the second, tissue weft. The colour scheme and drawing were the type that reformers disliked, but despite this, luxurious, realistically-woven floral patterns prevailed throughout this period.

25–7 Three colourways of a printed cotton rep manufactured by Cocheco in 1884, with the black and blue versions differing only in their background colour. Deep, bright colours such as these continued to be popular for furnishing fabrics into the 1920s. This detailed, naturalistically drawn design may have been procured from a European pattern supplier, for Diane Affleck's research indicates that Cocheco's was among the many American firms that subscribed to European sample services such as Homo & Cie, Jacob H. Sommer and J. Claude Frères. (Cocheco paid Claude Frères $160 for forty-two French printed samples in 1882.)

28 'Baveno' a silk terry (looped) and velvet designed by Owen Jones in about 1870, was woven by Warners in 1879, after the attendant technical difficulties had been overcome. Jones was often thought to oppose 'nature' in designs, but his objections to floral patterns (expressed in Proposition 6 in *Grammar of Ornament*) arose only when 'treated with *light and shade*, appearing to stand out from the *surface* on which they are worked, so as to destroy the form and unity of the object they decorate'. He proposed instead that 'beauty of form is produced by lines growing, out one from the other in gradual undulations'. In 1881 William Morris illustrated his own theories on 'branch' and 'net' designs with plates from Jones's *Grammar*.

25

26

28

27

29 This patchwork coverlet is composed of printed cottons obtained before 1880 by Henry J. Welsh from James, Kent, Santer & Co., a Philadelphia wholesale dry goods business of which he was a member. The fabrics are most probably of American manufacture, and provide a visual summary of the range of designs available in the 1870s, with Paisley patterns and small prints combined with rococo- and Renaissance-revival styles (far right centre and diagonally below to the left, respectively, for example). The lowest central square typifies designs that could be regarded as either medieval or Renaissance and which had been produced since the 1840s.

29

30, 31 Exhibiting almost identical neo-Renaissance shapes, both of these American valances of about 1870 were used with straight side panels (as shown in 31). Whereas the motifs in the green and gold damask valance (30) are appropriate to the neo-Renaissance style, emphasized by the wool-fringed braid, the valance and curtain set employs a chinoiserie stripe and pleated passementerie more in keeping with French eighteenth-century revival styles. The latter set is particularly interesting, since the design has been roller-printed onto embossed paper, a process that produced a cheaper but less durable product which may have been valued more for its novelty than for its low cost (much in the same way that paper dresses were in the 1960s).

30

31

32 With a satin ground and appliquéd satin motifs, this mid-sixteenth-century bed tester is a rare example of Renaissance secular embroidery (now in the Fondation Abbeg of Riggisberg, Switzerland). The geometric network of straight and curving 'strapwork' lines typify many of the details adopted by the Renaissance revival, either as applied bands at the edges of lambrequins, as darkened recessed areas on furniture, or incorporated into the patterns of prints,

weaves and laces, often with the inclusion of similarly drawn figures, masks and animals. Original pieces are now scarce because they were often used for upholstery and hangings in the second half of the nineteenth century. Manufacturers could produce such designs from one of the many 'grammars' which depicted Renaissance embroidery, such as C. J. Richardson's *Studies of Ornamental Design*, published in 1851.

33

33 These two alternative window treatments using the same elements were illustrated in *Godey's Lady's Book* in September 1859 as part of an advertisement by W. H. Carryl's, a major Philadelphia furnishings shop which specialized in French imports. Both schemes employ the same neo-rococo cornices and curtain pins and display a liberal use of fringe, cords and tassels. The lace curtains are not drawn back, as was typical until about 1890. With cords used to hold back but not drape the curtains, the simpler treatment shown at the left-hand window was the most fashionable, particularly when these windows were shown again in an advertisement of October 1866 (by which time Carryl's had been purchased by Walraven's). See Fig. 36 for a striped rep, gimp and tasselled cord of the same period.

34 With its many 'earth' colours and three distinct pattern areas on the walls and vaulted roof, the Chamber of State in the Chateau de Blois indicates the parallels between late Gothic and early French Renaissance decorative schemes and those created as 'reformed' Renaissance interiors in the years between 1865 and 1890. Built in the thirteenth century, Blois was restored in the 1860s by the French architect, Felix Duban, who appears to have based his reconstruction on fourteenth- and early-fifteenth-century French manuscripts.

32

34

35 The well-known East Coast painter Jonathan Eastman Johnson depicted a number of New York interiors during the 1870s, including this room, in which are assembled the Alfrederick Smith Hatch family, who lived on the corner of Park Avenue and 37th Street. This oil, in the Metropolitan Museum of Art, New York, illustrates the characteristics of many neo-Renaissance interiors, with its heavy, boldly delineated furniture, strapwork-edged curtains and draped lambrequins, and the predominance of red and brownish black. Painted in 1871, this room was a relatively early expression of a style which began in about 1865 and persisted into the early twentieth century (although not highly fashionable after c.1885).

36 Ogden Codman Jr. chose this wallpaper (right), fabric, gimp and tasselled cord for his Boston dining room in 1863, employing a rich colour scheme which, together with the wallpaper's pattern, was Renaissance in inspiration. There were two pairs of window curtains lined with buff silesia, ornamented with gimp and looped back over curtain pins with the tasselled cords, probably much as shown on the left in Fig. 33. The bill for these items, supplied by Leon Marcotte & Co. of New York, described the fabric as 'Striped Pékirsade reps'. Stripes remained fashionable curtain-fabric designs until the end of the century. Patterns such as the one on the wallpaper also appeared on printed and woven fabrics.

36

37 Based on a mid-sixteenth-century Italian velvet, this neo-Renaissance damask-type silk (damasquette) was hand-woven by Charles Norris & Co. for Crace & Son of Wigmore Street, London. The youngest member of the influential Crace decorating firm, John Dibblee Crace created a number of interiors and furnishings in Renaissance style, including the State Rooms at Longleat.

37

38

39

40

38 Called 'Venetian', this silk brocatelle was hand-woven by Daniel Walters & Sons in about 1860 and exhibited at the 1862 London International Exhibition, the sequel to the 1851 Great Exhibition. Walters were one of a handful of British fine furnishing silk-weaving firms operating between 1860 and 1890. In 1856 they had begun to build one of the first factories for furniture silk-weaving; by 1875, when the mill was complete, they had also installed twenty-three power looms.

39 Thomas Wardle, a silk dyer and printer based in Leek, Staffordshire, provided the initial knowledge required by William Morris to revive the use of vegetable dyes. Wardle was also influential by virtue of his interest in Persian and Indian designs and his importation of Indian silks. In this example, Wardle block-printed a Persian-style design on tusser (or tussah) silk, a cloth made from the more irregular and duller silk produced by undomesticated Asian silkworms. This small-scale design was first produced in about 1878, and versions were again printed in 1888 and 1890.

40 A design for a block-printed cotton, probably by Owen Jones, 1864. The border and filling elements can be compared to Grecian patterns contained in his influential *Grammar of Ornament* and the notation 'No. 2' is indistinguishable from Jones's inscriptions on several of his designs for woven fabrics. During the 1860s this type of formal layout also began to be more noticeable in floral chintzes, reflecting the trend towards neater, smaller, more simply coloured designs.

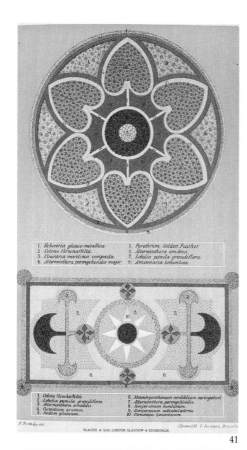

41

43

42

41 Increasingly formal arrangements typified both the most modern parks and the textile motifs of the 1870s and '80s. Containing elements which would have been equally applicable as fabric designs, this neo-Renaissance carpet-bedding plan was illustrated by Robert Thompson (in *The Gardener's Assistant*, 1881) and described by the author as one of the best examples to be found in London parks during 1875.

42, 43 By about 1860 a handful of British freelance designers had begun to break through the anonymity that had surrounded early Victorian designers. The work of two, Bruce Talbert and E. W. Godwin, are shown here. Talbert's 'Dominion' (c.1870, bottom 43) and an attributed design, 'Dragonfly' (c.1875, top), both silk tissues, were woven by Daniel Walters & Sons. The silk damask, 'Ely' (42) is attributed to Godwin and was woven by Warners in 1873. Talbert and Godwin trained as architects, designed furniture, carpets, wallpaper and textiles, and were also strongly influenced by Japanese art, which, in their textile designs, was expressed in the uniform dispersal of conventionalized motifs. All would have suited 'aesthetic' interiors.

45

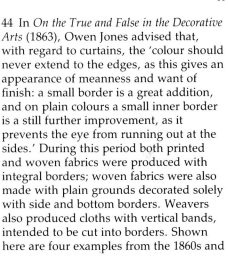

44

44 In *On the True and False in the Decorative Arts* (1863), Owen Jones advised that, with regard to curtains, the 'colour should never extend to the edges, as this gives an appearance of meanness and want of finish: a small border is a great addition, and on plain colours a small inner border is a still further improvement, as it prevents the eye from running out at the sides.' During this period both printed and woven fabrics were produced with integral borders; woven fabrics were also made with plain grounds decorated solely with side and bottom borders. Weavers also produced cloths with vertical bands, intended to be cut into borders. Shown here are four examples from the 1860s and

'70s. Woven by Daniel Walters & Sons, they include (top) 'Scotia', described as a six-over design (resulting in six borders, each 3½ inches wide, across a 21 inch-wide cloth), and 'The Malta 10-over' (third from top). Between the two is an unnamed design with an example (for the intended weave structures) attached.

45 Kate Hallyer's 'Sunflowers and Hollyhocks' (oil, 1883–98) could be taken as a guide to 'aestheticizing' an interior. Only the sunflower-patterned silk upholstery on the carved 'Louis' chair represents a substantial change to the setting; the vases, screen, shawl, flowers and draped gold-brocaded silk could

easily be added to any interior, and often were. Popular writers of the 1880s often suggested a 'cosmopolitan' parlour scheme, such as seen here, since to give an interior a distinct style required what the *Decorator and Furnisher* in May 1888 called 'a purse deep enough to gratify any passing caprice'.

46 Candice Wheeler, an important activist for American design reform, was a founder member of the New York Society of Decorative Art (1877) and Associated Artists. The latter, co-founded in 1879 by Louis C. Tiffany, Lockwood de Forest and Samuel Coleman, was until 1883 an interior decoration firm. Thereafter and until 1907 run by Wheeler and her family, Associated Artists specialized in textiles such as the one shown here. Now in the Metropolitan Museum of Art, New York embroidered with silk and metallic thread and appliquéd with silk velvet, this portière (74 by 50½ inches) of about 1884 typifies Wheeler's liking for overlaid detail and tone-on-tone effects. The silk base cloth is thought to have been produced by Cheney Brothers, for whom Wheeler designed a number of fabrics.

47 (detail), 48 Richly encrusted with block-printed pigment, couched metallic threads and gilt spangles, this 1880s portière hung in a house in Commonwealth Avenue, Boston. In keeping with fashionable interiors of the period, its pattern is divided into dado, dado-rail, filling and frieze. Less expensive substitutes were machine-woven in chenille, which provided a similarly textured surface.

46

47

48

49

50

50 Made in 1869 by Leon Marcotte & Co., New York, for Ogden Codman of Boston, this bergère is covered in what was described as 'garnet striped Cretonne chintz'. The bill (like the chair, in the possession of the Society for the Preservation of New England Antiquities) lists the chair as costing $70. The ten yards of fabric, seven yards of gimp and two wool and silk 'fringe rosettes' (only one remains) were an additional $20.80. The now-missing fluted flounce – from chair base to floor – was an extra $1.25. It clearly did not concern either maker or buyer that the stripe ('Oriental' in design, 'paned' in its layout) is extremely distorted by the deep-buttoning.

51 The design for this ebonized chair, by E. W. Godwin, was registered in 1876 by the cabinet-maker William Watt. Although the chair is Anglo–Japanese in design, the original worsted and silk upholstery, woven by J. W. & C. Ward of Halifax and also designed by Godwin, is neo-Renaissance in colouring and design. Leather upholstery was often preferred to cloth by many members of the reform movement in both Britain and, later, the United States, since it was flexible and hygienic and seldom needed to be re-covered. (The same preference was later held by Modernists.)

49 Homemade decorations had always existed for economical reasons; but as a result of the Arts and Crafts movement, they became more fashionable. According to Almon C. Varney, in *Our Homes and Their Adornments* (1882, p.261) silk rag carpets made attractive portières and curtains. 'Old silks are cut in strips as for carpet and either woven with a cotton warp, or better still [presumably since homemade], knitted upon fine wiry needles in stripes and tastefully joined together.' Shown here is a woven example, which Constance Cary Harrison noted (in *Woman's Handiwork in Modern Homes*, New York, 1881) could be made by a professional weaver for 28 cents a yard.

51

52

52 Between 1860 and 1890 folding chairs were the focus of much improvement and invention in both Britain and the United States. The most common folding chair during this period was of the type illustrated here, made by the Boston Furniture Company in 1870. Constructed from walnut, it is upholstered in wool velvet with an inset pane of printed wool velvet, intended to imitate more expensive chairs having central applied bands of tapestry or needlework.

53 A design for a machine-printed cotton, produced by Stead McAlpin in 1860 for Daniel Walters & Sons, successful silk weavers and fabric wholesalers based in Braintree, Essex. The orchids typify the interest in hothouse flowers, which, together with varieties of recently introduced climbers, were frequently used as sources for textile designs in the middle years of the nineteenth century.

54 In this 1885 portrait by George Elgar Hicks, Adelaide Maria, Countess of Iveagh, reclines in a large conservatory. The palms and flowering bushes are in keeping with the Turkish or Indian theme suggested by the couch and its fur cover, the casually arranged cushions, and the striped silk and silver-thread sash worn by the Countess. The folding chair, probably as common in outposts of the Empire as in Britain and the United States, completes the allusion to a luxuriously furnished tent or temporary encampment. During the late 1880s the informal richness of garden rooms such as this became a feature of previously more formal interiors.

53

55

56

55 The difficulties created by the Cobden Treaty (which in 1860 allowed French silks to enter Britain free of duty but retained a duty on English silks imported to France) encouraged some silk-weaving firms to extend their wholesale activities to prints, worsteds and stamped cloths, such as Utrecht velvets. One such firm was Charles Norris & Co., who nevertheless continued to weave some very elaborate silks in their factories in East London and Sudbury, Suffolk. This example – hand-brocaded, Jacquard loom-woven in 1883 – is typical of high Victorian neo-rococo design.

57 Chrysanthemums – which together with poppies and fruit tree blossoms were associated with the Orient – were often depicted by Arthur Silver, who founded an influential design studio in London in 1880. This printed textile design, drawn by Silver in about 1890, also shows the use of fashionable tertiary colours, with closely related tones of terra cotta and greyed blue-greens. It is thought to have been intended for Liberty's 'art' furnishing textiles range.

57

56 'Lyre Bird', a silk damask, was woven by Daniel Walters & Sons in the 1860s. Both printed and woven designs depicting palms and ferns were a subtle reflection of the British Victorian world, with their references to advanced technology (glasshouses), to man's control of nature (with forced growing and rearing of non-indigenous plants) and to imperialistic power, which encouraged importation of exotic plants (many by missionaries, who were often amateur naturalists). The fashion for jungle-like designs seems to have been established at the Great Exhibition in 1851, and continued for about two decades.

58 This lambrequin-like portière in Mrs. Gov. Wright's cottage, Martha's Vineyard, Massachusetts, was photographed by C. H. Shute & Son in 1870–75. Other photographs indicate that these were the summer hangings, which alternated with a heavier, darker lambrequin, suggesting that a similar change was made to the window curtains. Although in many homes during the winter heavy draperies were added to windows with arrangements such as shown here, others simply retained lambrequins and laces year round. The machine-made lace curtains imitated hand-made bobbin lace and were European, since lacemaking machines were not imported into the United States until the 1890s.

59 Carefully pleated curtain headings were still rare in 1890, when Felix Lenoir illustrated this selection in *Practical and Theoretical Treatise on Decorative Hangings, or the Guide to Upholstery* (Brussels and London). In the accompanying notes, Lenoir distinguishes box pleats (single, 10 and 11; double, 15 and treble, 13) as having the heading added to the curtain top, allowing a change in fabric and a slight downward drape between pleats. Flat headings (6 and 8, also called 'musical headings') were in one piece with the curtain, as they generally are today. The intention of these headings was to give complete coverage of the curtain rod (see simpler methods 1, 3 and 4). All were to be lined with buckram and 'must stand up quite straight'; to ensure this, one could use metal fittings as shown in 16, 17, 18 and 20.

58

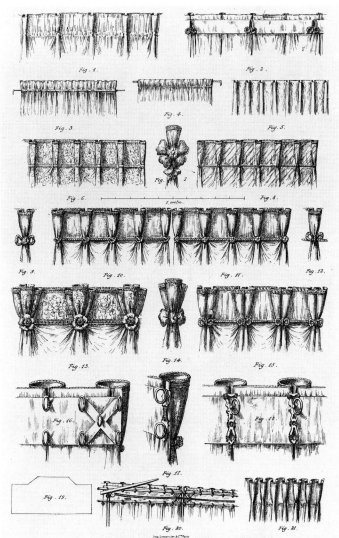

59

Chapter Five

Towards Simplicity

1890–1920

'Those sated and out of patience with ornament, whether mismanaged or simply super-abundant, have been known to fly to simplicity and plain surface for repose. Owen Jones so sought refuge from a jaded appetite for colour and form. A fashion for plainness and simplicity in decoration is convenient in more ways than one. It is convenient to the new-made *virtuoso*, who likes it because it may imply that he could have done the contrary if he had chosen; convenient to those born without taste, for it saves them fiascos; convenient to decorators who have crept into notice by good luck . . . for it saves them trouble.'
(Mrs. H. R. Haweis, in *The Art of Decoration*[1])

Mrs. Haweis offered the above remarks as an explanation of the growing popularity of Queen Anne furnishings, by which she meant almost anything *not* deep-buttoned Renaissance or rococo revival, and into which she included 'carefully discoloured and fatiguingly broidered napery', rush-bottom chairs, 'wretched hard "Sheraton" sofas', and 'the plain square patch of wall painted grey, or drab, or some of those nameless earth-tints which the "aesthetic" are vowed to'. In the late 1880s, as the pendulum of fashion moved away from the desire for ornamentation, such interiors were beginning to have a noticeable effect on the mass market. This coloured the views of Mrs. Haweis, who was a member of a fairly select circle which included the Alma Tademas, the Walter Cranes, a fair sprinkling of aristocratic families and fellow crusaders such as William Loftie (who, from 1878, edited a series of *Art at Home* books) and Lasenby Liberty, who at his own expense decorated the Haweis home for their 1881 'medieval' Christmas party. Naturally, therefore, her dissatisfaction with aspects of Queen Anne was that much of it was 'now provided by every upholsterer', a revealing remark made in her new edition of *The Art of Decoration* (1889).[2] By the 1890s 'Queen Anne' was (much to Mrs. Haweis's regret) a noticeably middle- and lower-class fashion, the first to secure wide popularity without having 'descended' from the highest social class.

The department and furniture stores which – even more so than the upholsterers – made this possible were able to do so only because of the demand. A contemporary American designer and writer, Candice Wheeler, witnessed the 'effects of the great race for wealth which

1 An emphasis on line characterized many 'New Art' textiles of 1895–1905. In the hands of a designer such as C. F. A. Voysey, lines could construct an entire pattern, as in the wool double cloth shown here (woven by Alexander Morton & Company from a design of about 1896, originally for wallpaper). Not surprisingly, since Morton's started in Scotland in 1867 as a leno wholesale firm, the same design was also woven as a madras muslin. Voysey, a British architect and painter, was one of the most influential turn-of-the-century designers, and produced numerous patterns for carpets, wallpapers, and printed and woven textiles, as well as for furniture and metalwork.

characterizes our time', noting that 'it is demanded that woman shall make it effective' by using income (great or small) 'to distinguish the family; and nothing distinguishes it so much as the superiority of the home'.[3] In 1889 Mrs. J. E. Panton (author of several popular books on interior decoration and daughter of the artist W. P. Frith) addressed *From Kitchen to Garrett* [sic] to the respectable British middle class, which had an income of £350 to £750 a year. Since in the 1890s an inexpensive but 'artistic' bedroom suite could be purchased for £9 9s (complete with mirrored wardrobe, dresser, washstand and two cane seat chairs), and £3 would secure an 'artistic' settee (fully upholstered with an appropriate fabric and often finished with studs), the mass-produced Arts and Crafts style was too readily available to remain fashionable for much longer. Prices were more or less the same in the United States, where, for example, chenille portières could be obtained in 1893 through Sears, Roebuck & Co. for between $2.15 and $5.25 (£1 1s). Thus, the more crowded, fully furnished version of 'Queen Anne' was also obtainable by many.[4]

As a complete look, 'Queen Anne' had therefore, by the 1890s, lost its cachet among the upper middle classes. By 1900 the division between the progressive and the tasteful-but-conservative upper-middle-class interior was complete. Ogden Codman, the influential American decorator who co-authored *The Decoration of Houses* (1897) with Edith Wharton, provides an excellent example of this: in 1897 he redecorated a room in his house, previously (c.1885) furnished with curtains and upholstery of William Morris's 'Brother Rabbit', replacing this densely patterned indigo discharge print with a scenic French toile. As an *idea*, however, 'Queen Anne' remained powerful; and the ideas were essentially upper middle class. 'Artistic', 'appropriate' and above all, 'simplicity' became the bywords for the fashionable taste of the years between 1890 and 1920. Simplicity, in

2 Inside the mock-Elizabethan Wightwick Manor, Staffordshire, is this great parlour, part of an 1893 extension to a building which was then only five or six years old. The wallcovering – 'Diagonal Trail', a woollen tissue designed by John Henry Dearle in about 1893 – was part of the original decoration; the chair in the foreground is upholstered in William Morris's 'Bird', a woollen double cloth designed in 1878; the inglenook sofa, in Morris's 'Tulip and Rose' of 1876, used sideways. Richly furnished interiors such as this were gradually watered down (compare, for example, Fig. 18) and eventually transformed into the 'Jacobean' interiors of the twentieth century.

particular, pervaded equally the four trends which were originally combined in 'Queen Anne', but which separated in this period into historicism, modernism, Orientalism and idealism.

One other aspect of 'Queen Anne' also persisted: textile designs of the 1870s and '80s remained in use for some time. In 1897 Rosamund Mariott Watson noted 'unhappily', that 'the same [reform] movement that dethroned the bloated commonplaces of the day before yesterday has given birth to more monstrosities, human and inanimate, than you may care to count'. Although not referring to textiles specifically, her description of distorted likenesses of irises and lilies, misbegotten sunflowers and poppies and 'inane sham-medieval dicky-birds' can be readily matched to the British designs of up to twenty-five years earlier. (The despised birds are possibly a reference to early 1880s designs by Morris, who had died the year before Watson published her comments.) Watson further expressed a hope that, having 'mainly ebbed out to the suburbs . . . the whole sorry company [may disperse] to their own place – the more or less decent obscurity of minor anthologies and cheap lodging-houses'. This is certainly what awaited many textiles commercially manufactured in Arts and Crafts style, although some – such as those designed by William Morris – never really ceased to appeal to those with intellectual, artistic or radical leanings or pretensions. And in 1913 the London *Times* could still truthfully remark that 'much of the present day style of decorated fabrics is stamped with the personality of William Morris in the design and colouring. . . .'[5]

The irony of Watson's condemnation of British design was that it was triggered by the achievement of one reform movement ideal – that good design could be made accessible to the general public. Many well-known and respected designers of the period, including C. F. A. Voysey, Lindsay Butterfield, Lewis F. Day, Walter Crane, G. C. Haite and Harry Napper, contributed to the output of leading British textile firms. G. P. & J. Baker, A. H. Lee, Morris & Co., Alexander Morton & Co., Simpson & Godlee, Turnbull & Stockdale, Warner & Sons, and Wardle & Co. were among the manufacturers who maintained a steady supply of variously priced, well-designed hand- and machine-made printed and woven fabrics. The interest in 'art' embroidery also increased; by the early twentieth century it was taught in schools as well as colleges. Many of the innovators in this design movement were members of the Arts and Crafts Exhibition Society (founded in 1888) – whose name, in shortened form, was henceforward applied to the 'reform/Queen Anne' movement.[6]

While retaining nature as a source of inspiration, the modern embroideries and repeating patterns of the period from 1890 to about 1910 were increasingly stylized or simplified. Line – whether as outlines or sinuous stems – became dominant. Texture remained 'appropriate': doublecloth (two-sided) weaves emphasized the bulk and softness of wool or wool and cotton blends; printed cloths showed their 'true' surface and were generally unglazed; and silks, whether printed, plain or patterned in the loom, were fine and light. Such fabrics were intended to be used in the simplest manner possible (and this was the simplicity approved by Mrs. Haweis;

3 The British typically preferred a more reserved form of Art Nouveau, as is evident in this Harry Napper design, for which Baker's cut printing blocks in June 1907. Napper, who worked for the Silver Studio from 1893 to 1898 before turning freelance, was a watercolour artist and also a designer of wallpapers, carpets, embroideries, furniture, metalwork and stencilled wall coverings. He was one of a number of British designers who supplied Art Nouveau patterns to Continental manufacturers.

she did not use the term to denote sparsely furnished rooms): window curtains hung straight – the only embellishment might be a gathered or pleated valance – and they or separate glass or 'casement' curtains hung to just above the window-sill. Upholstery was never deep-buttoned, and wooden-seat furniture perpetuated the reform movement's indifference to comfort with their hard squab cushions. In the most progressive interiors, by architects such as M. H. Baillie Scott and Charles Rennie Mackintosh, embroideries predominated over other textiles. Simulated modern embroideries, available by the bolt, were effective substitutes, as were the mass-produced fabrics bearing modern designs. However, these were not confined to use on modern furniture; for example, Liberty, in 1906, advertised an eighteenth-century-style wing chair covered in a woollen fabric designed in 'New Art' style by Allan Vigers and woven by Alexander Morton & Co.

From the 1880s to the early twentieth century, many designs included a stem meandering from side to side up the cloth. The use of a meandering line to organize pattern, often found in earlier textiles, now formed the basis of many new designs, both modern and traditional. Although British textile designers contributed to the use of increasingly energetic, whiplash-like stems, these became associated mainly with Art Nouveau, a Continental design movement which was prominently displayed at the 1900 Paris Universal Exhibition. Some of these designs, nearly always associated at the time with France, were also used in the United States. Comparatively few Art Nouveau textiles were manufactured in England, despite the fact that numerous designs in this style originated there (for example, many such designs by the London-based Silver Studio, founded by Rex Silver in 1880, were sold to the Scots, French, Belgians and Americans).

Art Nouveau had much wider use as a drapery style, interpreted in elaborate upper swags. The pattern of the fabric was inconsequential; what made this style 'modern French' was the asymmetrical arrangement: stiffened valances (sometimes covering only half of the window's width) or curtain rods were draped with irregularly arranged festoons, intended, according to *Practical Decorative Upholstery* (1889), 'to convey the idea that the whole is . . . simply thrown over. . . .'[7] In the 1890s and early 1900s these upper window treatments appear to have been equally popular in Britain and the United States, where they were often referred to as 'French shawl' draperies. The same drapery style was sometimes used with 'artistic' furniture and, inevitably, in what Codman and Wharton called 'the epidemic of "Marie Antoinette" rooms' [also called 'Louis XVI'], which had 'plenty of white paint, a pale wall-paper with bow-knots, and fragile chairs dipped in liquid gilding and covered with a flowered silk and cotton material'.[8] A related drapery style, also regarded as French, employed festoons and swags distinctly reminiscent of treatments popular in the first quarter of the nineteenth century.

By about 1900 the leading British textile designers had rejected the French style and turned instead to a more controlled, contained and often 'squared-off' format for their stylized floral motifs. This style, often

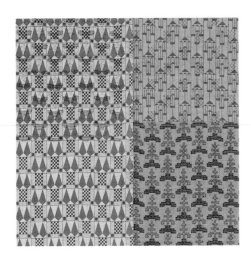

4 These linen fabrics block-printed with small two- or three-colour designs were bought by Baker's from Siebers of Vienna in about 1908, when Vienna was a centre of much innovation, not only in the decorative arts, but in science, music and the social sciences. Many subsequent modern textile designs can trace their roots to the work of the Weiner Werkstätte and other Austrian establishments and artists of this period.

called 'New Art' to distinguish it from Art Nouveau, influenced slightly later avant-garde movements in Austria and Germany. New ideas, flat designs and illustrations were continually transmitted through journals – most notably by *The Studio*, established in London in 1893 and until 1920 the most influential English-language art-decoration magazine. *The Craftsman*, published in New York under the editorship of Gustav Stickley, added another voice in 1901, and it too reported the progressive styles of the Weiner Werkstätte (founded in Vienna in 1903) and the Deutscher Werkbund (founded in Weimar in 1907). Firms such as G. P. & J. Baker, in London, and Cheney Brothers, in Manchester, Connecticut, produced a handful of modern Viennese designs in the early 1900s, but in both Britain and the United States, most people turned away from Continental developments.

This retreat from modernity requires some explanation, particularly in the case of Britain, which at the turn of the century was the acknowledged world leader in both quantity and quality textile production. Yet events of 1890 marked a turning point, for in that year the industry was unsettled by a general economic depression worsened by the implementation of the McKinley Tariff. This legislation, which imposed duties as high as 60 per cent on textiles imported into the United States, affected the well-made, mass-produced British goods most dramatically. (Wool textile exports to the US, for example, dropped from sixty-four million to nineteen million yards in one year.[9]) Those British cloths that continued to be exported to America now became much nearer in cost to similarly made French textiles and were unable to compete in the middle-class market for which they had been designed.

The impact of the McKinley tariff can be seen in relation to an American manifestation of the Arts and Crafts spirit – the 'Mission' or 'Craftsman' style of furniture, developed by Charles Limbert, the Roycroft community, Gustav Stickley and others. This style has been praised, in a

5 From *The Craftsman* magazine, published in New York between 1901 and 1916, this illustration (vol. IX, 1905–6) indicates the simple fabrics associated with Mission-style furnishings. The upholstery suggests Gustav Stickley's 'Craftsman canvas' (a plain-weave, piece-dyed jute and flax fabric) or 'antique linen' (using an irregularly twisted yarn in a loose, coarse weave). The latter, in green, was thought particularly suitable for willow furniture upholstery; in deep straw colour it was favoured for curtains, left unlined to transmit a warm glow into the room.

6 Designed in about 1900 by Henry Dearle, 'Elmcote', a wool and mohair lampas, was listed in the Morris & Co. catalogue of about 1910 as costing 18s. 6d. per yard. Dearle had joined Morris & Co. in 1878, and some ten or so years later began to design prints and weaves for the firm, having already contributed carpet and embroidery patterns. He became a director on Morris's death in 1896, and continued to design until his own death in 1932. (Morris & Co. closed shortly after the outbreak of the Second World War.)

recent study, for 'epitomizing an effort to capture the simplicity and harmony preached by William Morris and his followers'.[10] Yet English-made Arts and Crafts textiles were rarely used for upholstering Mission furniture. Instead, leather or leather cloth predominated, with occasional use of denim, canvas, or other durable jute- or hemp-woven textiles. This may have been partly due to a conscious desire to conform to the Southwestern/Spanish missionary allusions in the style, thought to have been first introduced in 1894 by Joseph P. McHugh & Co. of New York, or to the newly apparent desire for design autonomy; but it may equally have been caused by the high prices of English Arts and Crafts textiles. The influence of the 'reform/Queen Anne' school of thought in the United States after 1890 therefore shows less reliance on the products of the British Arts and Crafts movement than one might expect. Even in an emerging centre of progressive design such as Chicago, Morris & Co. textiles and wallpapers were not marketed until 1902, when the William Morris Room was opened in the Tobey Furniture Company showroom.

Innovative Arts and Crafts textiles were also becoming more exclusive in Britain, where, after about 1905, there was a noticeable trend towards hand-made fabrics, particularly weaves. Between 1890 and 1920 small weaving concerns were being run or set up by a new generation of designers, including Edmund Hunter, Ethel Mairet, Annie Garnett, Luther Hooper, Mr. and Mrs. Joseph King and Katie Grasett. Larger hand-weaving firms such as Gainsborough Silk Weavers (founded by Reginald Warner in 1903) and Warners (founded by Benjamin Warner in 1870), did not specialize in Arts and Crafts textiles but occasionally included them in their output. The many guilds of the period encouraged all kinds of crafts, from spinning to embroidery. Motivated by idealism rather than fashion, many of the Arts and Crafts fabric designers came to rely principally on colour and texture, or on designs based on traditional patterns. Morris & Co. continued to produce Morris designs and, from the late 1880s, embroidery and textile designs by John H. Dearle. Although some hand-made post-1905 Arts and Crafts fabrics were moderately priced in Britain, they were never produced in enough quantity to become widely used.

The interest in formal, stylized historic designs increased during this period, in part because the Arts and Crafts movement had also laid the foundations for a style which at its most expensive could be called 'baronial'. Rich, eclectic, but understated, these interiors were created mainly in re-claimed pre-eighteenth-century English buildings, 'prefera-bly', as John Cornforth has observed, 'a manor house or castle that had come down in the world'.[11] William Morris himself had preferred to live in old houses, but had furnished them anew with his own work. The 'baronial' interiors relied principally on antiques and – unlike the fully panelled, richly carved neo-Renaissance interiors of the same period – on plastered walls and exposed beams. Many were showcases for fine tapestries, needlework and other old textiles. New needlework, silks and velvets were used as necessary and chosen with an informed eye. Volumes such as Sydney Vascher's 1886 reproduction of textile patterns taken from fifteenth-century Italian paintings in London's National Gallery and

7 A Jacobean-style crewelwork pattern has been used in this woven panel, designed by the Silver Studio at the turn of the century and manufactured in northern France by Leborgne. Such pieces were intended for use as table carpets or wallhangings in conjunction with sixteenth- and seventeenth-century-style furnishings. In Britain and the United States machine-made 'tapestry' upholstery cloths were also often made, as here, with a worsted weft and a cotton warp. They employed similar (though frequently less detailed) designs and have continued to be produced throughout this century.

Arthur Silver's 1889 'Silvern Series' of photographs from the South Kensington Museum (now the Victoria & Albert Museum) provided manufacturers with documented designs for printed and woven textiles, many of which found their way into other types of interiors.

Between 1896 and 1920 *Country Life* devoted many pages to descriptions and illustrations of 'baronial' houses. Sensitive but not slavish homages to the past, they were part of the beginnings of the distinctly twentieth-century 'historic house' style, which sought to create an impression of age without recreating rooms of one specific period. The baronial style also served as one of the models for a new kind of suburban interior which was characterized by a juxtaposition of plaster walls and dark wood beams. Other models were the large houses in vernacular styles being built on both sides of the Atlantic. The new suburban interiors, which were still being created well into the 1930s, could be either mock-Tudor or pseudo-Spanish; these rooms were complemented by a group of mass-produced textiles which for convenience can be called 'Jacobean revival' (all having something identifiable as originating from c.1600) and which centred around carpet and crewelwork patterns. Surface interest was typical. Cretonnes, crashes, linens and velveteens were printed, and weaves often simulated tapestry or other cloths with a heavy, rough surface. Background colours tended towards the shaded, faded tones and were only rarely pure white. Many of these fabrics – particularly those inspired by carpets – were compatible with other decorating styles, such as 'Turkish' schemes which were overladen with a variety of textiles; but their use in suburban interiors tended gradually towards simplicity: plainly covered chairs, without excessive use of fringe, gimp or tassels, and straight-hanging short curtains. Similarly flexible were the non-pictorial, pseudo-baronial 'verdure' tapestries, machine-made in slightly 'faded' cottons and used both as hangings and upholstery. Elsie de Wolfe, the influential American decorator whose taste inclined towards neo-Georgian, approved of machine-made tapestries only if they employed foliage in soft greens, tans and browns on dark blue – in other words, the 'verdure' style.[12]

Out of the Arts and Crafts interest in traditional methods came a general interest in traditional style. The interpretation of 'appropriate' broadened, so that although it remained essential to the Arts and Crafts movement and to the American 'Mission' interiors of about 1900, it was also used to promote Jacobean revival styles, as well as the 'new' urban classicism. The light, small, late-eighteenth-century English furniture often called 'Adam', after Robert Adam (but, in reality, often after Hepplewhite or Sheraton), was, for example, said to be best for apartments; it was this concept of 'appropriateness', according to an observer in 1915, that had accounted for the 'mad onslaught' of this style, which had begun over a decade before.[13]

Both American and British manufacturers supplied the 'classical' market with roller-printed historical patterns (some more accurate than others), and the soft, clear colours, off-white or white grounds and glazed finish found on so many of the originals was returned to favour (although un-glazed cottons were also produced in this style). So common to

Lancashire printers were the pretty, small- to medium-scale patterns (with stripes, garlands and swags of flowers, little bouquets, ribbons and other 'eighteenth-century' motifs, such as baskets of flowers) that these became known as 'Manchester chintzes'. The dates assigned to many were incorrect, so that 1830s and '40s prints were often described as eighteenth century (not unnaturally, since some resembled the earlier patterns). A spate of books on the subject did little to correct these misconceptions. Manufacturers, who had long been in the habit of collecting old textiles for design inspiration, began to seek out old chintzes in earnest. The still prevalent criticisms of mid-Victorian designs they either simply ignored or avoided through incorrect dating. In 1912 the British writer Hugh Phillips addressed himself to any who may have still had reservations, describing old chintzes as 'articulate relics. So delectable are their soft, faded colours, so fascinating are the designs, and . . . so enchanting is the old-world musty scent which always clings to them, that it would be hard indeed to withhold one's affection. . . .'[14]

There were several room styles compatible with these roller prints, including the 'Marie Antoinette' interiors. By about 1910 a simpler type of eighteenth-century-style room had emerged. Variously dubbed 'Georgian', 'Federal' or 'French', this type of attractive, but too-uniform, inexact and sometimes bland adaptation of eighteenth-century furnishings was ubiquitous: Moreland's comment of 1890 that 'the larger number of rooms . . . represent no particular style of decoration' remained true until the First World War. Instead, as Moreland added, 'The desire is simply to produce harmony and good effect with a minimum expense'[15] and, one could add, a minimum of effort. In 1908, when the fictional Cecil Vyse, in *A Room with a View*, 'considered what might be done to make the Windy Corner drawing-room more distinctive', he concluded that 'it should have been a successful room, but the trail of Tottenham Court Road was upon it; he could almost visualize the motor-vans of Messrs Shoolbred and Messrs Maple arriving at the door. . . .'[16] The problem was not the room's appearance (which was probably late-eighteenth-century English in inspiration with matching upholstery and simply made curtains) but the fact that a graceful, tasteful interior could now be purchased easily. Perhaps even worse, from a class-conscious point of view, was the fact that the rooms of the middle class could now approximate, if only faintly, those aristocratic interiors that had remained fairly static since the late eighteenth century.

This convergence of taste can be traced back to about 1890, when in wealthier British houses, newly decorated interiors in the classical revival style were also adopting a more ordered manner. This is a well-documented change, but the new luxurious classicism was not inspired only by what could be literally described as aristocratic interiors. Although it was still a commonly held view in the 1890s that aristocratic fashions provided the model for the classes below, other influences were being felt. The British landed gentry were losing their financial muscle as a result of the agricultural depression of the last quarter of the century, and although still wealthy, were being outstripped, in this regard, by the new

8 This willow furniture appeared in *Craftsman Furniture Made by Gustav Stickley,* a catalogue of items available from Stickley's Syracuse, New York, showroom in 1910. At least one willow piece was suggested 'to lighten the general effect' in rooms otherwise furnished in Mission-style oak furniture. Of the eleven examples illustrated, ten had cushions covered with Stickley's Craftsman canvas, and a chintz or cretonne, as shown on the lower chair, was supplied only on request. The use of a printed fabric was thought suitable for a summer cottage or bungalow, but plain fabrics and leather remained the most common Mission-style upholstery.

industrialists – above all, by the even-richer visiting and resident Americans – whose wealth and 'high profile' made them the new trend-setters.

At the same time there came, from the United States, a separate and possibly more significant impulse towards simplicity, reflected in the influential Codman-Wharton book of 1897, *The Decoration of Houses*. Their book was concerned not with 'how to', but with 'why'. Reason, proportion and simplicity were their keys to decoration, which was always to reflect the architecture. The authors believed it to be a 'mistaken idea that defects in structure or design may be remedied by an overlaying of colour or ornament'. In practical terms this meant identical fabric for curtains (if used) and chair covers; no portières; no graduated shades of the same colour, no draped mantelpieces and no 'heavy stuff curtains, so draped as to cut off the upper light of the windows by day, while it is impossible to drop them at night'. (Of these, only portières continued to be recommended by other writers after 1900. In 1905, for example, they were thought best for city houses in the United States, where small reception rooms made doors an inconvenience. At about the same time the best portière fabrics (double-sided) were said to be in short supply in America, although Alice M. Kellog noted that 'many additions have been made during the past few years in [portières of] mercerized cottons, velours, reps, jutes and silk tapestries'. Even Elsie de Wolfe, who preferred doors to portières, allowed, in 1914, for 'honest' portières for simple houses, made of velvet or velveteen in a neutral tone.[17] In Britain they remained a common means of dividing the front and back hallway and were still being made, in chenille, by David Barbour & Co. Ltd. in Scotland in 1928.

While it could be argued that the styles favoured by Codman and Wharton were 'aristocratic', the concern for appropriate decoration – what they called 'suitability' – was an upper-middle-class concept. Their support of classicism as a *theory*, rather than a style, is demonstrated in their advice for those with little to spend on furnishings: 'Willow arm chairs with denim cushions and solid tables with stained legs and covers of denim or corduroy will be more satisfactory than the "parlour suit" turned out in thousands by the manufacturer of cheap furniture, or the pseudo Georgian or pseudo Empire of the dealer in high grade goods.' This could easily be taken as a recommendation of a Mission-style interior. Similarly, 'rational' principles were applied elsewhere, but with different results – in the furnishings from Heal's in London, for example, where well-crafted rural or Arts and Crafts-style furniture was sold alongside well-made Georgian revival pieces.[18]

The influence of American thought was felt directly in Britain; for many of the new 'country-house' interiors, created by the new breed of women decorators, were the handiwork of American women. The eighteenth-century style they created was characterized by greater informality and assured the place of the English chintz in the vocabulary of every subsequent decade's style. This predilection for chintz was fortunate for the British textile industry; for the American influence was on its way to becoming a dominant force in the industry, and without American support, this kind of textile printing might have been destined for oblivion.

9 A design for a traditionally styled print by Herbert Crofts of the Silver Studio, c.1908. The growing taste for both French 'neo-classical' and Jacobean interiors would have welcomed this type of scrolled, fully covered design, although its inspiration was probably French mid-nineteenth century tapestries, such as those hand-woven at Beauvais specifically for upholstery.

With the middle-class 'Windy Corners' and the upper-class homes now so similar in style, it was also fortunate for the European textile industry that the distinction between the fabrics used in middle- and upper-class interiors now rested not on style but on quality – whether hand-weaves, French toiles or British hand-block prints. Elsie de Wolfe, the prominent American decorator who was influenced by – or at least agreed with – Wharton's ideas, used so many English hand-block-printed chintzes that she could have single-handedly kept this branch of the industry alive.

The classicism of 1890–1920 had one other aspect – nationalism. At the Philadelphia Centennial Exhibition in 1876, displays of late-eighteenth-century interiors had focused interest on America's heritage. In the wealthiest American homes in the years approaching 1890 the revival style was overtly European; featuring tapestries, rich French or English hand-woven silks and fine antiques. Secure in their social position, the rich sought to proclaim their cosmopolitan style. Farther down the social scale, especially among those whose families had recently come from Europe, there was a strong wish to be seen to be American; and it was the American Federal and Colonial styles that conveniently provided a parallel but more fitting approach to classicism for middle-class and lower-class American interiors. Middle-class historicism in Britain took a similar turn; there it was the mass-produced 'Sheraton', 'Chippendale' or the less precisely-termed 'Adam' furniture, that satisfied a chauvinistic neo-classical taste. The Jacobean style, too, had the requisite 'English-ness'.

The textile industry must have sighed with relief as fashion abandoned innovation for thoroughly retrospective styles; for the McKinley Tariff and the depression of 1890, followed by several bad trading years in that decade, unsettled the industry – so much so that many firms considered combining together. The idea of a 'combine' was finally rejected by Philadelphia's textile industries; but the British Calico Printers Association (C.P.A.) was formed in 1899, in an attempt to bring together 85 per cent of Britain's massive textile printing capacity (which accounted for nearly two-thirds of the country's entire export trade). Reorganized in 1903 after an uneasy start, the C.P.A. was ill prepared for the next challenge – the cornering of the cotton market by the United States in 1904. Many English firms went onto half-time or closed as the price of raw cotton soared. Stabilized by about 1910, the C.P.A. was smaller in terms of both production and influence, comprising only about 60 per cent of the country's calico-printing firms.

By joining together, the members of the C.P.A. had a pool of unused designs which were now brought into production, and their demand for new designs fell. Even though the C.P.A.'s production had little to do with innovative design, the strength of the British 'down-market' textile industry had provided much of the confidence which permeated the higher-quality production. Without this broad, sound base, the entire industry became more cautious, and less willing to experiment with new designs. Since the American textile-printing industry still relied on European samples for inspiration, its own designs now reflected the new British conservatism.

10 'Extra Fine English Cretonne Yardage' roller-printed by Cocheco in the United States in 1890. Limited colour ranges, particularly the dull, warm shades seen in this detail, were both typical of many fashionable 1890s prints and also provided a means of reducing production costs. Designs such as this – essentially a 'chintz' pattern – were adapted to turn-of-the-century tastes by incorporating new colours and by omitting the glaze, a finish that was noticeably unpopular until about 1905–10.

It must also be remembered that textile manufacturers needed to make saleable fabrics, and that patterns with historical associations have always formed the basis of the industry's production. The upper classes, with few exceptions, always favoured these patterns; the rich middle class, who had previously purchased exclusive modern textiles, saw cheaply produced versions appearing with an almost imperceptible delay, and they, too, withdrew their support of modern design. Some people within the industry also noted the lack of young, well-trained designers. In 1909, when virtually all of the great late-nineteenth-century British textile designers had died, retired, or turned to other interests, the students at Macclesfield School of Art were told that 'the reproduction of period styles provides work for the draughtsman not the designer, and their frequent use is not so much due to their being preferred as to the scarcity of modern original designs equal in merit and pure in detail of motive and ornament'.[19]

For the first time, Americans also began to express dissatisfaction with their design sources and, in particular, with their reliance on European patterns. The criticism paralleled that heard in Britain in the 1840s and '50s, which suggests that there may be a relationship between a desire for good indigenous designers and industrial supremacy, for the latter was captured by America in the years around the First World War. As early as 1892 one American writer claimed that his country stood 'unrivalled in [calico printing], the art-department of commerce'. By that time there was more capital invested in all types of textile manufacture than in any other American industry; in terms of quantity, American silk weaving was second only to the French, and carpet weaving was unequalled. Machine-made lace production had begun in earnest, and by the early 1890s the most elaborate American lace curtains cost no more than $4.50 (wholesale). The years between 1900 and 1920 saw the height of prosperity for the Philadelphia woollen and worsted weavers, who combined large runs of plain upholstery plushes, mohairs (including corduroys) and velvets with (after 1898 and 1904 respectively) smaller amounts of patterned chenille (made on carpet looms converted for the purpose) and machine-woven tapestry.[20] These fabrics represented the most popular lines in both Britain and America during this period.

The American textile industry was certainly more efficient than the British; virtually identical printing machines produced on average 20,000 yards per week in the United Kingdom and nearly 75,000 yards per week in the United States. Quality remained another matter. An English writer – averting accusations of prejudice by quoting American print works' managers – claimed in 1903 that American cloth (for printing) was still far inferior to English, principally due to irregular spinning.[21] Also, the very high speed of American production largely precluded the manufacture of specialized goods. This left the upper end of the market open to firms such as Brunschwig & Fils, founded in France in 1880, exporting to America with such success that by 1926 they were to open a New York office, and Schumacher, founded in 1889 in New York as importers of fine French silks, which, in 1891, the *Decorator and Furnisher* noted, could cost up to $80 a yard (for a hand-woven brocade). Schumacher were also agents for the

11 A paper impression from a stencilled design, supplied to Turnbull & Stockdale by The Aerograph Co. Ltd. of Holborn Viaduct, London. Stencilled fabrics were available in London in 1897, but this design probably dates from the first years of the twentieth century. It appears to use a spray-gun technique, suggested by the shading of the roses and leaves and in the blurred edges of the black lines. This type of highly stylized rose remained the 'signature' of an avant-garde design until the mid-1920s.

English firm Foxton's, founded in 1903 by William Foxton and specializing in avant-garde prints. Other British firms specializing in high-quality textiles also found a ready market in the United States. Among them were Morton & Co., Warner & Sons and A. H. Lee; the latter opened a New York office in 1904 and survives in the present-day firm Lee Jofa.[22]

Although at the outset of the twentieth century the design of textiles still had its roots in the past, the textile industry was beginning to show signs of a modern spirit. In the United States this was expressed through greater efficiency, while in Britain it emerged in the interest in new techniques, fibres and dyes.

The British had long relied on technological improvements or novelties to maintain their markets, and in this period they continued this policy. Improvements in power-loom Jacquard weaving led to faster preparation and weaving times, while in hand weaving, luxurious three-pile velvets were achieved. In printing most of the interest lay in creating shaded tints, and several techniques from the past were explored, including rainbow printing, batik, warp printing and block printing over fabric with a woven pattern. The interest in blurred surface treatments was widespread; the Spanish-born designer Mariano Fortuny, for example, used a continuous stencilling machine of his own invention (in 1910) to create 'antiqued' textiles.

The interest in stencilling (derived partly from the Japanese prints which had been circulating in Europe from the mid-nineteenth century) was to have the most noticeable impact on textile printing of the twentieth century. A machine adapted for spray-painting fabric through stencils was patented by S. H. Sharp in 1894, although it is not known how widely it was used. Alice Kellog, writing in America in 1904, recommended bed coverings of plain linen stencilled with 'paints that when dry are capable of being laundered'. (Either the 'paints' were the relatively new small range of direct dyes, which reacted with fibre without an intermediate process, or the 'laundering' was really dry cleaning, which was now available on a commercial scale.) Whatever the exact method, stencilled fabrics were widely publicized and recommended at the turn of the century. Those designers known to have worked for their commercial production included, in Britain, Lindsay Butterfield and the Silver Studio; and it seems likely that Candice Wheeler experimented with the technique in America, for she certainly thought highly of the results, recommending stencilled muslin as a wall covering.[23] Although relatively few stencilled textiles were produced, the basic principle of stencilling was to play a significant part in today's industry, since it led eventually to screen printing. A method for screen printing was patented in 1907, but not developed commercially until after the First World War.

Attempts to mass-produce stencilled textiles also most clearly revealed the artistic interests of the period, incorporating flat decorative areas with broad outlines – a characteristic of stained glass, embroidered appliqué and illustrations of the same era. The relationship between designs for stained glass, appliqué and stencilling was recognized at the time, in the use of the latter two techniques on translucent curtain fabrics, to produce

12 Furnishing fabrics and wallpapers designed specifically for children began to be commercially made just before 1900. This 1903 Liberty & Co. 'Nursery Cushion' design, by a designer identified only as Houghton, is one of several which G. P. & J. Baker block-printed between 1900 and 1905. It measures 19 by 21 inches.

luminous areas of colour. Mass-produced textiles simulated this effect with designs printed on scrim or coarse muslin.[24]

Book illustration was particularly influential in turn-of-the-century textile designs and none more so than the children's books produced by Walter Crane, Kate Greenaway and Randolph Caldecott in the 1870s and '80s. The simplified, quasi-eighteenth-century interiors, fashions and gardens they depicted began almost to come to life shortly after 1900 – as if those brought up with these books sought to make their childhood fairy tales come true. Textiles were designed with 'storybook' images of topiary, orchards and figures – even houses – often combined out-of-scale. Some of these fabrics – for the first time – were designed for children's rooms, but others had a wider appeal. For children there were also cushion covers printed with scenes. Lithograph-printed cushion covers were produced in the United States – many of them depicting the fashionable 'Gibson Girl'.[25]

The interest in fibres focused on imitation silk, or 'Chardonnet silk' – the name given to the nitro-cellular fibre shown at the Paris Exhibition of 1889. Viscose rayon (which, unlike real silk, requires spinning) was patented in 1892 by the English chemists C. F. Cross and E. J. Bevan; and in 1904 Courtauld's purchased the production rights, supporting manufacture of the fibre in both Britain and America. The industry was not well established until the 1920s, so it was not until then that its impact was felt in the furnishing fabrics trade. Cottons were also given a higher and more permanent lustre through Horace Lowe's 1890 improvements to mercerization (a process that made cottons more receptive to dyes, perfected in 1850 by John Mercer).

With regard to dyes, the British had fallen behind the Germans, who controlled the supply of dyestuffs by virtue of their progress in the third quarter of the nineteenth century and their patents on the best man-made equivalent of madder (alizarin), the first direct cotton dye (Congo red), a water-soluble indigo-coloured blue (methylene blue) and the first green of real dyeing value (malachite green). By 1901 they had perfected the first so-called vat dye, which provided the fastest, clearest colour and which became – and remains – the most important colourant for high-quality prints.

British chemists had not been entirely idle, however; and with the outbreak of war in 1914, they were galvanized by the loss of German dyestuffs (and their essential 'drugs', or ingredients). A concerted, and successful, effort to provide colourfast furnishing fabrics was made during the war by the Scottish firm Morton Sundour (which was founded in 1914 by James Morton and which inherited Morton & Co.'s furnishing fabric production).[26] The rapid development of dyes between 1890 and 1920 led to brighter and clearer tints, evident in textiles by about 1905.

When F. A. Moreland noted in 1889 that 'the tendency at the present time is toward light furnishing, suggesting more or less the styles of the First Empire', he was noting only one aspect of the trend towards simplicity – the use of clear, often light colours. White or 'old ivory' woodwork and delicately tinted walls and ceilings were an important part

13 An 1898 design by Samuel Rowe, purchased by Turnbull and Stockdale, Lancashire fabric printers who sold their cloths under their own name throughout Britain, as well as through agents and under contract to London shops such as Liberty's and Maple's. Turnbulls were innovative printers and this design, probably for roller printing, suggests the use of a discharge process, since the design is deep red and white (completely bleached red) on a ground of light red (partially bleached red). The curling leaf-ends and flower-tips are typical of 'New Art' designs, and the wide spacing of the motifs made it appropriate for printing on a woven figured ground (which Turnbull's are known to have done with other designs which they manufactured for Liberty's).

of the new lightness, for the textiles themselves could be, but were not necessarily, pale. Moreland, for example, described the festooned drapery in his 'First Empire' room as intended 'to suit the airy tone . . . with [either] floral designs in natural colours, or more subdued colours in silks, brocatelles, etc. . . .'[27] Murkier, richer colours – tending towards browns or purples and with parchment-toned backgrounds, were typical of the Jacobean-style textiles used with darker, heavier woodwork. Even these rooms generally appeared lighter because fitted, single-colour carpeting was becoming popular (aided, no doubt, by the growing availability of vacuum cleaners) and because the domestic use of electric light was spreading.

It was colour, rather more than pattern, that formed the link between British and American Arts and Crafts-style interiors. William Morris's interest in natural dyes had centred on the madder-red, weld-yellow and indigo-blue palette. The influential English writer, Mrs. J. E. Panton, must have had these colours in mind in 1896, when she insisted that 'we cannot possibly have too much real colour, and . . . far from demanding the timid compromises so dear to English folk [excluding, of course, the Arts and Crafts followers], our climate and atmosphere clamour for real sealing-wax reds, deep oranges, clear yellows and beautiful blues.'[28] Candice Wheeler, one of the few American textile designers who can be identified as working in the Arts and Crafts tradition (for mass production) at the turn of the century, also favoured these colours. In *Principles of Home Decoration* (1903), she particularly recommended the virtues of indigo blue denim, which had long had 'its hold on the public use principally for the reason that it possessed a colour superior to all the chances and accidents of its varied life'. Several of her own designs were produced by the indigo discharge method. Stickley's 'Craftsman' canvas ('for a rugged effect') was available in a Morris-inspired range of colours: three tones each of wood-brown and golden-yellow, four shades of red, and a variety of foliage greens and ocean or Delft blues. For curtains Stickley recommended straw-coloured 'antique linen', a loose and coarsely woven cloth made from irregular linen threads 'that takes on almost an apricot tone when the light shines through it, giving the effect of a glow of sunlight in the room'. Gold, red or orange undertones were appreciated for the warmth they imparted to a room, and Wheeler suggested sheer silk curtains in these colours as 'corrective treatment' for a cold, viewless, or north-facing room.[29]

The psychology of colour was now drawn into the discussion of appropriate colour schemes, and also began to be used as an explanation of trends in taste. Commenting on the English upper-class fashion in 1909 for silks in grey, grey-green, grey-blue, heliotrope, purple and 'other shades of a rather quiet and depressing nature', Frank Warner surmised that this was probably due to the fact that 'the country is in a sad, gloomy and unsmiling mood'.[30] It was only the wealthy, in both Britain and the United States, who showed an inclination for very pale, dusty colours in reception rooms. Colour schemes crossed class barriers in bedrooms, however: dimity, lace, embroidery on a natural-coloured cloth or white-ground prints were the most approved choices. White ground prints for the

14 Although by 1890 many considered fully draped interiors unfashionable, they continued to be created and maintained into the first decade of the twentieth century. Photographed in 1894, the parlour in the New York home of Mrs. Leoni contains three shawls and a number of cushions; one close to the piano covered in a Near Eastern embroidery or carpet and two others (covered in what appears to be a silk damask) stacked on the floor in informal, 'Turkish' fashion. The portière – two double-sided, heavily fringed curtains with a simple Arts and Crafts pattern – is looped over a pole and caught up in the centre to create the upper drapery. Note also the 'hat' lampshades, which were often made of silk and chiffon and trimmed with handmade lace. Visible in the bedroom beyond are Venetian blinds, lace curtains and a counterpane with inset bands of drawn threadwork.

bedroom were among the 'gay chintzes' suggested by Elsie de Wolfe. Floral prints and matching wallpapers – a new and fashionable development of the period – were also intended principally for bedrooms.[31]

In 1893, *The Studio* quoted the architect C. F. A. Voysey's plea to 'reduce the variety of patterns and colours in a room'. By the early years of the twentieth century most writers agreed that colour was the first consideration in curtains and that it should follow the colours of the walls, with only one having a pattern (except where the walls were damask, in which case curtains were to be identical). The use of identical fabrics for upholstery and curtains also became more common; when they differed one fabric was generally a single colour. A sense of lightness was also achieved in interiors by removing some of the clutter. In the same 1893 article Voysey recommended, 'Instead of painting boughs of apple trees on our door panels and covering every shelf with petticoats of silk, let us begin by discarding the mass of useless ornaments and banishing the millinery that degrades our furniture and fittings.'[32]

The campaign against clutter had begun in the mid-1880s, and by the 1890s it had spread beyond the small circle of progressive, artistic upper-middle-class writers and decorators to the influential and more broadly based popular magazines. After 1900 the combination of sheer curtains, lace curtains and over-curtains fell from favour, although lace or net curtains were still considered essential in cities. In the country, sheer curtains on their own were preferred, to be combined with heavier curtains only in the winter. Elaborately patterned laces began to go out of fashion, with square-mesh nets and muslins taking their place. Attempts to simplify interiors extended to curtain fittings; cornices, exposed rods and large brass rings were banished by decorators and writers, if not by the general public. Rods were now covered with fabric, hidden by ruffled valances or simply shaped pelmets. Even glass curtains required a heading to cover

15 A block-printed linen manufactured by G. P. & J. Baker in about 1897, this design employs a seven-petal carnation or palmette motif reminiscent of Ottoman patterns of the late sixteenth century, but compressed into bold, flattened shapes in keeping with turn-of-the-century tastes. It has a small repeat – 7 by 3½ inches. The Baker family had trading connections with Turkey throughout the second half of the nineteenth century, and by the late 1870s were importing Turkish goods to London, including carpets, embroideries and other textiles. Their production of this print was a reflection of both their own natural interest in Near Eastern textiles and the more general vogue for such goods, which made commonplace the production of carpet, velvet and embroidery patterns in less expensive printed and woven form.

the rod from which they hung.[33] However, mantelpieces, dressing tables, mirrors, tables, pianos and chair and sofa backs continued to be draped with fabric until the First World War. Photographs from the 1890s and early 1900s indicate the persistence of this fashion, especially in lower-middle-class and working-class homes, where it produced an even more cluttered effect, since the rooms themselves were often small.

'Orientalism', another aspect of the 'Queen Anne' interior, was to blame for one form of clutter which survived in many American and British homes. At the beginning of this period the taste for Eastern patterns was focused on the 'Turkish corner', which evolved in about 1890 out of Queen Anne architecture, with its inglenooks, bay windows and cosy corners. The subsequent creation of these intimate spaces in progressive interiors used free-standing or built-in seating which projected from the wall at right angles and was fitted with loose or fixed cushions. To this somewhat rigid, architectonic concept of 'nook' or 'corner' the popular version added a more inviting 'Turkish' element, initially inspired by the entirely Moorish or Persian rooms of the recent Aesthetic movement and the interest in Near-Eastern textiles for upholstery and portières (which had reached fad proportions by 1890, and included rope and bead portières).

The essence of a 'Turkish corner' was the informal, slightly decadent effect of a completely upholstered space based on a window seat, a flat banquette or a 'Turkish divan' (a deep-buttoned backless couch with one end slightly raised) enriched with throws, mis-matched cushions and, if desired, draperies suspended from the wall or ceiling. Carved wooden grilles were also available to suggest further a division of space; these were often used at upper doors and windows as well. Many 'Turkish corners' (often placed in rooms with entirely different schemes) employed Near-Eastern woven textiles such as old shawls, or new kilims and coarsely embroidered panels; but carpet-patterned chenille, 'Ottoman' velvets and velveteens (with woven, printed or embossed ogee- or pomegranate-based designs), and other pile fabrics served equally well, as did the cotton furniture 'throws' mass-produced with imitation Turkish embroidery specifically for the purpose. This style was popular for day beds (placed, of necessity, against a wall), since – as an American writer pointed out in 1910, 'imitation Baghdad or other suitable couch covers in cotton fabrics are inexpensive, and a row of fancy pillows can be readily made of washable material at slight expense. Thus the entire couch and furnishing may be had at the cost of but a few dollars.'[34]

After about 1900, the Turkish aspect often disappeared, leaving only an entirely covered or upholstered, multi-patterned surface. 'Oriental' (which meant anything east of Germany and south of Italy) was, after all, associated with informality, a principle already established in Europe by the eighteenth century, if not earlier. Thus the careful positioning of two silk cushions on the floor – one on top of the other – in a 'Marie Antoinette' room also signified 'Orientalism' or informality, as did a comfortable overstuffed chair or sofa, particularly when covered in corduroy or a pile fabric.

The Orient was also represented by Chinese patterns, which appeared,

16 Although surface roller-printed by Arthur Sanderson & Sons, as part of their first 'Eton Rural Cretonnes' range in 1921, this design – particularly the 'finger-painted' stripes – is typical of the fashionable printed fabrics being produced in Britain between 1915 and 1920. Its rich colouring is Russian–Oriental in inspiration and suited those who – like the author of the Whitechapel Gallery's catalogue for their 'Exhibition of Household Things' in 1920 – believed that 'fabrics of vivid colour in strong relief are a tonic, and help to brighten a room tremendously'.

shortly after 1905, in a new form, with stylized lanterns, fretwork, and exotic birds printed in dark and bright colours made available by the new, inexpensive chrome and basic dyes. The black grounds so typical of these also soon appeared on chintzes and weaves with more traditional patterns. (The brighter colours were particularly popular in America, where the stronger natural light had already been associated with a preference for stronger colours.) The arrival of the Ballets Russes in Paris, in 1909, and their production of *Scheherazade* in the following year are often credited with launching a radically new Oriental style; but the brightly coloured, informally placed stylized flowers or irregular stripes and kimono-like plaids so characteristic of the new, naïve style, were essentially another facet of the previously established Orientalism. In modern interiors between about 1915 and 1920 these patterns were used with 'classical' furniture to create an informal, urban style and with overstuffed furniture to suggest rural simplicity. The seemingly casual juxtaposition of different patterns (particularly in 'scatter' cushions) was an essential part of this style in both its urban and rural forms. Before 1914, this type of patterning appeared mainly in Viennese and French textiles; and the full impact of the style was not to be seen until after the First World War, by which time the elements of overstuffed comfort, Russian–Oriental colouring and classical furniture shapes had been melded to create a new style.

By 1920 there was a fairly distinctive set of surburban interiors which were still modelled on fashionable themes, but in response to peer-group attitudes rather than those of any superior group. Thus the years between 1890 and 1920 can be seen as a period when styles were sorted out and loosely assigned to different classes; in modern terms, the targeting of specific markets began in earnest. The different strands within 1880s 'Queen Anne' interiors lent themselves to this development. Its element of stylization contributed to the Modernist movement (which remained an exclusive style more noted for its influence than for its use); its appreciation of old fabrics and furniture supported the 'reproduction' furniture industry (essentially a 'tasteful' middle-class style); and it imparted to the working- and lower-middle-classes a taste for pattern and texture (which so powerfully connoted 'richness' that even the most austere decades since have never removed these elements from the working-class home).

The formal or ceremonial associations which aristocratic interiors retained had been found to be something of an anachronism in an age which viewed itself as both unconventional and democratic. Informality – expressed both in the use of rooms (which no longer had such rigidly defined functions) and in their less complex, crowded furnishings – was more appropriate to a world which could no longer maintain such binding rituals as formal calls (for which the parlour was reserved), and keeping children and servants out of sight. The gradual introduction of restraint into textile designs and interiors – both traditional and modern – was sought as early as 1881, when Robert Edis posed the question, 'Why cannot people understand that good taste and simplicity go hand in hand with common sense?' By 1921, when Ethel Davis Seal's book *The House of Simplicity*[35] was published in New York, his plea had been taken to heart.

17

18

19

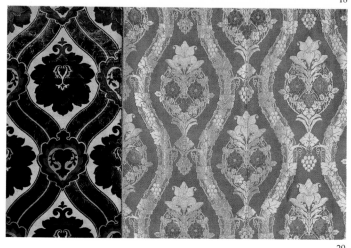

20

21

21 As furniture stores became influential providers of decorating services (as well as the furniture itself), they often issued illustrations of proposed interiors in several price-bands. This medium-priced drawing room, furnished for just over £81, was available from Waring's in 1910. Reproduction Hepplewhite furniture (including, at £43 6s., a 'stuffover settee' and chair covered in printed linen) has been combined with 'modern' cosy corners upholstered in velvet with a figured stripe; the wallpaper coordinates. The velvet curtains have applied borders.

17 Three samples of the same design with both Japanese (fruit blossom) and Arts and Crafts ('damask' ground) motifs, from the production records of the Hamilton Print Works, dated 5 December 1902. The choice of colours – particularly the red and blue backgrounds, also reflects the current vogue for shades of indigo and madder. Part of the Hamilton Manufacturing Company in Lowell, Massachusetts, the print works samples were sold through agents Joy, Langdon & Co.

18 This dining room, exhibited in 1906 by the London furnishings shop Warings, shows how Arts and Crafts-style furnishings were adapted for the early twentieth-century 'Jacobean' interior. The large carpet on a polished wooden floor, the table-runner and the chair with horizontal Eastlake-like banding – all relatively expensive but nevertheless mass-produced – were echoes of more exclusive interiors of ten to twenty years earlier (compare Fig. 2, for example). The matching cosy corner cushion and curtains (with characteristically simple valance) are of a fabric, (probably woven) with a large ogee pattern similar to one seen in Fig. 20.

19 With its continuous coiling stems, conventionalized flower-heads and 'damask' background, this American twilled cretonne, first roller-printed by the Cocheco Manufacturing Company in September 1889, shows the influence of William Morris designs of some five years earlier, an influence that was to continue unabated in the United States until the First World War. This use of British-style designs by Cocheco seems appropriate, since for many years their print works superintendents were British.

20 The nineteenth-century Gothic revival and the Arts and Crafts movement ensured that fifteenth- and sixteenth-century Italian designs remained classic patterns throughout the twentieth century. The examples shown, although made for the 1925 'Art Deco' exhibition in Paris, have pattern types already developed in the previous two decades. On the left is 'Braintree', a silk velvet designed by Bertrand Whittaker and hand-woven with three pile-heights, using a technique patented by Frank Warner in 1914. Whereas 'Braintree' is fairly true to its sixteenth-century antecedents, 'Whitchurch' (a brocade also by Warners) is more fashionably elongated, with 'New Art' elements such as coiling leaf-ends and stylized roses.

22

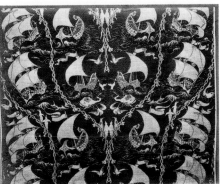

24

22 A design by Sidney Mawson, block-printed by Turnbull & Stockdale in 1911. Including exotic elements such as the pomegranate, this carpet-like design has a border which is unusual both for its narrow width and for its use at this date; except for revived chintzes, borders seldom appeared on prints.

23

23 Designed by Frederick R. Vigers in about 1905, this hand block-printed linen displays naturalistically drawn hedgerow and country-garden flowers which returned to popularity (for both suburban gardens and textile designs) early in the twentieth century (note the meandering line which is subtly suggested by the placement of the red flowers). It was possibly produced for Warners, who wove a Vigers silk damask design in 1904. A member of the Arts and Crafts exhibition society, Vigers was a versatile designer whose work also encompassed embroideries, furniture and wallpapers.

24 'Armada' was one of the first textiles designed by Alec Hunter. A silk damask, exhibited at the 1916 Arts and Crafts Exhibition, it was woven by his father's Letchworth firm, St. Edmundsbury Weavers, which had been founded in Haslemere in 1902. Edmund Hunter had been trained at the Silver Studio, and his firm – one of the new small Arts and Crafts-influenced firms – specialized in hand- and power-woven plain and figured fabrics, including dress silks for Liberty's and lining fabrics for Burberry's. Alec Hunter was to become a prominent designer-weaver after the war. In 1928 he helped to establish Edinburgh Weavers (a subsidiary of Morton Sundour), designing fabrics which were woven in Letchworth, and in 1932 joining Warners, where he remained head of design until his death in 1958.

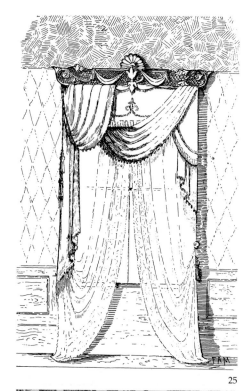

25

26

27

25 Illustrated by Frank A. Moreland in
Practical Decorative Upholstery (Boston, 1889
and 1890), this 'modern flat valance' was
modern by virtue of its asymmetrical over-
drapery; for, according to Moreland, 'flat
valances are things of the past except
when used in connection with festoon
work to heighten its effect.' The suggested
materials were plush with silk over-
drapery, lined or unlined. Although such
festoons were 'intended to convey the idea
that the whole is in one piece and simply
thrown over', Moreland advised that 'this
would be impossible to do except for some
very simple form of drapery in silk or
other reversible goods requiring no
linings'. Similar festoons were also used
over curtain poles. This treatment became
increasingly fashionable as the Art
Nouveau sensibility spread throughout
the 1890s; and it is tempting to think that
many existing valances and poles were
modernized in this way. Similar curtain
designs were still being published in 1914.

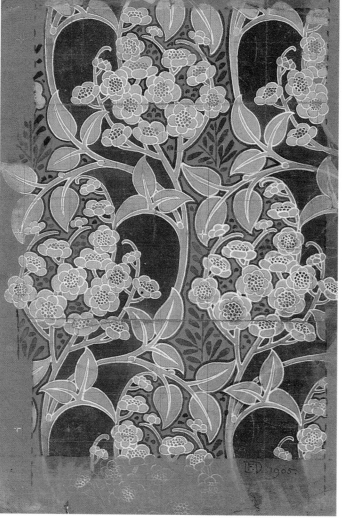

28

26 With peacocks and poppies in 'aesthetic' taste, sinuous lines which anticipate Art Nouveau and a layout based on the c.1760 treatment of a meandering stem, this hand block-printed fabric demonstrates the way in which traditional and new design styles merged in the last two decades of the nineteenth century. It was first produced on a glazed cotton in the mid-1880s and by 1896 was being printed on the then-more fashionable linen (as seen here). The fabric was sold through Warner & Sons (previously Warner & Ramm), and a matching wallpaper was produced by Knowles.

27 A Silver Studio design for a woven textile, or tissue, 1897. The lower green band represents the warp colour, while the two outer vertical bands indicate weft colours used over the entire repeat. The inner vertical band shows a third weft (sometimes called a tissue weft), which changed in colour as the weaving progressed, suggesting a brocaded effect. This design is not entirely successful, since the object was to disguise the presence of the striped third weft. The 'damask'-patterned background, suggesting a broad vertical meander, adds subtle Morris-like variation.

28 A design for an indigo-discharged textile by Lewis F. Day, an extremely successful designer, writer, lecturer and publisher who became artistic director of Turnbull & Stockdale when the firm was founded in 1881. Designed in 1905, when Day was 60, this pattern is a reminder of the long popularity of Morris-like meandering bands with 'damask' patterns. The flattened, stylized flowers are typical of turn-of-the-century designs.

29 Fine, lightweight silks were used in turn-of-the-century 'artistic' homes, often as bedcovers and hangings. This example of a bedcover, hand-block printed by G. P. & J. Baker in about 1895 from a Voysey design of about seven years earlier, was probably sold through Liberty's. The compression of the main flower-heads into a near square was a tendency that increased until about 1905.

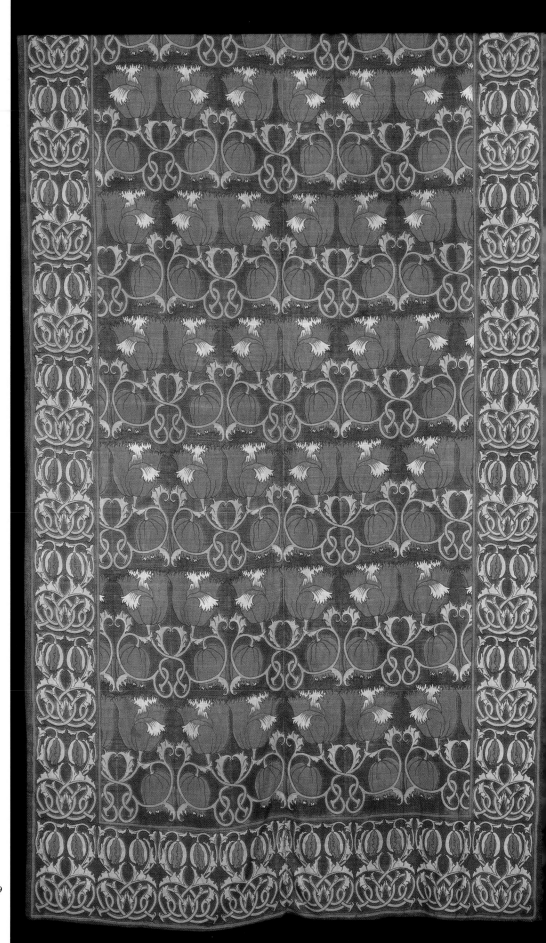

30 When the large London store Whiteley's included these chairs in their 1912 catalogue, there was very little difference in price between printed and woven upholstery fabrics (except silks), and the same type of chairs as shown, if covered in cretonne, cost only about three shillings less. The machine-woven 'tapestry' upholstery cloths shown here range from conservative to 'new art' (lower left) in design. The relatively neutral chair shape could therefore be adapted to interiors of any style by the choice of fabric, a practice still prevalent.

EASY CHAIRS AT POPULAR PRICES.

No. W1516. **Easy Chair** in Tapestry.
£3 5 0

No. W1518. **Easy Chair**, in Tapestry.
£3 15 0

No. W1519. **Easy Chair**, in Tapestry.
£3 18 6

No. W1517. **Easy Chair**, in Tapestry.
£2 19 6

No. W1522. **Easy Chair**, in Tapestry.
£3 10 0

No. W1520. **Easy Chair**, in Tapestry.
£3 2 6

WM. WHITELEY, Ltd., Westbourne Grove and Queen's Road, LONDON, and PARIS.

30

31

31 Between 1890 and 1920, rich colours and bold patterns were often used in textiles intended for interiors with panelling or dark oak furniture. These two fabrics, both hand-woven by Warners in 1914, exhibit both of these qualities ('Knowle', shown full-width on the right, is 56 inches wide). Both are also examples of attempts to economize: 'Cymric' (left) is woven from spun silk (from silk wastes, pierced cocoons or floss) and 'Knowle' is woven in cotton and wool. Compared to silk, the latter two fibres not only were cheaper to buy throughout this period but also, in Britain, cost less to send by rail.

32, 33 The use of real and imitation Turkish or other Near and Far Eastern textiles reached its peak in the 1890s. The stairhall in the Blakely Hall House, 11 West 45th Street, New York (below, photographed in 1896), contains several such fabrics, and the room beyond the stairhall has a fully draped and tented 'Turkish' room. Nevertheless, European textiles were also used, as on the two hall chairs and the couch cushions. Noteworthy are the two panels made from five coarsely woven and embroidered bands sewn together, one used as a half-visible portière on the left and the other used to cover a 'Turkish' couch. Inexpensive imitations of these panels were also available; the example shown above is a reversible machine-woven cotton, produced in the United States at the turn of the century.

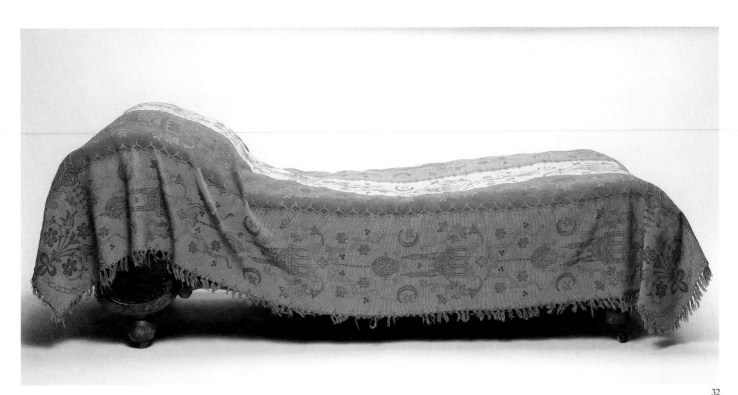

32

33

35 Taken from an Arnold Print Works pattern book, this sample, dated 5 September, 1911, was manufactured exclusively for S. M. Schwab. Based in North Adams, Massachusetts, Arnold's produced both dress and furnishing prints. The example shown here is a furnishing fabric, with the 6-inch-high four-colour design roller-printed onto a cloth woven with a black warp and pink weft. It typifies manufacturers' attempts to create elaborate surface treatments which gave the finished cloth a handmade or antique appearance.

36 Isolated Persian and Indian floral patterns such as these had been illustrated by Owen Jones in *The Grammar of Ornament* and had been printed on tussore silk by Thomas Wardle and sold through Liberty's from the late 1870s. This block-printed cotton was produced by G. P. & J. Baker in or shortly after 1893, when Baker's acquired the Swaisland Printing Company in Crayford, near London. The selvage indicates that it was produced for Heal & Son, the influential London shop which shared a Tottenham Court Road address with several other major furnishings stores. The design itself shows the approved form of floral patterns, with evenly spaced conventionalized motifs (based on the general principles of a flower or leaf shape, but not on any specific, variable detail).

35

36

37

38

37 Aymer Vallance noted in one of his frequent contributions to Britain's *Art Journal* (1892) that light-coloured fabrics were suitable for the country – notably 'fresh and homely . . . old fashioned white dimity' – whereas smoky towns required cloths with patterns that would not show the dirt. His comments reflect the growing perception of the character of fabrics (as opposed to their actual use) as suggestive of 'country' or 'city'. Thus, this white painted, pastel-toned bedroom, designed by the British architect M. H. Baillie Scott, is designated as for a 'country cottage', meaning a large house in vernacular style. (Compare Fig. 56, a city bedroom.) Illustrated in *The Studio* (vol. XXV, 1902), it contains curtains, bed furnishings and a cosy corner cushion which are embroidered or, possibly, stencilled.

39

40

38 This student's room at Barnard College, New York, was photographed in 1901. Out of her bed and what is probably a trunk, she has created a 'Turkish corner', employing a machine-woven counterpane and at least fourteen cushions. Note also the 'Turkish' table and coffee urn.

39, 40 A comparison between Walter Crane's illustration from his *Beauty and the Beast*, 1873–4, and one sofa from Lord Brabourne's suite of twenty pieces, shows the close relationship between the Empire style as imagined in the 1870s and the neo-Empire style of twenty to forty years later. The furniture itself dates from c.1830, but some fifty years elapsed before the painted and gilt finish was added. In 1913 it was re-upholstered with the black-ground English silk upholstery fabric (with a design first produced in 1874). Such dramatic interpretations of neo-Empire styles contributed to a fashion that eventually became known as Art Deco.

41 Between 1890 and 1920, the overriding influence in interiors was the neo-classicism of a century before. Even completely different types of interiors – from elaborately draped 1890s boudoirs to architect-designed 1900s built-in furniture – had common antecedents, as this plate (dated 1794) from Thomas Sheraton's *Drawing Book* shows.

42 This parlour in the George Grey residence, in Stockton, California, photographed c.1890, shows a lavish use of controlled Empire-revival drapery which preceded and coexisted with more asymmetrical 'thrown over' arrangements (see Fig. 43). The window and door draperies each differ from each other in detail, although each appears to be made from the same material and employs identical fringe. The presence of the low Turkish chair and the carved grille just visible above the doorway are fashionable references to the East.

41

42

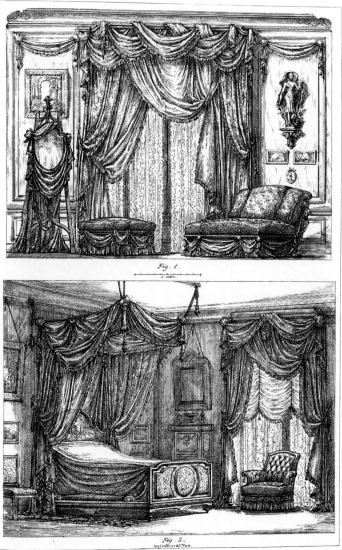

43

43 Felix Lenoir's 1890 *Treatise* (see also Fig. 52, Chapter 4) included decorative schemes in a number of historical styles, but, like the two 'Louis XVI' interiors shown here, all were equally overwhelmed by asymmetrically arranged drapery. For the bay window (Fig. 1) Lenoir suggested two different fabrics (one plain, one figured) for upholstery and windows, the latter with an additional pattern provided by the lace curtains. Three curtains also appear in the bedroom, the centre one of which was now referred to as an 'Austrian shade'. The bed, draped 'à l'antique', was fully upholstered, with stuffed and embroidered head- and foot-boards. Only the lack of buttoning on the 'Turkish' seating in the bay window gives evidence of the more restrained treatment of 'historical' interiors which was soon to come.

44 These five heavily glazed English roller prints of 1905–10 are typical of small scale neo-Georgian patterns of the period, and were often called 'Manchester chintzes' because of the concentration of roller-printers in and around that city. Soft but clear tones were typical of these chintzes, and each design had another colourway which substituted lilac for deep pink. Note the shading on the right-hand piece, which was produced by very fine gradations in the depth of the engraving. All were produced for Warners.

45 This 1911 Silver Studio sketch for a block-printed cotton bedspread shows the ground and one corner of the border. Featuring rosebuds and ribbons, it was probably intended for use in a room furnished with floral chintzes, such as those seen in Fig. 44. Machine-embroidered bedcovers were available in similar designs and were popular substitutes for their more expensive hand-embroidered counterparts.

44

45

46 Canon Valpy, a member of the Chapter of Winchester Cathedral and a man of considerable means, lived at 3, The Close, Winchester, with his wife and a full complement of servants. His drawing room, captured in watercolours by B. O. Corfe in about 1900, typifies the more ordered form of classicism that had begun to appear in wealthy homes about ten years earlier. Furniture, predominantly from the eighteenth century, is grouped together with seating loose-covered in what is probably a hand-block printed chintz. The simply made sets of damask and lace curtains do not impede the entry of midsummer light and air, nor do they have any upper draperies to compete with the carved coving. Edith Wharton and Ogden Codman Jr., whose *Decoration of Houses* (1897) promoted a similarly restrained style in America, would, one feels, have approved.

46

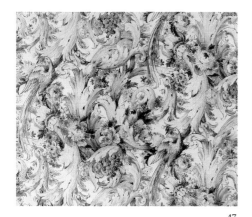

47

47 This 1914 design for a printed textile was worked in pencil and crayon by Herbert Crofts of the Silver Studio. It demonstrates the high level of draughtsmanship expected of studio designers, who could readily turn from modern to traditional patterns. Both this and Fig. 9 show the continued taste for coiling acanthus leaves popularized in more austere form by William Morris.

48 As illustrated by 'After the Meeting', an oil of 1914 by the American artist Cecilia Beaux, traditional patterns and methods of using fabrics not only survived the reform and 'aesthetic' movements' influence but also were returned to popularity with the new classicism of the turn of the century. Here the loose cover of chintz – probably hand-block printed – has employed a design of the mid-nineteenth century which is coloured according to early twentieth-century taste.

48

51

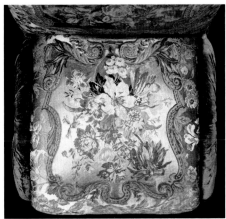

52

49 The new classicism of 1890–1920 assisted the silk industry, since it renewed the appreciation of lustrous surfaces. Among the hand-loom Jacquard-woven silks, one of the most favoured patterns throughout the period was derived from brocades of 1755–65. Extremely expensive, they nevertheless found buyers in both the United States and Britain. In particular, many London townhouses (in their last period of social and decorative importance) were decorated in similar, so-called Louis XVI silks. The same silks were used in fashionable evening dresses in the late 1880s and 1890s, suggesting that their revival owed much to the popularity of fancy-dress balls, for which original eighteenth-century gowns were often altered or entirely remade. This example was woven in 1920 by Warners.

50 This 'baronial' room set in the New York store W. & J. Sloane, 1902, shows a set of furniture upholstered in what is probably machine-made woollen tapestry. Linens printed with similar patterns could be obtained at lower cost, and were more typical in suburban interiors, in which could be found similar furniture in less ornate style. A tantalizing glimpse of a neo-classical room set on the left, and an Art Nouveau room on the right, are a reminder that furniture shops and department stores were exercising growing control over the decoration of interiors and yet, at the same time, were seldom willing to promote a single, preferred style.

51 Opulent grandeur such as this is often associated with late Victorian and Edwardian interiors – and with reason, for it was not uncommon in the American and British houses that were built or redecorated during this period by the extremely rich. Completed in 1905, this ballroom in Manderston, then the Berwickshire home of Sir James and Lady Miller, is furnished entirely with silks. The curtains, a Warners hand Jacquard-loom-woven silk tissue with gold and silver threads, was based on a fifteenth-century Italian textile, whereas the upholstery fabrics are all eighteenth century in style. The walls are covered in a silk brocatelle, its design also based on eighteenth-century (c.1730) patterns. This type of classical-revival interior was emulated by those who were less affluent but nevertheless had incomes large enough to make them 'comfortable'; lightweight power-woven silk damask for wall panels, for example, was provided by many furnishing and decorating firms, and power-woven upholstery fabrics were available in similar styles, but with less expensive yarns, such as cottons and worsteds, wholly or partly replacing the silks (see Fig. 52).

52 While printed fabrics revived French eighteenth-century patterns in greatly simplified form, many woven fabrics of 1890–1920 continued to employ much more elaborate 'eighteenth-century' designs, such as this example, covering a 1907 pillowback chair from the Voight House in Grand Rapids, Michigan. The silk and worsted machine-made 'tapestry', probably produced in Philadelphia, was intended to suggest either real tapestry (in style it is French, c.1860) or richly hand-brocaded silks which were also available from American firms such as Schumacher. Fabrics which alluded to French styles were generally in light, sweet colours – in this case the predominant tone was peach. The side rolls of silk-pile velvet were typical of padded edges added to fully upholstered furniture during this period.

53 Freely drawn, broad outlines often appeared on printed textiles between 1890 and 1920, adding a flattened, stylized appearance to floral designs even when, as here, they are fairly naturalistically drawn. This block-printed linen of about 1918, sold by an unidentified American firm, has a background of narrow stripes (which had been popular since about 1905); in the years around the First World War many similar designs were printed on a black ground.

54 A printed textile design by Harry Napper, sold through the Silver Studio in 1918 to the British manufacturers Simpson & Godlee, who in the 1880s had block-printed avant-garde patterns such as those which A. H. Mackmurdo and Herbert Horne had designed for The Century Guild. Reflecting a similar shift in design tendencies, Napper – well known at the turn of the century for 'New Art' designs (see Fig. 3) – turned to a more naturalistic form of stylization in the 1910s, as demonstrated in this pattern. Note especially the broad, loosely drawn outlines, a dominant theme in textiles and other decorative arts throughout the first quarter of the twentieth century.

55 In 1907 George Mann Niedecken founded a Milwaukee interior design firm, Niedecken-Walbridge, and about five years later he produced this ink and watercolour scheme for the Armin A. Schlesinger residence. In its blend of traditional and modern elements (in this case sixteenth- and eighteenth-century classicism and the American Arts and Crafts style), it epitomizes the comfortable yet stylish simplicity which decorators from the United States contributed to many twentieth-century interiors. (Niedecken's interior designs were also commissioned by Frank Lloyd Wright, and they married well with the principles set down by Frank Alvah Parsons [in *Interior Decoration*, New York, 1915], founder of the Parsons School of Design.) Later to become known as a mural painter, Niedecken probably intended to execute the frieze, elements of which are echoed in the carpet and fabric borders. The plainly covered, modernized 'Hepplewhite' wing chair and sofa and the 'Sheraton' desk chair may have come from W. & J. Sloane, New York, one of several of Niedecken's sources of ready-made furniture that, in keeping with the decorative ideals of the period, advertised reproduction pieces as handmade in the best traditions of the cabinet-maker's art.

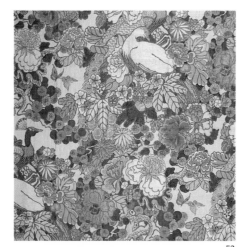

53

54

55

56

57

56 An exotic note has been added to a simply furnished British bedroom by the use of woven curtains and a bedspread in 'Oriental' colours. Produced between about 1910 and 1914, these cloths were manufactured in England by William Foxton, whose firm, founded in 1903, specialized in artist-designed prints and weaves. The cottage-style furniture was available from firms such as Heal's.

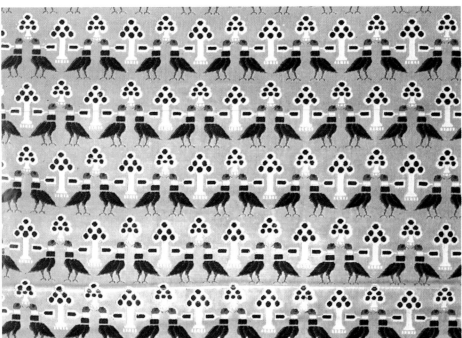

58

59

60

57 Periods dominated by historical styles often create 'new' designs which unconsciously contain undertones of the revived fashion. In this hand-block printed cretonne (unglazed medium-weight cotton), the vivid colours (possibly printed in chrome dyes), the seemingly casually drawn and rendered outlines, and the exotic flowers and birds reflect the Russian–Oriental style of 1910–20, when this fabric was produced. Yet its design is actually remarkably close to the 'arborescent' printed textile patterns of 1760–80, when similarly gnarled branches with irrationally mixed 'Indienne' blooms and birds were fashionable. So this fabric is not really at odds with the pretty pastel prints of the 1910s, which were obvious revivals of mid- to late eighteenth-century patterns.

58 The bright 'Oriental' colouring of this British roller print of about 1918 had become increasingly fashionable throughout the 1910s. Many such colours were produced with the recently extended range of basic (or coal tar) synthetic dyes, which required a tannic acid mordant when printed on cotton, and produced particularly brilliant colours which faded when washed or exposed to light.

59 This handwoven silk velvet and terry, produced by Warners in 1915, employs confronting birds characteristic of many textiles of the fifteenth century and earlier. However, its rigid arrangement, small scale and sombre colouring align it with avant-garde Austrian designs of 1908–15.

60 'The Best Bedroom of Hampton's Ideal Home Exhibit' at Olympia, in London, 1920. Despite the Chinese lampshades and the Russian–Oriental colouring of the curtains and upholstery, this bedroom is described as Jacobean, because of the ladder-back chair, casement window, ceiling cross-beam and Hampton's simple wooden furniture with 'Jacobean' barley-twist legs. The furnishing fabric is a printed cretonne with a fashionable black ground. Made to suggest sixteenth- or early seventeenth-century crewelwork, bedcovers such as shown were machine chain-stitched, printed or hand-embroidered. (Hand-embroidered textiles were one of the most persistant legacies of the Arts and Crafts movement.) Note also the absence of pattern on the carpet and walls, save the decorative border.

BRITISH
ACHIEVEMENT
IN
DESIGN

Chapter Six

Contrast and Variety

1920–1950

'Which do you want – a contrast between curtains and coverings, or to have them both the same? Usually contrast and variety are the most pleasing to the eye in a lasting way.'
(Mary Shaw, in *Buying For Your House: Furnishing Fabrics No. 1*[1])

1 An interest in the 'primitive' underlines many of the textile designs produced between 1920 and 1950, whether Oriental, African or European in inspiration, textural or figurative in interpretation. Spanning the decade between 1936 and 1946 are these five furnishing fabrics, one of which (top left) exemplifies the Rural Industries Bureau's efforts to revive the floundering and often antiquated Welsh woollen mills. Designed by Marianne Straub c.1936 and sold by Gordon Russell Ltd., this woollen double cloth was woven by Holywell Mills until after the war. The remaining four fabrics typify the peasant-art style and the revival of figurative weaves in the 1940s. Continuing clockwise they are 'Framlingham', by Olga Forbat, a Warners cotton gimp and rayon tissue, 1946; 'Bird and Vase', a cotton damask by Heal's, 1944; 'Songster', a Warners hand-screen-printed linen, 1944 and 'Roundabout', by Warners' staff designer Albert Swindells, a cotton and rayon tissue, 1946. The Heal's fabric was also produced into the mid-1950s. (Note the absence of wool in the woven cloths designed in the 1940s.)

If the textile industry were to be imagined as a human being, it could be described during this era as having reached its thirties – having left the intensity of young adulthood behind it around 1915. Hard knocks, considerable success and greater experience had given a cautious edge to its willingness to experiment; and although many manufacturers were responsive to fashion, they were at the same time somewhat wary of it. A similar contradictory current ran through decorative schemes. This was the era of interiors that ranged from the scholarly to the surrealistic – on the surface very different from each other. But the impulses that led, on the one hand, to witty revivals and, on the other, to suburban modernity were the same: the need for order, simplicity, convenience, comfort and – in most cases – economy. These very domestic requirements moderated the 'jazz age' styles and made historically based interiors less overpowering than they might otherwise have been.

The effect was far from bland. Despite the economic traumas of the period – or perhaps to counteract them – the prevailing styles were offhand, charming, relaxed or confident, never too earnest. Shortly after the end of the First World War an American writer summarized the prevailing attitude to traditional decoration in his comment on choosing fabrics, stating that 'it is not obligatory to limit ourselves slavishly to the designs and materials of the particular period, provided there is no incongruity.' By 1946 the advice of Dan Cooper (an American designer and manufacturer) was bolder: 'Never buy sets of furniture. They give the effect of oppressive monotony.'[3] Throughout this period it was variety and contrast in style, texture, colour or pattern that dominated, whether creating stylishness out of economy or providing a backdrop for sophisticated ease.

The Wall Street Crash of 1929 was the last in a series of events which set the tone for the years encompassed by the two World Wars. Wall Street had already shaken in 1907, after which prices had begun to rise. Philadelphia manufacturers of woven textiles, for example, increased their prices by 10–40 per cent in that year. British exports of prints (always a good indication of the stability of the industry as a whole) began to fluctuate downwards. With the outbreak of the war, yarns for furnishing fabrics, especially woollens, were in short supply, and access to German dyestuffs was cut off. Prices soared – and not only those of textiles. By 1920 the cost of living in Britain and the United States was roughly twice that of 1910.

The events of 1910–20 established two significant and related changes in the way textiles were made and purchased. At the turn of the century, department stores, upholsterers and furniture manufacturers had held stocks of fabrics. As costs rose they tended to order smaller amounts, but more frequently. This trend was briefly reversed in the 1919–21 postwar 'boom', when both retailers and manufacturers paid high prices to build up their depleted stock and satisfy the demand for fabrics. However, when the buying spree ended abruptly in 1921, prices dropped and textiles were sold at a loss. Few retailers thereafter were prepared to take risks; rapid turnover became the goal, and many of them requested samples and no more, unless a customer placed an order. In the long run, this forced manufacturers away from the middle ground – variously priced fabrics, economically produced in various amounts – to a reliance on a narrower range of cloths, all made at more or less the same cost. In the short term, new, fashionable designs were most affected by this trend, since both consumers and manufacturers became more conservative.

Large runs of fabrics were the most economical, but these could be supported only by guaranteed (or at least fairly assured) trade. Britain's printers in 1907 had this kind of trade in their export cloths, which included specialized fabrics such as machine-printed batiks. Although the latter were produced for Africa, some found their way into avant-garde shops, including Roger Fry's Omega, which in its short life (1913–19) sold mainly a wide range of artist-designed items, including hand-painted and commercially made fabrics. (Batiks made by hand were also available from artist-designers in Britain and the United States well into the 1920s.) Limited amounts of other Third World export cloths also found their way into the Western market. Following a fairly steady decline, by 1933 Britain's export sales had declined by nearly 90 per cent, crippling its printing industry and removing its somewhat fortuitous contribution to the variety of designs available at a reasonable cost.

In contrast, American manufacturers fared better, benefitting from their nation's much larger population, chain stores and mail-order businesses; low-cost, high-volume production increased during the 1910s and '20s, particularly in the new mills being established in the South. Nevertheless, competitive prices were often more important than designs, which tended to be simplified copies of well-established, conservatively styled, higher-priced fabrics or a continuation of once-popular patterns and colours. In this climate the introduction of new designs progressed more slowly, as became apparent during the brief economic reprieve of the second

2 Both designed in 1925, 'Decima' (top, spun silk and rayon) and 'Peterson' (below, cotton and rayon) were woven by Warners. They typify the attempts to economize that were being made by firms that had traditionally woven silk fabrics. 'Peterson' was one of a dozen cloths that the firm exhibited at the 'Art Deco' exhibition in Paris.

3 This early 1930s design, by John Churton of the Silver Studio, employs whirring lines which owed much to French modern and Russian Constructivist art of the period. It was intended for production as a woven cloth, which compared to prints used more purely abstract patterns.

building boom in 1924 and 1925, when, according to *Modern Interiors Today and Tomorrow*, 'New [American] houses were being rapidly filled with the same taupe-mohair, three-piece, overstuffed suites which had pocked the face of America for more than a decade.' Cheap, over-elaborate, and poorly constructed, the worst of these were known in the trade as 'borax' or 'Bronx Renaissance'.[4]

Both the Americans and the British were made very conscious of their conservatively patterned mass-produced textiles by the *Exposition Internationale des Arts Décoratifs et Industriels Modernes*, held in Paris in 1925. The exhibition gave its name (in retrospect) to Art Deco, the Russian-Oriental-French-'Empire' style. The Americans declined to exhibit, believing they had nothing modern to show (which was not true). The British participated, but only in a limited way. One reason for their caution was that they had just expended a great deal of energy and money in 1924 on the British Empire Exhibition at Wembley. In addition, they recognized that such large international exhibitions were essentially trade fairs through which countries tried to increase their exports, and many British manufacturers saw little hope of extending their sales in France.

Although it had the impact of a new style when shown at the Paris exhibition, Art Deco was really the culmination of the Empire-modern style, which had been built upon the prewar fashion for Orientalism (expressed literally in lacquer, fringed lantern-like lampshades and standing screens, and metaphorically in high colour, well-padded shapes and artfully scattered cushions). The Empire element prevailed only in the shape of Art Deco furniture, which by 1925 had become more bulbous, the rounded shapes occasionally counter-balanced by an angled edge. Many textile designs showed the same inclinations, with motifs stylized into circles and set against squares or into overlapped, angled planes.

It was the increased angularity and abstraction that was perceived as new, although in textile designs this had already been seen in the products of England's Omega Workshops, in the Egyptian motifs briefly fashionable in the years around the opening of Tutankhamun's tomb in 1922 and in the 'revolutionist' textiles from the Soviet Union. Despite the American government's view that the United States had nothing new to offer in 1925, abstract patterns had been developed as part of the campaign to create an indigenous style based on 'primitive' objects in American museums. Between 1916 and 1922 this led to designs based on African and Peruvian textiles and pottery, American Indian sand paintings, and Southwestern basketry and pottery. Patterns with stepped or jagged edges, abstract symbols or geometric motifs were produced by hand techniques such as batik, or made available by a limited number of American manufacturers, such as H. R. Mallinson, Belding Brothers and Cheney Brothers. Just after the war, some of these American fabrics were exported to London and Paris, where they contributed to the growing interest in abstract 'cubist' patterns.[5]

As interpreted in the design of interiors, the Art Deco style also remained consistent with some of the prewar trends. Curtains, for example, continued to be straight-hanging, although many now fell beyond the

4 A 'modified classical' living room, first suggested to Americans in the 1929 edition of Thorne and Frohne's *Decorative Draperies and Upholstery*. The curtains, showing an existing fabric, are of linen printed in modern or Art Deco style. The green velvet upholstery was also proposed for other furniture, with the addition of deep purple or ultramarine blue. Note the neo-classical 'draped' details: the upper supports to the wrought-iron tables, and the metal cornice and frieze. The latter two were to be finished in 'verde antique' green or made from carved wood and finished in a metallic colour. (Ironic elements such as these became part of 'traditional-modern' interiors, particularly the baroque-modern style more prevalent in the 1930s.) The 'Nefertiti' vase is a reminder of the recent vogue for Egyptian decorative details.

windowsill to the floor, as the emphasis returned to the vertical. Gathered valances also remained popular as an informal style; rigid pelmets were used in more formal settings. Often the latter were of wood, either painted the colour of the walls or covered with fabric. In the most modern interiors such pelmets were used to disguise light fittings placed above windows.

The decorative potential of electric light was an important focus of attention throughout this period. Its more uniform illumination and comparative lack of colour 'flattened' surfaces that had once been enriched by shadows. Expensive modern furniture offset this flattening with reflective surfaces – lacquer, veneer, marble or glass – while fabrics contributed much-needed richness to a room – either through bold patterns or through subtle shifts in colour. Many writers and decorators recommended fabric-covered walls or panels, in agreement with an American writer who, in 1926, proposed that 'all background surfaces should reveal a marked effect of texture . . . because large areas of flat color are not only tiresome and unbeautiful in themselves, but also totally unsympathetic backgrounds for the people and things that appear against them'.[6]

In its pure form, Art Deco was an expensive, luxurious and international style – deliberately outrageous in both cost and effect. It appeared in a very limited number of homes in Europe and the Americas. Many of the fabrics for these interiors were exported from France; in New York, for example, they were available from stores such as B. Altman, Wanamaker, Stern Brothers and Arnold Constable, or directly from the Bianchini-Ferrier or Ducharne branches opened there in 1923. French designs were also available from American manufacturers: Cheney Brothers, for example, maintained their own studio in Paris during the 1920s, and from 1926 Schumacher produced designs by prominent participants at the Art Deco exhibition, such as Henri Stéphany. For the handful of British who required them, French fabrics and designs were also available in Britain.

When finally adopted in 1927–28 as a mass-produced style (mainly for prints), Art Deco did not differ significantly from the previous 'modern' style, relying principally on the addition of areas of geometric patterns to the background, creating a busy, 'jazzy' effect. Although the popular press and the public greeted these fabrics enthusiastically, others such as the influential writer and critic, Nikolaus Pevsner, had reservations. Because the French had dominated the Art Deco exhibition, they were able to claim as their own the bold, flattened, and often naïvely drawn motifs which in truth owed a great deal to Austria, Germany, Russia, Britain and the United States. Having skilfully appropriated all the modern styles as their own, the French presented a problem for American and British design critics and manufacturers alike. The wide publicity afforded the exhibition (and the display of some of the pieces in New York soon afterwards) promoted an interest in modern design, but continuing nationalistic sentiments (and the desire to extend exports) demanded that each country have its own style.

As a result, there were a number of distinct modern trends, none of which succeeded in becoming identified with one particular country until after the Second World War. There was Empire-modern (already passé by about 1927 but still popular ten years later), baroque-modern, streamlined-modern and rustic-modern, as well as new interpretations of overtly historical and nationalistic themes. Many of these styles overlapped each other in their use of colour or pattern and in their repudiation of the new aesthetic of Functionalism, which emphasized practical utility and the exclusion of ornament. Eventually identified as the 'serious' modern style and associated with the German Bauhaus (a design school which existed from 1919 to 1933) functionalism played only a very small role in British and American interiors in the 1920s and '30s.

In keeping with the contradictory nature of this period, interiors described as 'modern' could contain antique, reproduction or entirely new furniture and textiles. Although novel styles were developed throughout this period, the interpretation of traditional themes was far more prevalent and revealed much more about the changing attitudes and circumstances of both the 'new poor' and the 'still rich'.

Of lasting importance to traditionally styled textiles was the heightened interest in American furniture, which had been slowly growing since the 1870s. This culminated in the opening of the Metropolitan Museum's American Wing in 1924, the restoration of Colonial Williamsburg, begun in 1926 by John D. Rockefeller, and, by 1931, the existence of period rooms in museums in Boston, Philadelphia, Brooklyn, Baltimore and St. Louis. The private collections of Henry Francis du Pont and Francis P. Garvan, already substantial by the late 1920s, were later to become the great teaching collections at Winterthur (Delaware) and Yale, respectively. These and other private collections contributed to a new approach to scholarship – which considered objects within their cultural context as well as in relation to twentieth-century taste. Because they were also the furnishings of wealthy homes, such collections gave impetus to a new

5 A 'simple but smart' scheme for a 'new poor' cottage interior of the 1920s and '30s from *Decorative Draperies and Upholstery*. The painted woodwork, mid-nineteenth-century patterned chintz, and ruffles typified this tyle. Note the shirred inset panel of the loose cover. The curtains have been designed for use with in-swinging windows, so the valance is in two sections.

6 Described by Derek Patmore in *Colour Schemes for the Modern Home* (London, 1933) as an illustration of how the clever use of fabrics can modernize and decorate a period room, this morning room by the British decorator John Hill has swagged pelmets and curtains of white satin, the latter stencilled with a large abstract leaf design, which, like many of the first hand-screen-printed textiles, has limited colour and detail. Both the curtains and sheer under curtains puddle on the floor, in keeping with the Regency flavour of the pelmet. The solid-coloured antique wing chairs are modernized with fringed piping. The modern armchair, with what may be a loose cover, employs a woven fabric probably designed by Marion Dorn, an influential American designer working in England in the 1920s and '30s.

'Americana' style. At the same time, the need for appropriate furnishing fabrics for such rooms generated an academic interest in historic textiles, which laid the foundation for subsequent research.

The interest in American antiques also underpinned a 'rural' revival, which was a godsend to the 'new poor', since it relied for effect, as Ethel Davis Seal noted, on 'such ancient simplicities as field-beds dressed in calico, wayside antiques, new rooms from old pine, and early American spindles and chintzes'.[7] Prominent features of this style were painted farmhouse furniture, rag rugs, Windsor chairs and Victorian-style chintzes or cottons printed with birds, flowers or foliage in modern colour ranges (such as soft orange, rose, yellow and turquoise on a grey ground). Ginghams, plaids, stripes, toiles and muslin were particularly popular, since they had been identified as authentic early American fabric types. As evident in 1920 as it was in 1950, the hallmark of 'early American character' was the use of ruffles on loose covers, dressing tables, bedspreads and curtains (the last three often given double or triple ruffles), followed closely by scalloped, piped edges for window, dressing table and bed valances. (Bedcovers tended to extend half-way to the floor and therefore had two valances: the gathered side of the bedcover itself and another beneath it attached to the mattress.) The dressing of tent beds with a ruffle-edged canopy and no curtains seems also to have originated out of this style.

Certain aspects of the rural style were part of the American 'decorator' style. Chintzes, toiles and canopied beds for example, were often used by Elsie de Wolfe, Ruby Ross Wood, Rose Cumming, Elinor McMillen Brown and Dorothy Draper. However, the 'decorator' style differed from the rural style in its Anglo–European tastes; the 'found' objects were not farmhouse pieces, but fine antiques, many procured from the large European houses whose contents were dispersed during and after the

First World War and for which sympathetic surroundings had to be created. And the traffic was not all one-way, for the Americans continued to contribute to the British interpretation of traditional interiors. There were two distinct sides to the American influence. The first and older one was described in 1882 by Mrs. Haweis as being 'less posé than French taste, more subtle than English. The prevailing impression of the house is softness, refinement, harmony. There is nothing bizarre or eccentric, to startle and . . . annoy.'[8] The second American contribution was the new 'found' style, which could be classed as eccentric in its juxtaposition of modern and antique fabrics and furniture.

The more established American approach was already part of the English country-house style. Houses treated in this manner received scholarly sympathy; they were not expected to look new – the aim, rather, was to restore life and at the same time achieve comfort. The 'new' American style was more radical. In the hands of the British decorator Ronald Fleming, for example, it resulted in eighteenth-century armchairs covered in plain red American cloth (a waterproofed cotton).[9] Together the two styles shared credit for the introduction of the square-cushioned simply-shaped modern sofa into traditional interiors, where it remains prominent today. In country houses its cover was silk damask or chintz loose covers; in McMillen Brown rooms it was often covered in a modern-style fabric, while period pieces had appropriate traditional cloths. Fleming's room with the red chairs was accompanied by this type of sofa, covered in natural holland piped with scarlet.

Fleming's interior had been created for publication in British *Vogue*, which in both its fashion illustrations and features on interiors promoted the contrast of new and old furnishings.[10] Regency furniture was often used in this way, particularly after 1924, when Edward Knoblock had displayed his black-and-gold Thomas Hope furniture in the '1815' room at the Wembley exhibition. Knoblock, an American, had acquired his taste for this style while living in Paris shortly before the war, and was one of a handful who appreciated early nineteenth-century furniture. His Hope collection had been purchased in 1917 from the auction of the contents of The Deepdene in Surrey, and although he created sympathetic surroundings for them, many of the other readily available Regency pieces were incongrously placed in sparsely furnished, white-walled rooms in conjunction with modern sculpture, paintings, rugs and furniture.

Regency furniture was not alone in being rediscovered in this period. In the early 1920s there was also a renewed interest in baroque art, but it was not until the mid-1930s that its decorative features influenced interiors. The so-called 'baroque-modern' style shared with the original baroque its inherent extravagance, but was often otherwise devoid of any antique or reproduction furniture.

Both the scholarly and the innovative approaches to traditional interiors made use of old fabrics. Many of the textiles now at Winterthur, for example, were acquired as 'stock' for re-upholstery. Nancy Tree (the American who, after the Second World War, purchased the London decorating firm Sybil Colefax Ltd. from Lady Colefax) made good use of

7 Sybil Colefax's first-floor showroom at 24 Bruton Street, London (photographed c.1938, shortly after she had been joined by John Fowler) is shown decorated in the 'Vogue Regency' style. Typical of the style, for which Fowler was to become known, is the contrasting fringe on the drapery, also used as tie-backs, and the window covering made of chintz simulating a Venetian blind, the pattern adapted from a design of about 1840. Fowler had similar faux-blinds in his own home and continued to use this pattern for a number of years, even hand painting it on plain cloth when supplies ran out during the Second World War.

8 In October 1928, *Furnishings* (U.K.) lamented the existence of the 'salesman in the soft furnishing department [who] picks up a little about "Old needlework", some smattering of "Louis", and the rest is slumped together under that most convenient and horribly misused term, "Jacobean"', despite the fact that fabrics showing 'the real spirit of the handworkers of one to three hundred years ago' could be obtained. One such fabric, shown here in detail, is a linen weft and silk warp damask sold by Messrs. Cowtan & Sons Ltd. in May 1927 for 50 shillings. The linen weft has been allowed to show through to suggest some antiquity. Cowtan's, one of a number of nineteenth-century London cabinet-makers who extended their business to all aspects of interior decoration, had taken over Crace & Son in 1899. The order and pattern books of Cowtan's from 1824 to 1938 are in the Prints and Drawings Department of the Victoria & Albert Museum.

old fabrics, both for her bed at Kelmarsh Hall, Northamptonshire (made by Mrs. Guy Bethell – herself an influential decorator) and at Ditchley Park, Oxfordshire, where the furnishings included original early nineteenth-century bed hangings and newly installed old fabrics supplied and made into curtains by the Paris firm, Jansen.[11] In the 1920s old fabrics were (observed *The House Beautiful Furnishing Annual*) 'procurable, in better or worse states of preservation, and, in the case of those of the seventeenth and eighteenth centuries, in some numbers'. Besides considering them 'effective in combination with good modern fabrics', an American writer noted that 'they usually must be so used; for it is difficult and costly to get sufficient old material in good condition to hang an entire room or even to make a set of draperies.'[12]

The interest in antique fabrics led, as in the past, to reproductions. Some were so good that the *House Beautiful* writer quoted above also felt obliged to warn readers that 'it is best to take care . . . if you purchase seventeenth-century damask, that you do not pay too much for merely a fine modern reproduction', adding shrewdly that 'the difference lies more in the texture than in design or even in colour' (a new silk has a 'brisk' feeling which diminishes with age). Block prints could also be deceptive, since many were produced in the 1920s and '30s from blocks originally cut fifty to eighty years earlier. Here again, the handle was the crucial difference – few could appreciate the very stiff glaze applied to nineteenth-century chintzes.

The taste for old fabrics (real or reproduction) stimulated some textile manufacturers to create new fabrics that seemed to have acquired the patina of age. This was particularly true with regard to weaves, which were made with strie (shaded) grounds, with silk warps and woollen wefts, on linen warps (exposed in areas to give the appearance of wear) and using slubbed yarns. Fabrics made with slubbed yarns were described in 1925 by the *Textile Mercury* as interesting because of the 'wonderful "shabby" effect that has been achieved. None of these [cloths] looks in the least new . . . and . . . appear as having been mellowed by time.'[13]

Slubbed yarns were also useful for creating a hand-made appearance. The distinguishing features of artist-made 1920s and '30s fabrics were spontaneity, naïveté or irregularity. Printing blocks, for example, were simply, even crudely, cut (often from linoleum); and the pressure applied to them could be allowed to vary considerably. New patterns could be created by combining blocks in different ways. When manufacturers of mass-produced printed textiles wished to capitalize on the growing fashion for hand-made goods they were limited by the regular pattern repeat and pressure required by the machinery; and it was only by using cloths made with irregular or fancy yarns, and thus printing onto a rough or uneven surface, that a hand-crafted appearance could be obtained. Velvets, slubbed satins, dobby weaves and 'basket weaves' were therefore not uncommon surfaces for prints between the two World Wars. The delight in texture was so pervasive that many traditional floral designs had 'textures' printed as backgrounds, where once there had been broad stripes and other more clearly articulated 'fancy' grounds.

Hand-crafted textiles were still prized for their exclusivity, in spite – or because – of their implicit incongruity with modern (i.e. machine-age) design. There were many such fabrics, which varied enormously, since they were supplied mainly by individuals who produced small quantities of hand-woven, embroidered, stencilled, batik-printed or block-printed pieces. The best-documented of these, in the 1920s, were made by English craftswomen such as the hand weaver Ethel Mairet (who set up her own dyeing, spinning and weaving workshop, called Gospels, in 1920) and the block-printers Phyllis Barron, Dorothy Larcher, Enid Marx, Mrs. Eric Kennington and Joyce Clissold (the last two founder and designer-manager respectively of Footprints, established in 1925). But there were many others on both sides of the Atlantic whose work still awaits study.

Of the various trends current in the 1920s, including Art Deco and the vogue for old fabrics, it was the interest in hand dyeing, spinning and weaving that had an enormous impact on the subsequent development of mass-produced weaves. Direct influence was evident in Germany, Finland and Britain, where, by the early 1930s, hand-weavers were producing prototypes for machine production. Indirect influence was noticeable in the increased use of yarns with hand-spun qualities – slubs, snarls, gimps, finger-thick cotton chenille yarn and others.

The interplay between man-made and textured natural fibres was also important. The rising cost of natural fibres made it cost-effective to use rayon (the most important man-made fibre of the period), particularly after 1933 (the lowest point for the textile industry), when the costs of natural fibres increased but rayon prices continued to fall. Rayon had initially been combined with cotton (both twisted into a double-ply warp

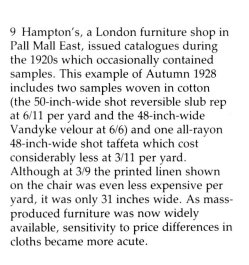

9 Hampton's, a London furniture shop in Pall Mall East, issued catalogues during the 1920s which occasionally contained samples. This example of Autumn 1928 includes two samples woven in cotton (the 50-inch-wide shot reversible slub rep at 6/11 per yard and the 48-inch-wide Vandyke velour at 6/6) and one all-rayon 48-inch-wide shot taffeta which cost considerably less at 3/11 per yard. Although at 3/9 the printed linen shown on the chair was even less expensive per yard, it was only 31 inches wide. As mass-produced furniture was now widely available, sensitivity to price differences in cloths became more acute.

yarn or used separately with the cotton as a warp), because it then lacked the strength required of a warp yarn. Into the mid-1920s rayon alone produced a stiff, very glossy cloth which was difficult to dye in dark colours without producing a metallic effect, but by the late 1920s all these problems had been overcome, and rayon was appreciated in its own right. It was the most 'modern' of all furnishing fabrics; it was thought (erroneously) to shed dirt; and its lustre was appreciated under electric lights. Because it was also inexpensive, it brought into many homes, for the first time, a sheen comparable to that of silk.[14] The combination of rayon with other fibres also created inexpensive new effects: for example, in neutral-coloured cloths the brilliance of rayon could be contrasted with a textured natural yarn. Rayon could also replace silk in cross-dyed fabrics (woven from two different fibres and immersed in a dye which affected only one).

The improvements in dyestuffs (for all fibres) were furthered by the need to procure dyes for man-made yarns; and by the early 1930s experimentation had produced ranges of both bold and subtle colours which had greater resistance to the effects of sunlight and washing. Matching different fabrics now became much easier. The practice of producing a design (whether woven or block-printed) on a figured ground and also producing the figured ground alone, or a plain companion fabric, became widespread, and ceased to be the province of 'exclusive' manufacturers. And the new matching colours were applied to cloths of very different qualities, ranging from plain rayon and cotton to silk velvet and slubbed linen (which was by this time a rather expensive fabric). In 1932 the available colour palette was likened by Grace Lovat Fraser (a perceptive British journalist and widow of the artist and designer Claude Lovat Fraser) to that of 'the most fastidious painter', and this, combined with the interest in the effect of electric light (which accentuated the difference between lustrous and matt surfaces), contributed to the vogue for 'monochrome' rooms, which were based around a single colour such as sky blue, apricot, cyclamen, willow green or off-white.[15]

Within both the American and British industries the concept of introducing new, coordinated colour 'stories' each season was growing; in the mid 1920s it had been suggested first for the American silk industry by Cheney Brothers and was taken up on a broader basis by the British Colour Council in 1930. The industry's interest in colour was motivated partly by the importance of colour in post-First World War interiors. Paint was particularly useful as a means of modernizing a room or individual pieces of furniture, but fabric colours were used in the same way (as in the radical 'decorator' styles such as baroque-modern). Although in general it could be said that the colour taste moved from dark-brights, through greyed neutrals to clean, 'tangy' pastels, colour trends until the late 1930s were less distinct than they are today. Between 1920 and 1950 certain colours were consistently used – among them black, brown-black, orangey-pink, and bright, true yellow. The last-named was seen as 'Chinese', a theme which survived its Art Deco phase and remained popular in fretwork designs and willow-patterns (which were not dissimilar from 'toile' copperplate designs).

10 This British living room designed in the early 1930s by Betty Joel and pictured in *Colour Schemes for the Modern Home* exemplifies what was regarded as a monochrome colour scheme, which with few exceptions included accents of complementary colours – in this case the small amount of blue in a predominantly cream and apricot interior. The bleached blonde wood and the lack of distinction between the painted walls and ceiling focus interest on the Modernist rug and overstuffed chairs, one of which retains an Oriental touch with its fan-shaped cushion. In her chapter in *The Conquest of Ugliness* (London, 1935), Joel announced that 'the so-called "modern movement" is already out of date'. Disliking interiors entirely controlled by the architect, she preferred 'the gradual perfecting of . . . surroundings', in which the owner's taste and views could be expressed through the addition of craftsmen's work. At this date Joel's firm, founded just after the First World War to sell furniture, had a Knightsbridge showroom, from which were sold French-made textiles and Chinese-made carpets of her design.

In 1926 the British architect and designer Basil Ionides had predicted that 'there is bound to be a great revolution in the textile trade shortly, and already signs of this are showing. The influences of chemistry and engineering are so strong to-day that new yarns and new looms and printing processes, assisted by chemical dyes, are completely altering materials.'[16] He predicted correctly, for the textile industry expressed the spirit of modernism principally through technology.

In fact, for every 'ism' of the period, textile engineers and chemists produced an '-izing'. New in the 1930s were Sanforizing (to prevent shrinking), Vitalizing (to reduce wrinkles), Everglazing (creating a washable lustre), and Bellmanizing (a permanent stiffening – principally for muslin). 'Scotchgarding' and other waterproofing treatments were improved, with rubberized taffetas and ginghams taking interior decoration into kitchens and bathrooms (which were now standard in American homes, but not in British ones). The weaving of moquette, 'a material', said Ionides, 'that was truly hideous during the last generations and only fit for railway carriages',[17] was improved in the mid-1920s, when its previously very stiff, carpet-like quality was transformed into a fabric suitable for both upholstery and curtains. By the 1930s the new quality was manufactured in large amounts in both Britain and the United States, having become very popular, although only for upholstery.

By the early 1930s other aspects of interiors were beginning to adapt industrial techniques and materials such as rubber and tubular steel. This style was more prevalent in the United States, where it became known as streamline-modern. The principal upholstery for this style was leather, patent leather or, at less expense, leather cloth; and the interiors were intended to express, in the words of Paul T. Frankl, 'a new ideal of beauty today . . . speed'. This was conveyed mainly through 'horizontal lines,

11 In *Inside Your Home* (New York, 1946), Dan Cooper advised that 'if you can afford only one good upholstered piece at a time, buy only one, and cover it with a strong neutral material so that it will stay covered as long as you want to use it. Homespuns are wonderful for this purpose. Some have been known to last on sofas for twenty years and more.' His conception of 'neutral' may well have included this 50-inch wide silk and nylon homespun, which he designed in about 1947, when boldly coloured 'mis-matched' pieces of furniture were just becoming popular.

12 Illustrated in *The Flat Book*, an excellent guide to British rustic-modern style published in 1939, this cane chair is by Dryad Ltd., and with its removable upholstered pad cost £5 7s. 6d. The fabric typifies mid- to late-1930s weaves, with their emphasis on texture and structure and their absence of motif. Similar fabrics shown elsewhere in the same publication were priced at between 10 and 20 shillings a yard.

straight and uninterrupted'. True to the contemporary ambivalence regarding machines, Frankl's recommended lightweight curtains with horizontal stripes ('to accentuate the longitudinalism') were invariably woven by hand, or in the style of a hand-weave, with the stripes created by a textured or looped yarn.[18] Similarly horizontal in emphasis were Venetian blinds, considered essential to control the light streaming through large areas of glass in modern buildings.

As with many other avant-garde styles, streamline-modern was more noticeable as an influence than in fully realized form. The 'club' chair, already common in modest American and British homes, gained a new, less bulbous interpretation, distinguished as modern by its leather-cloth, moquette or tweed upholstery (or a combination of two of these). Contrasting piping was often incorporated – to suggest the speeding line – and became ubiquitous. Streamline-modern also provided a forum for American hand-weavers and upholstery tweed manufacturers, which by the late 1930s included Boris Kroll, Dorothy Leibes and Dan Cooper.

Many of the fabrics considered suitable for streamline-modern interiors were also found elsewhere; the horizontally striped 'hand-weaves', for example, often provided a touch of modernity in traditional interiors. Venetian blinds were similarly versatile, since they had been widely used prior to 1850. The baroque-modern style, with its dramatic, surrealistic use of light and shade, trompe l'oeil effects, antiques, chrome and glass, included an inclination towards animal-skin upholstery – both real and fake – as did streamline-modern.

The rustic-modern style also shared with streamline-modern the use of seemingly hand-woven cloths, absorbing the interest in hand-made textiles which had been – and remained — associated with Art and Crafts and Mission furniture. Rustic-modern, despite its paradoxical name, was the closest the British came to European Functionalism. Unlike streamline-modern, this style favoured wooden furniture (although metal-framed furniture was also accepted). The emphasis was on structure rather than ornament, and the upholstery was chosen 'for its hardwearing qualities and [was] either washable or removeable for cleaning or [had] a close patterned cover of small squares, checks, stripes or spots which will not require constant cleaning'.[19] Firms such as Donald Brothers, Edinburgh Weavers (an offshoot created in 1932 by Morton Sundour), Helios (created in 1937 by Barlow & Jones), the Welsh mills (trading through the Rural Industries Bureau) and Warners became known for their provision of suitable cloths in this style, which relied on neutral colours and bold interpretations (by machine) of hand-spun yarns and hand-weave effects. There was a concerted effort in the 1930s to promote British rustic-modern through exhibitions and journals, such as *Architectural Review*; and in the process the hand-woven look, as interpreted by designers such as Arundel Clark, Alistair Morton, Alec Hunter and Marianne Straub, attained something of a cult status.[20]

A salient feature of the modern trends for weaves in both Britain and the United States was the rejection of figurative pattern. Loraine Conran expressed the avant garde view when she wrote in Britain's *Architectural*

Review that 'pictorial representation must be abandoned in woven mater-ials and the business of design must be left to someone closely connected with the manufacturing process'.[21] Not surprisingly, by the late 1920s naturalistically patterned Levers lace curtains (which were machine-made with Jacquard-controlled patterns that imitated every kind of handmade bobbin lace) were no longer fashionable, and many lacemaking firms did not survive the Depression. Less expensive, more crudely patterned nets, machine-made with coarse yarns and a square mesh (often called filet nets) nevertheless remained an important feature of even the most im-poverished homes. In her autobiographical series of books, Helen Forres-ter recounted the Depression years in Liverpool, where her once-affluent parents – forced, as were many others, to live in damp, cold and cramped quarters – maintained a pretence of respectability by hanging filet net curtains at the front window. Behind the curtains, the room was often empty, the furniture having been repossessed.[22]

At the same time, plain-woven sheer curtains became increasingly popular. Both rustic- and streamline-modern proponents shared an inter-est in natural light, and among the curtain fabrics they recommended were many that were sheer or semi-sheer. Loosely constructed 'hand-woven' fabrics were unlined, so that light could shine through. This practice conformed with a general inclination towards translucent or lightweight fabrics for curtains.

Among the muslin-like fabrics used at windows in the 1930s and '40s were organdie (stiffened), voile (soft and fine) and scrim (coarse and cheap and in the opinion of an American writer, 'rather clumsy'[23]). All but the last of these were produced in white and coloured cotton, silk, rayon and mohair. Leno and mock-leno fabrics (with crossed-over warp threads creating open areas), reed and bamboo slat roller blinds, and thin silk or rayon taffetas were equally appreciated as 'filters' of natural daylight. Full-length sheers and/or semi-sheers were sometimes used double, one set as glass curtains and another to be drawn open during the day, an arrange-ment that seems to have been particularly approved for American sky-scraper apartments which were not overlooked. It was also possible to have a third pair of stationary 'dress' curtains at the sides – in which case there was normally a pelmet to match.

In woven fabrics, between 1920 and 1950, modernity decreed a gradual increase in the emphasis on variation in texture, weight and density. Prints also followed the same trend, using heavily textured base-cloths, as well as thin silks and rayons, which were admired for their luminous quality and soft drape.[24] Chintzes were given a textured form by means of machine quilting. At the beginning of the 1930s, however, weaves were still the dominant fabrics in both modern and traditional interiors.

The gradual introduction of commercial hand screen printing in the 1930s set the stage for a reversal of this trend. Faster than block printing, requiring less investment than roller printing and more easily adapted to fabrics of different thicknesses, hand screen printing also offered an attractive prospect to artist-designers, since it could produce a wide range of effects. Although the method was not widely practised in the United

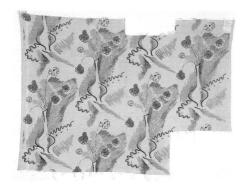

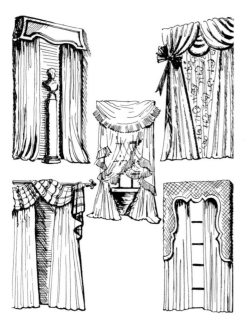

13 'Burlesque', Donald Brothers' hand-screen print on linen, was designed by Grace Peat in 1938. It typifies the lull in design developments caused by the Second World War, in that it was being sold in 1951 (in exactly the same colours) through Dan Cooper, a New York designer-manufacturer of avant-garde fabrics.

14 Although the American decorator, broadcaster and writer Dorothy Draper declared herself satisfied with simple, straight-hanging curtains, occasionally trimmed with a wide, bulky fringe, she chose to illustrate these five window treatments in her 1944 book *Decorating is Fun!* The centre and upper right curtains and draperies show the excesses associated with the baroque-modern style, which despite its name stressed effect rather than any particular period.

States until the 1940s (when firms such as Ben Rose and Dan Cooper took it up), in Britain, in the '30s, it quickly became the favoured medium for modern printed designs.[25] Many of the early designs were highly stylized two-colour naturalistic motifs printed on plain medium-weight cotton, but the technique was quickly adopted for printing velvets, slubbed satins (including rayons) and chintzes. The chintz finish, accentuated by contrasting watercolour-like images with stark, deeply coloured solid grounds, quickly became popular in baroque-modern interiors.

Towards the end of the 1930s the baroque-modern style became more light-hearted, under the influence of decorators such as Elsie de Wolfe and Dorothy Draper, in the United States, and Betty Joel and H. G. Hayes Marshall in Britain. Antique and modern were combined in a whimsical, offhand way. Curtain treatments became noticeably eclectic, with sheer Austrian blinds, for example, placed underneath severe, straight-hanging curtains. Early-nineteenth-century festoons and swags were reinterpreted in defiantly crisp fabrics, as flat 'silhouette' pelmets and even in glass. Yet a purely modern effect, achieved with simply gathered or pleated curtain headings on a curtain track, was also a popular treatment for baroque-modern rooms. Curtains might just touch the windowsill or 'puddle' on the floor. Dorothy Draper's suggestions ranged from simple curtains with a wide bulky fringe to lambrequins covered with fabric, wood or imitation leather. She also proposed that 'rough white brocade curtains could be lined with coral-pink satin, or chintz curtains could be lined with red, or solid red lined with chintz'.[26] The latter practice, she claimed, was widespread in England.

The theatrical nature of many baroque-modern interiors may have owed much to the stage, and even more to films, both of which often used this style for sets. Looking back from the vantage point of 1952, Barbara Worsley-Gough described a 'baronial' variant of baroque-modern as 'always containing a Knole sofa and armchairs covered in red brocade or velvet, heavily trimmed with galon and fringe; table lamps made of Spanish baroque church candlesticks with shades made of old maps or deeds on parchment; cigarette boxes made of the covers of calf-bound books; and wrought iron standard lamps and wall brackets and andirons supporting electrically powered imitation logs on hearths of vast proportions. . . . The general effect', she concluded, 'was that of a Hollywood set for *The Conti*', adding that London's Curzon Street was the centre of supply for these articles.[27]

Baroque-modern suited the years just before the Second World War, when, for a brief period, optimism reigned. Aside from the prominent use of wrought iron, printed textile designs also reflected the preference for Spanish baroque interpretations, with their large, bold tropical plants, enormous bouquets of freshly coloured garden flowers and trompe l'oeil effects, which included bunting-like swags draped between columns or floral sprays. These were particularly popular in 1937, the year of the Coronation of George V – and perhaps the best of all the inter-war years for the British textile trade, since 'Coronation fever' boosted exports of chintzes, especially to America.

15 An inter-war scheme from *Decorative Draperies and Upholstery* employing basic cloths as a complement to a machine woven tapestry, this room set was sketched in the United States from fabrics then available. Single-colour or two-toned cloths were often recommended in the 1920s when precisely matched shades were wanted. The sofa is covered with red silk damask, and the curtains are satin with a fringe of blue, green and red. The valance, with a walnut cornice, is embellished with fringe and embroidery (there still existed a number of British and American firms that did both embroidery and appliqué to order), while the chair is upholstered in leather. Sofas of this shape were added to many 'country-house' interiors during this period, and have since remained a standard accompaniment to eighteenth-century furniture. Wall panels were regarded as substitutes for pictures, and among the fabrics recommended for this use were seamed and braid-edged panels of Fortuny fabric, supplied by A. H. Lee in both the United States and Britain.

Despite the enthusiasm for modern interior design in this period, the most-used textile designs were undoubtedly the conservative ones. The majority of these were of the type prevalent in 1910 and compatible with Jacobean, Spanish and (in the United States) Colonial revival interiors. Retaining the slightly muted colours of now-faded originals, these fabrics were predominantly printed cretonnes based on samplers, crewelwork and other types of embroidery. Their widespread popularity was due partly to the number of houses built in these styles, but a contributing factor must have been that, as *The Decorator* observed two years after the Wall Street Crash, 'needlework patterns convey a certain sense of comfort'.[28] In the late 1930s some printed cottons and cretonnes adopted baroque scrolls and Victorian-rococo motifs, but many designs survived unchanged, in production throughout the inter-war period.

The outbreak of war did not significantly affect textile design and decorating trends. Nevertheless, the appearance of British interiors was, of necessity, altered by the need for blackout curtains (which had to have enough density to block any light, but were not required to be black). Many net, muslin and lace curtains were converted to a more practical use, being pasted to window panes to prevent any shattered glass from spraying inwards.

Decorating *per se* virtually ceased in Britain, but in America it continued, more often than not on a do-it-yourself basis, since labour was in short supply. In 1941 an American writer, seeking to alleviate the monotony of home-made curtains, recommended 'dressmaker touches', suggesting that 'rows of colored bias binding or rickrack braid, grosgrain or picot-edged ribbon, ball fringes and cut fringes, appliqués of motifs inspired by those on wallpaper or chintzes [and] novelty tiebacks will make an ordinary curtain a topic of conversation . . .'[29]

Furnishing textiles continued to be made by British textile manufac-

16 Simple weaves served a dual purpose in Britain during the 1940s, marrying well with the fashion for 'folk weaves' and primitive peasant-art designs and at the same time able to conform to colour and cost requirements set for Utility fabrics. Note that the Utility ginghams in this Empire Stores (Bradford) catalogue for Spring/Summer 1945 are advertised as suitable for both clothing and curtains.

turers whose mills had not been converted entirely to war-related work, although, like other raw materials, the supply of yarns for furnishing fabrics was restricted. As stocks were depleted many made curtains from blankets, which were not rationed. Americans also gradually began to see imposed changes. Although bright 'Pan American' colours were popular in the United States in the first years of the war, by about 1943 dyes were used in weaker solutions here, as well as in Britain; colour-matching was once again unreliable and the coverage of colour in prints was restricted. A British writer, commenting in 1943 on the 'process of elimination to the extreme limit of austerity and utility', looked forward to 'a future where possessions which have neither the merit of beauty nor usefulness have no place'.[30] These sentiments paraphrased the principles behind the British Board of Trade's Utility scheme (for which Enid Marx began designing small-patterned four-colour weaves in 1943) – principles which had themselves descended through a chain of craftsmen and designers leading back to William Morris and the Arts and Crafts movement. American designers also wrote and lectured about the opportunities which lay ahead, engendering a sense of optimism which balanced the design restrictions that prevailed for most of the 1940s.

The diversion of materials into the war effort stimulated a search for alternative fibres for furnishing fabrics. Nylon, a synthetic fibre perfected by E. I. du Pont de Nemours & Co. in 1938, and in production by 1939, was restricted solely to war-related products, but experiments were made with cellophane and other non-essential substances. This was the reason for the emergence of mohair – one of the few fibres not requisitioned by the American armed forces – as the basis of the most readily available furnishing fabrics in the United States. Mohair was blended with rayon or cotton; mohair weaves, previously including moquettes, velvets and modern textures – such as those designed by Dorothy Liebes for Goodall Decorative Fabrics – were extended to include sheers and plain fabrics (both of which were sometimes printed).

In the long term, roller-printing firms were the section of the textile industry which was most seriously affected by the War. Since metals were diverted to war-related production, copper and base metals for new printing cylinders were soon in short supply. During the last years of the War, both American and British printers were asked to give up any cylinders which had not been used in recent years. This depleted the stock of patterns which had built up over a number of years, and left printers facing substantial replacement costs (the price of copper also doubled between 1940 and 1949). Once the War was over this gave a further advantage to screen printers, who had suffered no similar losses.

At the end of the War there was naturally a desire to return to normality, but for many people the re-decoration of homes had to wait. Furnishing textiles remained in relatively short supply, with silks and linens particularly difficult to obtain. This was true even in 1949, when the American government rescinded the requirement of an import licence for foreign upholstery and drapery fabrics.

If the 1940s contributed little in terms of new designs, the period

17 David Whitehead Ltd. became known in the immediate postwar years for their range of inexpensive, well-designed prints. Eight examples of 1947 are shown here, roller-printed on cotton and rayon cloths. The designs were created under the direction of the British architect John Murray, who had joined Whitehead's in 1946. *Design* magazine, in December 1950, cited the Whitehead range as proof of 'a fundamental tenet of the modern faith that the cheap need not be cheap-and-nasty'.

nevertheless crystallized an awareness of the importance of well-designed, mass-produced goods – the primary objective of Functionalism, rustic-modern and streamline-modern. The influence of these movements had already been felt in the late 1920s and the 1930s, when furniture designed specifically for smaller living spaces began to be produced. Although most modern-style interiors remained relatively expensive, there was a growing recognition of the needs of the mass-market. In 1939, an American writer (after discussing Italian, Spanish, seventeenth-century English, Georgian, Colonial, French and nineteenth-century decorative styles) mentioned low-rental housing, proposing that 'a certain price structure for furnishing according to taste, income and rent must be established. This is an entirely new and modern approach to furnishings and is just as much a part of the movement as the designs and materials themselves'.[30] This issue, and others related to it, had to wait until the 1950s to be resolved.

The years between 1920 and 1950 were the last in which the vast majority of luxury fabrics were produced by commercial firms employing hand-printers or hand Jacquard-weavers. Thus the dissatisfaction with the 1920s mass-produced taupe mohair for 'Bronx Renaissance' furniture expressed a comparison which was invalid – based, as it was, on the assumption that mass-produced fabrics should emulate hand-made ones. The attempt to reconcile the conflict between hand-made 'quality' and machine-made 'borax', and to find a legitimate role for both, can be recognized in all the new interior styles evolved in this period, in which new and old, modern and traditional were so often mixed. It was after 1950 that the principles of 'honest' mass production bore fruit, nurtured by the experimentation of the inter-war years. Inevitably, as Functionalism was subsumed by the post-Second World War International style and in this 'new' form came increasingly into play, the 'delightful anachronism'[31] which had characterized the years encompassed by the two World Wars was bound for exclusion from mainstream interiors.

18

18, 19 Both of these surface-roller-printed 'Eton Rural' fabrics were among the first textiles printed by Sanderson's at their printworks, built in 1921 at Uxbridge, outside London. The design of 19 shows what *The Journal of Decorative Art* called (in a review of Sanderson's display of cretonnes in November 1921) 'all the harmonious freedom and abandonment which is jazz'. The arrangement of tulips and daffodils in 18 (probably first produced in 1922) anticipates the late 1920s preference for designs based on horizontal lines. The 'Eton Rural' range was, like many other manufacturers' modern collections, made unprofitable by the sudden drop in demand which followed the 1919–21 postwar 'boom'.

20 Sold in the United States by an
unknown manufacturer, this mid-1920s
block-printed cotton epitomizes the large,
bold, naïvely drawn and richly coloured
motifs associated with modern French
designs. It may nevertheless have been
designed in America, where studios such
as Ericson & Weiss were producing similar
designs in the second half of the 1920s.

21 Lace curtains were to become
unfashionable in the 1930s, but in 1920,
when the Pennsylvania lace and filet net
manufacturers, Scranton, produced this
advertisement, they were an essential part
of the Empire-modern style which had
begun before the war. The interior shows
other aspects of 1920s Empire-modern as
it approached the style to be known as Art
Deco: the table with a white lacquered
surface, sharp coloured lines, glass top
and bulbous legs counterbalanced by
massive square and oblong areas, the
printed cotton curtains with fat, naïvely
drawn motifs, and the vertical emphasis
in the lace curtains themselves. The latter,
together with the advertisement's border,
employ 'grotesque' motifs which alone
can be said accurately to reflect designs
used in the first Empire period. The
stylishness of this and many other
interiors of the inter-war years depended
on the contrast between new and
traditional elements.

19

21

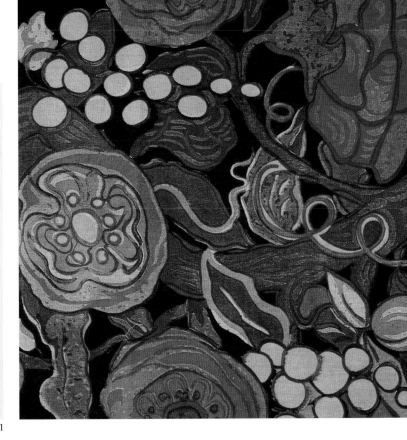

20

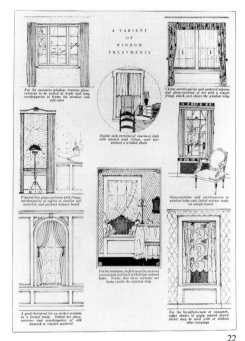

22

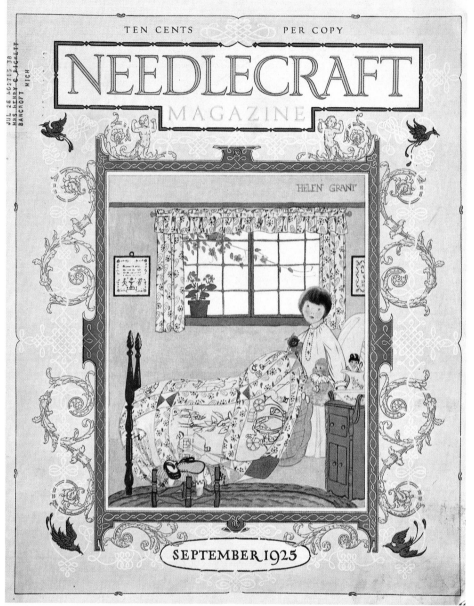

23

22 These eight window treatments, illustrated in *The House Beautiful Furnishing Annual* (Boston, 1926), represent the curtains typical of the majority of inter-war interiors. Simple in appearance, each nevertheless has at least two contrasting textures or colours – even the double sash casement cloth curtains (centre top, also called 'Double Dutch' curtains) have a coloured wool fringe. Completed curtains in identical styles – intended to be 'dignified yet simple enough to make everybody feel at home' – were illustrated in Bess M. Viemont's *Window Curtaining*, which, under the auspices of the American Bureau of Home Economics (Washington D.C., 1930, 2nd. ed.), was widely circulated. Viemont dismissed 'extreme and faddish window decorations', formal damasks, brocades and tapestries and 'tiresome' roses 'natural enough to pick'. Instead she suggested richly toned patterned cretonnes, hand-block-printed linens and plain materials (which were, in fact, the most widely used).

23 A 'cottage' bedroom featuring an embroidered pieced coverlet, for which instructions were included in the September 1925 issue of *Needlecraft Magazine*, published in Augusta, Maine. The coverlet is made from cotton fabrics (with no wadded interlining); the patterned 'bars' were specified as either chintz or cotton. Typical of an informal room of the period, the matching curtains hang to just below the sill, supported by a rod hidden by a valance gathered onto a second pole with simple decorative ends.

The use of painted (and possibly second-hand) furniture, the rag rug and the framed samplers all contribute to an Early American look.

24 Chequerboard motifs appeared in many textile designs of the 1910s and '20s, and were often associated with Viennese prewar avant-garde design. This printed textile design (1926) by Madelaine Lawrence, of the Silver Studio, has alternatives to the chequerboard areas attached in the top row. The small scale of this pattern gives it an informal quality, and its simplicity belies the fact that it employs overlapping to create eleven 'perceived' colours from only eight different colours.

24

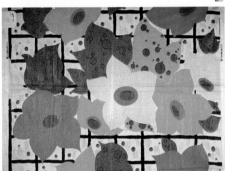

25

26

27

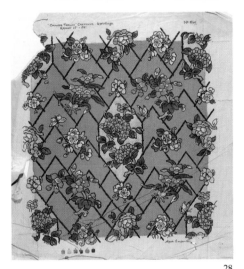

28

29

25 'Butterflies', a silk lampas, was designed by Séguy and exhibited at the 1925 'Art Deco' exhibition. It was subsequently produced for exclusive sale by Schumacher in New York. Séguy was one of a handful of French designers who published pattern books which also provided designs for American manufacturers. The work shown by Edgar Brandt at the 1925 Paris exhibition was equally influential in New York, since immediately afterwards he had designed wrought-iron entrance and window decorations for the New York office of the silk-weaving firm Cheney Brothers (who in 1929 produced a series of fabrics for automobile interiors based on Brandt's work). Schumacher also produced a design showing gazelles amid wrought-iron-like scrolls c.1927, and in smaller scale this damask was used in the Waldorf-Astoria in 1934.

26 This hand-block-printed cotton was designed by Paul Poiret and produced for Schumacher in 1930. Initially a fashion designer, Poiret first sold furnishing textiles in 1912, when he established Maison Martine in Paris. This interior decoration firm closed in the after-effects of the Wall Street Crash, but had already established a reputation for naïvely drawn and boldly coloured textiles (many of which had been designed by the young students of Atelier Martine, founded in 1911). Poiret's name was widely known in the United States; his 1929 collection for Whiting and Davies, New York, had been well publicized in *Harper's Bazaar*.

27 Fruit was one of the popular patterns for printed textiles of the mid- to late-1920s. This American example was block-printed on cotton in 1928–9 by Everfast Textiles.

28 'Chinese Trellis', by Alfred Carpenter, was probably designed shortly before his death in 1912, but not produced by Turnbull & Stockdale until 1919/20. This type of Chinese pattern – particularly the 'keyed' motif in the background – remained popular throughout the 1920s and '30s, being thought especially suitable with reproduction Chippendale furniture.

29 'Cowslip' is a roller-printed cotton produced in 1932 by the British Calico Printers' Association in fast vat colours. The addition of the Modernist background to a floral design was an often-used device at this time, employed in the hope that it would appeal to both modern and conservative tastes. The faded-denim blue remained an important colour until the Second World War and, together with the equally popular faded-madder peach, reflected the influence of natural dyes on 1930s colours.

30 This late 1920s public sun lounge from *Decorative Draperies and Upholstery* has been designed to satisfy a variety of tastes and is therefore neither overtly modern nor traditional, as were the majority of private interiors of the period. The large bowl of flowers on hand-block-printed linen has been centred in each panel of the valance, which has intermediate cascades of gold rep and, together with the curtains, is trimmed with a wool fringe. The curtains were stipulated as one-and-a-half times wider than the windows, and the depth of the valance was dependent on the pattern size on the fabric (fabrics ready-woven with valance designs were also available). Block-printed fabrics were still easily obtainable in the 1920s and '30s, and the height of the pattern (consisting of several 'stacked' motifs) could often reach 4 feet. The draw-curtains underneath were to be of a pongee casement cloth, while the split-reed sofa was to be upholstered in chintz, shown here in mauve with appliquéd strips of green.

31 Sixteenth- and seventeenth-century needlework patterns remained popular sources of woven and printed textile designs throughout the inter-war period and into the early 1950s. This example, 'The Four Marys', was hand-block-printed in 1929 by Baker's. Also typical of the period was the use of a linen base cloth both to suggest age and to emphasize the irregularity of the drawing. This particular shade of deep lilac was fashionable in both the 1910s and the 1920s.

32 These samples are from an Arnold Print Works (Massachusetts) record book containing fabrics roller-printed especially for S. M. Schwab. Dated 12 February, 1926, the design, shown here on swatches of cotton satin, was also printed on other cloths, including cotton flannel. All are richly coloured, and the two left-hand samples illustrate the continued practice of deriving different colourways by changing the background colour. The same firm also printed similar designs on duplex machines, which simultaneously printed both sides of the cloth, thus simulating a woven fabric and being suitable for unlined curtains and portières.

30

31

33 'Mandarin', a hand-loom Jacquard-woven silk, was produced by Warners in 1930 for Carter's Grove, a plantation house near Williamsburg, Virginia, where it was used for upholstery. The pale apricot colour was hand brocaded. Reminiscent of scenic printed toiles (which were also fashionable), its design – characteristic of the inter-war years – suited the current taste for both chinoiserie and the late eighteenth century.

34 Machine-made tapestry remained a popular upholstery cloth throughout the inter-war years; in 1923 Hampton's chose one in 'crewelwork' style for this walnut bergère chair and settee. Furniture in this price range (nearly £23 for the settee) normally had only its lining upholstery until sold; to enable customers to select the final covering Hampton's sent 27-inch square samples by post, for which they charged a non-returnable fee of 2/3 each.

32

33

Hamptons' Easy Chairs and Settees.

Hamptons' No. S 15326. Carved Walnut Bergère Easy Chair with caned sides and back. Upholstered all hair. Two loose feather cushions. Covered with Tapestry. £13 15s. 0d.

34

35 In this dining area, designed by H. G. Hayes Marshall of Fortnum & Mason Ltd., the Queen Anne-style chairs have silver legs and real zebra skin upholstery, and the silvered wrought-iron table has a black Vitrolite top. Typical of dramatic, extravagant baroque-modern interiors, such schemes represented a reaction against Functionalism. In 1939, in the introduction to *Decoration for the Home* (from which this illustration comes), Herman Schrijver pronounced the modern interior with fitted furniture and indirect lighting to be 'quite *vieux jeu*' and decried the 'appalling progression in standardization today'. As if with this interior in mind, he added that 'good decorating is extremely expensive and has always been so'.

35

36

37

36 During the 1930s the growing interest in craftsman-printed textiles (and the related liking for ethnic, particularly African, patterns) encouraged commercial manufacturers to produce naïve, spontaneous-looking block prints which were, by the standards of professional block-printers, imperfectly printed. These three 1937 examples, hand-printed on linen by Warners for Fortnum & Mason, were selected by H. G. Hayes Marshall from designs by 10–15-year-old students at the London Central College. Perhaps because of the fashion for animal-skin upholstery and their printed imitations, 'Snakeskin' (below) was the most successful of the three.

37 The interest in handmade textiles during the inter-war years created a small but steady market for panels such as these, both hand-printed in natural dyes from small, hand-cut wooden blocks. Designed by Enid Marx (left) and Phyllis Barron (right), both were produced in about 1925, the same year in which Marx joined Barron and Dorothy Larcher in their hand-block printing workshop, where they printed to commission and sold lengths through a handful of London craft galleries and exhibitions such as those mounted by the Red Rose Guild.

38 The influence of the fine arts was apparent in textile designs of the inter-war years, as typified by 'Welwyn Garden City', which was exhibited at the International Exhibition of Decorative Metalwork and Cotton Textiles, held at the Metropolitan Museum of Art in 1930. It was designed in England by Doris Gregg and hand-block-printed by Joyce Clissold, the designer-manager of Footprints. Both women were familiar with the decorative arts that emanated from Paris during the 1920s, when fabrics by artists such as Raoul Dufy were being printed with modern 'toile' scenes similarly compressed and stylized. Many such designs (they were also created in the early 1930s by, among others, Marion Dorn in England and Ruth Reeves in the United States) depicted scenes as if viewed from above, a natural inspiration, given the enthusiasm for machinery – including aeroplanes – expressed in Futurist, Constructivist and 'simultaneous' art of the 1920s.

39 'The Fabrics of 1937', according to Britain's *Decoration* magazine, included these prints and weaves from Gordon Russell Ltd. (top) and Donald Brothers (below), a Dundee firm well known for its linen furnishing fabrics. Gordon Russell was one of Britain's leading furniture designers, and in the late 1930s his London showroom was also well known as a fabric shop.

40 Reflecting the revived interest in hand-batiked cloths and the avant garde's taste for mass-produced batik-like fabrics (actually intended for British export markets), this roller-printed cretonne, in 'Indonesian' or 'African' colours, was designed by Albert Griffiths and produced by Foxton's in 1922.

38

Above: A group of fabrics made exclusively for Gordon Russell. Back left: a banded fadeless curtain material in rayon and cotton, also supplied in brick-red, yellow and brown. Right: two colourings of a bold floral print on a spun rayon. Front left: an interesting heavy fadeless weave, suitable for upholstery. Centre: a cushion in printed rayon rep. Right: a Welsh tweed suitable for upholstery. Below: a group of Old Glamis Fabrics. Left to Right: "Tyndrum" and "Seagulls," both printed linens; "Grange," a guaranteed fast cloth suitable for most purposes; "Totland," another printed linen; "Kilmany," a fadeless cloth, and "Coopersdale," a printed crash (Donald Brothers).

39

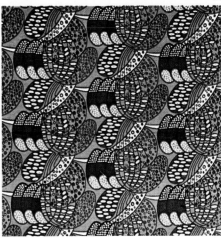

40

41

42

41 The upholstery on this American club chair is patterned in the style of the rich brocades and velvets shown by the British at the Paris exhibition in 1925. A voided cotton velvet, it has been overprinted to suggest added richness and texture (see Chapter Four, Fig. 46 for the type of velvet it imitates). Together with machine-made tapestry cloth and moquettes, voided cotton velvets had been popular middle-class furnishing fabrics since the end of the nineteenth century, but in the 1930s their production in the United States was gradually directed towards the automobile industry.

42 The interest in textured weaves as a base for printing is well demonstrated in this hand-block-printed 'herringbone weave', designed and produced by Michael O'Connell in about 1937/8. O'Connell also designed for firms in New York, Australia and New Zealand, and his work included theatre drop curtains. His own hand-printed fabrics were sold under the trade name of Mael.

43 In the second half of the 1930s a number of artist-designed textiles were produced in Britain, partly to help boost exports and partly because the development of hand-screen printing allowed more direct translation of artwork to fabric. Allan Walton Textiles became known for such innovative designs (Walton was himself a painter), and this Walton hand-screen-printed satin was designed in about 1938 by Kenneth Martin, a painter who had studied at the Royal College of Art in London and whose work was well known in the 1930s.

44 Several factors combined to bring many more artist-designed fabrics onto the British market in the 1930s – among them the ability of screen printing to capture the spontaneous marks made in the original design. Two artists who took advantage of this were Duncan Grant and Vanessa Bell, who designed the fabrics (produced by Allan Walton Textiles) included in their painted music room, exhibited at the Alex Reid and Lefevre Gallery, London, 1932, and illustrated by Patmore (see Fig. 6) in the following year. Trompe l'oeil effects, as seen in the wall painting and the loose-cover skirts, were to remain a prominent element of printed textile designs for another two decades. (According to *The Christian Science Monitor*, 28 August, 1931, the idea of printing lose chair covers with designs planned to fit individual chairs originated with Celandine Kennington, the founder of Footprints.) This room was again illustrated by Derek Patmore in *Colour Schemes and Modern Furnishing* in 1945.

43

45 Both of these designs were first block-printed in 1935 by Baker's. The cotton chintz 'Large Lily' was manufactured for A. H. Lee, a New York wholesale fabric firm which also supplied Fortuny fabrics. 'Ferns', based on botanical prints of 1743, was by Joseph M. Doran, a well-known British freelance textile designer, and remains in the Baker range of a screen-printed linen and cotton fabric. Informally placed flora and fauna designs which avoided the use of 'chintz' flowers, such as roses, were typical of sophisticated prints of the 1930s and '40s.

46 Throughout the 1930s and early 1940s this hand-block-printed chintz was supplied to Dorothy Draper, who illustrated it as loose covers and gathered four-poster bed valances in *Decorating is Fun!* (New York, 1944). Commission-printed for Warners, 'Maryport' had been in their range since the late nineteenth century, at which time it had also been produced as a hand-loom Jacquard-woven silk. It has remained in production throughout this century, latterly as a screen print.

47 Plain fabrics were a particularly noticeable feature of many 1930s interiors and often suggested modernity, even when used in pseudo-Regency interiors, such as can be seen in this caricature of Emily Post, the well-known American writer and successor to nineteenth-century authors of etiquette books, whose publications included *The Personality of a House* (New York, 1930). In providing this illustration for the December 1933 issue of *Vanity Fair*, Miguel Covarrubias captured the stark, flattened treatment given to many neo-Regency and baroque-modern interiors of the period. The only decorative touches are the pink tie-backs and fringe added to the pelmet and curtain hem, and the faintly drawn trompe l'oeil panelling on the walls. Note the spring roller blind, with its ring covered with buttonhole stitch, a feature common until plastic replaced metal for rings in about 1960.

45

46

47

48

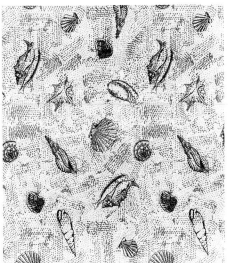

49

49 This cotton furnishing fabric 'Conchotas', was produced in the 1940s by Jim and Leslie Tillet, who, in the late 1930s, had established a hand-screen printing factory in Mexico, one of the first in North America. Many 1930s screen prints had a short, wide pattern (here it is just short of the 35½ inch cloth width and 17¾ inch high), since this made the screen a convenient size for the printers.

50 As remodelled by Frank Lloyd Wright in 1937, this office in Kaufmann's Pittsburgh department store (now in the Victoria & Albert Museum) contains carpets and upholstery designed by the architect and woven by Scandinavian weavers in the Studio Loja Saarinen at the Cranbrook Academy of Art, outside Chicago. Wright supervised the weaving of the mercerized cotton, rayon and cotton chenille upholstery cloth and the hand-knotted flax warp and wool pile rugs.

48 In 1948 Edith Hernandez, a New York interior decorator, furnished her showroom with a bamboo blind – a new and fashionable window treatment – and a printed fabric which in its pattern reflects the character of the mobile nearby. Patterns such as these featured prominently in the range of roller prints designed by Juanita Hall and produced by D. N. & E. Walter & Co., San Francisco. Similar designs achieved widespread use in both Britain and the United States and remained popular until the late 1950s.

51 This room set in an unidentified New York store, photographed in 1949, still shows evidence of the restrictions imposed during the war. The curtains are printed with a design that conforms to the limited colour coverage regulations, and both patterns on the woven upholstery employ an economically scaled repeat and what appears to be a 'filling' yarn – which has non-fibrous material added to increase the bulk of the fabric. The design of the curtain fabric reflects one philosophy of the day, which held that unless used flat, fabric patterns should appear to be supple and pliant, in keeping with the folds of the cloth. The blond wood and leather upholstery were to remain fashionable into the early 1960s, dictating colours softer than those used with reddish or dark woods.

50

51

54

These two rooms, one large and one small, are arranged as comfortable living-rooms, with space reserved for dining-tables, where meals can be conveniently served from kitchen to table by means of the hatch. Both rooms have solid-fuel, continuously burning fires. Notice the table-lamp and adjustable ceiling light in the room below.

The gas kitchen above, with its dining-alcove, is an excellent example of the use of modern equipment planned to fit into a small space. The kitchen-living-room below, with walls and dresser painted cream to reflect the light, has a modern combination grate for heating and cooking. The table can be moved near the fire in winter.

52

53

55

52, 53 Two living-dining rooms and two kitchen-dining rooms illustrated in *Modern Homes*, 1947, offering suggestions for medium and small spaces in British homes. The reliance on 'basic' fabrics is noticeable in both, with floor-length curtains in the large living room described only as 'heavy', and sill-length curtains in the other rooms made from horizontally striped fabric, recommended to give the

effect of width. These rooms differ little from the type of interior found at the end of the 1930s, when, for example, widthways stripes were also popular for curtains and were often associated with streamlined furniture. Note the Venetian blind, with brightly coloured straps, and the plaid cotton tablecloths, the latter a fashionable accessory for informal dining, new to the mid- to late-1930s.

54, 55 Coordinated fabrics – often accompanied by wallpapers – were a well established part of American interiors by the late 1940s. Among Tamis Keefe's coordinates for Golding Decorative Fabrics were these two screen-printed cottons of c.1949, typical of the years around 1950, with a smaller all-over motif on one cloth and a larger, more openly spaced design on the other. Often fabrics were coordinated only by colour, as when an abstract floral was paired with a plaid.

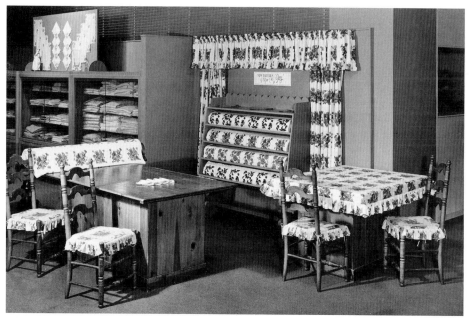

56

56 On display in Bullock's, an influential Los Angeles department store, are Elza Sunderland's printed cottons 'Strawberry', designed in 1943, and 'Ivy', designed in 1946. Through her textile converting firm, Elza of Hollywood, Mrs. Sunderland produced a range of informal dress and furnishings fabrics which received nationwide publicity and achieved equally widespread use; 'Strawberry' sold over 250,000 yards in the decade after it was launched.

57 The fashion for depicting everyday objects on printed furnishing fabrics began just after the Second World War and persisted for about ten years. 'Déjeuner', an American hand-screen print of 1946–50, has been printed in vat dyes, which were soon to become the standard dye for all good-quality prints. It may well have been designed by Richard Dillon, Jr., who produced (for Jofa Inc., New York) a series of 'hand prints that appeal not only to the eye but also to our sense of humor' (illustrated in 1954 in *American Textiles* by Paul T. Frankl). Of the three colourways shown two differ only in the alteration of the background gingham 'check' from grey to pale red.

57

58

59

58 In the second half of the 1930s hand-screen-printed 'decorator' chintzes (for use in baroque-modern or neo-Regency settings) often employed brilliantly coloured backgrounds, against which subtly coloured tropical plants and flowers were highlighted. Printed by Warners (who began hand-screen printing in 1932), both of the chintzes shown here were designed by Lewis Jones, in 1937 (left) and 1938 (right). Jones was employed by the Silver Studio, from 1910 (aged 16) until his death in 1953 (except during the world wars, in which he served). A skilled draughtsman, he was equally at home with traditional designs, which remained in great demand throughout his career.

59 This group of fabrics is typical of the range created by Marianne Straub for Helios, an independent subsidiary of Barlow & Jones which operated from 1937 to 1950. All dobby-woven, they were created from five or six standard yarns dyed in up to ten or twelve colours, six of which are shown. The tablecloth ('St. Mary', 1937) is an all-cotton seersucker, the apron ('Griesdale', 1946) an all-cotton 'bird's eye' pattern; the napkin and swatch ('St. Hilier', 1937, and 'Goathland', 1946–9) have cotton wefts and unevenly spaced warps of Nuralyn (a yarn of ramie and cotton created by Felix Lowenstein and confined to Helios except for knitting). The Helios range was the first in Britain created specifically to provide well-designed, reasonably priced woven fabrics. (Until about 1960 firms such as Edinburgh Weavers and Warners tended to concentrate on architect- or decorator-commissioned work.)

THE SATURDAY·EVENING
POST

NOVEMBER 18, 1950   15¢

Chapter Seven

Individuality

1950–1980

'The kind of ambiance most people want today [is] an elegance gently tempered by nostalgia, by fantasy, by romance. The interesting thing about these temperings is that . . . they are wholly individualistic.' (American *House and Garden*[1])

The postwar building boom, the creation of giant multi-national textile manufacturers and increased education contributed to the twinned desires to procure and provide which characterized the period from 1950 to 1980. In the Western world, newly freed from the trauma of war, much of the zeal that propelled society forward was based on an acute sense of the value of the individual. Increasingly dominated by the media, cajoled by advertisers and tempted by 'designer' names, consumers were at the same time urged to express themselves.

For over one hundred years, as mass production had increased, the need to distinguish one interior, or one textile from another had also been growing. So, too, had the importance of the designer, who was increasingly viewed as the key to this distinction. This had been acknowledged in the 1930s, when a review of the fabrics at the British Industrial Art Exhibition of 1933 admitted that 'the problems and penalties of standardisation and mass production haunt us to-day with their insistence. Essential though mass production un-doubtedly is, we must not let it detract our attention from the body of individual and creative work which is still being carried on.'[2] The industry was clearly at a crossroads, uncertain in which direction lay a successful future. The choice was not only between machine and hand production, traditional and modern design, but whether – and, if so, to what extent – to combine different approaches to style and manufacture. To compound the problem further, the definition of 'modern' was by no means agreed.

The intervention of the Second World War delayed the resolution of these difficulties, turning attention in the 1940s to the broader issue – the meaning and function of good design. The American industrial designer Raymond Loewy proposed that 'a good design will open up new markets, but it must progressively sustain that market for re-sale'; it must create and foster 'a public taste that demands an increasingly high standard of design and engineering perfection'. This reasoning appreciated style for its ability to sell products and sell the services of the designer. It did not promote the 'serious'-modern style of the prewar years, which Loewy himself disliked;

1 This *Saturday Evening Post* cover by Norman Rockwell celebrates the return to normal domestic life which was still a high priority in both Britain and the United States in 1950. The chair is covered with a fabric printed with scenes of American rural life. Similar textiles were produced in America by Riverdale Fabrics. They were nicknamed 'Grandma Moses' fabrics, because they borrowed images from the work of the primitive artist of that name. The haphazard placement of motifs, the thick cotton chenille piping (recommended among the 'dressmaker touches' for home furnishings) and the deep, irregular box pleats suggest that this is a homemade loose cover.

2 For the Festival of Britain, 1951, a
number of products – including textiles –
were created with designs based on
crystallography. To inspire and develop
patterns, participating firms (known as
the Festival Pattern Group) were issued
with die-lines of over twenty different
crystal structures, of which three, based
on insulin, are shown.

many of the 'cold, uninspiring examples of so-called Functionalism', he
asserted, 'are rebukes to the profession of Industrial Design'.[3] The British
Council of Industrial Design, founded in 1944, interpreted good design in
a similar way, 'encouraging fresh thought and design in both the old craft-
based and the new technical industries', whether the inspiration for a
good design was original or traditional.[4]

The desire to increase public awareness of good design was not entirely
motivated by a desire for commercial gain; there also existed a genuine
belief in the democracy of design. Reminiscent of William Morris was the
conviction that more pleasant surroundings created a better life; new to
the 1940s and '50s was the optimistic theory that class barriers were
disappearing and that new products could both serve and satisfy a
classless society.

In this idealistic climate, exhibitions in both Britain and the United
States set out in the 1940s and '50s to educate the public. The 'Britain Can
Make It' and Festival of Britain exhibitions in 1946 and 1951, respectively,
and the series of Good Design exhibitions, the first held at New York's
Museum of Modern Art in 1940, displayed modern products selected for
their superior design. This in itself was not new, but the educational,
almost evangelical, approach to the subject was. In retrospect, it is clear
that the museum- and government-sponsored programmes, intended to
raise the quality of life through design, probably brought greatest satisfaction to those who created the objects, or selected, displayed or promoted
them. Nevertheless, the resulting celebration of mass production, the
prevailing spirit of the years around 1950, firmly (if temporarily) established engineering, science and machine production as the guiding
principles for textile manufacturers and designers. The term applied to
the resulting style for household goods was 'contemporary'.

Apart from providing an ideological basis for design, the 1940s had also
contributed stylistic and technical innovations, many of which were not
widely apparent in homes until the 1950s. Among the new products were
printed rayon taffeta shower and matching window curtains, treated, as
the American magazine *Interiors* proclaimed, 'with the same mildew and
water repellant process used by Textron on jungle hammocks for the
South Pacific'; fiber glass marquisettes and printed curtain fabrics (which
did not shrink, rot, burn or need ironing); and vinyl compounds used in
sheet form (thin for curtains, thicker for upholstery), as a fabric coating,
and as a filament, or yarn, for weaving. Experimentation with new fibres
had continued throughout the war; the Americans had Aralac (made of
casein, or milk protein, also used in plastics), as well as other fibres, man-
made by chemical treatment of the proteins in soybeans and peanuts.[5] By
the 1950s it was clear which were to be the most important developments;
joining the first synthetic yarn, nylon, were the newer synthetic acrylics,
modified acrylics and polyesters – the last-named invented by John
Whinfield and J. T. Dickson of Britain's Calico Printers Association in 1941
and first produced in America from 1946 by E. I. du Pont de Nemours &
Co. (Du Pont), who developed it under the brand name Dacron.

Rayon and acetate (man-made from plant cellulose) were not imme-

3 In Paul T. Frankl's introduction to *American Textiles Today* (1955), he noted that hand-weaving had 'recently established a new place for itself and by so doing has added prestige and variety to the textile market'. 'The public response,' he continued, 'has been so rewarding that we find machine-made textiles imitating the materials woven by hand, even to the point of aping the imperfections that are so characteristic of the originals.' (see, for example, Fig. 43). Shown here is the work of three weavers associated with this trend (clockwise from bottom): a window blind of about 1950, by Dorothy Liebes, of bamboo splits, wooden dowels, rayon, cotton and metallics; 'Magnum', by Jack Lenor Larsen, 1970, a mirrored, Mylar polyester film, machine-embroidered with coloured cottons and rayons; and a 1951 fabric by Evelyn Hill, woven in wool, viscose rayon and synthetic raffia. Also shown is a hand-screen-printed linen designed in 1955 by Marianne Strengell. Called 'Double Print', since the same screen is used in opposite directions to create the design, it also demonstrates the exploration of techniques so typical of the 1950s.

diately threatened by the new synthetic fibres (made entirely from chemical substances), which did not drape well, yellowed and attracted dirt. They also had design limitations because they were difficult to print (a problem still not resolved successfully for acrylics). Far more influential in 1950s interiors were the vinyls, which, like the parallel developments for moulded and extruded furniture, were greeted as signs of an efficient, egalitarian machine age. An American writer even ecstatically predicted the day when 'junior romps into mother's boudoir, leans a jam-sandwich-clutching fist against the pale, quilted satin walls, grabs filmy draperies with another grimy paw, steadies a grease-covered knee on a white upholstered chair, and just gets beamed at by his doting mother . . .' – all through the miracle of vinyl and vinyl-coated fabrics.[6]

By 1950 vinyls were being embossed in imitation of elephant hide, straw, rope, velvet and quilting, or finished like patent leather. These 'fabrics' were stylish: Schumacher's weather-resistant fabrics were selected by James Amster to accompany his nostalgic wrought-iron furniture and featured in American *Vogue*'s February issue in 1949. Knoll Associates, one of the most influential American furniture manufacturers, included plasticized woven upholstery fabrics in their 1950 range, together with fabrics woven from filament saran (a vinylidene chloride copolymer – melted mixtures of resins – which the Dow Chemical Company began developing in 1937).

The first signs of disenchantment were not apparent until about 1959, when, for example, *Design* magazine (the mouthpiece of Britain's Council of Industrial Design) commented that despite changes in colour or pattern, the basic character and texture of vinyls and vinyl-treated fabrics could not substantially be altered.[7] Thereafter, vinyls were increasingly

4 Two Tootal furnishing fabrics of 1957 show the most popular colour combinations of the second half of the 1950s, whether applied to designs in traditional or, as here, modern style. (The 1950s interpretation of Regency relied heavily on red, greyish-black, and cream or white – particularly for the ubiquitous striped wallpapers and woven fabrics.) Here the theme is 'modern-rural', as emphasized by the Morris-like chair, upholstered in a woven fabric. The use of bright turquoise as an accent colour was common throughout the 1950s; it was one of the new dye shades perfected by ICI during the war. Hanging behind the chair, 'Arlequino' (a 48-inch-wide hand-screen-printed cotton satin) was moderately priced at £1 per yard.

reserved for outdoor furniture, shower curtains, and contract use in cars, aeroplanes and offices. Saran has since become better known in America as part of the generic term 'saran wrap' or cling-film, while the related polyvinyl chloride (PVC) provided an important rubber substitute in applications as diverse as electrical wire casings and raincoats.

Stylistically, the wartime concentration on engineering and science also had an impact. The crystal-structure patterns which formed the keynote of the Festival of Britain testified to the interest in science-based curved and geometric shapes; related to engineering and electronics were images generated by cardiographs and radar screens, as well as the more typical skeletal, section and outline drawings, including drawings of buildings, cross-sections of fruit and vegetables, or everyday objects sketched in outline form. There were of course also traditional designs to suit the still-fashionable neo-Georgian interiors. Many such designs incorporated modern taste by using lightly sketched details, while scenic toiles needed no adaptation, having the requisite fine-line drawing. In some instances fine lines were applied to compensate for a lack of textured fabrics; due to yarn shortages they were printed on rayon, for example, to give the impression of a herringbone tweed.

Metallic colours and surfaces were another legacy from the war. These included battleship-grey dyes, metallic prints and metallic yarns such as Lurex, developed by Doebeckman in the United States and available worldwide by the early 1950s. The metallic yarns were particularly popular, both for opaque woven upholstery and curtains and for sheers. Developments in the dyestuffs industry during the war had led to a wider range of fast colours (and the possibility of matching curtains to plastic furniture and utensils). Vat dyes, previously restricted to cottons, were extended to woollens and fine delicate fibres. Deep reds, oranges, yellows, purples, greens, aquas and black were also made available in cheaper reactive dyes which linked chemically with fibres during fixation (a post-printing process). From 1956 these began to replace the non-fast and inexpensive chrome dyes on cotton and acetate. They were also found to be useful for printing polyester (which was easier than cotton to dye, but had been difficult to print using previously known methods).

The crisp, austere lines of many designs of the 1950s were balanced by these bright colours. Most contemporary designs used no more than three or four colours, one of which was a neutral – grey, white or, typically, black. The restriction of colours had been a means of economizing for the British, and in the 1950s remained a distinctive feature of their printed and woven fabrics, whether produced in limited quantities by 'upmarket' firms such as Heals, Edinburgh Weavers, Warners or Liberty, or in much larger amounts by Sandersons, Sekers, Horrockses, David Whitehead, Donald Brothers or Storeys of Lancashire (whose printing plant was the first to use photo-engraving in the early 1950s.

In the United States such limiting of colours was not financially necessary. There, however, it was maintained as a distinguishing feature of avant-garde design, which tended towards a feeling of clarity and spaciousness. Designers refrained from covering the cloth completely with

5 Among the many abstract textile designs in the years after the Second World War were those that used fine lines in a manner that suggested mathematical symbols, transistor-board diagrams or scientific notations. This example of about 1953 was hand-screen-printed in black on natural by Laverne Originals, a New York-based firm which had been founded in about 1937. Some of its shapes also echo the lines of the steel tubing legs of chairs designed shortly after the war by Charles and Ray Eames, Eero Saarinen and others.

pattern in order to emphasize the fabric itself. The use of a limited number of colours on an uncoloured ground was particularly noticeable in the early-1950s hand-screen-printed abstract designs in the ranges of Angelo Testa, Laverne Originals, Ruth Adler Schnee, Knoll Associates, Schiffer Prints and Elenhank Designers. Such highly stylized prints were aimed specifically at the American architect and furniture designer whose contemporary tastes could not abide what Angelo Testa described as 'Nature in all her splendor . . . supremely represented on all of the furniture and furnishings.'[8]

Hand screen printing entered the 1950s with two advantages: novelty and prestige. It was still a relatively new technique; and it was already associated with the designer-craftsman tradition. The economics of machine printing militated against innovation; and although a few roller-printing firms were sufficiently encouraged by the enthusiasm for modern design to invest in artist-designed fabrics, most were forced to hesitate until the cost of setting up an engraved design seemed likely to be justified by volume sales. Among the early 1950s contemporary prints, the majority were therefore still hand-screen-printed, and in terms of price were comparable with (and sometimes more expensive than) power-woven cloths. However, this was soon to change.

Screen prints were pushed to the fore by several other factors, all of which came into play in the mid-1950s. As wide picture windows and patio doors became more common features in new homes, bold, bright straight-hanging curtains with large pattern repeats were promoted. Entire walls of such curtains were fashionable in both large and small rooms, providing a focal point in rooms with central heating (and therefore, often, no fireplace) and compensating for the lack of architectural details such as coving or panelling. Jacquard weaving and block printing had previously been the only techniques that allowed long repeats (engraved rollers were limited to a design height of about 24 inches or 60 centimetres). Flat screens, which were cheaper to set up, maintain and use than Jacquards or blocks – and were also capable of stretching to a design height of 60 inches (153 centimetres) or more – therefore had an advantage.[9] They were also less threatened by Japan's and India's massive increase in basic yarn and cloth production, which undermined cotton spinning and weaving in Britain to such an extent that the Lancashire industry collapsed. There, between 1954 and 1957, more than 250 weaving mills closed. The United States was affected in a similar but less dramatic way, and by about 1965 both countries were using more imported than domestically produced fabrics.

Despite the efforts of avant-garde print designers, most of the 1950s upholstery fabrics were weaves – maintaining, for modern furniture, a tradition established in the 1930s in Britain and Scandinavia. However, several developments in the mid-1950s counteracted the tendency to regard printed cottons as informal fabrics, unsuitable for the more formal role ascribed to sofas and chairs. Silicone treatments were introduced to make printed cottons and linens soil-resistant, eliminating one objection to their use as fixed upholstery. Attitudes also changed with the ap-

6 The interest in designing for dual-use spaces, evident since the 1920s, had by 1950 become a matter of necessity. In this studio apartment, designed by George Nelson for the Brooklyn Museum's 1957 exhibition 'Home Furnishings, Old and New', an entire wall of curtains suggests an expanse of glass and provides a visual focus, while the remaining textiles supply additional colours and textures. The early-nineteenth-century furniture and accessories from the museum were said to harmonize successfully with the modern elements 'because of a common quality of elegance.' Nelson, one of America's most influential architect/designers, was appointed in 1946 as the first design director of the furniture firm Herman Miller, and here may well have utilized Miller fabrics, which from 1952 until the late 1960s were designed under the direction of Alexander Girard.

pearance of cottons in postwar French and British *haute couture* – advocated by the British Cotton Board's 'Colour, Design and Style Centre' and accomplished with the help of Zika Ascher's innovative dress prints. Finally, as mechanized forms of screen printing (perfected before the war) began to be introduced in the mid-1950s, the price of screen prints gradually dropped. These factors, in conjunction with the enthusiasm for vinyl fabrics and un-upholstered plastic, wood or metal furniture, resulted in the most dramatic change in interiors over the next twenty-five years: the virtual disappearance, in many homes, of non-printed fabrics.

In 1955 'the recent sharp effect in prints' was also noted by a British writer as part of 'the trend for "contemporary" [which] has been particularly kind to cotton'.[10] Kinder still to British cotton prints was the abolition of purchase tax early in the same year. This reduced the cost of all household textiles and furnishing fabrics (other than woollens) by 25 per cent and launched the consuming 'boom' which was already noticeable in the United States, where 'daily, our advertising celebrates in prose and song the advantages of maximum production and consumption.' The more rapid replacement of furnishings also favoured prints over weaves (which are generally more durable), so that Arthur Drexler – whose just-quoted comment on mass manufacture was written in 1956 – could also note that 'the rich and the not rich may equally pride themselves on owning fabrics our grandfathers would have regarded as poor investments, because they will not last at least ten years'.[11]

The increased demand reinstated variety in design. Immediately, British *Vogue* noticed 'greater imagination, more adventure and experiment in curtainings', adding that 'manufacturers seem willing to print designs quite unlike those of their competitors and to make sales on individuality'.[12] Demand in Britain was nevertheless tempered by the economic need to export – a factor that often made it easier to purchase a high-quality British-made fabric in the United States than at home. Many British firms specializing in high-priced cloths survived largely due to their exports, and so it did not really matter to their business that, for example, 'the treasures of Edinburgh Weavers are usually limited, for the general public, to what can be seen through their great glass doors'.[13] This comment, by a *Sunday Times* journalist, could equally have applied to companies such as Heals, Warners or Liberty, for in 1957 the retail prices for their good-quality power-weaves and hand-prints ranged from 22 to 33 shillings per yard, more than twice the price of a machine print or a coarse 'folk weave'. (At the exchange rate of $2.80 to £1, however, they averaged $3.75 per yard, a middle-market price in the United States.) By the early 1960s British wages were rising faster than retail prices, leaving more disposable income for textile companies to pursue. By March 1963 *Ideal Home* could comment, of the British, 'we're not yet as decoratively fashion-conscious as some Americans, who re-scheme their rooms annually, but manufacturers are doing their very best to tempt us to spend our money on curtains', adding that mass-producers were now making original and beautiful fabrics – citing as an example Cepea, with their inexpensive range of roller-printed designs by Audrey Levy, Roger Nicholson, Humphrey Spender and students from London's Royal College of Art.

Much of the variety available in textile designs of this period resulted directly from the presence of a designer, either in a controlling position in an already-established, small avant-garde firm, or working freelance. While this may seem self-evident, it was the promotion of fabrics by the designer's name that allowed greater diversity within each range; one artist-designer was not expected to produce work like another but was, rather, encouraged to create his or her distinctive style. This was not a new idea, but it received more attention during the 1950s and early 1960s because it went hand-in-hand with the educational aims of exhibitions, awards, and magazine articles, many of which continued to stress the value of good design (and good designers) to the renewal and maintenance of industrial prosperity. The emphasis on individuality was also a natural corollary to the increased provision of professional training for aspiring textile and interior designers.

In recognition of the press-worthiness of a 'designer' label, collections without this cachet began to be grouped into 'themes'. In the United States, Greeff Fabrics was one of the first to exploit this device, which allowed manufacturers, particularly in America, to aim merchandise at a specific market. One of Greeff's 1955 collections, for example, was 'For Men Only', and comprised ten designs based on c.1900 images including cars and women, and intended for dens, clubs, studies and restaurants.

Having long been assumed to be uninterested in interiors, men now began to be recognized as influential in the purchase of fabrics and furniture. More men had also begun to enter the field of interior decoration; in 1955, one of them, William Pahlmann, commented, on behalf of fellow American men, that 'a little trimming goes a long way, and it should be used with taste and discretion. . . . There is nothing worse than finding

7 The sense of freedom that swept through the Western world at the end of the Second World War was expressed partly in a desire to travel. Between 1950 and 1980 first-hand experience of foreign cultures became possible for a much larger section of the population than ever before, and textiles throughout this period have reflected tastes broadened in this way. In the years around 1950 Paris was a particularly fashionable destination, and apart from inspiring the 'New Look' and many Hollywood films, such as *Gigi* and *An American in Paris*, it promoted café curtains, gingham tablecloths and wrought-iron 'café' furniture. Evoking a number of these themes is 'Grand Hotel', a hand-screen-printed cotton satin designed by Sylvia Goodale and produced by Warners in 1950.

8 Photographed in the late 1960s, this living room in one of Liberace's homes reflects, in its conspicuous display of wealth and its necessity for well-behaved inhabitants, the persistence of baroque-modern as a principle of decorating. True to prewar examples of this style, the objects and furniture are from a mixture of periods, authentic and reproduction, but the modern furniture has been covered in modern fabric (a white damask with integral fringing, created by cutting long floating threads after weaving), while the 'Louis' chair has traditionally styled machine-made 'tapestry' upholstery.

a hapless man wading around in a sea of flounces, ruffles and ball fringe.'[14] This was partly an attack on the lingering and often frothy baroque-modern – considered unsuitably grand and a little too foreign – and partly an attempt to curtail the 'dressmaker' touches applied by amateur decorators.

The last stronghold of 1930s and '40s froth was glass curtains, which were recommended by some writers up to the early 1960s as a means of presenting a unified appearance from the outside. Many different fabrics were available for these curtains. Typical was one list of 1959 with twenty-five recommended fabrics for bedroom glass curtains, including (among the sheers, or 'nets', as they are often called in Britain) dimity, cheesecloth, chiffon, dotted swiss, nylon and metallic 'plaids' and *point d'esprit*, and (among the opaque fabrics) Chinese silk, handkerchief linen, rayon dress fabrics and madras cotton. Within each type of fabric was even more variety. Dotted swiss, for example, was available in white with coloured dots, including red, yellow, green and black, or in pastel shades with self-coloured or white dots. Many of these fabrics were available as ready-made glass curtains – plain, ruffled or tiered.[15]

However, many cross-over sheer curtains were replaced in the 1950s by sheer or opaque half-length 'café' curtains, initially fashionable for both dining rooms and living rooms and part of a fascination with Paris which was also reflected in wrought-iron 'café' chairs and printed fabrics featuring Parisian scenes. They were used alone, or with curtains set in front of the window frame, or upper swags or a valance. However, by the early 1960s draw curtains alone were far more common in living rooms – sometimes stretched across more than one window to suggest a non-existent picture window.

A wide variety of fabric types for opaque curtains and upholstery were also still being made into the early 1960s. Block printing, roller printing, fancy yarn spinning and hand weaving had not yet become the highly specialized and limited production techniques that they are today. (They were, however, already becoming relatively more expensive; at Warners, for example, a simple power-woven cloth in 1961 cost about 16 shillings; a hand-woven silk damask was 15 times more; and a hand-brocaded silk 46 times more, costing over £36 a yard.) The provision of variety was also in the mind of Tibor Reich (whose English firm Tibor Ltd. was better known in the 1950s for its Jacquard weaves) when he produced 'textured' prints in over a dozen colourways. These were designed to be used either as two curtains in different colours, each capable of covering the window and therefore offering a choice of effect, or in curtains made of seamed panels in different colour combinations.[16] The latter practice had a brief vogue in both Britain and the United States in the years around 1960, although it seems to have been more commonly done with completely plain fabrics.

Signs of the more limited choice just over the horizon were nevertheless visible as early as 1951, when one writer complained that 'dimity seldom appears in the decorative market in any range of patterns and sometimes cannot be found there at all. It is usually available among the dress goods.'[17] The limitations were not in surface design, which continued throughout this period to change rapidly, but, rather, in the surface itself, which became increasingly standardized. This occurred as a result of a second industrial revolution, which, between 1946 and the early 1980s, employed both new methods and increased mechanization of known methods to boost spinning speeds by eight times and weaving speeds by five. Fully mechanized rotary (or roller) screen printing, introduced in the mid-1960s, used, with very few exceptions, a standard plain-weave base or 'grey' cloth. All of the economic, social, technical and architectural changes, when taken together, ensured that for most of the forty years after the war, screen-printed fabrics were the preferred form of patterned textiles. As a result, particularly in the second half of the 1960s and throughout most of the 1970s, there were few textured fabrics to be seen in the mass-market manufacturers' ranges.

There were, however, exceptions. Expensive modern furniture (though often upholstered in leather) continued to display predominantly plain (off-white or bright) textural dobby-weaves, produced by a number of up-market firms, including those of Boris Kroll, Jack Lenor Larsen, Herman Miller and the Knolls in the United States and the established weaving firms in Britain. As the International style gained ascendancy, the furniture forms of the 1940s lost their splayed and often thin legs, and now tended to 'float' above tubular steel supports, a form of construction that emphasized the shape of the seat and back, and demanded upholstery which enhanced the boldness of form. Subtle weave structures, with a rich interplay of colour and texture which printing could not duplicate, were ideally suited to this task. International style furniture, prominent in corporate offices, never replaced in homes the more moderately priced, mass-produced Scandinavian and British modern wooden-framed sofas and chairs; and after about 1960 the interest in both styles began to wane. Sheer dobby-woven curtains until the early 1970s were one of the few types of innovative woven cloths to attain wider use in domestic interiors.

9 When, in 1964, Courtauld's took over Edinburgh Weavers, the latter's stylist, Isabell Tisdall, founded Tamesa to cater for the exclusive British market, which was increasingly buying expensive woven fabrics from the Continent. The fabrics shown here, designed between 1964 and 1970, give an indication of the range of weaves sold (printed fabrics were also stocked). Third from the top is 'Allegro', designed by Frank Davies in 1968; the remainder were designed by Marianne Straub. Included are (from top) first, a worsted mock-leno; fourth and fifth, cotton/viscose cloths with irregularly spaced warps (part of a group of correlated curtain and upholstery fabrics produced between 1967 and 1969); and sixth, a worsted curtain fabric of 1966, selected by British Rail for their Midland Region trains. All were woven for Tamesa by Warner & Sons Ltd.

10 As the baby boom generation began to furnish their own interiors, they applied a noticeably new set of criteria. By about 1964 buying-to-last had been replaced by buying-for-now, and the relatively inexpensive furniture made to satisfy these new demands (and often bought in kit form) generally relied for effect on brightly painted surfaces or a visually aggressive upholstery cloth. In this British interior a plywood sofa, from (or after) Max Clendenning's Maxima range of 1966 for Race Furniture Ltd., is upholstered with a boldly coloured cotton screen print. The deep apple-green colour in both the print and the shag rug was – used in this quantity – unique to 1960s interiors.

Mass-produced furniture began to be fully upholstered in the early 1960s – the dominant (and still-fashionable) style being the two- or three-cushioned sofa popularized by decorators before the war. As the 1960s progressed, these were typically covered in a printed cotton. As with base-cloths for printing, mass-produced furniture forms relied for variety on the pattern printed on the cloth. This provided another impetus for frequent updating of textile designs, which by the end of the 1950s were already turning to 'Americana' and 'Victoriana' themes, including the revival of William Morris patterns.

The 'serious' Modernist style – esteemed by some for over thirty years – began to be regarded as history. As Elizabeth Benn commented in the London *Daily Telegraph*, in 1966, 'Every five years or so furniture and decorating styles begin to change. Since 1950 we've been through Festival [of Britain] and Scandinavian decor and now that we are comfortably surrounded by Victoriana people are beginning to ask: what next? Judging by the amount of chromed metal furniture and jazz-patterned fabrics creeping into the shops it looks as though we are going back to the ''modern'' style of the Thirties.'[18] Although this relegation of Modernism to the status of just another fashion offended its disciples, and was disputed by manufacturers who, convinced of its timelessness, revived inter-war furniture by designers such as Le Corbusier, Mies van der Rohe and Marcel Breuer, the philosophy of Functionalism no longer dominated interior design. Instead, the impetus was provided by pop art, which freely extracted, flattened and intensified elements from a wide range of sources, including – in textile designs – the 1930s, Art Nouveau, op art, the traditional floral and even, incestuously, the work of pop artists. Andy Warhol, Roy Lichtenstein and Richard Hamilton were among the artists who both influenced and responded to the design of household items. The bold outlines and felt-tip-pen-like colours of many textile designs of the 1960s also owed a great deal to graphic designers, among whom the most influential was the American Peter Max.

Whereas modern-style interiors of the 1950s and early '60s acquired a measure of individuality through the use of a single striking 'designer' fabric (whether by a fine artist or a well-known professional designer), in the following ten years or so, this element was achieved through a medley of patterns and furniture types. A contrast between intense colours and bold patterns extended to the walls, which up to the early 1960s had exemplified the preference of the International style for light, plain surfaces. As a sense of insecurity began to seep through the veneer of postwar optimism, some found this effect inappropriately reserved. As one British journalist put it in 1964, 'You begin to yearn for a bit of colour in all the whiteness like you yearn for a bit of humour in Simone de Beauvoir – it is as urgent as that. And who do we think we are kidding anyhow, all this stark simplicity in the middle of the boom time for complexes!'[19] Rooms as a reflection of character could be 'masculine' (leather and tweed), 'romantic' (mirrors, silvered walls and floral patterns) or 'fantasies' (glitter and fur). 'Young' interiors stressed disposable or 'found' items – including bead or bamboo curtains, paper chairs and circular inflatable plastic cushions. These and other inexpensive furnishings, such as pre-formed laminated timber furniture (painted, typically, red, white or green) were no longer purchased from established shops, but from import warehouses or boutiques.

While their appearance was changing rapidly, the *use* of furnishing fabrics changed little at this time. No distinctively new drapery or upholstering techniques were introduced; the only significant innovation was the revival of the fabric-covered wall, perhaps partly because it provided the sound insulation found necessary in newly built apartments. What had changed was the *attitude* to interiors. The careful, well-judged style of the 1950s (represented by the concern that curtains should appear uniform from the outside), gave way to an *ad hoc* method of decorating. At the luxury end of the market, some rooms used extremely expensive materials, such as fur, or high-style minimalist furniture as an adjunct to an art collection. In the middle were mainstream interiors with coordinated fabrics (to contrast rather than match); and at the other extreme were the 'throwaway' interiors, with their ironic mixture of modern, traditional and 'found' objects.

Printed fabrics survived well through these trends, despite the fact that 'young' interiors often included such items (recommended in the American *House & Garden* in 1968) as vinyl pouffes at $5, Paper Moon paper tables ($30) and chairs ($15), moulded plastic and folding cane chairs ($40) and director's chairs ($15).[20] Only the last-named included a textile – a plain-dyed canvas. It was this kind of weave which, along with denim, was most

11 In the years around 1970 the complementary developments of free-form furniture and stretch-knitted fabrics proved a serious threat to manufacturers of woven fabrics. Interiors such as this, furnished with Turner T-furniture upholstered in Jack Lenor Larsen's 'Contour' (wool stretch fabric) and 'Firebird' (hand-screen-printed stretch Caprolan nylon), were intended to emphasize the theme of sensuous curves, curvilinear forms and contrasting textures which are repeated in the fabric-covered shell. Larsen's phosphorescent casement, used on either side of the chimney breast, completes the moon-like allusions by transmitting what was described as an 'ethereal blue' onto the vaulted ceiling.

popular in 'young' interiors of this period. Even the avant garde turned to legless free-form furniture, exploiting Plexiglass, injected foam and moulded plastics. Free-form seating, when upholstered, generally used a double jersey knitted fabric, which could be stretched to conform to rounded edges.

Double jersey knitting – developed in Eastern Europe – had begun on a commercial scale in the West in the late 1950s, supported by the synthetics manufacturers, who saw double jersey as a natural end product for their yarns. In the heyday of synthetics (from about 1951 to 1972), the production of these yarns supported much of the new technology which accounted for the standardization and amalgamation of the industry. Large conglomerates had existed before the War, but after 1950 their characteristics changed from horizontal (concentrating on one aspect of the product) to vertical (extending from manufacturing to sales). Firms such as Courtaulds, Coats Patons and ICI, in Britain, and Westpoint Pepperell, Burlington, Spring Mills and Textron, in the United States, also became giant international concerns, controlling the major supplies (and therefore the appearance) of yarns, dyestuffs and household textiles, such as sheets and towels. Many of the small avant-garde firms which had provided design leadership and variety were absorbed into these large firms, losing their identity in the process.

Faced with the need to inject personality into their mass-produced products, multinationals began to commission fashion designers such as Christian Dior, Bill Blass and Mary Quant to design sheets and towels, the printing of which had become economically and aesthetically viable around 1963 with the perfection of photographically engraved seamless nickel cylinders. (The use of pigment dyes on polyester-cotton sheeting was introduced at the same time, and is now a universal practice.) The Americans were first to market their household textiles as part of the fashion sector, and in doing so re-introduced the *en suite* bedroom (and invented the *en suite* – that is, coordinating – bathroom), providing sets of designs for the mass market which embraced such items as curtains, quilted bedcovers, towels and bathmats.

Despite the great advances made in synthetic fibre performance by the mid-1960s, market research revealed that although people appreciated these fibres' easy-care qualities, they preferred the feel of cotton and linen.[21] In response to this attitude, further developments led to texturized synthetics and more advanced techniques for blending synthetics with natural fibres. As a result of these improvements, weavers began once again to have a wider range of 'fancy' yarns at their disposal, although this advantage was initially taken up more noticeably in the fashion industry, particularly in knitwear, than in furnishing textiles. By 1971 an American writer could advise that 'it is almost unnecessary to learn to recognize traditional weaves and fibers; usually you must read the label. . . . For instance, a leather I admired lately turned out to be a cotton coated with polyurethane.'[22]

Just as the manufacturers of synthetic fibres were introducing yarns and blends with a more natural appearance, which might ultimately have led

12 In about 1963 Stork, a textile engineering firm in Amsterdam, perfected a seamless nickel cylinder for rotary screen printing. This new cylinder eliminated the restrictions on designers that the existing welded cylinders had imposed, and was also capable of greater fineness of detail. (Today ninety per cent of all fabrics worldwide are printed by this system.) It also made printed sheets economically viable, which in turn supported the sustained growth of polyester-cotton bed furnishings. By the late 1960s sheetings had become fashion-sensitive and have since reflected the trend towards fully coordinated interiors. With a quilted coverlet (preferred to duvets by the American mass market), this Springmaid bed-set was produced by Spring Mills Inc. in 1979, as part of their 'Newburyport' range, which was based on a French mid-eighteenth-century design. The marketing of ranges on the strength of their historical associations had been part of Springs' policy since the early 1970s.

13 In the late 1960s and early 1970s the trend towards short-lived interiors intensified. Many began to display what the English writer and design critic Reyner Banham described (in an address to the Design and Industries Association's annual conference, 1969) as elements of surprise, of variability, of exploitable imperfection – resulting in a personal statement as unique as its maker. This interior is capable of endless rearranging and is made up of elements that anyone could construct (and thousands of students did). The fabric-covered dado and bedspread are both Indian hand-block-printed cotton; the cushion covers include batiked silks and Kutchi embroidery. These, with their intrinsic imperfections, are contrasted with the bright 'acid' colours and smooth, controlled surfaces of the short-pile fabrics on the remaining cushions.

to the replacement of pure cotton as the principal printing base, the recession of 1971–73 was beginning to have a dramatic effect. Industrial and social unrest had been rife since the mid-1960s, and by about 1970 economic growth had begun to slow down. This was exacerbated by the oil crisis in 1970–71, by which time it was clear that many of the large conglomerates had far more capacity to produce than the public had to consume. Turning their attention to the introduction of less labour-intensive – and therefore ultimately cheaper – methods of production (such as shuttle-less looms), the United States maintained its production of synthetic and blended fabrics, such as sheeting, but Britain, with its smaller market, could not. As the entire industry contracted in both countries, the result was high unemployment; in Britain, for example, 65 per cent of the textile labour force was made redundant (or not replaced on retirement) in the decade following 1972. Weaving was once again the sector most seriously affected; screen printing was the only process that did not decline in Europe and the United States during the 1970s.

The recession had a marked effect on interiors. In 1975, Britain's *Drapery and Fashion Weekly* noted that 'The huge boom in do-it-yourself, make-it-yourself and the revival of crafts underlines the psychological switch people have made . . . from leisure pursuits outside the home to new interests inside it.'[23] As fewer people moved home or bought new furniture, there was an increasing interest in modifying interiors, as opposed to redecorating completely; and this was reflected in the design trends of the 1970s, which reinterpreted themes that had already appeared in the previous decades. Among these were Near Eastern, Oriental and other ethnic patterns. One writer pointed to the 'Beatles/Maharishi Yogi influence, plus a fashion-craze for caftans' in 1968 as the source of interest in Persian and Indian patterns, which at the time were produced in rich

'Mediterranean' colours, becoming paler as the 1970s progressed.[24] (However, such patterns had already existed in psychedelic, highly stylized form in the mid-1960s.) Equally influential were the inexpensive Indian bedspreads imported into Britain and the United States in vast numbers, which brought with them an acceptance of muted colours and crude, blurred printing and inspired many tented interiors, large floor cushions and soft-edged *'Indienne'* prints in the years around 1970. Chinese elements also existed in designs throughout the 1950s, '60s and '70s – in the latter two decades owing a great deal to the revival of interest in the 1920s, when Oriental details had also been fashionable in interiors.

The crafts revival, also, was not new, having existed in two forms since the 1950s. One of its manifestations was the making of individual textile pieces, initially employing mainly the tapestry technique, but gradually incorporating such off-loom methods as wrapping, coiling and plaiting to achieve a more sculptural effect. The other manifestation was the revival of Arts and Crafts patterns, which also had persisted since the late 1950s. The most striking example of this is the continued production of William Morris designs by several British firms over the past thirty years.

14 The architect Steven Yakeley's own home in Cambridge, photographed in 1978, epitomizes the use of 'natural-look' fabrics, which had recently returned to fashion. With the exception of the bold Marimekko print on the wall behind the piano, the remaining fabrics are woven. The hand-spun yarns in the cushions and the striped upholstery cloths provide textures to balance the glass and chrome table and the boldly articulated spaces. Warm tones such as these characterized many interiors of the period.

On both sides of the Atlantic the nostalgic interiors of the 1970s also perpetuated an interest (first evident in the 1960s) in the styles of the inter-war years. Tubular steel furniture was now available at reasonable cost (and therefore widely used), but interpreted in a French 'Provençal' manner, best exemplified by Terence Conran (whose influence began to spread with the publication of his first Habitat catalogue in 1971). Cane seating, baskets, dried flowers, canvas, ticking, trellis-work prints, patch-work coverlets and duvet covers – all in warm and soft or clear colours – were part of an updated urban-rural fashion which mixed sleek 1930s Functionalist furniture with peasant artefacts and which increasingly placed more emphasis on the look than on the philosophy of good design. The simple, 'old-fashioned' rural style of the 1970s, epitomized by Laura Ashley, was merely the other side of the coin, adapting the 'new poor' interiors of the 1920s and '30s, which had similarly been based on floral prints and farmhouse furniture. The main difference between inter-war 'new poor' and 1970s 'old-fashioned' was in the 1970s' vogue for natural pine, which necessitated stripping off layers of paint probably applied in the 1920s or '30s.

The emphasis on natural woods was characteristic of the 'baby boom' generation, who had come of age in the mid-1960s and by the 1970s were focusing on environmental issues, paving the way for further changes in the textile industry. Dyers were forced to use procedures that minimized or purified effluents; later some black dyes ceased to be used when identified as possibly carcinogenic. The return to a preference for natural fibres was in sympathy with 1970s social trends; but an increase in cotton fibre production and weaving in Europe and the United States was also directly caused by the loss of indigenous manufacturers' sales in syn-thetics, which were being made in greater quantities in Near- and Far-Eastern countries, where labour costs (and therefore final costs) remained substantially lower. Since by 1977 cottons were more expensive than polyesters, few British and American manufacturers were competing in the production of all-synthetic, low-cost cloths, and thus were concentrat-ing, by the late 1970s, on the middle and upper end of the market.

More complex blends and weaves also satisfied the manufacturers' need for cloths that justified the middle-to-high price dictated by the economics of production. At the same time, the use of textured yarns and cloths both contributed to a 'natural' look and provided scope for incorporating synthetic and man-made fibres. One result was that, from the mid-1970s onwards, velvets and other pile fabrics gradually became more widely available. These ranged from linen velvets and silicone-treated cotton velvets to sculptured and embossed pile fabrics and simulated furs made from rayon or synthetics. Acrylic velvets gained such popularity for inexpensive curtains and mass-produced three-piece suites of furniture in Britain that Dralon – the brand name of the German firm, Bayer, for their acrylic pile fabric – has become synonymous in Britain with furnishing velvet. By about 1980 texture had also become prominent in prints (especially sheeting), which often included effects such as stippling, hatching or uneven lines and tones.[25] In the case of nostalgic designs, the

15 The renewed interest in texture in the late 1970s meant the return of moquettes to the luxury upholstery market. This example, woven in France for Clarence House of New York, is all-cotton. Based on a Kelim carpet, 'Turkestan' was designed with a single 5-inch border, intended to be cut off and re-applied at the discretion of the designer. In 1989 it was still in the Clarence House range.

16 Offering a 'grown-up' alternative to ethnic decor, romance returned to interiors in the 1970s by way of the bedroom, where 'mini' half-testers, lace, frills and bows began to re-appear in about 1968 (having been unfashionable for a little over a decade). Looking perfectly at home, Zsa Zsa Gabor sits amid an example of 1970s escapism, complete with the crisp, fresh-looking field flowers found on many printed textiles of the period and offset by the equally fresh and fashionable colours used in the silk taffeta half-tester. The increased provision of printed fabrics with large areas of white ground and overprinted white details was a testament to the improved colourfastness and dirt-repelling treatments of the 1970s.

desire for complexity brought larger and more sophisticated patterns, requiring a well-judged use of colour and richly detailed motifs – found particularly in revived Regency and Victorian designs.

Nostalgia and market forces therefore combined in the late 1970s to bring the English chintz style greater attention. Today we equate it with the country-house style and 'as-it-used-to-be' restorations (although it should be noted that many of the restorations of the 1960s – such as that undertaken at Audley End, north of London – owed more to the enthusiasm for artificial fibres and low cost than to authenticity). The long-established policy, among some manufacturers, of basing collections on museum objects had also continued in the United States. In the 1940s and '50s the interest had gradually shifted from museums to historic house collections, remaining there into the 1980s; and this trend, too, occasionally pushed an 'authentic' chintz into the limelight during the 1960s and '70s. It also reinforced many British manufacturers' and wholesalers' appreciation of their own archives as sources of 'document' designs. But the real impetus behind the restoration of chintz (both as a finish for cottons and as a design style) had less to do with such trends within the furnishing fabrics industry than with those in fashion.

The influence of fashion on the development of furnishing colour ranges and designs had been noticed just before the War, and its role in the promotion of cotton has already been commented on. Between 1952 and 1954 French *couture* designers, including Schiaparelli and Christian Dior, used large floral screen prints for evening gowns, establishing a taste for nineteenth-century floral designs and also for less literal, watercolour-like interpretations. However, these tended to be printed silks. It was the Colour, Design and Style Centre in Manchester that played the most crucial part in the resurgence of English chintz designs on glazed cottons, with its exhibition of these fabrics in 1955 (intended as a promotion of cottons to high-quality garment makers). This was the basis of a larger exhibition tracing the history of British cotton printing which was held at the Victoria & Albert Museum in the summer of 1960. 'Suddenly', the *Tatler* announced, 'there's a revival in English chintz.' Variations on, or, occasionally, straight reproductions of designs first block-printed in the nineteenth century (and very like the high-fashion fabrics of six or seven years before) were said to have outsold abstract design in that year.[26] And they continued to gain popularity.

In 1966 it was reported that despite the vogue for rich contrasting colours and generous, abstract designs, modified by distinctive, slightly geometric outlines, floral chintzes were the best British fabric exports, particularly to the United States. In both countries during the 1950s and '60s, however, the original colours were seldom used, and chintzes were updated with contemporary colourways or produced in monochrome schemes. By the early 1970s there was greater concern for authenticity, although monochrome versions remained popular, probably due to the fact that – as the magazine *The Ambassador* put it – 'the moderns' conception of things is more like ideas of them, in black and white, like TV'. With the arrival of the recession and the associated romantic revival, *The Times*

17 Given to the Preservation Society of Newport County in 1972, Kingscote, a Newport, Rhode Island, summer house, was designed for George Noble Jones by Richard Upjohn in about 1840 and enlarged by Stanford White in 1881–2. With its crisp pinch-pleated curtains, chintz covers, marcella-type quilted bedspread and a colour scheme which was the height of fashion for retrospectively styled modern rooms, the bedroom's decoration provides a visual summary of the historical 'eye' of the 1960s and early 1970s.

could report in 1974 that 'no matter how purple, orange or red dominate the current scene, more people go back for floral chintzes than for any other kind of furnishing or curtain material'.[27]

The romantic trends so characteristic of the 1970s had also been present, since the 1950s, in the United States, where the interest in restoration and heritage combined to keep small-scale 'calico' prints and imitation patchwork or stencilled designs continually in the marketplace. Although by the mid-1970s the fashion for 'old-fashioned' floral furnishing prints was fairly universal, initially the interest in Americana was stronger in New England than in other regions. In fact, another aspect of the individuality prevalent in interiors of this period was the more noticeable regional variations. The Western states, for example, retained an interest in the International style, perhaps because both the climate and the local vernacular architecture were so compatible with white or light-coloured plastered walls and lightweight textured curtains. By 1972, when the American *House & Garden* acknowledged that the American 'desire to preserve what's good of all periods is as active in Texas and California as it is on Long Island and in Massachusetts', the editors could include factory-built modular homes as part of this trend by viewing them 'as right in the middle of American tradition with its implied attitude that when there's a lack there's technology to fill it'.[28]

With so much nostalgia in the air, it was odd that lace-like net curtains had such a bad time of it in the 1960s and 1970s. As a British observer noted, they came to be regarded 'with the kind of sneer usually reserved for leatherette sofas, teak-look television cabinets and nodding doggies in

18 Throughout the 1970s, Laura Ashley cottons were single and, later, two-colour prints, typically with small-scale patterns such as seen in the green 'Wild Clematis' (1976/7), 'Nutmeg' (1976) and (in the cup) 'Cottage Rose Sprig' (1979). Influential in restoring 'petite' patterns to interiors, these designs have become classics, still produced by Laura Ashley (founded 1953) and widely imitated by other firms.

19 Decorated between 1958 and 1959 and modified slightly until 1982, this great barrel-vaulted room, in a Georgian building off Brook Street, London, was undoubtedly the most influential traditional interior of the postwar period. Nancy Lancaster's library, created with the assistance of John Fowler, epitomizes the 'English country house' style, with its easy, elegant arrangement of chintz-covered chairs, loose, ticking-covered seating and fine furniture. The choice of yellow as a dominant colour is enhanced by the light shining through the unlined silk taffeta curtains. The dense but informal arrangement of seating – here providing a balance to the symmetrical placement of the interior elements – and the floor-length table cover were elements gradually assimilated into many interiors.

the rear windows of Austin Allegros' – to which could have been added ready-made Dralon curtains, sculpted rayon velvet-covered sofas and printed stretch-nylon furniture covers.[29] The downfall of nets had begun after the War, with the introduction of the German Raschel machine, which used artificial fibres to produce nets with a large mesh the size of which, once programmed, could not easily be changed. The crudeness of these ubiquitous cheap fabrics gradually gave all nets a bad image, in a sort of aesthetic 'guilt by association'.

In the mid-1970s however, real lace and old machine-made lace curtains began to appear in antique markets – again following the influence of fashion. Machine-made madras laces, made with a gauze base and Jacquard woven areas of supplementary weft pattern, long dormant in a handful of up-market fabric showrooms, returned to prominence, featuring as floor-length covers to both dining and sofa tables and at windows as glass curtains or stiffened to make roller blinds. Soon bedrooms were being swathed in lace, a style that could hardly have been more different from another fashionable type of interior, 'high tech'. The range of furniture and fabrics available by 1980 also included the 'grown-up' ethnic fabrics imported mainly from India – slubbed thin silks, dhurries and coarsely spun cottons. Within all these choices the voice of Modernism was lost – not as one of several alternative styles, which it remained, but as the ruling aesthetic of all genuinely modern interiors. It had proved itself to be too earnest, too demanding and too uniform for an age in search of identity.

Summing up the approach to interior design in the 1980s, the textile designer Jack Lenor Larsen has written: 'Today, then, furnishings have new major roles [including]. . . . To individualize space, and to personalize it. Conformity is *not* the answer, as the more alike those shoebox spaces become the more distinguishing the furnishings must be! How do we *feel* in a space? How do we relate in it? Secure? Happy? Homey? Does it reinforce our identity? Does it accommodate? Is it considerate?'[30] Written in 1985, these remarks reflect the gradual changes that occurred over the thirty-five years following the Second World War, changes which steadily increased the average person's freedom to concentrate on individual expression in interiors. This freedom owed a great deal to the multinationals, who suffered their own identity crisis in the early 1970s but who nevertheless had already sponsored research (and continued to do so) that enabled consumers to rely on high-performance fabrics, fast to light and washing and relatively free of faults. No longer buying to last, or selecting by dictates of 'good design' (as defined by Functionalism), consumers decorated as they dressed – choosing from 'ready-to-wear', pre-coordinated interiors or, if they could afford it, paying a higher price for *'haute couture'* decorator touches. The challenge presented to the interior design and furnishing trades in the 1980s was that of satisfying the desire for distinction and creative innovation at the upper end of the social scale while simultaneously providing for an ever-more-sophisticated mass market which demanded the latest fashions and, in acquiring them, quickly made them unfashionable.

20 During the 1950s the Philadelphia textile firm, Stapler Inc., produced a number of fabrics based on objects in the collection of the Philadelphia Museum of Art (see also Fig. 38), and in doing so maintained a practice established in America in the 1910s. Shown here is a 36-inch-wide Stapler cotton chintz of 1951, based on the Marquand rug from the Museum's McKilhenny Collection.

21 'Daisy Chain', shown here in twelve colourways, was designed by Pat Albeck for Cavendish Textiles (John Lewis) in about 1964, and has been in production ever since. Even in 1989 John Lewis still had six or more requests for this fabric every week. Trained at the Royal College of Art, Albeck was described by fellow designer Eddie Pond (in his essay, in *Did Britain Make It?*, Design Council, 1986) as 'one of the UK's most successful and versatile textile designers.'

22 Described by *Design* magazine in August 1955 as 'possibly the most beautiful chintz on the market', 'Hollyhock' had been (in 1852) one of Sir Henry Cole's examples of 'False Principles of Design'. It was one of a number of traditional chintzes which prospered under the attention created by the 1955 and 1960 exhibitions (in Manchester and London respectively) of English chintz. It has since become a classic pattern and is still hand-block-printed by Edward Turnbull & Sons Ltd. for Lee Jofa in New York and Pallu & Lake in London.

20

21

22

24 These five printed furnishing fabrics, produced by Greeff between about 1950 and 1957, show a variety of colourants and base cloths which disappeared as standardization progressed in the 1960s. 'Destination', centre, a chintz designed by Francis Dearden in 1956, was typical of prints intended specifically for 'masculine' rooms such as dens or libraries.

23 European designers had a sustained influence on the appearance of fabrics and furnishings throughout this period. Typical of the many freely interpreted floral patterns that originated from the French design studios is this hand-screen-printed chintz, designed by Dubois in 1961 and sold in America until the late 1960s by Jofa Inc. (now Lee Jofa). The unnatural colouring is typical of 1960s florals.

23

24

25

25 When *Design* magazine illustrated these five Heal's printed furnishing fabrics in their May 1958 issue, Geoffrey Salmon praised the painterly, organic images present in some, noting that 'with the luxury of subdued lighting goes an emphasis on the formal values of furniture and floor coverings and hence the use of wall coverings as informal large scale backcloths, often brilliantly lit. A richer, more dramatic conception is demanded for these background fabrics.' He liked 'Oak' (fourth from left, a hand-screen print designed by Dorothy Carr) and 'Sweet Corn' (second, a roller print by Barbara Brown, who remained an important contributor to the Heal's range into the 1970s. The pattern on 'Voyagers' (first left, a screen print by Gordon Dent) was, Salmon felt, wasted when folded, whereas 'Plantation' (centre, by Lucienne Day, the most prominent English pattern designer of the 1950s and '60s) was congratulated for its Scandinavian look. 'Furrows' (right, a roller print by Ellen Fricke) he correctly predicted was to become ubiquitous. Put together by Tom Worthington (director of Heal's Wholesale & Export Ltd. and a great influence on British textiles by virtue of his selection of designs), the range was priced from 27/9 (for screen-prints) to 11/9 (for roller prints).

26

26 From the late 1950s to the early 1960s there was a marked interest in painterly textiles that demonstrated the unique potential of screen printing, with its ability to capture the quality of brush-stroked colour. 'Northern Cathedral', designed by the British artist John Piper, and produced in 1960 by Sanderson Fabrics, also epitomizes the individuality for which British manufacturers had become known (compare to Fig. 27, included by Sanderson's in the same year's range). The belief that such diversity was particularly important for export trade slowed the acceptance of coordinated fabrics, which were already a prominent feature of many American ranges.

27

27 In 1960 Sanderson's celebrated their 100th anniversary as wallpaper suppliers, and to mark the event they organized a competition which attracted more than 3,000 entries. Shown here is one of the two winning entries in the textile section, designed by Robert Dodd. Then a recent graduate of the Royal College of Art, Dodd was one of several designers trained at the R.C.A. in the 1950s and early 1960s who subsequently influenced the look of British textiles.

28

29

28 The contents of Wilsford Manor, Wiltshire, the home of Stephen Tennant, were auctioned by Sotheby's in 1987, when this photograph was taken. It shows a room which, with the help of friends such as Cecil Beaton and decorators such as John Fowler, evolved mainly during the decade after the end of the Second World War. This interior could be described as an evolution of baroque-modern, with its startling juxtaposition of, for example, Empire-style wallpaper (put up in about 1950) and a soldier-bedecked printed cotton 'portière' of about 1955. It is nevertheless a foretaste of alternative interiors of the 1970s (with its Chinese shawls and other 'ethnic' objects) and 1980s (with a hint of creative salvage). Serving as a reminder that most 1900–1940 styles have had continued influence on post-1950 interiors, it also exemplifies a taste for opulence which has survived to the present day.

29 Many postwar decorating firms have had designs exclusively produced. Shown here is the design for 'Rope Lattice', since 1950 continuously offered, on chintz, by the London firm, George Spencer.

30 Subtle and fairly neutral colour schemes, such as that shown in this 1963 British magazine illustration by Anne Moorey, were welcomed as a relief from the violent colours of preceding years, although exactly matching upholstery was still unfashionable. Under the influence of the International style, the 1960s emphasis on light and space often led to the use of soft, sheer curtains such as those shown here. Note the relatively high cost of the French fabrics imported by Elizabeth Eaton, a London decorating business founded in 1946 by Mrs. Joy King (who is still a director of the firm).

31 Both the 1960s interest in designs of the 1910s and '20s and the use of contemporary colours to update a design are illustrated in these two textiles, both produced by Baker's. On the right is a hand-block-printed cotton manufactured in 1913 and on the left, a rotary screen-printed cotton of 1969. The later version typified a vogue for Orientalized birds on floating 'islands' which was particularly strong in the late 1960s and the '70s, and which persists today in much-changed colours.

30

31

32

32 English chintzes in updated colourings were a major export to America during the 1960s. Shown here (from left) are 'Dorchester' for Bailey & Griffen, 'Ribbon Swag' for Thorpe, 'Rose and Fern' for Cowtan & Tout, and 'Brompton' for Stroheim & Romann. Below are two colourways of 'Bird and Butterfly' for Scalamandre. All were available from these American firms in 1965.

33 Soon after printed cottons began, in about 1960, to be more widely used for fixed upholstery, border prints such as this one were developed (see Fig. 30 for a

similar pattern on the sofa). They originated in the United States, but have since also been designed in Britain, becoming, apart from floral chintzes, the most long-lasting type of postwar print design. Many were developed in tandem with furniture manufacturers, having the width and placement of the borders (often along both selvages and down the centre) calibrated to provide borders for seat and back cushions and kick pleats in an economical manner. During the 1970s 'bird and border' patterns were also fashionable wall coverings, as seen in this bedroom of about 1977.

33

34 Relying almost entirely on contrasting slabs of colour, this contemporary room, advertised by Harrods in the 22 November 1956 *Country Life* supplement, epitomizes the aggressively tailored interiors of the 1950s. Although the furniture is described as Continental, its upholstery reflects George Nelson's observation (in *American Fabrics*, vol. 38, Fall 1956, p.54) that designers were 'beginning to look at fabrics and to see them as new things for which we may presently have unexpected uses in our continuing struggle to do more with less'. Differing from 1960s minimalist interiors, those of the 1950s emphasized juxtaposed masses – often relieved, as here, by curtains of printed cotton.

35 Hard-edged designs of the mid-1960s expressed the last wave of enthusiasm for Modernism and the new and briefly felt influence of abstract expressionism and Op art. These three boldly patterned screen-printed cottons (from left) are 'Kernoo' by Victor Vasarely, made in 1963 by Edinburgh Weavers, 'Impact' by Evelyn Brooks and 'Caprice' by Barbara Brown, both made for Heal Fabrics in 1966 and 1964.

36 Long before strong geometrics invaded the mass market in about 1960, firms such as New York's Knoll International had included such textiles in their range, as this 1952 photograph of their Stuttgart showroom indicates. Managed from 1943 to 1959 by Florence Knoll, an architect and graduate of Cranbrook Academy (a primary source of America's leading postwar weavers) the fabric range was by a number of designers, including Angelo Testa, Eszter Haraxzty (director of weaves from 1949 to 1955) Evelyn Hill, Astrid Sampe and Marianne Strengell.

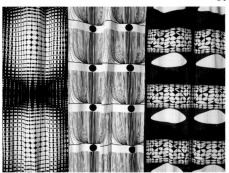

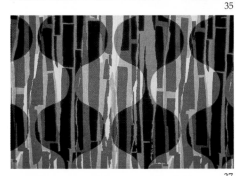

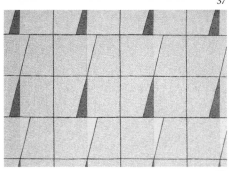

37 In *Printed Textile Design* (London and New York, 1957), Tibor Reich commented that very few modern textiles were 'coloured with dignity, being mostly over-coloured, which tires one very easily as the eye has nowhere to rest.' Demonstrated in this 1972 Tibor Fabrics screen print is his further observation that 'the purpose of pattern in printed textiles should be expression of flow and rhythm which will move sympathetically with its surroundings, distribution of colour areas, and to give pure visual pleasure and tranquillity on the one hand, and interest and thrill on the other.' Such analysis of design in abstract terms typified the continued influence of the Bauhaus, acknowledged by Reich (who was educated in Hungary and, in the 1930s, in Vienna) for 'its simple, straightforward thinking of a lineal character'.

38 'Point on Point', a 1955 Stapler Fabrics screen print on fibreglass, was based on a 1931 painting of the same name by Sophie Taeuber-Arp, in the A. E. Gallatin Collection at the Philadelphia Museum of Art. The relatively small scale of the repeat (14 by 12 inches) is typical of many 1950s abstract designs.

40 Illustrated in a Grace Lovat Fraser article in *Ideal Home Book 1952–3* (published by the *Daily Mail*), these sketches illustrate her comment that fabrics were among the most important and versatile elements in an interior. In particular, she advised that curtain fabric must drape well. Both rooms contain fabrics that provide contrasting textures and colours; note the dining room's orange accents (a colour seldom used in quantity in this period, but greatly liked as an enlivening touch). Typically for this period, the upholstery fabrics are weaves (drawn from Morton Sundour's range), whereas the draped fabrics are prints (from Sundour's subsidiary, Edinburgh Weavers).

41 Illustrated in the Empire Stores catalogue of 1954, the bottom two cotton counterpanes were probably produced in Lancashire, which ceased making such elaborate Jacquard-woven items when the cotton industry collapsed. The 'smart taffeta' bedspread at the top was probably made of rayon or nylon, and would have been embroidered by machine. Up to about 1970 in the United States, candlewick bedspreads were the more popular form of woven coverlet.

39 Dorothy Liebes was one of several innovative American designers of woven fabrics, and like others, she included among her interests the use of metallic and synthetic yarns, as well as traditional fibres. During the 1940s and '50s she was one of the 'celebrity' designers, becoming well known for her work with mohair, one of the few yarns freely available throughout that period. This small sample, hand-woven by Liebes in about 1950, was probably a prototype for a mohair cloth by Goodall Fabrics, who retained Liebes as a designer.

39

A most interestingly woven material, with alternating plain and slightly crinkled stripes is used for the chair seats. Its soft sheen contrasts pleasantly with the slightly textured surface of the printed curtain material, the same colours appearing in both fabrics. (Material for the chair seat: *Morton Sundour Fabrics.* Curtain material: *Edinburgh Weavers.*)

Light-weight printed material is here contrasted with heavy basket-woven one. The delicacy of the printed fabric is enhanced by the texture of the heavier cloth. (Curtain material: *Edinburgh Weavers.* Bedspread material: *Morton Sundour Fabrics.*)

40

D.3622. Smart Taffeta Bedspread, with embroidered designs. Rose, Green or Gold, Approximate size 90 in. x 100 in. **£2/0/0**

D.3633. As above, but approximate size 72 in. x 90 in. **£1/13/3**

D.3652. Cotton Jaspé Bedspread. In Pink, Gold or Green. Approximate size 80 in. x 100 in. **£1/18/3**

D.3648. As above, but approximate size 70 in. x 90 in. **£1/13/0**

D.3644. Attractive Cotton Counterpane, with assorted woven designs in Rose, Blue, Green or Gold. Approximate size 80 in. x 100 in. **£2/14/0**

D.3643. As above, but approximate size 70 in. x 90 in. **£2/8/0**

D.3647. Smart Counterpane in heavy Cotton, with woven designs. In Rose, Blue, Green or Gold. Approximate size 80 in. x 100 in. **£2/14/0**

D.3651. As above, but approximate size 70 in. x 100 in. **£2/8/0**

Page 63

41

42

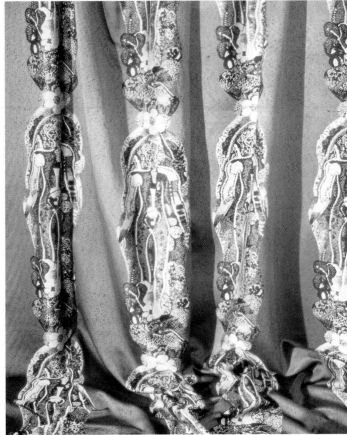

43

44

44 This Manhattan interior, designed in
the mid-1970s by Luis Villa Design,
contains elements which epitomize the
International Style: metal-frame furniture,
leather and textural-weave upholstery,
and semi-sheer woven curtains.

42 The postwar interest in scientific
images was expressed in several subtle
ways by textile designers. Here, in a
1955/6 Liberty's hand-screen-printed
cotton, large leaves have been depicted in
skeletal form. This delight in microscopic
detail married well with a simultaneous
interest in graffito-like designs which
appeared to have layers of colour through
which scratches had penetrated. The leaf
image itself was also employed on many
mid-1950s textiles.

43 Until Edinburgh Weavers were taken
over by Courtauld's in 1964, they
maintained a reputation for innovative
design and high-quality cloths. 'Adam',
an Edinburgh Weavers cotton and rayon
damask designed by Keith Vaughn in
1958, won the Design Council award for
'Best Weave' of that year. It typifies many
1950s weaves, with its emphasis on
texture and its almost 'illegible' figurative
design (very few realistic patterns were
produced in weaving after this date). Like
many other firms Edinburgh Weavers
increased the proportion of its prints
during the 1950s, to accommodate the
rising costs of high-quality weaving yarns
and the popularity of prints.

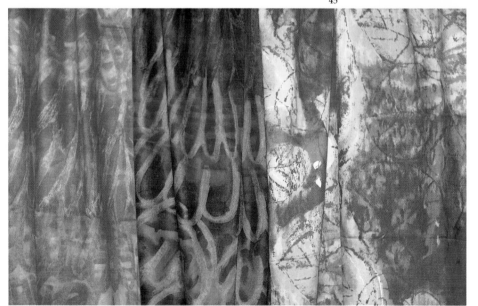

47 'Jungle Legend' and two colourways of 'Fresco' (both 1961) are typical of Althea McNish's bright free-form designs. McNish, a Trinidadian who remained in London after training at the Royal College of Art, supplied printed textile designs to a number of firms in the 1960s and '70s (turning to contract and one-off designs in the 1980s), including Liberty's, Heal's and Cavendish Textiles, who produced the fabrics shown.

45 Glass fibre curtain fabric, generally known as fibreglass, after Corning's trade name Fiberglas, was advertised in Empire Store's Spring/Summer 1970 catalogue as a 'wonderful' fabric that did not shrink, stretch, wrinkle or sag, was fireproof and never needed ironing. The patterned fabrics were generally available in, at most, two colourways and ranged in price from 13/11 to 15/11. They were available by the yard or as ready-made curtains, up to a maximum of 70 by 90 inches. Although fibreglass curtains enjoyed wide popularity from the 1950s to the early 1970s (in the United States they were particularly popular in off-white 'bouclé'-like weaves and casement cloths), the 'natural' tastes of the later 1970s made them unfashionable for domestic use.

46 'Swedish modern' remained an important interior style until it was subsumed in the rural styles of the 1970s. This British interior, designed in 1969 by Peter Aldington of the architectural firm Aldington, Craig & Collinge, typifies the last stages of Swedish-influenced interiors, with an emphasis on pine, plain-woven curtains, built-in, brightly upholstered banquette seating and natural-coloured woollen carpeting. The wire chairs covered with jersey-knitted fabric were by this date design classics, created in the previous decade by Harry Bertoia for Knoll Associates.

49 In *The Sunday Times*, 28 February 1971, Elizabeth Benn posed the question, 'Which is the Warhol?' She was referring to the then still-popular Greeff Fabrics poppy designs which had first been introduced in 1963, a year before Andy Warhol painted the same subject in a similar manner. The group of screen-printed cottons shown here were part of two Greeff mid-1960s ranges which evolved from their influential 1963 collection. All were designed under the direction of Virginia Nepodal, who started the Cheney print range, joining Greeff in 1952 when the two firms became one. Shown are three colourways of 'Poppies', a bold design the width of the cloth (48 inches) and 32½ inches high; its coordinate, 'Violas and Violets' (right); and 'Wind Song' a chintz made in 1967.

48

49

50

48 From 1960 to 1972 Shirley Craven both designed and commissioned work for Hull Traders' range of screen-printed textiles, creating a reputation for design excellence matched in Britain only by Heal's. Among the graphic, boldly styled, award-winning fabrics she produced is this 1969 screen-printed cotton, 'Memories'.

50 This group of Warner fabrics, designed between 1962 and 1967, illustrates the diverse themes which could be found on modern textiles of the period. The three screen prints are, from left, 'Circuit' (on cotton, 1967), designed from printed copper foil circuit boards by Warner's head designer, Eddie Squires; 'Mucha' (on cotton, 1962), an Art Nouveau-inspired design by Friedlande di Colbertaldo Dinzl, a freelance designer based in Italy; and 'Rhapsody' (on linen, 1963), from a late-1930s design by Eva Crofts. The Op-inspired cotton and Lurex damask (second from left) was designed in 1962 by Warner's wovens manager, Frank Davies.

51 The London-based interior designer Eva Jiricna designed this living room in her own home (now sold) in 1981. Representing the high-tech style, the room includes silver-anodized aluminium blinds, green studded-rubber and foam-backed PVC on the walls, perforated plastic tile flooring and perforated metal seats and tables. However, in keeping with the renewed appreciation of natural fibres, the settees are covered with a cotton chintz from Parker Knoll's fabric division (founded c.1950 as a complement to their furniture manufacturing). The quilting was done to order.

51

52

53

52 The expansion of Habitat began in 1967, when a Manchester branch was added to the two stores in London. Like the fashion boutiques in the Kings Road and Carnaby Street, Habitat offered instant 'good taste', based on Terence Conran's intuitive understanding of the youth market. Interiors were neither modern (as defined by the International design movement) nor traditional, and many were based on modular units to allow an element of self-designing and tailoring to space and budgets. This living room, illustrated in Habitat's 1977/78 catalogue, does, however, reflect the

International style's last phase, when neutral-toned plain weaves predominated.

53 One of the advantages of hand screen printing which enabled it to survive the introduction of rotary screen machines was its ability to print very large vertical repeats by dividing the image into two or more screens. This mural print is 80 inches high, but has been designed so that the height could be adjusted to any required measurement. Called 'Countryside', it was designed in 1975, but is still produced by Farmhouse Studios, a small firm run by Skif Peterson

in West Lafayette, Indiana. The Studios maintain a tradition started by Eleanor and Henry Kluck, who founded Elenhank Designers Inc. in 1946. After having established a reputation in the 1960s for their panel designs (including laminated pieces such as those used as counter fascias in Chicago's O'Hare Airport), they sold their business and designs to the Petersons in 1981.

54

55

56

56 'Saki', a rotary screen-printed fabric designed by Pat Albeck, was produced by Cavendish Textiles in 1976, it combines a liking for simplified motifs, the revived interest in patchwork and the use of trellis-work. In her book *Printed Textiles* (1969), Albeck stressed that 'the designer who thinks it is wrong to get ideas directly from other things, whether historical reference, or nature, or man-made forms, is mistaken', adding that a designer who relies 'entirely on designing what he believes to be individual . . . ends by becoming monotonous'.

54 The large internal market in the United States has supported the production of 'Americana' designs since the end of the Second World War. In and around the Bicentennial year of 1976, such patterns became increasingly popular. Many took their inspiration from historical textiles, but just as many were derived from other decorative arts. Here, Brunschwig & Fils' 'Devonshire' coordinates (1975) echo stencilled patterns in the chair seat and back. The relatively narrow border on the accompanying fabric was typical of many new 'historical' prints of the period, which had just begun to re-employ this device, after some sixty years during which it was seldom seen.

55 The alternative lifestyle of the early 1970s, which supported the use of imported 'ethnic' textiles and craftsmen-made batik and tie-dye fabrics, soon influenced the design of mass-produced textiles. This group of Warner screen prints includes designs inspired by African, Moroccan, Indonesian, Turkish and American Indian hand-decorated cloths (or in the latter case, leather). 'Africa', shown flat, was designed by Graham Smith in 1977, and the remainder were produced between 1975 and 1979.

Chapter Eight

Retrospection
1980–1990

'It is neither new, nor uncreative, to refer back to the past for models and inspiration. People have been doing so throughout history, possibly because past styles have an air of being resolved, which is helpful to artists and designers floundering in a sea of uncertainties.'
(Jocasta Innes, *Decorators' Directory of Style*[1])

Historical reference of some kind underlies most furnishing textiles of the 1980s. The touchstone of the decade has been authenticity, embodied in the faithful revival of the period textile document. Wearing its history, so to speak, on its sleeve, the document design has been married to the single most pervasive interior style of the decade, that of the English country house.

The publicity given to the painstaking restoration and correct interior decoration of important historic houses in Britain and the United States first raised awareness of the diversity and appeal of period textiles. Cloth specially woven or printed for a particular project and then put into the manufacturer's collection, was able to trade upon the added piquancy of its history.

Few projects carried more romantic associations than that with which Tissunique, London, were involved in 1985, when they were asked to help with the refurbishment of Newstead Abbey, in Nottinghamshire, once the home of Lord Byron. Their task was to reproduce an accurate copy of the small chinoiserie design that the poet had chosen in 1808 for his bed hangings. The new fabric had to capture the drab colouring typical of the period, including the unevenness of the green, which was originally overprinted blue on yellow. 'Lord Byron's Chintz' then went on general release.

When Brunschwig & Fils, New York, were researching less formal damask patterns for their 1982 collection, they picked out an embossed wool ivy-leaf design of the early nineteenth century from the Brooklyn Museum archive. This was reproduced as 'Hambledon' with the permission of the Museum and that of the Winterthur Museum, who also had the same document in another colour. Not long afterwards the Baltimore Historical Society asked Brunschwig if they could supply a wool damask with an ivy-leaf pattern for a restoration project. There was mutual delight when it turned out to be the same design that the Society had in scarlet on an American Empire settee. 'Hambledon' was successfully reborn as

1 All folds and fringe, 'Aldwych' by Titley & Marr (UK) and Clarence House (USA) was one notably successful trompe l'oeil print of the 1987–88 season. The design and colouring are closely based on a flamboyant English block print of 1856.

2 'Lord Byron's Chintz' was one of six designs in Tissunique's 'Historic Prints' collection of 1986 which used historic associations and authenticity as a promotional asset. The collection was supported by a brochure in which each design was illustrated in colour and by word painting making reference to the original setting or provenance. For this design the description turned to the poet's life and art. 'In 1808 just before he set out on his Grand Tour to Greece and to Turkey, that was to have such an effect on his poetry and his life, Lord Byron refurnished, with no expenses spared, his ancestral seat at Newstead Abbey. French silks, chintzes and trimmings of the highest quality were hung, helping to put the young Lord even deeper into debt.' Sole survivor of all the magnificence at Newstead Abbey is the fabric of the bedhangings in the chinoiserie print, subject of this reproduction. Besides the original green, it was also printed in 'an Etruscan red, and a blue and white in the spirit of Chinese porcelain.' To draw full measure from the romantic associations the poet inspires, a companion print, backprint from the main design, was named 'Allegra', after Byron's natural daughter.

3 Country house style for the 1980s made adventurous statements in the hands of American decorators such as Beverly Jacomini, who designed this interior of a nineteenth-century cook-house in Houston, Texas, as a rural hideaway with manorial overtones. Although many of the ingredients of the scheme – good rugs, fine document chintzes and a mix of patterns including traditional check and paisley – are the stock-in-trade of the country house room, the finished effect shows far more bombastic eclecticism than the British would tolerate. The printed cotton on the chair and ottoman, 'Tredwell Garland' by Brunschwig & Fils taken from a block print dated 1820–30, is coloured in the true chintz palette of red, green and yellow on an opaque ground that Americans love but the British find hard to accept.

'Bacchus' in 1989 in a heavier quality for the contract market, which in the second half of the decade responded to the movement towards greater formality in interiors.

Document designs chosen from company or museum archives for inclusion in commercial collections are now generally first reproduced in the original colourway. Alternative colourways painted in studios reflect current colour preferences. These are markedly different for the British and American markets. The British are the less adventurous. They choose colours that will not offend so will not need to be changed frequently.

4 The drawing room at Horsted Place, Sussex, decorated in the 1960s, expressed the gracious comfort and charm of the English country house style at its best and encapsulated many of the stylistic aspirations that professional decorators and amateurs strove to capture in interiors of the 1980s. It also explains visually why the style is so difficult to get right. The Victorian Gothic room begins by offering a suitably commanding setting and the quantity and quality of the furniture – sofas, chairs of various styles, stools, small tables and important pictures acquired by the family over the years – gives a sense of sufficiency that is at the heart of this style. The apparently casual hand with which the room was put together and the unstudied arrangement of furniture and family photographs diffuses the grandeur of the individual components, and the rich mix of textiles softens a potentially formal image. Chintz curtains and wallcovering are 'Roses and Pansies' by Colefax & Fowler. Also made up as slipcovers for some of the chairs, the less than perfect fit on the chair to the left, and the track of bare boards between the two carpets is typical of the careless grace of a country house room that has more than money can buy.

Every studio knows that a good document design revived from any period between 1800 and 1920 and coloured in soft greens, dusky pinks and a touch of muted blue (including as it does three popular carpet colours) is destined for success in Britain. More adventurous colourings have had considerable publicity and some impact on British taste in the second half of the 1980s but, reckoned in terms of metres sold, the deep pastel is still firmly entrenched.

Document prints coloured for the American market have a bright clarity and panache which alarms the British. Ground colours such as pumpkin orange, red-brown and mauve, with unusual blends of colour on top, are expected and embraced in the United States. The British call them 'decorator colourways' because only the professional decorator knows how to cope with them. There is plenty of professionalism in the highly charged world of American interior decoration, and the bold colouring of the document print is one medium through which the English country-house style has found widespread acceptability there.

The country-house look, which Sybil Colefax and John Fowler among others are credited with having invented in the 1930s, has been safely ensconced ever since in English houses of a certain distinction, especially those that have been occupied continuously by generations of the same family. The style became so desirable because it is exclusive and easily eludes capture. The country-house interior should imply organic growth, preferably over many generations: nothing should look too new or too smart. It also requires good furniture of differing periods, good pictures and generous helpings of chintz. The adoption of this style into the mainstream of interior decoration was accomplished early in the 1980s.

Possibly because the style is linked with the sensitive issue of class, the question of who gets it right generates some friction on both sides of the Atlantic. Harry Hinson, of the fabric house Hinson & Co., is one American colourist who thinks the 'muddy' tints the English favour for their document prints are wrong. Discussing his 1988 fabric collection with *Architectural Digest*, he claimed that the English take their colours from 'Adamesque' walls and dusty, faded period chintzes. The same fabric printed for an English company and an American company will look totally different, 'once the American company has corrected the printing of the colour to its taste'.[2] Fresh apple green was his colour of that year.

The British respond that Americans do not understand the subtlety and understatement that is the key to the English look. Imogen Taylor of Colefax & Fowler, the British decorators who still have their finger on the pulse of the country house, much where John Fowler placed it, explained in *Country Life* magazine why she never uses sharp greens or fresh, pure colour in country houses. 'It quarrels with the English countryside. Our quality of light is best suited by colours with a slight dirtiness, as in the blend from an artist's palette.'[3]

Document prints at the disposal of the burgeoning country-house style at the beginning of the 1980s were dominated by big birds sitting on branches or picking their way amongst lotus leaves. Many were inspired by fragments of Chinese textiles or hand-painted eighteenth-century

5 The Chinese influence was selling well in the early 1980s when 'Canton' was featured in this advertisement for the British market by G. P. & J. Baker. Taken from a linen in the Baker archive, itself inspired by an eighteenth-century Chinese wallpaper, 'Canton' was first launched in 1915 as a block print on linen and included a background of thick bamboo copied from the textile document. The design was redrawn and the bamboo background omitted when it was screen printed on linen in 1964 and on cotton in 1970. Launched once again in 1982, this time on easycare cotton, it matched the mood of the moment when the popularity of large Chinese designs was at its height and recognition of its success was this advertising boost in 1984. The wording of the advertisement gave the print its historical credentials – a significant marketing strategy throughout the 1980s – but the phrase 'taken from a document' acknowledged that the design had been reworked and was not being promoted as an accurate document revival.

wallpapers. However, even at the beginning of the decade it was already apparent that no individual trend would match the overwhelming popularity of the floral document prints which outflanked every transient fashion and sustained public esteem throughout the 1980s.

Bird prints peaked out around 1984, and although many individual designs continued to flourish, the search was on in company and museum archives for other effects that could be put to the service of traditionally decorated rooms. Between 1985 and 1987 came a season of ribbons and bows, followed by a series of trompe l'oeil effects based on swagged, festooned and draped fabric. In 1986 and 1987, the fashion for ropes, tassels and *passementerie* was part of a general demand for printed fabrics that were less romantic. Flowers appeared in the context of rococo scrollwork, urns and pillars.

The heavier nature of many of these designs commanded a stronger colour palette, even in Britain. There was also a wide use of under-printing with crosses, dots and 'vermicelli' used to break up plain backgrounds which, unless specifically coloured, moved away from pure white to off-white and aged tea-stained tints. Pleasing decay – the look of applied antiquity – was then at its height in Britain, where magazines advised how surfaces could be distressed and fabrics dipped to mute and age the colours.[4]

Archive revivals for 1988–9 showed a move towards much larger florals (some with metre-long repeats), a harvest festival of fruits and the rise of the small filler print as accessory to large designs, particularly mid-nineteenth-century minor patterns based on seaweed, coral and small leaves as well as the oaks and acorns of the early 1800s.

Document sources for the prints of 1990 include novelties such as early Victorian 'Portuguese' stripes, with flowers juxtaposed with hats, swans and even bagpipes. Some prints have light apparently cast into them in the manner of a Fragonard painting. But the major shift has been towards prints with some architectural quality. This coincided with an upsurge in original (i.e. non-document) late 1980s print collections with a strong architectural bias, based on classical ornament, Gothic or heraldic motifs. Although these designs are derived from some historic point of reference, they are not necessarily based on past textiles and are open to wider and more vigorous interpretation.

This less slavish, more openly creative, use of historic sources is generally accepted as an indication that the great days of the English country-house style, with its dependence on document designs, are over. Decorators talk of being 'fed up with chintz' (meaning chintz the glaze as much as chintz the print), sentiments unthinkable in 1985. Through its wide dissemination as a decorator style, the look acquired unwelcome polish. Decorators paid lip-service to the essential element – called 'shabby chic' – without which no country-house interior could win its spurs, but many failed to deliver any shabbiness at all. Country house conventions began to merge with the more generalized rural nostalgia of the middle market and were widely copied.

The downward slide of the country-house style was part of the general

6 Rooms that revelled in soft textile effects and pastel colours were a source of inspiration for a new romanticism at the beginning of the 1980s. Abundance of fabric was the rule, skimping prohibited. The Austrian blinds in this bedroom are typically generous, gathering far more fabric into their billowing festoons than any furnishing textbook would think proper. Walls lined with gathered chintz soften the elevations, full-length lace curtains filter the light and the bedside table has an overcloth flaring gracefully into a pool of fabric at the hem. The discipline comes in the detailing; the blinds delicately edged with lace, the cushions covered in antique cutwork, crochet and drawn threadwork, accented by a judicious input of flowers and accessories.

7 Festoon and Austrian blinds lost their decorator status when they began to appear in the furnishing pages of mail order catalogues in standard sizes, garish colours and poor quality fabrics.

popularizing movement, described in somewhat contemptuous terms by Angela Huth in the *Mail on Sunday* magazine in the spring of 1988. 'Once modest little streets proclaim their first steps into a more prosperous world with a mass-made knicker blind at every window. And, as always happens when a minority taste hits the mass market and becomes fashionable, the cognoscenti are the first to see it has become a ubiquitous cliché, a bad joke, and quickly steer themselves towards something else.'[5] That obituary for the Austrian blind could equally well have applied to the frilled valance or the circular cloth for the side table, which sped rapidly downmarket, where tables were constructed of slot-together chipboard, and the cloths, of polyester-cotton.

The 'something else' for the cognoscenti was to be a robust update of classicism. The mood for change could be observed from the mid-1980s, with its new interest in traditional damask, cut velvet, brocade and tapestry. Although these fabrics lent themselves to the country house too, a current towards classicism had begun to flow, especially in the United States. Much top decorator work in America at the end of the decade is in the eighteenth-century classical tradition, with damask-dressed windows, and silk-covered chairs. American classicism eighties-style is based on the French eighteenth-century model with a preponderance of strong Empire reds, greens and blues. It spans eighteenth-century chinoiserie patterns too, again in the French manner. Collections of prints being launched by several design houses in Britain late in 1989 for the 1990 season tap the same French neo-classical tradition. The distinctive delicacy of these spacious, symmetrical arrangements of medallions, urns and garlands also makes a topical response to the commemoration of the bicentenary of the French Revolution going on across the channel.

Classicism has been the inspiration behind many of the original textiles of the 1980s, as well as the revivals of eighteenth-century silks and prints. The flurry of attention paid to Post-Modernism, with its symbolic use of classical architectural motifs, extended to other kinds of decorative pastiche, including textiles that mimicked natural materials such as granite, gravel, and, most importantly, marble. Timney Fowler's monochrome classicism caused a stir when they opened their first shop in London in 1983 and launched 'Emperors' Heads', with a huge 42-inch or 104-centimetre pattern repeat, and 'Columns' in which pillars twist up the cloth like swizzle sticks, their capitals entwined with naturalistic acanthus leaves. Retaining the startling purity of these classical images by printing always in black on white, they are now straying into eighteenth-century territory in new experiments with hand-blocked silk velvet.

Seriously re-working a specific eighteenth-century idiom, the 'Bizarre' collection from Osborne & Little, London and New York, explored and interpreted themes from the strangely exotic early eighteenth-century bizarre silks. These abstract motifs, superimposed over plaids and checks, created an important new look for 1989.

The disillusionment with Modernist architecture, especially in Britain where environmentally destructive post-Second World War rebuilding despoiled many city centres and small towns, has been mirrored by a

8 Black, white and classical, Timney Fowler's prints took architectural and ancient history as a source book, putting grand images in unlikely marriages with an assured and contemporary eye. Left to right, from the Neo-Classical collection, 'Urns and Drapes' dates from 1987; the best-selling 'Emperors' Heads' and 'Columns' from 1985 and the architectural miscellany called 'Medici', from 1986. They all share an ample sense of scale and put the case for wit as a valid attribute of the printed textile.

suspicion amongst the public of textile designs with Modernist implications, popularly dismissed with their associated furniture as 'cold and clinical'. But there has been a sustained fascination throughout the 1980s with the most familiar and least alienating geometrics – the stripe and the check. Stripes of every kind from the classically simple to figured stripes, pinstripes, freehand lines and ticking are used alone or alongside other patterns. Revival of interest in traditional furniture checks has been a feature of the second half of the decade. Tartans and ginghams have always been well used in American decorating circles and have begun to shed their car-rug and cheap-tablecloth image in Britain and to be used intelligently in interiors.

Other designs with a geometric character that have had wide currency in the 1980s are ikat prints and weaves, particularly the Indian ikats commissioned by Conran, and flamestitch in both heavy weaves and print interpretations. Other important non-floral themes reworked in terms of printed textiles have been paisleys, Oriental kelim and Aubusson carpet patterns, and medieval embroidery, all of which share a density of pattern and potential for the merging and blending of rich and striking colours, typical of the closing years of the decade.

The quest for a new simplicity in interiors has been met by several style sources running parallel in the second half of the 1980s. The cool northern rococo of Sweden's Gustavian period (1770–1810, roughly spanning the reigns of two kings of that name) and the humane domesticity of Carl Larsson's interiors, known through his paintings of his own country house, published in the 1890s, have brought two strands of Swedish style to occupy the void left by the departure of Scandinavian teak and folk weave. On both sides of the Atlantic there is renewed interest in furniture, fabrics and interior styles of the late-Victorian Arts and Crafts movement which bridged the gap between high-Victorian opulence and early Modernism. Reflecting similar tastes, the profound austerity of early nineteenth-century Shaker furniture, well known in the United States, is being copied for the British market for the first time.

Interiors conceived around Gustavian, Larsson, Shaker or Arts and Crafts ideas rely heavily on a few pieces of the correct furniture, but the textiles are easy. Light, airy fabrics, simple stripes and checks complement Larsson or Shaker; Gustavians are also allowed delicate ribbon-and-bow floral stripes. The Arts and Crafts interior, with oak floors and furniture, Oriental rugs and tapestry, calls for the fabrics of William Morris and his successors which – though over-exposed in Britain from thirty years of sustained popularity – are enjoying a revival in the United States.

A small but influential number of the design community in Britain and America have espoused aspects of these styles for themselves, choosing overtly cheap calico and muslin for curtains and bedhangings, plain natural linen or ticking stripes for covers and old or finely crafted new furniture, or even creative salvage, the decade's most dismissive gesture in the direction of high decorator glitz.

Another fashionable antidote to the whims and fluctuations of decorator styles is to use only antique textiles. Bernard Nevill, designer and first

9 When the *New York Times* devoted a section of its Home Design magazine (16 October, 1988 issue) to Arts and Crafts style, it indicated the level of interest existing in the United States in the furniture. fabrics and hand-blocked wallpapers of the movement. Decorator Jed Johnson whose Manhattan apartment, furnished with Arts and Crafts pieces, was reviewed in the magazine, paid tribute to the extraordinary level of craftsmanship and attention to detail in the fabric designs of William Morris. Almost simultaneously, A. Sanderson, who own the original blocks for many Morris & Co. designs, used this setting illustrating Arts and Crafts fabric and wallpaper in the context of an American craftsman-style interior of 1910–20, in their advertising campaign in the United States.

10 The revival of interest in woven tapestry as an upholstery cloth for traditional interiors was mirrored by the rise of the tapestry print. Bernard Nevill's 'Montrose' for Romanex de Boussac in 1985, was one of a collection of prints well received in Britain and the United States that was drawn, coloured and printed to convey the depth and substance of a heavy weave. Tapestry prints fuelled the general movement towards the deeper, grander colours of the second half of the decade and became the ideal medium for experiments in the use of printed colour to convey vibrancy faded by age.

professor of textiles at London's Royal College of Art prefers the mellow presence of old textiles. He has no new fabrics in his own house, designed in the Queen Anne Revival style by Philip Webb in 1869. Fabrics are contemporary with the house; genuine William Morris and friends, including woven wool curtains from Morris's Merton works and sofas covered in *gros point* and tapestry.[6] All were the genesis of his richly evocative 'tapestry by the metre' prints of 1985 for the French fabric house Boussac, which have had wide distribution in Britain and the United States. Decorators and talented amateurs all use antique textiles too when they can find them. Eighteenth-century silk curtains and embroidered hangings are the sort of pieces that have survived and, according to the London shop Heraz, if the English can get them up without them falling apart, they seldom want them mended. American customers come looking for faded gentility, but when they see it, they run away. As owner Malcolm Puttick explained in 1985, 'We have one range in pristine condition for the Americans and another in less immaculate condition, "The English Country House" look.'[7] It is his opinion that the English have a less transient view of their interiors; American customers operate in the manner of eighteenth-century cognoscenti, the ones who built new houses and wanted new textiles to go in them: 'No-one wanted old textiles then.'

Heraz is not alone in taking scissors to damaged Aubusson carpets and cutting them up to cover sofas, stools and cushions. Needlework carpets are thrown over tables in post-Renaissance manner. As traditional paintings become more expensive and less easy to find, walls are once more hung with tapestries which can fill a large area, such as the drop of a stairwell, with comparative economy.

In a decade that has been dominated by the printed textile, the importance of texture as an attribute of cloth has been of secondary importance. But texture began its rehabilitation with a resurgence of interest in damasks and a concern with the particular qualities of natural fibres. Linen has been the subject of attention because it makes such a positive contribution to the character of a base-cloth and a complex weave. Being springy, it will not frill, but its tendency to crease can be controlled in knife-edge pleats. Linen is a muscular yarn, employed in blends with other fibres to provide strength and character, and control sheen. Cotton is being used

11 Window treatments throughout the 1980s were a tribute to the ingenuity of decorators and the skill of their workshops. This also led to conspicuous consumption of fabric and expensive braids and trimmings, evidence this exquisite and complex pelmet and drapes in a setting designed to promote 'Brodick Castle' from the Laura Ashley Decorator collection. Once the lower end of the market had taken on board the idea of window dressing, many decorators began to employ such a level of detail and originality in curtains and pelmets that even other workshops keen to add something similar to their repertoire sometimes failed to break the code.

more ambitiously in heavy Jacquards and moquettes, these latter usually called epinglé weaves, a term borrowed from the French – to disassociate them from old-style railway carriage upholstery. Silk, which has always been used for prestigious interiors and historic restoration work, has been descending the ladder of accessibility throughout the decade and major collections of plain and shot taffetas, stripes and checks are coming to compete with synthetic dupions.

The absence of well-trained staff in most retail establishments has continued to stimulate the development of sophisticated coordinated collections. What began tentatively in the 1940s with related fabrics and wallpapers has come of age in this decade with composite collections of several printed fabrics offered with a choice of wallpapers and wallpaper borders, and heavyweight plain cloths as an option for upholstery and loose covers. By the end of the 1980s, collections were being designed with a much looser, less rigid coordination. Constituent fabrics and papers work together, but the pattern and colour matching is less precise, so that schemes have the look of being individually designed, not put together on a one-stop shopping excursion.

The search for style, and the public's desire, stimulated by magazines, to be seen to have acquired it, led to much trend-labelling, and bred the instinct to out-date a style as soon as the label stuck. Minimalism, high- and low-tech, Bloomsbury, Beidermeier, Mission and Santa Fé rusticity are a few of the sub-dominants that have been talked about more than lived with. But there are always many strands and minglings of style worth spotlighting in a magazine article or gratifying with a fabric collection. In the United States, with its enormous potential market and a public avid for choice, major manufacturers can launch as many as six new collections four times a year. Many more specialist collections can be supported and theming, to cater for the nautical look, for example, or the Provençal style, is well established. Schumacher's 1985 collection of designs based on Frank Lloyd Wright's diagrams and working drawings and the same firm's strongly Art Deco 'Radio City Music Hall' collection of 1987 could not be sustained in a limited marketplace. The thread that connects clothing fashion trends a season or two later with furnishing textiles and interiors (fashionable brown for clothes in 1988 being the interior colour to watch for 1990) saw the classic country and sporting look refined by Ralph Lauren's fashion reflected, for instance, in Stroheim and Romann's 'Sporting' collection for 1988. Horses and hounds, pheasants, tennis rackets and sailing ships all came together with complementary plaids.

Described metaphorically in terms of painting, the colours and impact of furnishing fabrics during the 1980s began in watercolour and ended in oils. The pastels of the early decade, muted in Britain, bright in America, graduated to deep rich colours and effects that attracted such epithets as 'Venetian', 'Renaissance', 'Victorian' and 'Pompeiian'. The prettiness of the frilled curtain, the flounced valance and voluptuous festoon have been challenged both by a backward glance to the eighteenth-century grandeur of swags, tails and lambrequins, and by a new simplicity based upon custom-made furniture and low-key textiles.

12 Towards the end of the decade the frills and festoons that served both romantic and country house rooms of the early 1980s were being tailored into a more rigorous elegance. When Karen Armstrong designed this setting for the London Interior Designers Centre in 1987, she chose a bold printed linen, 'Lenoble' by Charles Hammond, as walling above the dado and for a formal window treatment that shows off the textural quality of the cloth to advantage. 'Lenoble' is one of those classic French patterns dating from the very end of the eighteenth century and repeated almost continuously over the last 200 years, slightly adapted each time to the tastes of the period. This version recreates a mid-nineteenth-century revival in the coral red of the document. The check, 'Boulogne' covering the sofas is similar to furniture checks from the eighteenth to mid-nineteenth century. Except for the furniture arrangement – the unique 1970s-and-after use of confronting sofas – this is an informed pastiche of what rooms looked like prior to 1860. Note the chair backed with a self-coloured weave, following the eighteenth century assumption that it would be placed against the wall.

13 'Watercolour' launched in 1979-80 by Designers Guild was one of the first fabric collections to exploit the technical possibilities offered by nickel-coated mesh Galvano screens. With their studio frequently working in watercolour rather than the more usual gouache, Designers Guild investigated the potential of the Galvano because the printing of tonal effects is limited using conventional screens. 'Paper Roses' from this collection of delicate translucent prints was also one of the most significant contemporary flower prints of the decade – an English rose for the '80s. The delicacy of the image, especially in this multi-pastel colourway, was outstandingly successful worldwide, sustaining an undiminished popularity from 1980 to 1990.

12

13

14 Medallions, stars, sunbursts and chequered diamonds from the gilded pageantry of the Renaissance were emblems reworked and coloured with appropriate splendour for 'Romagna', an historically derived but non-document collection of prints launched by Osborne & Little in 1988.

14

15

16

16 'Villa d'Este', a document revival, chosen for 1989/90 by Ramm Son & Crocker (UK) and Baker Knapp & Tubbs (USA) shows the late decade twin tendencies – despite its Italian name – to pick designs from French sources and with an element of ornament, in this case a vase and rococo scrolls. Derived from an Arthur Silver document of the 1870s but based on a French eighteenth-century panel, these two new colourways illustrate the still differing demands of the Americans and the British at the end of the 1980s. For the American market, especially the West Coast, where brilliant light dissipates fabric colour and tones it down, the strong Roman-red ground or such alternatives as hunter green or dark gold are late '80s favourites, while a large section of the British market still holds to soft, muted tones.

15 'The Real Thing?' was the query in the title to this setting devised to show some of the new trompe l'oeil passementerie prints in the *Fabric Styles of 1987* supplement to the November issue of 'Homes and Gardens' magazine. Walls were clad with 'Curzon', a swagged trellis bound with braid and decked with cord and tassels, by Titley & Marr (UK) and Payne Fabrics (USA). Cord and tassels take a linear arrangement in 'London Tassels' by Warner Fabrics, used for the curtains. Blind and floor runner featured 'Sandringham', a picot-edged ribbon trellis, and the single cushion was covered in 'Hadleigh', an embroidered ribbon maze, both by Titley & Marr.

18

18 Susan Collier and Sarah Campbell were one of the smaller design teams that found success on both sides of the Atlantic in the 1980s. Their prints are recognisably rooted in the medium of painting. In the United States, Collier Campbell are best known for bed linen designs marketed under their own name. 'Silk Passage' made a sensational debut for them there in 1982. Seemingly handpainted in dull moody tints, it sold 100,000 sets in its first season. In Britain, their names are associated with prints such as 'Cote d'Azur' (1983) illustrated here by the original artwork. Its bright Mediterranean imagery, inspired by the genius of Matisse and Dufy, proved that not everyone in Britain was scared of living with strong bright colour.

17 In the stronger colour palette of the late decade, Designers Guild's 1988/89 'Tapisserie' print collection put a contemporary interpretation on a merging of themes and motifs from Aubusson carpets, tapestries and embroideries. The jewel-bright colours of the prints and companion weaves carry across the wallcovering to dragged and distressed paintwork and furniture. By eliminating the stark contrast of white or pastels in this room, the richness of colour remains undiluted and effectively mellows the heady impact of strong tones used on all surfaces. The changing pattern of furniture arrangement at this date can be observed in the non-matching chairs, variously covered, and in a progression of furniture levels from lowest stool to highest wing chair so that the image of the room is perceived in a series of layers.

19 The simplicity of some mid-1980s interiors contained more than a hint of distaste for high decorator styles and made an alternative statement with the least expensive fabrics and effects. This room spells out uncluttered calm with a low colour input, plain calico-covered seating, wood floor and tall display columns. The window is sumptuously decked, however, using self-lined raw calico (calico being cheaper than lining fabric) in a Grecian-draped pelmet and very full curtains pulled back, then draped and held with matching calico ties.

19

20 The image of a room for 1990 takes a classic fabric and creates a simple, theatrical effect. Homage is paid in passing to a most favoured accessory of the period, the cherub. Curtains are a damask by Gainsborough Silk Weavers, Suffolk, in a pattern taken from an Italian cut velvet of about 1700, reverse woven with as many as four colours in the warp and five in the weft to imitate the shading of Fortuny silks. The interplay of minor colours in addition to the dominant green and gold of this colourway subtly suggests the depth and weight of a pile fabric in certain lights and from certain angles. Looking beyond the elegant stereotype of swags and tails, the curtains have a loose drapery attached to the heading itself, and the full effect swings from heavy poles.

Notes

Chapter 1

1 H. W. Arrowsmith, *The House Decorator and Painter's Guide*, London, 1840: 118
2 David Pearce, *London's Mansions*, London, 1986: 170–71
3 The Victoria & Albert Museum's textile collection includes a silk with this design (483–1897), made by Bailey & Jackson in Spitalfields in the 1840s. A very similar design was used in America in about 1810 on a Duncan Phyfe sofa, and elsewhere as curtains. As wallcovering, this pattern-type was in use at the same time in England, at Audley End
4 Rosamund Mariott Watson, *The Art of the House*, London, 1897: 152
5 A Philadelphian in 1765 described dining room chairs covered in a plain haircloth as looking as well as paduasoy, a rich and heavy silk. Franklin Papers, 12: 296, cited in Florence Montgomery, *Textiles in America, 1650–1870*, New York, 1984: 225
6 George Hepplewhite, *The Cabinet-Maker and Upholsterer's Guide*, London, 1789: 2
7 J. Arrowsmith, *The Paper-Hanger's Guide*, Philadelphia, 1852: 94
8 Catalogue, James Shoolbred and Company, London, April 1891, the mecca velvets were 'New Material for covering Furniture, suitable for Dining Room, Hall, Smoking Room, and Library Furniture', the deep pile velvets were recommended for curtains: 758–62, and *passim*
9 Port Folio II, 28 August, 1802: 268
10 John Bradshaw papers, 1797–1858, Bolton Museum, Lancs. (48–29, 1–14, 1827)
11 Dorothy Draper, *Decorating is Fun!*, New York, 1944: 70
12 J. C. Loudon, *An Encyclopedia of Cottage, Farm and Villa Architecture*, London, 1833: 1075
13 H. G. Hayes Marshall, *Within Four Walls*, Essex, 1948: 93
14 J. Arrowsmith, *op. cit.*: 93
15 F. A. Moreland, *Practical Decorative Upholstery*, Boston, 1889: 320
16 Ogden Codman Jr. and Edith Wharton, *The Decoration of Houses*, London and New York, 1978: xiii
17 Peel papers, Bolton Museum, Lancs., 12 May, 1807, referring to twelve years earlier.
18 *Cassells Household Guide: being A Complete Encyclopedia of Domestic and Social Economy and forming a guide to Every Department of Practical Life*, London and New York, early 1870s: Vol. II, 131
19 Codman and Wharton, *op. cit.*: 16
20 This point was made in 1787, when the first British Copyright Bill was under discussion. See Ada K. Longfield, 'William Kilburn & the earliest Copyright Act for Cotton Printing Design', *Burlington Magazine*, July 1953: 73
21 J. C. Loudon, *op. cit.*: 1079
22 J. Arrowsmith, *op. cit.*: xii; George Smith, *A Collection of Designs for Household Furniture*, London, 1808: 90
23 Mrs. Charles Andrews and Mrs. E. F. Southwork, *Hints for Housekeepers*, New York, 1904: 67

Chapter 2

1 George Smith, *A Collection of Designs for Household Furniture*, London, 1808: v
2 George Rudé, *Revolutionary Europe 1783–1815*, London, 1971: 83
3 George Hepplewhite, *The Cabinet-Maker and Upholsterer's Guide*, London, 1788, 1789, 1794; reprinted in New York, 1969: 18
4 Abbott Lowell Cummings, *Bed Hangings: A Treatise of Fabrics and Styles in the Curtaining of Beds 1650–1850*, Boston, 1961: 14
5 Smith, 1808 (on grandeur): *op. cit.*: v; Rudolph Ackermann: *The Repository of Arts, Literature, Commerce,*

Manufactures, Fashion and Politics, London, October 1810: series I, volume 4, p.246, pl.24
6 Hepplewhite, *op.cit.*: 24
7 Smith 1808, *op.cit.*: 1, pl.2
8 Hepplewhite, *op.cit.*: 2
9 Inventory of David Hinckley, no date, New England. Cited in Jane Nylander, 'Bed and Window Hangings in New England', in *Upholstery in America and Europe from the Seventeenth Century to World War I*, New York, 1987: 179. Another room in the same house was similarly furnished in yellow instead of blue.
10 Pauline Agius: *Ackermann's Regency Furniture & Interiors*, Marlborough, Wilts., 1984: 18
11 Ackermann, *op. cit.* December 1825: III, 6, p.162, pl.35
12 Gillow business records 1731–1832, Westminster Reference Library, 344/100, 1815–22 estimate sketch book, regarding a 'Rutland' chair.
13 Hepplewhite, *op. cit.*: 3
14 Peter Thornton, *Authentic Decor: The Domestic Interior 1620–1920*, London, 1984: 156, citing Scottish Record Office GD1/377/40, bundle 1, item 23, and National Library of Scotland, Acc 4796/26/2, being 1799 striped linen samples for the Assembly Room loose covers and Lady Helen Hall's correspondence.
15 Thomas Sheraton, *The Cabinet-Maker and Upholsterer's Drawing Book*, London, 1793, 1794, 1802, reprinted in New York, 1972: 155–6. The SPNEA, for example, owns a loose cover for a Grecian couch, owned by Nathan Appleton (a Boston textile merchant) and printed at Bannister Hall between 1818 and 1825 (the pattern possibly revived from about 1805).
16 Crompton Papers ZCR series, Bolton Public Library, Lancs. (bedstead and hangings valued in 1799 and 1802 at £1/1/0; bed quilt in the same years at 7/0; curtains valued in 1805 at 2/0 and two bed quilts at 30/0. Re. Pennock, Edward de N. Mayhew and Minor Myers Jr., *A Documentary History of American Interiors*, New York, 1980: 115
17 Thomas Martin, *Circle of Mechanical Arts*, London, 1813
18 See Thornton *op. cit.*: 155, and Mayhew, *op. cit.*: 90 Paper blinds were raised and lowered from the top by string (as were cloth blinds) and also were fitted to boxes at the window base, from which they were drawn up.
19 *The Housekeeping Book of Susanna Whatman, 1776–1800*, National Trust Classic reprint, Century, London, 1987: 38–9
20 Thomas Sheraton, *Cabinet Dictionary*, London, 1803: 23
21 Smith, 1808, *op. cit.*: 4, pl.12
22 *The Palladium*, Boston, 22 May, 1810
23 Sheraton, *Cabinet-Maker, op. cit.*: 408, pl.51
24 Smith, 1808, *op. cit.*: pl.8; Ackermann, October 1810, *op. cit.*: I, 4, p.246, pl.25; and Ackermann, March 1815, 13, p.179, pl.12
25 Ackermann, March 1809, *op. cit.*: I, i, p.188–9, pl.14
26 Ackermann, September 1816, *op. cit.*: II, 2, p.182, pl.14. Peter Thornton, in *Authentic Decor*, p.154, suggests that the French fashions – influential in the 1790s in setting the trend for extravagant use of fabric – were devised to aid the ailing Lyonnaise silk industry.
27 Smith, 1808, *op. cit.*: xiii
28 Hepplewhite, *op. cit.*: 18, p.98, suggested green silk linings to dove-coloured satin curtains.
29 Advertisement by S. Cole & Co. at the Peacock Corner of Bedford Street and Maiden Lane: 'Public Advertiser', 18 February 1769
30 See Barbara Morris, 'The Classical Taste in English Wood-Block Chintzes', *Connoisseur*, April 1958: 93–7
31 George Smith, *A Collection of Ornamental Designs after the Manner of the Antique*, London, 1812: 1

32 See Florence Montgomery, *Printed Textiles: English and American Cottons and Linens 1700–1850*, London, 1970: 212–14 and *passim*
33 Thomas Hope, *Household Furniture and Interior Decoration executed from designs by Thomas Hope*, London, 1807
34 Charles Percier and Pierre-François-Leonard, *Recueil de Décorations intérieures comprenant toût ce qui a rapport à l'ameublement*, Paris 1801–12
35 Pierre de la Mesangere, *Meubles et Objets de Goût*, Paris, 1802–35
36 Sheraton, *Cabinet-Maker, op. cit.*: 16
37 Ackermann, May 1814, *op. cit.*: I, 11, p.283, pl.29
38 Peel day book, 1806–21: Bolton Museum, Lancs. Established by Robert Peel in 1764 and continued by his son, Robert Jr., and other partners, the Peel company ran a printworks from 1772 to 1840 at Church, near Accrington, as well as other businesses, including another printworks at Bury and wholesale firms in London.
39 Elijah Bemis, *The Dyer's Companion*, New York, 1806 and 1815, re-printed in 1973: 96
40 Peel day book, *op. cit.*: 2 May, 1807 and 4 February, 1807
41 Bury MSS: letter from John Bury to J. Bury, September 1813
42 *Orders in Council and Minutes of Evidence on Petitions*, 1808–12: 143, evidence of John Inglis to a Select Committee of the House of Commons in April, 1808. Inglis was a London merchant, exporting to America and India, and was a Director of the East India Company.
43 David J. Jeremy, *Transatlantic Industrial Revolution*, Massachusetts, 1981: 18
44 See Barbara M. Tucker, 'The Merchant, the Manufacturer, and the Factory Manager: The Case of Samuel Slater', *Business History Review*, Autumn 1981, vol.LV, No.3: 298–313. Slater was the first to introduce the factory system successfully to America, founding a spinning mill in Pawtucket, Rhode Island, in 1790. Until about 1820 yarn was turned over to partners who sold it both directly and through merchants, or put it out to local weavers for manufacture into cloth.
45 Winterthur broadsheet, quoted in Harrold & Gillingham: 'Calico and Linen Printing in Philadelphia', *The Pennsylvania Magazine of History & Biography*: vol.LII, 1928, No. 2, 109
46 Clarance Day, *A History of Maine Agriculture*, Orono, Massachusetts, 1954: 155
47 Ackermann, December 1818, *op. cit.*: pl.100; Smith, 1812, *op. cit.*: pl.42; Smith, 1808, *op. cit.*: pls.5–6

Chapter 3

1 Hermann Muthesius, *The English House*, BSP Professional Books, Oxford, London, 1979: 154 (reprint of *Das Englische Haus*, Wasmuth, Berlin, 1904–05)
2 H. W. and A. Arrowsmith, *The House Decorator and Painter's Guide*, London, 1840
3 Mark Girouard, *Sweetness and Light: the 'Queen Anne' Movement 1860–1900*, New Haven and London, 1977: 12
4 E. Potter, *Calico Printing as an Art Manufacture: A Lecture Read Before the Society of Arts*, 1852: 27, note 7
5 Ackermann, February 1821, *op. cit.*: II, 11, p.128, pl.9
6 Ackermann, February 1822, *op. cit.*: II, 13, p.120, pl.9
7 Ackermann, September 1824, *op. cit.*: III, 4, p.183, pl.16
8 *cf* P. and M. A. Nicholson, *The Practical Cabinet-Maker*, London, 1826; and Smith, *The Cabinet Maker and Upholsterer's Guide*, London, 1826
9 Webster and Parkes, *An Encyclopedia of Domestic Economy*, New York, 1848: 251; J. C. Loudon, *An*

Encyclopedia of Cottage, Farm and Villa Architecture and Furniture, London, 1833, regularly reissued until 1867: 1076 (on dust); and J. Arrowsmith, *The Paper Hangers' Companion*, Philadelphia, 1852: 96 (on moreen)
10 The entire textile industry faced industrial disputes throughout the first half of the nineteenth century; see B. L. Hutchins and A. Harrison, *History of Factory Legislation*, 1911, and H. A. Turner, *Trade Union Growth, Structure and Policy: a comparative study of the cotton unions*, 1962.
11 The Jacquard 'factory' system soon developed, but at first retained home weavers, who hired or borrowed the Jacquard and cards from their employer. Since they continued to be paid on piece rates they were still, in effect, self-employed. Home weavers gradually dwindled, but a few were still working in and around London in the early twentieth century.
12 Norwich had been the centre of worsted furnishing fabric weaving, but in 1833, when the Jacquard was introduced there, it was used principally for making shawls. By this date other Norwich fabrics were also for clothing, as the new silk and worsted fabric introduced in 1819 and similar to bombazine, and challis, a slightly later development, sold as woven (plain) or block printed in London (see *Journal of Design*, London, no.16, June 1850: 106).
13 A Lady, *The Workwoman's Guide*, London, 1838: 204
14 At the 1853 industrial exhibition in New York, the Melville Manufacturing Company of Melville, Massachusetts, displayed Jacquard-woven fancy cassimeres which they had recently begun to make. See George Wallis's 'Special Report' in the *New York Industrial Exhibition: General Report of the British Commissioner*, Harrison & Sons, London, 1854: 16
15 Lancashire Record Office (DD Ht/12), letter to Jonathan Morris, joiner near Bolton, 8 March 1834
16 Lancashire Records Office (DD Ht/12.1), letter to Jonathan Morris, 30 November 1829, from William Morris, including copy of letter dated 19 October 1829 from Andrew Morris, in the United States
17 Lancashire Records Office (DD Ht/12.16)
18 James Ackroyd & Son used the term 'French figures' to describe 'a damask made 6/4 wide, of single worsted warp, and fine English or merino weft . . .', cited in Florence Montgomery, *Dictionary, op. cit.*: 377
19 J. Emerson Tennent, *A Treatise on the Copyright of Designs*, 1841: 23, note 16, cited in David Greysmith, 'Patterns, Piracy and Protection in the Textile Printing Industry 1787–1850', *Textile History*, 14(2), 1983: 173. French designers earned between £320 and £400 a year.
20 Isabella L. Bishop, *The Englishwoman in America*, London, 1856: 340
21 Winterthur broadsheet, 1 October, 1841
22 Ackermann, August 1809, *op. cit.*: II, no.8, 132
23 Miss Eliza Leslie, *The Lady's House Book*, Philadelphia, 1841: 188
24 Christopher Columbus Baldwin, *Diary*, the American Antiquarian Society, 1901: 301 (11 May, 1834, entry on a visit to the home of George A. Tufts in Dudley, Massachusetts)
25 George Smith, *The Cabinet Makers and Upholsterer's Guide*, London, 1828
26 Mrs. William Parkes, *Domestic Duties: or Instructions to Young Married Ladies*, New York, 1829: 182–3
27 Leslie, *op. cit.*: 306–07
28 J. C. Loudon, *op. cit.*: 1080
29 Leslie, *op. cit.*: 303–04
30 The Workwoman's Guide, *op. cit.*: 196
31 Loudon, *op. cit.*: 334 (tent beds), 330 (half-testers)
32 Loudon, *op. cit.*: 1080; Leslie, *op. cit.*: 303–04
33 *The Workwoman's Guide, op. cit.*: 197; Leslie, *op. cit.*: 306
34 Kax Wilson, *A History of Textiles*, Colorado, 1979: 262
35 Sandra R. Walker, *Country Cloth to Coverlets*, 1981: 15
36 Edward Baines Jr., *History of the Cotton Manufacture in Great Britain*, London, 1966: 358
37 Pauline W. Inman, 'House Furnishings of a Vermont Family', *Antiques*, USA, August 1969: 228–33
38 Baines, *op. cit.*
39 Delores H. Connolly, *Home Weaving, Professional Weaving and Textile Mills in Southeast Iowa 1833–70*,

Iowa State University, 1982 (unpublished thesis): 68; and Sandra R. Walker, *Country Cloths to Coverlets*, 1981: 8–10 (the following values are quoted from Pennsylvania accounts: muslin, 1827, eighteen cents a yard, twill weave, 1853, fifteen cents a yard and the same price in 1865).
40 *The Workwoman's Guide, op. cit.*: 192
41 J. Arrowsmith, *op. cit.*: 90
42 Only 6 of 300 exported in 1840 were English – see David Greysmith, note 19
43 Jeremy, *op. cit.*: 40–45
44 David Smith, *The Practical Dyer's Guide*, 1850: 124
45 George Dodd, *The Textile Manufacturers of Great Britain*, 1844: 56
46 Window curtains were less likely to survive, since they took the brunt of both sunshine and dampness. Such patterns may also have been made for export to the United States.
47 *Knight's Unique Fancy Ornaments*, London, 1834: 137 and *The Architectural Magazine*, London, July 1834: 313 (review of *Locke, Johnson and Copeland's Ornamental Designs*)
48 See Barbara Morris, 'Audubon's Birds of America', *Antiques*, LXXII, December 1957: 560
49 The peak period for 'floramania' was in the 1850s, although from the 1820s until the end of the century between four and six dozen publications made the emblematic significance of plants and flowers widely known. Also at its peak in the middle of the century was the interest in glasshouses – expressed in the Crystal Palace, built for the Great Exhibition in 1851. The mid-century *Journal of Design* urged the usefulness of botanical studies for designers, while the Royal Horticultural Society, founded in 1804, published its first *Journal* from 1846–54 and its new garden at Kensington Gore was opened by Prince Albert in 1861.
50 *Journal of Design*, No.16, June 1850: 97
51 *Ibid*, vol.II, September 1849–February 1850: 122 ('Hints for the Decoration and Furnishing of Dwellings')
52 *Ibid*: 120 Crace presumably excluded from this comment the Pugin silks which his firm made.
53 In 1854 (*The Behaviour Book*: 78) Miss Leslie recorded that it was only half a day's journey from Philadelphia to New York, although in California's central valley it remained an eighteen- to twenty-four-hour trip from Bakersfield to Los Angeles (145 miles) until after the First World War.
54 J. Arrowsmith, *op. cit.*: 98
55 Leslie, *op. cit.*: 311
56 H. W. & A. Arrowsmith, *op. cit.*: 118
57 Loudon, *op. cit.*: 1361
58 Loudon, *op. cit.*: 325; Parkes, *op. cit.*; and Andrew Jackson Downing, *The Architecture of Country Houses*, New York, 1850, reprinted 1969: 169

Chapter 4

1 Harriet Beecher Stowe and Catharine E. Beecher, *The American Woman's Home*, New York and Boston, 1869: 84
2 Stead McAlpin production record books, 1862, and correspondence from their London agent, William McDowall, 7 April, 1862
3 Harriet Beecher Stowe and Catharine E. Beecher, *op. cit.*: 87 French glazed prints were recorded as 75 cents a yard
4 Geoffrey Turnbull, *A History of the Calico Printing Industry of Great Britain*, 1951: 81 (600 million yards in 1851) and 114 (between 1,500 and 2,000 million yards in 1889); and George Dodd, *The Textile Manufacturers of Great Britain*, London, 1844: 67
5 *cf* Harriet Prescott Spofford, *Art Decoration Applied to Furniture*, New York, 1877: 198–9, where primary colours are called 'crude'
6 *Cassells Household Guide . . . etc.*, London and New York, 1870–75: 360 The available colours were magenta, mauve, violet, puce (a fleshy rose), purple, canary, cerise, scarlet, orange, blue, pink, green, crimson, brown, black, lavender, slate and grey. According to George J. Henkles, *Household Economy*, Philadelphia, 1867, before the perfecting of aniline dyes, plushes were only available in green and shades of red.
7 *Ibid*: 126 Very good quality damask was less than

three shillings a yard, double width. Rep, at double the cost, was suitable only for 'lofty and large' rooms.
8 *Official Illustrated Catalogue* (of the International Exhibition), printed for Her Majesty's Commissioners, London, 1862: 23
9 William R. Bagnall, *The Textile Industries of the United States*, Massachusetts, 1893: 1792
10 Charles L. Eastlake, *Hints on Household Taste in Furniture, Upholstery and Other Details*, London, 1878, reprinted New York, 1969: 100
11 Mrs. H. W. Beecher, *All Around the House: or how to make a home happy*, New York, 1879: 51 Geoffrey Turnbull, in *A History of the Calico Printing Industry of Great Britain*, 1951, p.167, describes the printing of cretonnes as a dying industry in 1850, the revival of which he also attributed to good design, particularly later in the century, when Morris, Voysey, Crane and Day were working.
12 E. C. Gardner, *Home Interiors Illustrated*, Boston, 1878: 60 See also Alex J. Warden, *The Linen Trade*, London, 1864: Jute cloth, burlap and hessian are all made from jute, a plant fibre.
13 Owen Jones, *On the True and False in the Decorative Arts*, London, 1863: 83
14 Mrs. H. W. Beecher, *op. cit.*: 51
15 *Ibid*: 52
16 *cf* Eastlake: 129 (for leather valances to bookcase shelves, which when 'scalloped and stamped in gilt patterns . . . add considerably to the general effect') and Clarance Cook, *The House Beautiful*, New York, 1881: 126, for mantleshelf decoration.
17 *The Young Ladies' Treasure Book*, Ward Lock & Co., London, undated but probably 1881–2: 161–2, quoted from John Gloag's *Victorian Comfort*, London, 1961: 40
18 Henry James, *Portrait of a Lady*, London, 1881, reprinted by Penguin Books, London and New York, 1981: 63
19 Mrs. H. R. Haweis, *The Art of Decoration*, London, 1889: 222–3; *Cassell's Household Guide, op. cit.*: vol.II, 251; and Mrs. C. S. Jones and Henry T. Williams, *Household Elegancies*, New York, 1875: 227 Tie-backs in this period held back but did not lift up the curtains.
20 H. W. Arrowsmith, *The House Decorator and Painter's Guide*, London, 1840: 118
21 Including Spofford, *op. cit.* (whose book was based on articles in Harper's Bazaar); Clarance Cook *op. cit.* (from articles in Scribner's Monthly); and, in part, Robert W. Edis, *Decoration and Furnishing of Town Houses*, London and New York, 1881
22 Eastlake, *op. cit.*: 96
23 Eastlake, *op. cit.*: 99, and Florence Montgomery *Textiles in America, 1650–1870*, New York, 1984: 144 (both references from the 1880s)
24 Quoted in Peter Thornton, *Authentic Decor: The Domestic Interior 1620–1920*, London, 1984: 225
25 Almon C. Varney and others, *Our Homes and Their Adornments*, Cincinnati, Chicago, St. Louis, Philadelphia, 1882: 262
26 *Cassell's Household Guide, op. cit.*: Vol.I, 337
27 William H. Kanlet, *The Architect: A Series of Original Designs for Domestic and Ornamental Cottages*, New York, 2 vols, 1849: design no.62
28 Varney, *op. cit.*: 259
29 Haweis, *op. cit.*: 27
30 Haweis, *op. cit.*: 52
31 Angela Thirkell, *Angela Thirkell . . . Recalls*, Three Houses, London, 1936: 64
32 Mrs. H. W. Beecher, 1879, *op. cit.*: 25
33 Robert Edis, *Decoration and Furniture of Town Houses*, London, 1881: 157
34 Varney, *op. cit.*: 277
35 Frances Cranmer Greenman, *Higher Than the Sky*, Harper & Bros., 1954: 12 (speaking of her mother); Varney: 263, noted that cotton flannel or 'fashion drapery' was 90 cents a yard in 1882, and double-width, alike on both sides so it needed no lining; stamped velveteen was between $1.25 and $2.00 a yard and cotton and woollen, 50" wide, momie-cloths, $1.10 and $3.00 a yard respectively.
36 See Harriet Beecher Stowe and Catharine Beecher, *op. cit.*: 88; and Spofford, *op. cit.*: 179–80
37 *Cassell's Household Guide, op. cit.*: 313
38 E. C. Gardner, *op. cit.*: 235–6; and, on prices, Gail C. Winkler and Roger W. Moss, *Victorian Interior*

Decoration, New York, 1986: 169 and 236–7 (note 19)
39 Eastlake, *op. cit.*: 102 (the 'muslin' was probably bobbinet decorated with machine chain-stitch); Edis, *op. cit.*: 211; and the Beechers, *op. cit.*: 38, also noting that muslin was 37 cents a yard, six being needed for the average window.
40 Mrs. H. W. Beecher, 1879, *op. cit.*: 63 (recommending dotted Swiss over blue cambric); also Spofford, *op. cit.*: 208 and H. T. Williams and Mrs. C. S. Jones, *Beautiful Homes; or, Hints in House Furnishing*, New York, 1878: 97–8
41 *Cassell's Household Guide*, *op. cit.*: vol.III, 272
42 Edis, *op. cit.*: 211, and Owen Jones, *On the True and False in the Decorative Arts*, London, 1863: 87–8
43 Mrs. T. W. Dewing, *Beauty in The Household*, New York, 1882: 119–20
44 Varney, *op. cit.*: 263, also 288, commenting that the average American home had carpet too costly for the other furniture in the room; and *The Decorator and Furnisher*, editor, A. Curtis Bond, published in New York between 1882 and 1898, which had Clarance Cook, Robert Edis, and Lewis F. Day as frequent contributors
45 Haweis, *op. cit.*: 54
46 Haweis, *ibid*: 219
47 *Cassell's Household Guide*, *op. cit.*: 126
48 Linda Parry: *William Morris Textiles*, London, 1983: 147, 'probably adopted from range of J. Aldam Heaton, Manchester . . . Available from Morris & Co in at least 14 colourways'; and Edis, *op. cit.*: 167, referring to Gillow's decoration of the Prince of Wales Pavilion at the Paris Exhibition of 1880
49 *The Advertiser*, Southport, Connecticut, March 16, 1888: 4, also Varney, *op. cit.*: 262, 'Velveteen is a desirable material for either portières or curtains . . . Plush is the richest material in use'
50 Varney, *op. cit.*: 262–3
51 *The Advertiser*, *ibid*, and Varney, *op. cit.*: 260
52 Isabella L. Bishop, *The Englishwoman in America*, London, 1856: 340 (for example, a gold brocaded cloth sold to the St. Nicholas Hotel for £9 a yard)
53 See Mary Schoeser, *Owen Jones Silks*, Warner Fabrics plc, London, 1987. Warners, founded in 1870, wove over 20 designs by Jones and retain samples of many in their archive
54 See Barbara Morris: *Inspiration for Design: The Influence of the Victoria & Albert Museum*, London, 1986, for a full discussion of the impact of the museum's collection on textile designs. Japanese objects were shown at the 1851 Great Exhibition and again in 1873 in London, in the Paris 1867 exhibition and the Philadelphia 1876 exhibition
55 Eastlake, *op. cit.*: 103
56 Edis, *op. cit.*: 178
57 Walter Smith: *Examples of Household Taste*, New York, c.1876: 197
58 Mrs. H. W. Beecher, 1879, *op. cit.*

Chapter 5
1 Mrs. H. R. Haweis, *The Art of Decoration*, 2nd edition, 1889: 51
2 *Ibid*, and 53: The Amber House in St. John's Wood, London, where the Haweis lived from 1878–83, had a hall fresco of heraldic sunflowers and a large stuffed peacock hiding a grate she disliked. Loftie's series, published in London by Macmillan, included *A Plea for Art in the House*, by Mr. Loftie, *Suggestions for House Decoration in Painting, Woodwork and Furniture* by Agnes and Rhoda Garrett, *The Drawing-room* by Mrs. Orrinsmith, *The Bedroom and Boudoir* by Lady Barker and *The Dining-room* by Mrs. Loftie.
3 Candice Wheeler, *Principles of Home Decoration*, New York, 1903: 10–11
4 From catalogues held in the Silver Studio Collection, Middlesex Polytechnic, London, including William Wallace & Co.'s of c.1895. Workmen's wages made the purchase of such items a matter of very careful budgeting – by 1903 the average British textile worker still made about £120–£150 a year. In America the same type of job paid about $1400 a year, and an upholstered divan could be purchased from Sears, Roebuck & Co. for about $14 (equivalent to £3). Accommodation was more expensive in America, but there was nevertheless a more affluent working class.

5 Rosamund Mariott Watson, *The Art of the House*, London, 1897: 9; *The Times*, London, special number on the textile industry, 1913
6 Linda Parry: *Textiles of the Arts and Crafts Movement*, London, 1988, for a complete discussion of the society. She comments (71) that, 'the decade 1893–1903 proved to be the most significant period in the development of textiles of the Arts and Crafts movement'.
7 F. A. Moreland, *Practical Decorative Upholstery*, Boston (three editions) 1889 and 1890; reprinted as *The Curtain Maker's Handbook*, New York, 1979: 50
8 Ogden Codman Jr. and Edith Wharton: *The Decoration of Houses*, London and New York, 1978: 27
9 See George S. Cole, *A Complete Dictionary of Dry Goods*, Chicago, 1894: 431–40, which contains an extract of those portions of the McKinley Tariff which affected the dry goods trade; see Phyllis Bentley, *O Dreams, O Destinations*, Victor Gollancz Ltd., London, 1962, for a personal account of the impact of the McKinley Tariff in West Riding, Yorkshire.
10 Wendy Kaplan and others, *'The Art that is Life': The Arts & Crafts Movement in America, 1875–1920*, Boston, 1987: 185, with reference to the McHugh furniture displayed at the 1901 Pan-American Exposition.
11 John Cornforth, *The Inspiration of the Past: Country House Taste in the Twentieth Century*, London, 1985: 20 'So many castles and manor houses were restored between about 1890 and 1930 that they form a distinct group in the history of the country house.'
12 Elsie de Wolfe, *The House in Good Taste*, New York, 1913: 85
13 Benjamin Russell Herts, *The Decoration and Furnishing of Apartments*, London and New York, 1915: 161
14 In Arthur Hayden, *Chats on Cottage and Farmhouse Furniture*, T. Fisher Unwin, London, 1912: 341. Many of the incorrect dates of fabrics illustrated in this book were deduced from the date of the furniture on which they were found. This helps to explain how designs actually created in the nineteenth century escaped the general condemnation (which still persists) that they tended to be 'hideous', 'base', and 'inartistic perversions' (388)
15 Moreland, *op. cit.*: 11–12
16 E. M. Forster, *A Room With A View*, first published by Edward Arnold, London, 1908; Penguin Books Ltd. edition 1978: 108
17 Codman & Wharton, *op. cit.*: 20–29; Alice M. Kellog, *Home Furnishings Practical and Artistic*, New York, 1905: 162–3; de Wolfe, *op. cit.*: 85
18 English hand block prints were said to be as expensive as velvets by about 1900. Even mass-produced goods were 'price sensitive': Sears Catalogue No. 104 (1897) included a six-piece parlour suite, for £24 upholstered in cotton tapestry, and $33 if in 'fine brocatelle or choice silk damask' (the prices for imported corduroy, crushed plush or silk tapestry fell in between these two figures).
19 Frank Warner, *Lecture to Macclesfield School of Art*, 16 December, 1909: 9 (manuscript in the Warner Archive)
20 Cole: *op. cit.*: 53–54
21 T. M. Young, *The American Cotton Industry*, New York, 1903: 119 and 127, originally published in the *Manchester Guardian*. America's weaving (except of fine grade yarns) was also much more efficient, with 85,000 automatic looms in use in 1903. British weavers were resisting them, since between 15 and 20 looms could be tended by only one man.
22 I am indebted to Richard Slavin and Judy Straeten for information on Schumacher and Brunschwig respectively.
23 Kellog, *op. cit.*: 170, also published by Butterick in 1904 and 1905. See also Parry, *op. cit.*: 53–4. Candice Wheeler's discussion of stencilling is in *Principles of Home Decoration*, *op. cit.*: 209
24 See for example America's Arnold Print works production records at RISD, including 1912 samples made especially for J. W. Woods, and including New Art or Mission designs.
25 Lithography had been used for the production of pictorial handkerchiefs from the 1830s. Its use for printing textiles has never been extensively studied.
26 See Jocelyn Morton, *Three Generations in a Family Textile Firm*, London, 1971

27 Moreland, *op. cit.*: 11–12
28 J. E. Panton, *Surburban Residences and How to Circumvent Them*, London, 1896: 125–6
29 Wheeler, *op. cit.*: 147 and *passim*; Stickley Craftsman Furniture Catalogs, Dover Publications, New York, 1979: 97 (from a reprint of *Craftsman Furniture Made by Gustav Stickley*, 1910), noting 50"-wide 'Craftsman' canvas at $1.25 per yard
30 Hester Bury, *A Choice of Design . . .* etc., London, 1980: 19
31 de Wolfe, *op. cit.*: 197; Kellog, *op. cit.*: 169–70; Wheeler, *op. cit.*: 143, 156
32 *The Studio*, London, 1893: vol.I, 234, quoting C. F. A. Voysey.
33 For example, Frank Alvah Parsons, *Interior Decoration: Its Principles and Practice*, New York, 1915: 269, recommending hidden rods, the wooden curtain pole with brass ends and other trimmings to be discarded along with carved frills 'and other atrocities'; and Kellog, *op. cit.*: 152–5, on top hems and double brass rods (one for a ruffle, one for curtains of bobbinet, white nainsook or – for the unconventional – fishnet).
34 Sidney Morse, *Household Discoveries*, 1908, quoted in Katherine C. Grier, *Culture and Comfort: People, Parlours and Upholstery 1850–1930*, Massachusetts, 1988: 197
35 Edis, *op. cit.*: 109; Ethel Davis Seal, *The House of Simplicity*, New York, first published in 1921.

Chapter 6
1 Mary Shaw, *Buying for your House: Furnishing Fabrics No.1*, London, 1945: 13
2 Stratton Holloway (ed), *The Practical Book of Interior Decoration*, Philadelphia, 1919: 314
3 Dan Cooper, *Inside Your Home*, New York, 1946: 66
4 Emily Genaner, *Modern Interiors Today and Tomorrow*, New York, 1939: 14
5 See M. D. C. Crawford, *The Heritage of Cotton: The Fibre of Two Worlds and Many Ages*, Fairchild Publishing Co., New York, 1948, regarding the *Women's Wear/ American Museum of Natural History/Metropolitan* series of competitions, exhibitions, lectures and articles intended to encourage American design. No extensive study of American exports of this period has been made, but the catalogue of the 1919 exhibition of industrial art and costume noted the export of avant garde American fabrics.
6 Bernard C. Jakway, *The Principles of Interior Decoration*, New York, 1926: 178
7 Ethel Davis Seal, *The House of Simplicity*, New York, 1921: x, 207–8 and *passim*. A $300 sofa, Seal said, was bought for £120.
8 Mrs. Haweis, *Beautiful Houses*, London, 1882: 237, speaking of G. H. Broughton's house in Campden Hill, designed by Norman Shaw.
9 Included in the decor for an apartment in *Vogue*, 1927, noted in Martin Battersby, *The Decorative Twenties*, Studio Vista, London 1969, reprinted Herbert Press, 1988: 134, as having a scarlet floor, white distempered walls, a deep brown rug and cubist paintings.
10 See, for example, the cover of American *Vogue*, 15 April, 1925. Osbert Lancaster satirized black Regency pieces used with modern furniture and fabrics as 'Vogue Regency'.
11 John Cornforth, *The Inspiration of the Past*, London, 1985: 116–125
12 *The House Beautiful Furnishing Annual*, Boston, 1926: 85
13 *Textile Mercury*, 7 November, 1925: 483
14 'most modern . . .' *The Ideal Home*, July 1928: 9; dirt 'literally slides off' rayon, *Town and Country Homes*, summer 1929: 11; on electrical or 'cubist lighting', *The Ideal Home*, September 1928: 173. Prices in 1930, (proportionally) were for heavy upholstery fabrics (moquette or natural fibre flat weaves), 100%, for printed linen 75%, for rayon taffeta 50%. Because cost was crucial, many magazine articles list prices in this period.
15 Grace Lovat Fraser, 'A Progressive British Industry', *The Sunday Times*, London, 30 October, 1932: 25. Advertised on the following page is a 71-day trip to Burma for £128.

16 Basil Ionides, 'Textiles', *Architectural Review*, London, April 1926: 183
17 *Ibid*. Moquette in 1926 was 50s a yard, double width, when a shot silk was 22/6 (50" wide)
18 Paul Theodore Frankl, *Space for Living*, New York, 1938: 14
19 J. L. Martin and S. Speight, *The Flat Book*, London, 1939: 13
20 See M. Schoeser, *Marianne Satraub*, London, 1984: Chapters 3 & 4
21 Loraine Conran: *Architectural Review*, November 1934: 183
22 Helen Forrester, *Lime Street at Two*, Fontana, Glasgow, 4th ed. 1988: 22, in which a beshawled neighbour is recorded as saying, 'All lace curtains and nothing in the larder – that's your Mam and Dad.'
23 Ethel Lewis: *Decorating the House*, New York, 1942: 283
24 *Good Furnishing*, New York, March 1928: 165, illustrating Cheney Brothers printed silks
25 The introduction of hand screen printing in Britain coincided with the high protective tariffs which became effective in 1931 in both Britain and America. Designs were also taxed, encouraging manufacturers to find indigenous designers, many of whom were artists and industrial designers whose post-depression incomes needed supplementing.
26 Dorothy Draper, *Decorating is Fun!*, New York, 1939: 70
27 Barbara Worsley-Gough, *Fashions in London*, Allan Wingate, London, 1952: 68
28 *The Decorator*, April 1931: 35. For more affluent homes there were real embroideries, crewel work and needlework, some of which were made for upholstery on pre-marked pieces, to ensure the correct placement of motifs. See Basil Ionides, *op. cit.*
29 Harry Trethowan, 'Decorative Art 1893–1943', *The Studio*, London, 1943: 146. Trethowan was a glass and pottery designer and a director of Heal's newly founded Wholesale and Export Company, which was shortly to produce some of Britain's most avant garde furnishing fabrics.
30 Gladys Miller, *Your Home Decorating Guide*, New York, 1947: 33
31 Gladys Miller, *Decoratively Speaking*, New York, 1939: 280

32 *The Queen*, 1933: 34, speaking of the printing on rayon of 'fine old patterns'.

Chapter 7
1 *House & Garden*, USA, January, 1968: 74
2 *Decoration*, September 1933: 137; offered as testimony to the survival of the designer and craftsman was the Allan Walton range of hand screen prints, which included designs by Paul Nash, Duncan Grant, Vanessa Bell, Frank Dobson, Keith Baynes, Cedric Morris, Walton and others.
3 Raymond Loewy, 'Selling through Design', *Annual Report*, 1953: vol XC, no.2604
5 *Interiors*, October 1944: 78; and January 1943: 63
6 *Interiors*, December 1945: 77. The rate of production of vinyl film for curtaining was over 15 million square yards per month in 1949, having been only 40,000 in 1941.
7 *Design*, no. 127, 1959: 36. Prices cited ranged from 12s/6d to 18s/6d for vinyls and vinyl-coated fabrics 48–50" wide.
8 Angelo Testa, 'Designs vs Monkey Business', *Interiors*, February 1948:84
9 Between c.1954 and c.1965 most mechanized screen printing was done on a flat table (the movement of the screen was mechanized as was – sometimes – the action of the squeegee, which dispersed the dye or pigment. Hand screen printing also continued, although on a very limited scale after 1960, and in either table (or flat-bed) method large repeats could be obtained by splitting the image over two or more screens for each colour.
10 *Furnishing World*, October 1955: 51
11 Arthur Drexler, *Textiles USA*, 1956: 3
12 *Vogue*, Export No.2, 1955: 38
13 *The Sunday Times*, 24 March, 1957
14 William Pahlmann, *The Pahlmann Book of Interior Design*, New York, 1955: 96
15 Kay Hardy: *Room by Room*, New York, 1959: 147
16 See, 'Foxteur', *Design*, UK, 100, April 1957: 46–53
17 Lucy D. Taylor, *Know Your Fabrics, Standard Decorative Textiles and Their Uses*, New York and London, 1951: 21
18 Elizabeth Benn, 'Back to the '30s?', *The Daily Telegraph*, London, 1966

19 The *Evening Standard*, London, 26 March, 1964: 16
20 *House & Garden*, USA, May 1968: 119
21 *Drapery and Fashion Weekly*, UK, 25 November 1966
22 Ellen Liman, *The Money Saver's Guide to Decorating*, New York, 1971: 221–2
23 *Drapery and Fashion Weekly*, 11 July, 1975: 12
24 *Good Housekeeping*, London, April 1968: 46
25 Textural prints were also used in transfer printing, a method developed in France in 1968, which used dyes printed onto paper and then transferred to a polyester fabric under pressure and at a high temperature.
26 Maureen Williamson, 'A Comeback for English Chintz', the *Tatler and Bystander*, London, 21 September 1960, noting also that although the 'Everglazing' process was American and that the UK manufacturers paid a royalty to use it, it was nevertheless more often used in Britain even, ironically, on chintzes destined for the United States.
27 *The Ambassador*, UK, no.7, summer, 1966: 67; and *The Times*, London, 15 February, 1974: 16
28 *House & Garden*, USA, February 1972: 35
29 Robert Tewdwr Moss, the *Sunday Telegraph* Weekend magazine, 19 November, 1988: 57
30 Jack Lenor Larsen, 'The New Importance of Furnishings', *Textiles for the Eighties*, Rhode Island School of Design, 1985: 6

Chapter 8
1 Jocasta Innes, *Decorators' Directory of Style*, London, 1987: 8
2 Harry Hinson, *Architectural Digest*, 'AD at Large', October 1988: 314
3 Imogen Taylor, *Country Life*, 'Scales that do Justice', 1 October, 1987: 156
4 *Homes and Gardens*, 'Decorating Trends – Faded Splendour', April 1986: 66
5 Angela Huth, *Mail on Sunday* magazine, 'The Rise and Fall of the Knicker Blind', 24 April, 1988: 16
6 *The World of Interiors*, 'Private View', September 1985: 116 (also in conversation)
7 Malcolm Puttick, *The World of Interiors*, 'Herazmattaz', November 1985: 73 (also in conversation)

Further Reading

Contemporary Sources:
Ackermann, Rudolph, *The Repository of Arts, Literature, Commerce, Manufactures, Fashion and Politics*, R. Ackermann, London, 1809–28.
— *A Series Containing Forty-four Engravings of Beds, Sofas, Ottomans, Window-Curtains, Chairs, Tables, Book-Cases, &c*, R. Ackermann, London, 1823.
Albeck, Pat, *Printed Textiles*, Oxford University Press, Oxford, 1969.
Andrews, Mrs. Charles and Southwork, Mrs. E. F., *Hints for Housekeepers*, Women's Auxiliary of the Hospital of the Good Shepherd, Syracuse, New York, 1904.
Arrowsmith, James, *An Analysis of Drapery; or, The Upholsterer's Assistant, Illustrated with Twenty Plates to Which is Annexed a Table, Showing the Proportions for Cutting One Hundred and Thirty Various-sized Festoons*, London, 1819.
Arrowsmith, J., *The Paper-Hanger's Companion*, Philadelphia, 1852.

Arrowsmith, H. W. and A., *The House Decorator and Painter's Guide*, London, 1840.
Bagnall, William R., *The Textile Industries of the United States*, Riverside Press, Cambridge, Massachusetts, 1893.
Baines, Edward Jr., *History of the Cotton Manufacture in Great Britain*, London, 1835. Re-issued, Frank Cass & Co. Ltd., London, 1966.
Barron, James, *Modern and Elegant Designs of Cabinet and Upholstery Furniture*, W. M. Thiselton, London, 1814.
Beck, S. William, *The Draper's Dictionary: A Manual of Textile Fabrics*, Warehousemen & Drapers' Journal Office, London, 1882.
Beecher, Catharine, *A Treatise on Domestic Economy*, Marsh, Capon, Lyon and Webb, Boston, 1841.
Beecher, Mrs. H. W., *All Around the House: or how to make a home happy*, D. Appleton & Co., New York, 1879.
Beecher Stowe, Harriet and Beecher, Catharine E., *The*

American Woman's Home, J. B. Ford & Co., New York, and H. A. Brown, Boston, 1869.
Beecher Stowe, Harriet and Mitchell, D. G. (eds.), *Hearth and Home*, Pettengill, Bates, New York, 1868–1875 (weekly).
Bemis, Elijah, *The Dyer's Companion*, New York, 1806.
Bendure, Zelma and Pfeiffer, Gladys, *America's Fabrics*, Macmillan, New York, 1946.
Bischoff, James, *A Comprehensive History of the Woollen and Worsted Manufactures*, Smith, Elder, London, 1842.
Bishop, Isabella L., *The Englishwoman in America*, John Murray, London, 1856.
Brothers, Samuel, *Wool and Woollen Manufactures of Great Britain: A Historical Sketch of the Rise, Progress, and Present Position*, Piper, Stephenson & Spence, London, 1859.
Burns, George C., *The American Woolen Manufacturer: A Practical Treatise on the Manufacture of Woolens, in Two Parts*, E. L. Freeman, Central Falls, Rhode Island, 1872.

Candee, Helen Churchill, *Weaves and Draperies*, New York, 1930.

Cassell's Household Guide, being A Complete Encyclopedia of Domestic and Social Economy, and forming a guide to Every Department of Practical Life, four vols., Cassell, Petter & Calpin, London and New York, 1870–75.

Charles, Richard, *Three Hundred Designs for Window-Draperies, Fringes, and Mantle-Board Decorations*, R. Charles, London, 1874.

Church, Ella Rodman, *How to Furnish a Home*, D. Appleton & Co., New York, 1881.

Codman, Ogden Jr. and Wharton, Edith, *The Decoration of Houses*, Scribner, New York, 1902. Reprinted by W. W. Norton & Co., New York, 1978.

Cole, George S., *A Complete Dictionary of Dry Goods*, J. B. Herring Publishing Co., Chicago, 1894.

Conran, Terence, *Printed Textile Design*, The Studio Publishers, London and New York, 1957.

Cook, Clarence, *The House Beautiful: Essays on Beds and Tables, Stools and Candlesticks*, Scribner, Armstrong, New York, 1881.

Cooper, Dan, *Inside Your Home*, Farrar, Straus & Co., New York, 1946.

Cooper, Thomas, *A Practical Treatise on Dyeing and Calicoe Printing*, Dobson, Philadelphia, 1815.

Croften, J. S., *The London Upholsterer's Companion*, London, 1934.

Decorator and Furnisher, New York, 1892–8.

Design, Council of Industrial Design, London, 1946–present (monthly).

Dewing, Mrs. T. W., *Beauty in the Household*, Harper & Bros., New York, 1882.

Dodd, George, *The Textile Manufacturers of Great Britain*, Charles Knight & Co., London, 1844.

Downing, Andrew Jackson, *The Architecture of Country Houses*, New York, 1850.

Draper, Dorothy, *Decorating is Fun!*, Doubleday, Doran & Co., New York, 1939 and 1944.

Dresser, Christopher, *Principles of Decorative Design*, London, 1873.

Drexler, Arthur, *Textiles USA*, Museum of Modern Art, New York, 1956.

Eastlake, Charles L., *Hints on Household Taste in Furniture, Upholstery and Other Details*, Longmans, Green & Co., London, 1868. Reprinted in New York, Dover Publications, 1969.

Edis, Robert W., *Decoration and Furnishing of Town Houses*, C. Kegan Paul & Co., London and New York, 1881.

Elder-Duncan, J. H., *The House Useful and Beautiful: Being practical suggestions on furnishing and decoration*, London, 1911.

Faulkner, Ray, *Inside Today's Home*, Henry Holt & Co., New York, 1956.

Fishburn, Angela, *Curtains and Window Treatments*, Van Nostrand Reinhold Co., New York, 1982.

Frankl, Paul T., *Space for Living*, Doubleday, Doran and Co., New York, 1938.

— *American Textiles*, F. Lewis, Leigh-on-Sea, Essex, 1954.

Gardner, E. C., *Home Interiors Illustrated*, James R. Osgood & Co., Boston, 1878.

Genaner, Emily, *Modern Interiors Today and Tomorrow*, New York, 1939.

Gibbs, Charlotte M., *Household Textiles*, Whitcomb & Barrows, Boston, 1914 (9th edn.).

Gloag, John, *Simple Schemes for Decoration*, London, 1922.

Godey, Louis, *Godey's Lady's Book*, 1830–98 (title varies), Philadelphia until 1892, then New York.

Hardy, Kay, *Room by Room*, Funk & Wagnalls Co., New York, 1959.

Hargrove, John, *The Weavers Draft Book and Clothiers Assistant*, I. Hagerty, Baltimore, 1792. Reprinted by the American Antiquarian Society, Worcester, Massachusetts, 1979, with an introduction by Rita J. Adrosko.

Hayes Marshall, H. G., *Within Four Walls*, F. Lewis, Leigh-on-Sea, Essex, 1948.

— *British Textile Designers Today*, F. Lewis, Leigh-on-Sea, Essex, 1939.

— *Interior Decoration Today*, F. Lewis, Leigh-on-Sea, Essex, 1938.

Haweis, Mrs. H. R., *The Art of Decoration*, Chatto &

Windus, London, 1881. Revised and reissued in 1889.

— *Beautiful Houses*, Sampson & Low, London, 1882.

— *The Art of Housekeeping: A Bridal Garland*, Sampson & Low, London, 1889.

Henkles, George J., *Household Economy*, King & Baird, Philadelphia, 1867.

Hennessey, W. J., *Modern Furnishings for the Home*, Reinhold Publishing Co., New York, 1952 (vol.I) and 1956 (vol.II).

Hepplewhite, George, *The Cabinet-Maker and Upholsterer's Guide*, London, 1788.

Herts, Benjamin Russell, *The Decoration of Apartments*, G. P. Putnam's Sons, New York and London, 1915.

Holloway, Edward Stratton (ed.), *The Practical Book of Interior Decoration*, J. B. Lippincott Co., Philadelphia, 1919.

— *The Practical Book of Furnishing the Small House and Apartment*, J. B. Lippincott Co., Philadelphia and London, 1922.

Holloway, Laura C., *The Hearthstone; or, Life at Home*, Bradley, Garretson, Philadelphia, and Wm. Garretson, Chicago, 1883.

Holly, Henry Hudson, *Modern Dwellings in Town and Country Adapted to American Wants and Climate with a Treatise on Furniture and Decoration*, Harper & Bros., New York, 1878.

Home Furnishings Preview, Crooker Co., Providence, Rhode Island, 1930s.

Hope, Thomas, *Household Furniture and Interior Decoration, Executed from Designs by Thomas Hope*, Longmans, London, 1807.

The House Beautiful Furnishing Annual, The Atlantic Monthly Co., Boston, 1926.

Jackway, Bernard C., *The Principles of Interior Decoration*, Macmillan, New York, 1926.

Jones, Mrs. C. S. and Williams, Henry T., *Household Elegancies*, H. T. Williams, New York, 1875.

— *Beautiful Homes: or Hints in House Furnishing*, H. T. Williams, New York, 1878.

Jones, Owen, *The Grammar of Ornament*, London, 1856.

— *On the True and False in the Decorative Arts*, London, 1863.

The Journal of Design and Manufactures, Chapman & Hall, London, 1849–52.

Kanlet, William H., *The Architect: A Series of Original Designs for Domestic and Ornamental Cottages*, New York, 1849.

Kellogg, Alice M., *Home Furnishing, Practical and Artistic*, Frederick A. Stokes Co., New York, 1905.

King, Thomas (attributed), *The Upholsterer's Accelerator; Being Rules for Cutting and Forming Draperies, Valances, &c.*, Architectural and Scientific Library, London, c.1833.

Knight's Unique Fancy Ornaments, London, 1834.

La Valette, John de (ed.), *The Conquest of Ugliness*, Methuen, London, 1935.

A Lady, *The Workwoman's Guide*, Simpkin, Marshall & Co., London, 1838.

Lardner, Dionysius (ed.), *The Cabinet Cyclopaedia: A Treatise on the Origin, Progressive Improvement, and Present State of the Silk Manufacture*, Longmans, London, 1831.

Leslie, Eliza, *The Lady's House Book: A Manual of Domestic Economy*, Philadelphia, 1841.

— *The Behaviour Book*, Philadelphia, 1854.

Lewis, Arnold and others, *The Opulent Interiors of the Gilded Age: All 203 Photographs from 'Artistic Houses'*, Dover Publications, New York, 1987.

Lewis, Ethel, *Decorating the House*, Macmillan, New York, 1942.

Lewis, F. (ed.), *British Designers and Their Work*. F. Lewis Ltd., Leigh-on-Sea, 1941.

Liman, Ellen, *The Money Saver's Guide to Decorating*, Macmillan, New York, 1971.

Locke, Johnson and Copeland's Ornamental Designs, London, 1834.

Loudon, John Claudius, *An Encyclopedia of Cottage, Farm and Villa Architecture and Furniture*, London, 1833.

Martin, J. L. and Speight, S., *The Flat Book*, Shenval Press, London, 1939.

Martin, Thomas, *Circle of Mechanical Arts*, London, 1813.

The Merchant World and Journal of Fabrics, New York, 1871–88.

Miller, Gladys, *Decoratively Speaking*, Doubleday, Doran & Co., New York, 1939.

— *Your Home Decorating Guide*, Grosset & Dunlap, New York, 1947 (first published in 1941 as *Room Make-up*).

Moreland, F. A., *Practical Decorative Upholstery: Containing Full Instructions for Cutting, Making and Hanging All Kinds of Interior Upholstery Decorations*, Lee & Shepherd, Boston, 1889, reprinted as The Curtain Maker's Handbook, E. P. Dutton, New York, 1979.

New York Interiors at the Turn of the Century in 131 Photographs by Joseph Byron from the Byron Collection of the Museum of the City of New York (text by Clay Lancaster), Dover Publications, New York, 1976.

Nicholson, Peter and Nicholson, Michael Angelo, *The Practical Cabinet-Maker, Upholsterer, and Complete Decorator*, H. Fisher, Son & P. Jackson, London, 1826.

Noetzli, E., *Practical Drapery Cutting . . . for Upholsterers, Cutters and Apprentices*, B. T. Batsford, London, 1906.

Pahlmann, William, *The Pahlmann Book of Interior Design*, Thomas Y. Crowell Co., New York, 1955.

Panton, Mrs. J. E.,
— *From Kitchen to Garrett*, London, 1889.
— *In Garrett & Kitchen*, London, 1919.
— *Suburban Residences and How to Circumvent Them*, London, 1896.

Parkes, Mrs. William, *Domestic Duties: or Instructions to Young Married Ladies*, J. & J. Harper, New York, 1829.

Parsons, Frank A., *Interior Decoration: Its Principles and Practice*, Doubleday, Page & Co., New York, 1915.

Patmore, Derek, *Colour Schemes for the Modern Home*, The Studio Ltd., London and The Studio Publications Inc., New York, 1933. Revised and reissued in 1936.

— *Decoration for the Small Home*, Putnam, London, 1938.

Peterson, Charles J. (ed.), *Ladies National Magazine* (widely known as *Peterson's*), Philadelphia, 1842–95 and New York, 1895–8.

Rees, Abraham (ed.), *The Cyclopaedia; or, Universal Dictionary of Arts, Sciences, and Literature*, Bradford, Fairman *et al*, Philadelphia, 1810–24.

Schrijver, Herman, *Decoration for the Home*, F. Lewis, Leigh-on-Sea, Essex, 1939.

Seal, Ethel Davis, *The House of Simplicity*, D. Appleton Century Co., New York, 1921, subsequent editions in 1924, 1925, 1926 and 1934.

Shaw, Mary, *Buying for your House: Furnishing Fabrics No.1*, Council of Industrial Design, London, 1945.

Sheraton, Thomas, *The Cabinet-Maker and Upholsterer's Drawing Book*, London, 1793.

— *Cabinet Dictionary*, London, 1803.

— *The Cabinet-Maker, Upholsterer and General Artist's Encyclopedia*, London, 1804–7.

— *Designs for Household Furniture*, T. Taylor, London, 1812.

Smith, David, *The Practical Dyer's Guide*, Simpkin & Marshall, London, 1850.

Smith, George,
— *The Cabinet-Maker and Upholsterer's Guide*, Jones, London, 1828.

— *A Collection of Designs for Household Furniture*, J. Taylor, London, 1808.

— *A Collection of Ornamental Designs after the Manner of the Antique*, London, 1812.

Smith, Walter, *Examples of Household Taste*, R. Worthington, New York, c.1876.

Smithells, Roger, *Fabrics in the Home*, Herbert Jenkins, London, 1950.

Spofford, Harriet Prescott, *Art Decoration Applied to Furniture*, Harper & Brothers, New York, 1877.

Stickley, Gustav, *Craftsman Homes*, Craftsman Publishing Co., New York, 1909.

— (ed.) *The Craftsman*, New York, 1901–1916.

Taylor, Lucy D., *Know Your Fabrics, Standard Decorative Textiles and Their Uses*, John Wiley & Sons Inc., New York and Chapman & Hall Ltd., London, 1951.

Tennent, J. Emerson, *A Treatise on the Copyright of Designs*, London, 1841.

Textiles USA, Museum of Modern Art exhibition catalogue, New York, 1956.

Thorne, Edward and Frohne, Henry W., *Decorative Draperies & Upholstery*, Garden City Publishing Co., Garden City, New York, 1929 and 1937.

Throop, Lucy A., *Furnishing the Home of Good Taste*, McBride, Nast, New York, 1912.

Townsend, W. G. Paulson, *Modern Decorative Art in England: Its Development & Characteristics* (vol.I), B. T. Batsford, London, 1922.

Tulokas, M. (ed.), *Textiles for the Eighties*, Rhode Island School of Design exhibition catalogue, 1985.

Varney, Almon C. and others, *Our Homes and Their Adornments*, Jones Brothers & Co., Cincinnati, Chicago, St. Louis and Philadelphia, 1882.

Viemont, Bess M., *Window Curtaining*, U.S. Department of Agriculture, Farmer's Bulletin No.1633, Washington D.C., 1930.

Warden, Alex J., *The Linen Trade*, Longman, Green, Longman, London, 1864.

Watson, Rosamond Mariott, *The Art of the House*, George Bell & Sons, London, 1897.

Webster, Thomas and Parkes, Frances B., *An Encyclopedia of Domestic Economy*, London, 1844, Harper & Bros., New York, 1845.

Wheeler, Candice, *Principles of Home Decoration*, Doubleday, Page & Co., New York, 1903.

Whitaker, Henry, *House Furnishing and Decorating Assistant*, H. Fisher & Son, London and Paris, 1847.

Whitaker, Henry and Nicholson, Michael Angelo, *The Practical Cabinetmaker, Upholsterer and Decorator's Treasury of Designs in the Grecian, Italian, Renaissance, Louis-Quatorze, Gothic, Tudor and Elizabethan Styles*, Peter Jackson, London, 1850s.

White, Gleeson (ed.), *Practical Designing*, George Bell and Sons, London and New York, 1893.

Whittock, Nathaniel, *The Decorative Painter's Guide*, London, 1827.

de Wolfe, Elsie, *The House in Good Taste*, The Century Co., New York, 1913.

Yapp, G. W. (ed.), *Art Industry: Furniture, Upholstery, and House-Decoration*, London, 1879.

Yerbury, F. R. (ed.), *Modern Homes Illustrated*, Oldhams Press Ltd., London, 1947.

Young, T. M., *The American Cotton Industry*, Charles Scribner's Sons, New York, 1903.

Periodicals: .
Ambassador (UK)
Architectural Review (UK)
Decoration (UK)
Furnishing World (UK)
Good Furnishing (USA)
Homes and Gardens (UK, from 1919)
House & Garden (UK & USA)
The Ideal Home (UK)
Interiors (USA)
The Studio and *Studio Yearbooks* (UK)
Town & Country Homes (UK)
Vogue (UK & USA)

Histories and Retrospective Surveys:
Adrosko, Rita J., *Natural Dyes in the United States*, Smithsonian Institution Press, Washington D.C., 1968.

Affleck, Diane L. F., *Just New From the Mills: Printed Cottons in America*, Museum of American Textile History, North Andover, Massachusetts, 1987.

Alexander Giraud Designs: Fabric and Furniture, Goldstein Gallery, University of Minnesota, 1985.

Brightman, Anna, *Window Treatments for Historic Houses, 1700–1850*, National Trust for Historic Preservation, Washington D.C., 1968.

Brown, E., *Sixty Years of Interior Design: The World of McMillan*, Viking Press, New York, 1982.

Burnham, Dorothy. T. *Warp and Weft: A Textile Terminology*, Royal Ontario Museum, Toronto 1980.

Bury, H., *A Choice of Design 1850–1980: Fabrics by Warner & Sons Ltd.*, Warner & Sons Ltd., London, 1981.

Calloway, Stephen, *Twentieth Century Decoration*, Weidenfeld and Nicolson, London, 1988

Clabburn, Pamela, *The National Trust Book of Furnishing Textiles*, Viking, London, 1988.

Coatts, M., *A Weaver's Life: Ethel Mairet 1872–1952*, Crafts Council, London, 1983.

Coleman, D. C., *Courtaulds: An Economic and Social History* (vol.II), O.U.P., Oxford, 1969.

Cooke, Edward S. Jr. (ed.), *Upholstery in America and Europe from the Seventeenth Century to World War I*, W. W. Norton & Co., New York, 1987.

Coons, Martha and Koob, Katherine, *All Sorts of Good Sufficient Cloth: Linen-Making in New England 1640–1860*, Merrimack Valley Textile Museum, North Andover, Massachusetts, 1980.

Cooper, Grace R., 'The Copp Family Textiles', *Smithsonian Studies in History and Technology*, Smithsonian Institute Press, Washington D.C., 1971.

Cooper, Jeremy, *Victorian and Edwardian Furniture and Interiors: From the Gothic Revival to Art Nouveau*, Thames and Hudson, London, 1987.

Cooper, Nicholas, *The Opulent Eye: Late Victorian and Edwardian Taste in Interior Design*, Architectural Press, London, 1976.

Cornforth, John, *The Inspiration of the Past: Country House Taste in the Twentieth Century*, Viking, London, 1985.

— *English Interiors, 1790–1848: The Quest for Comfort*, Barrie & Jenkins, London, 1978.

Coulson, A. J., *Bibliography of Design in Britain 1851–1970*, London, 1979.

Cummings, Abbott Lowell, *Bed Hangings: A Treatise of Fabrics and Styles in the Curtaining of Beds 1650–1850*, Society for the Preservation of New England Antiquities, Boston, Massachusetts, 1961.

Davidson, Caroline, *Women's Worlds: The Art and Life of Mary Ellen Best 1809–1891*, Crown Publishers, New York, 1985.

Davies, Karen, *At Home in Manhattan*, Yale University Art Gallery, New Haven, Connecticut, 1983.

Detroit Institute of Arts, *Arts and Crafts in Detroit 1906–1976: The Movement, the Society, the School*, 1976.

Detroit Institute of Arts & Metropolitan Museum of Art, *Design in America: The Cranbrook Vision*, Harry N. Abrams, New York, 1983.

The Domestic Scene: George M. Niedicken, Interior Architect, Milwaukee Art Museum, exhibition catalogue, 1981.

Dornsife, Samuel J., 'Design Sources for Nineteenth Century Window Hangings', *Winterthur Portfolio 10*, University Press of Virginia, Charlottesville, 1975.

Dunwell, S., *The Run of the Mill*, David R. Godine, Massachusetts, 1978.

Durant, Stuart, *Ornament*, Macdonald, London, 1988.

Edwards, Michael M., *The Growth of the British Cotton Trade 1780–1815*, Manchester University Press, and Augustus M. Kelley, New York, 1967.

Gervers, Veronika (ed.), *Studies in Textile History in Memory of Harold B. Burnham*, Royal Ontario Museum, Toronto, 1977.

Goodden, S., *A History of Heal's*, Heal & Son Ltd., London, 1984.

Girouard, Mark, *Sweetness and Light: The 'Queen Anne' Movement 1860–1900*, Yale University Press, New Haven, Connecticut and London, 1977.

Gloag, John, *Victorian Comfort*, A. and C. Black, London, 1961.

Greysmith, David, 'Patterns, Piracy, and Protection in the Textile Printing Industry 1787–1850', *Textile History 14(2)*, The Pasold Research Fund Ltd., Bath, 1983.

Grier, Katherine C., *Culture and Comfort: People, Parlours and Upholstery 1850–1930*, Strong Museum and University of Massachusetts Press, 1988.

Hanks, David A., *The Decorative Designs of Frank Lloyd Wright*, E. P. Dutton, New York, 1979.

Harris, J. Hyde, S. and Smith, G., *1966 and All That: Design and the Consumer in Britain 1960–69*, Trefoil Books, London, 1986.

Heisinger, K. B. and Marcus, G. H. (eds.), *Design Since 1945*, Philadelphia Museum of Art, 1983.

Innes, Jocasta, *The Decorators' Directory of Style*, Windward (Marshall Cavendish for W. H. Smith), 1987.

Jeremy, David J., *Transatlantic Industrial Revolution*, MIT Press, Cambridge, Massachusetts, 1981.

Joy, Edward, *English Furniture 1800–1851*, Sotheby Parke Bernet Publications, Ward Lock, London, 1977.

Kaplan, Wendy and others, *'The Art that is Life': The Arts & Crafts Movement in America, 1875–1920*, Museum of Fine Arts, Boston, 1987.

King, D., Rothstein, N., and Hefford, W., *Textile Design in the Victoria & Albert Museum*, vol.II, Gakken Co. Ltd., Tokyo, 1980.

Lackschwitz, G., *Interior Design and Decoration: A Bibliography*, New York Public Library, New York, 1961.

Larsen, J. L., *Jack Lenor Larsen: 30 Years of Creative Textiles*, Jack Lenor Larsen Inc., New York, 1981.

Lasden, Susan, *Victorians at Home*, Weidenfeld & Nicolson, London, 1981.

Little, Frances, *Early American Textiles*, The Century Co., London and New York, 1931.

Mayhew, Edward de N. and Myers Jr., Minor, *A Documentary History of American Interiors*, Charles Scribner, New York, 1980.

Mendez, V. and Parry, L., *British Textile Design in the Victoria & Albert Museum, Vol.III*, Gakken Co. Ltd., Tokyo, 1980.

Middlesex Polytechnic, *A London Design Studio 1880–1963: The Silver Studio Collection*, Lund Humphries, London, 1980.

Montgomery, Florence, *Printed Textiles: English and American Cottons and Linens 1700–1850*, Thames and Hudson, London, 1970.

— *Textiles in America 1650–1870*, W. W. Norton & Co., New York and London, 1984.

Morris, Barbara, *Inspiration for Design: The Influence of the Victoria & Albert Museum*, Victoria & Albert Museum, London, 1986.

Morton, J., *Three Generations in a Family Textile Firm*, Routledge & Kegan Paul, London, 1971.

Nylander, Jane, *Fabrics for Historic Buildings*, The Preservation Press, Washington D.C., 1983.

Nylander, Richard C., 'Documenting the Interior of Codman House: The Last Two Generations', *Old Time New England*, vol.LXII, Society for the Preservation of New England Antiquities, 1981.

O'Connor, Deryn and Granger-Taylor, Hero, *Colour and the Calico Printer*, West Surrey College of Art and Design, exhibition catalogue, 1982.

Parkinson, C. Northcote (ed.), *The Trade Winds: A Story of British Overseas Trade during the French Wars, 1793–1815*, George Allen & Unwin, London, 1948.

Parry, Linda, *William Morris Textiles*, Weidenfeld & Nicolson, London, 1983.

— *Textiles of the Arts and Crafts Movement*, Thames and Hudson, London, 1988.

Pearce, David, *London's Mansions*, B. T. Batsford Ltd., London, 1986.

Perkins Centenary London: 100 years of Synthetic Dyestuffs, Pergamon Press, London, 1958.

Peterson, Harold L., *Americans at Home*, Charles Scribner, New York, 1971.

Phillips, L. (ed.), *High Styles: Twentieth Century American Design*, Whitney Museum of American Art, New York, 1985.

Pool, M. J. and Seebohm, C. (eds.), *20th Century Decorating, Architecture and Gardens . . . from 'House & Gardens'*, Weidenfeld & Nicolson, London, 1980.

Praz, Mario, *An Illustrated History of Furnishing from the Renaissance to the Twentieth Century*, George Braziller, New York, 1964.

Schiffer, Margaret B., *Chester County, Pennsylvania, Inventories 1684–1850*, Schiffer Publishing, Exton, Philadelphia, 1974.

Searle, William, *Recreating the Historic House Interior*, American Association for State and Local History, Nashville, Tennessee, 1979.

— *The Tasteful Interude: American Interiors Through the Camera's Eye 1860–1917*, Praeger, New York, 2nd edn., 1981.

Schoeser, Mary, *Marianne Straub*, Design Council, London, 1984.

— *Fabrics and Wallpapers: Twentieth Century Design*, Bell & Hyman, London, 1986.

Schorsch, Anita (ed.), *The Art of the Weaver*, Universe Books, New York, 1978.

Simpson, W. H., *Some Aspects of America's Textile Industry*, University of South Carolina, Colombia, 1966.

Smith, G. and Hyde, S. (eds.), *Walter Crane 1845–1915: Artist, Designer and Socialist*, Lund Humphries, London, 1989.

Thornton, Peter, *Authentic Decor: The Domestic Interior 1620–1920*, Weidenfeld & Nicolson, London, 1984.

Tucker, Barbara M., 'The Merchant, the Manufacturer, and the Factory Manager: The Case of Samuel Slater', *Business History Review*, vol.LV, No.3, Harvard Graduate School of Business Administration, autumn 1981.

Turnbull, Geoffrey, *A History of the Calico Printing Industry of Great Britain*, John Sherratt and Son, Altrincham, 1951.

Turner, Mark and Hoskins, Leslie, *Silver Studio of Design: A Design and Source Book for Home Decoration*, Webb & Bower, London, 1988.

Victoria & Albert Museum, *Catalogue of a Loan Exhibition of English Chintz*, HMSO, London, 1960.

— *Catalogue of an Exhibition of Victorian & Edwardian Decorative Arts*, HMSO, 1962.

— *Designs for British Dress and Furnishing Fabrics: 18th Century to the Present*, London, 1986.

— *From East to West: Textiles from G. P. & J. Baker*, London, 1984.

Walker, Sandra Rambo, *Country Cloth to Coverlets: Textile Traditions in 19th Century Central Pennsylvania*, The Oral Traditions Project of the Union County Historical Society, Lewisburg, Pennsylvania, 1981.

Walton, Karen, *The Golden Age of English Furniture Upholstery, 1660–1840*, Temple Newsom House, Leeds, exhibition catalogue, 1973.

Ware, Caroline F., *The Early New England Cotton Manufacture*, Houghton, Mifflin Co., Cambridge, Massachusetts, 1931.

Warner, Frank, *The Silk Industry of the United Kingdom, Its Origin and Development*, Drane's, London, 1921.

Wilson, Kax, *A History of Textiles*, Westview Press, Boulder, Colorado, 1979.

Winckler, Gail C. and Moss, Roger W., *Victorian Interior Decoration*, Henry Holt & Co., New York, 1986.

Wingate, Isabel B. (ed.), *Fairchild's Dictionary of Textiles*, Fairchild Publications, New York, 1974.

Woods, C., *Sanderson's 1860–1985*, Arthur Sanderson & Sons Ltd., London, 1985.

Periodicals:
Antiques (USA)
Burlington Magazine (UK)
Connoisseur (UK)
The Old House Journal (USA)
Traditional Interior Decoration (UK)
The World of Interiors (UK)

Appendix

The names given to fabrics have changed over the past two hundred years, and are still not standardized. However, for twentieth-century terms, the Fairchild Publications' *Dictionary of Textiles* (1915, with subsequent editions in 1920, 1924, 1959, 1967 and 1974) is useful; for the previous century Florence Montgomery's *Textiles in America 1650–1870* is invaluable. The basis of identifying fabrics lies in an understanding of their construction. An indispensable aid in this is Dorothy K. Burnham's *Warp and Weft: A Textile Terminology* (1980). However for those who are unfamiliar with the processes involved in weaving and printing, this section offers a brief introduction to the major methods of production.

Simple Weaves

Weaves can be divided into three categories – simple, dobby and complex. The simplest weave structure (**plain** or **tabby** weave) has yarns in the loom (the **warp**, or end) which are spaced at intervals roughly equal to those in the **weft** (or pick), which is passed back and forth from selvage to selvage, alternately over and under each warp and reversing the over-under sequence on the return journey. A wide range of cloths are made in this way, including **taffetas** (crisp, closely woven cloths of silk or silk-like fibres such as rayon), **muslin** (lightweight, widely spaced cotton), **canvas** (strong, firm and closely woven, usually cotton), **baize** (loosely woven and napped) and some **tweeds**. A plain weave is identical on both sides.

Among the variations on plain weaves are stripes, **ginghams** and **plaids**, created by altering the colours of the warp and/or weft yarns; **basket weaves**, made by treating two or more warp and weft yarns as one; **seersuckers**, with alternate bands of tight and slack warps resulting in a 'puckered' effect; and some horizontally ribbed fabrics (including **rep** and **poplin**) that use thick and fine yarns together (the thick yarns creating the rib).

Twills and **satins** are made by floating the warp over more than one weft, moving under wefts diagonally for twills and in a more random order for **warp-faced** satins (which have a fine, closely set warp so that the weft hardly shows on the surface). **Denims** are twill-woven, **herringbone weaves** are twills which continually reverse horizontally or vertically creating a diagonal 'grain' which appears to go in two different directions. '**Birds eye**' weaves with small 'lozenges' of pattern can be made by reversing the twill in both directions.

Dobby Weaves

Simple weaves, such as plain, satin and twill, continue uninterrupted across the cloth and are produced on simple or **cam** looms. Small patterns which appear at intervals are made on a loom with a **dobby** mechanism. This controls the movement of the 'harnesses' through which the warp threads are passed. Every thread in each harness (which may number, typically, 4, 8, 12 or 16 threads) is raised simultaneously, so the dobby is less flexible than the **Jacquard** loom, which can control threads singly. Dobby looms cannot produce full-width repeats; their province is smaller-scale geometric designs that are often called 'dobbies'. Making them on Jacquards would be uneconomical. In all weaving the pattern size is always a proportion of the selvage-to-selvage measurement: full width, one-half, one-quarter, one-eighth and so on. Patterns also tend to fall in diagonal grids, in order to prevent uneven uptake of the warp.

Compound Weaves

Unlike plain-weave and some twill cloths which are named to distinguish the weight and density of the fibre or the finish of the cloth, fabrics which combine two or more weave structures have names which generally indicate their characteristic construction, regardless of their weight or fibre content. This makes plain the distinction between, for instance, 'muslin', which always indicates a light, plain cotton weave, and 'damask', which can come in a wide variety of weights and fibres, but always has the same characteristic compound weave structure. **Compound** weaves are used to create contrasting textures and the more elaborate patterns and colour effects, and are generally produced on a loom with an attached Jacquard or a Jacquard-like computer.

The use of different weave structures in a cloth of one colour is generally associated with **damasks**, in which a warp-faced satin weave is used for the ground and reversed for the design (or **figure**) so that on the back of the cloth the pattern appears in a satin weave. In a **single damask** the satin weave is tied down by every fifth weft, while in **double damask** this occurs at every eighth weft, creating a firmer, more lustrous cloth. Where two colours appear, the warp is generally one colour and the weft the other. Any fibre can be used in a damask cloth, and other weaves may be incorporated.

Related to the damask weave is **brocatelle**, which normally has a satin or twill figure on a plain or satin ground. It has areas which appear raised, since it contains a **double warp** (too many warp threads to lie together in one plane). Like damask, it seldom uses more than two colours.

Multi-coloured, compound weave fabrics are often known by the term **lampas**, a French derived term denoting a figured fabric with additional warps or wefts, used in the patterned areas to create extra colours and, when not required, woven into the back of the cloth. In some English firms lampas weaves are broken down into more specific types: the term **tissue** distinguishes the cloth with an extra colouring weft, **lisere** (contrary to its French meaning, selvage) denotes a figured weave with a striped additional warp, while **damasquette** indicates an additional single-coloured warp which usually matches the weft, so that in, for example, a green warp/white weft damasquette, an extra white warp will create areas of pure white where it crosses the weft (in a damask the single green warp would 'colour' any predominantly white areas). A lampas can be distinguished from a damask by the presence of two or more areas of unblended colour and by the back of the cloth, which is not, as in damask, a reverse of the front. In a **brocade** an entirely different process is used: the additional colours are added by hand-held bobbins and resemble a form of embroidery, being an addition to, rather than an integral part of, the cloth.

Other compound weave fabrics include machine-made '**tapestry**', in which the multi-coloured warp lies mainly on the surface and the weft is largely unseen. **Striped tabaret** is also a compound weave, the stripes (which can, but need not, be of different colours) being of different weaves, typically satin and a vertical rib.

Loop and Pile Fabrics

A simple ground weave with intermittent loops is the basis for a number of fabrics. **Terry** has the loops intact. **Plush**, **velvet**, **velveteen** and **velours** all have cut loops; in plush the pile is long and less densely placed than in other pile fabrics. Like velvet, plush pile is made from the warp threads; velveteen, often erroneously used to mean cotton velvet, has a pile made from weft loops. 'Velours' originally indicated a fabric similar to plush, but today is the term for a cloth like a cotton velvet but with a thicker, softer pile.

There are many variations of loop and pile fabrics and, like simple cloths, their names are often associated with a particular fibre content. **Corduroy** has areas of pile placed in horizontal stripes and is generally made of cotton; **moquette** has a warp pile – generally of wool or mohair – that can either be all cut or have some loops left uncut. **Terry cloth** refers to a loosely looped cotton; **terry velvet** to a densely looped cloth, originally of silk.

Yarns

The yarns used in a weave also determine its appearance. They can be dyed before spinning, or prior to weaving or, as is often done with less expensive cloths, woven 'grey' that is, undyed, and dyed in the piece. They may be textured, snarled, unevenly spun, or spun from yarns of different fibres or colours. Today synthetic and natural fibres are often spun together. There is an important distinction between **wool** and **worsted** yarns. Both are made of wool, but the worsted yarn is combed before spinning, so that the fibres lie in the direction of the yarn and therefore are smoother and reflect more light. **Chenille** yarn begins as a fabric woven with groups of four or more closely set warps; the finished cloth is cut horizontally and the four warps twisted, leaving the severed wefts to create the pile, which protrudes on all sides of the yarn which is then re-woven.

Non-Woven Patterns

To create patterns independent of the weave structure, either the yarns can be patterned before weaving, by printing or dying, or a design can be pressed or stamped into the finished cloth. **Moiré** patterns are a well-known watered effect caused by passing a ribbed fabric through high-pressure cylinders; **Utrecht velvets** are pile fabrics, with a pattern created by crushing areas of the pile, a process which, since a French patent of 1828, has been done by engraved rollers. **Gauffering**, the name by which this process is sometimes known, is also used to produce relief designs – such as **honeycomb** or '**waffle**' – on non-pile fabrics.

Printed Fabrics

Plain, textured and figured weaves may be printed. If the principle of weaving might be related to engineering, by the same token printing can be looked on as a branch of chemistry, involving a series of steps that permit the colourant to become absorbed by or attached to the fibres. Patterns are created by direct means (treating the area to be coloured) or indirect means (treating the area to remain clear, either by resisting colour or bleaching it out).

Block printing, using carved wooden blocks that retain raised pattern areas which can also incorporate raised wood-edged areas of felt, or metal insertions, can be detected by the presence of '**pin**' marks (small dots which guide the printer) at regular intervals. Technically there is no limit to the size of the finished design, although for practical reasons the block itself is seldom larger than 16 inches in height or width. **Cylindrical surface rollers** are one means by which mechanized block printing was achieved. They also have raised wooden pattern areas, but complete repeat heights, dictated by the size of the roller, never exceed about 22 inches, and there are no pin marks.

Printing from **engraved** or **etched metal** is an **intaglio** process, technically the reverse of block printing because the colourant is carried in the depressed rather than the raised areas. **Hand printing** by individual **flat plates** (up to about 38 inches in height or width) was only occasionally done in more than one colour, and any additional colours were added by hand or by blocks. Whereas block and surface printing coexisted, flat plate printing was superseded early in the nineteenth century by **roller printing** (like surface roller printing, limited to a design height of between 20 and 22 inches, the diameter of the roller), Fine lines, hatching, stippling and subtle shading are characteristics of intaglio printing techniques.

Screen printing is a form of stencilling. The screen presents a barrier to the dye or pigment. Initially mechanized by powering the movements of flat screens, subsequent improvements developed a cylinder of the mesh or screen. Today many roller 'screens' are actually a solid metal cylinder, with the 'mesh' etched only into areas through which colour must pass. **Hand screen printing** has no design height restrictions, and its mechanized counterpart can produce designs up to about 39 inches high.

Since screens can be 'engraved' photographically, they carry the same capacity to imitate as all photographic printing. This capacity has mainly been used to imitate other textile printing techniques. However, mechanized screen printing is a wet process (one colour does not have time to dry before the other is applied) and therefore colours do no overlap, as they can do in hand printing, whether by block or by screen. Apart from the design height, mechanical printing by surface, engraved or screen rollers can often be detected by the repetition of errors, such as misregistration of colours. Because printing is an addition to the cloth, rather than part of its structure, designs need not be a proportion of cloth width and can be unevenly dispersed over the fabric.

Principal Weave Structures

The warp is shown in white, the weft in black

Plain Weave

Twill Weave

Satin Weave

Photo Credits

Index